Communications in Computer and Information Science 2850

Series Editors

Rationale

The CCIS series is devoted to the publication of proceedings of computer science conferences. Its aim is to efficiently disseminate original research results in informatics in printed and electronic form. While the focus is on publication of peer-reviewed full papers presenting mature work, inclusion of reviewed short papers reporting on work in progress is welcome, too. Besides globally relevant meetings with internationally representative program committees guaranteeing a strict peer-reviewing and paper selection process, conferences run by societies or of high regional or national relevance are also considered for publication.

Topics

The topical scope of CCIS spans the entire spectrum of informatics ranging from foundational topics in the theory of computing to information and communications science and technology and a broad variety of interdisciplinary application fields.

Information for Volume Editors and Authors

Publication in CCIS is free of charge. No royalties are paid, however, we offer registered conference participants temporary free access to the online version of the conference proceedings on SpringerLink (http://link.springer.com) by means of an http referrer from the conference website and/or a number of complimentary printed copies, as specified in the official acceptance email of the event.

CCIS proceedings can be published in time for distribution at conferences or as post-proceedings, and delivered in the form of printed books and/or electronically as USBs and/or e-content licenses for accessing proceedings at SpringerLink. Furthermore, CCIS proceedings are included in the CCIS electronic book series hosted in the SpringerLink digital library at http://link.springer.com/bookseries/7899. Conferences publishing in CCIS are allowed to use our online conference service (Meteor) for managing the whole proceedings lifecycle (from submission and reviewing to preparing for publication) free of charge.

Publication process

The language of publication is exclusively English. Authors publishing in CCIS have to sign the Springer CCIS copyright transfer form, however, they are free to use their material published in CCIS for substantially changed, more elaborate subsequent publications elsewhere. For the preparation of the camera-ready papers/files, authors have to strictly adhere to the Springer CCIS Authors' Instructions and are strongly encouraged to use the CCIS LaTeX style files or templates.

Abstracting/Indexing

CCIS is abstracted/indexed in DBLP, Google Scholar, EI-Compendex, Mathematical Reviews, SCImago, Scopus. CCIS volumes are also submitted for the inclusion in ISI Proceedings.

How to start

To start the evaluation of your proposal for inclusion in the CCIS series, please send an e-mail to ccis@springer.com

Huizilopoztli Luna-García ·
Vanessa Agredo-Delgado · Pablo H. Ruiz
Editors

Human-Computer Interaction

11th Iberoamerican Workshop, HCI-COLLAB 2025
Zacatecas, Mexico, May 7–9, 2025
Revised Selected Papers

Springer

Editors
Huizilopoztli Luna-García
Universidad Autónoma de Zacatecas
Zacatecas, Mexico

Vanessa Agredo-Delgado
Universidad del Cauca
Popayán, Colombia

Pablo H. Ruiz
Universidad del Cauca
Popayán, CAUCA, Colombia

ISSN 1865-0929 ISSN 1865-0937 (electronic)
Communications in Computer and Information Science
ISBN 978-3-032-31222-8 ISBN 978-3-032-31223-5 (eBook)
https://doi.org/10.1007/978-3-032-31223-5

This Springer imprint is published by the registered company Springer Nature Switzerland AG
The registered company address is: Gewerbestrasse 11, 6330 Cham, Switzerland

Preface

This volume constitutes a substantial contribution to the development and consolidation of the Human-Computer Interaction (HCI) field in the Ibero-American context, as it compiles a rigorous selection of the most relevant works presented at the 11th Ibero-American Conference on Human-Computer Interaction (JIHC 2025), held from May 7–9, 2025, in the city of Zacatecas, Mexico.

The event, organized by the Autonomous University of Zacatecas, the Zacatecan Council of Science, Technology and Innovation, and the HCI-COLLAB network, was held in a hybrid format that enabled broad international participation while strengthening academic exchange among researchers, professionals, and students across the region.

Since its inception in 2015, the Ibero-American HCI Conference has established itself as a key forum for the HCI-COLLAB academic community, promoting scientific exchange, inter-institutional collaboration, and the development of an interdisciplinary community focused on the study, design, and evaluation of human-centered technologies. In this regard, the eleventh edition reaffirmed its role as a strategic platform for bringing together researchers, educators, students, and professionals from diverse countries.

The thematic focus of this edition, "Human–Technology Interaction in the Era of Artificial Intelligence," marked a turning point in the discipline, characterized by the increasing integration of intelligent systems into everyday life. From this perspective, HCI extends beyond interface optimization, emerging as a key field for understanding and designing complex sociotechnical relationships in which artificial intelligence reshapes human experiences across work, education, and cultural domains. Accordingly, the volume emphasizes the need to address human–technology interaction from ethical, inclusive, and sustainable perspectives.

The academic program of JIHC 2025 included keynote lectures delivered by international experts, specialized workshops, technical sessions, and training activities, with the "UX Summer School for Students (UX-EVE)" standing out as a key initiative to foster the next generation of HCI researchers and professionals.

The event was structured around multiple thematic tracks and workshops addressing contemporary challenges and emerging areas in the field. It fostered discussion and experimentation on intelligent interactive systems, accessibility and digital inclusion, cognitive and interaction processes, and applications related to Industry 4.0. Furthermore, dedicated workshops explored video game analysis and design, gamification strategies, and collaborative work and learning in technology-mediated environments.

Taken together, these spaces contributed to disseminating scientific and technological advances, fostering new research collaborations, and advancing interdisciplinary approaches that significantly strengthened the HCI ecosystem in the Ibero-American context.

The editorial process underpinning this volume followed a rigorous double-blind peer-review model involving 136 national and international experts, thereby ensuring the scientific quality, methodological rigor, and relevance of the selected contributions.

Out of 105 submitted papers, 23 were accepted following an exhaustive evaluation process in which submissions received three reviews each on average. Collectively, these contributions represent significant advances in the state of the art across both theoretical and applied domains.

The contributions gathered in this volume reflect the thematic and methodological diversity of contemporary HCI, encompassing areas such as multimodal interaction, artificial intelligence, user experience, accessibility, extended reality, and collaborative systems. This diversity highlights the transversal nature of the discipline and its ability to engage with pressing technological and societal challenges.

The editors gratefully acknowledge the valuable contributions of the Program Committee, reviewers, authors, and organizers, as well as the support of the collaborating institutions and the Ibero-American academic community. Appreciation is extended to Springer for enabling the dissemination and visibility of these works.

This volume not only documents the advances presented at JIHC 2025 but also enhances the international visibility of the event while reinforcing HCI as a strategic field for human-centered technological development. It is expected to inspire new research, foster interdisciplinary collaboration, and strengthen academic networks that drive innovation across the region.

It consolidates its position as a leading academic and scientific forum, advancing the development of inclusive, ethical, and human-centered technologies in a global context driven by the rapid evolution of artificial intelligence.

May 2026

Huizilopoztli Luna García
Vanessa Agredo-Delgado
Pablo H. Ruiz

Organization

General Chair

Huizilopoztli Luna García	Universidad Autónoma de Zacatecas, Mexico
Cesar A. Collazos	Universidad del Cauca, Colombia

Program Committee Chairs

Huizilopoztli Luna García	Universidad Autónoma de Zacatecas, Mexico
Vanessa Agredo-Delgado	Universidad del Cauca, Colombia
Pablo H. Ruiz	Universidad del Cauca, Colombia

Steering Committee

Luis A. Flores Chaires	Universidad Autónoma de Zacatecas, Mexico
José María Celaya Padilla	Universidad Autónoma de Zacatecas, Mexico
Jorge Isaac Galvan Tejada	Universidad Autónoma de Zacatecas, Mexico
Hamurabi Gamboa Rosales	Universidad Autónoma de Zacatecas, Mexico
Toni Granollers Saltiveri	Universidad de Lleida, Spain
Jaime Muñoz-Arteaga	Universidad Autónoma de Aguascalientes, Mexico

Program Committee

Silvana Vanesa Aciar	Instituto de Ciencias Astronómicas de la Tierra y el Espacio,Argentina
Abhinav Mehta Aditya Gupta	Amazon Web Services, USA
Vanessa Agredo	Universidad del Cauca, Colombia
Raúl Antonio Aguilar Vera	Universidad Autónoma de Yucatán, Mexico
Sergio Albiol Pérez	Universidad de Zaragoza, Spain
Cibelle de la Higuera Amato	Universidade Presbiteriana Mackenzie, Brazil
José García Alonso	Universidad de Extremadura, Spain
Patricia Appel	Technische Hochschule Ingolstadt, Germany
Jeferson Arango López	Universidad de Caldas, Colombia
José Guadalupe Arceo Olague	Universidad Autónoma de Zacatecas, Mexico

Luis Alberto Flores Chaires	Universidad Autónoma de Zacatecas, Mexico
Leandro Flórez Aristizábal	Institución Universitaria Antonio José Camacho, Colombia
Ismar Frango	Universidade Presbiteriana Mackenzie, Brazil
Sandra Gallardo Baldassarri	Universidad de Zaragoza, Spain
Carlos Eric Galván Tejada	Universidad Autónoma de Zacatecas, Mexico
Alicia García Holgado	Universidad de Salamanca, Spain
Francisco José García Peñalvo	Universidad de Salamanca, Spain
Alfredo García Suárez	Benemérita Universidad Autónoma de Puebla, Mexico
Juan Enrique Garrido	Universidad de Castilla - La Mancha, Spain
William Joseph Giraldo Orozco	Universidad del Quindío, Colombia
Alexandre Gomes de Siqueira	University of Florida, USA
Ricardo Mendoza González	Instituto Tecnológico de Aguascalientes, Mexico
Claudia Blanca González Calelleros	Universidad Veracruzana, Mexico
Juan Manuel González Calleros	Benemérita Universidad Autónoma de Puebla, Mexico
Julián Grigera	Universidad Nacional de la Plata, Argentina
Toni Granollers	Universidad de Lleida, Spain
Josefina Guerrero García	Benemérita Universidad Autónoma de Puebla, Mexico
Alexander Guerrero Avendaño	Universidad Francisco de Paula Santander Ocaña, Colombia
John Alexis Guerra Gómez	Northeastern University, USA
Francisco Gutiérrez Vela	Universidad de Granada, Spain
Oscar Alberto Henao Gallo	Universidad Tecnológica de Pereira, Colombia
José Miguel Herrán Suárez	Universidad Nacional Abierta y a Distancia, Colombia
Javier A. Jiménez Toledo	Universidad CESMAG, Colombia
Cesar Jaramillo	Universidad Tecnológica de Pereira, Colombia
André Luiz Satoshi Kawamoto	Universidad Tecnológica Federal de Paraná, Brazil
Carlos Javier Latorre Rojas	Universidad Militar Nueva Granada, Colombia
Jessica Lorena Leal Pabón	Universidad Simón Bolívar, Colombia
Germán Ezequiel Lescano	Universidad Nacional de Santiago del Estero, Argentina
Fulvio Lizano Madriz	Universidad Nacional de Costa Rica, Costa Rica
María Lozano	Universidad de Castilla - La Mancha, Spain
Huizilopoztli Luna García	Universidad Autónoma de Zacatecas, Mexico
José Antonio Macías Iglesias	Universidad Autónoma de Madrid, Spain
Beatriz Eugenia Marín Ospina	Institución Universitaria Antonio José Camacho, Colombia

Rosa María Gil Iranzo	Universidad de Lleida, Spain
Ramon Mas Sansó	Universidad de las Islas Baleares, Spain
Daniela Marques	Instituto Federal de São Paulo, Brazil
Nicolás Esteban Matus Palma	Pontificia Universidad Católica de Valparaíso, Chile
Carlos A. Meneses Escobar	Universidad Tecnológica de Pereira, Colombia
Jorge Alejandro Morgan Benita	Universidad Autónoma de Zacatecas, Mexico
Alejandro Moreno Cruz	Universidad Autónoma de Aguascalientes, Mexico
Marcelo Morandini	Universidad de São Paulo, Brazil
Fernando Moreira	Universidade Portucalense, Portugal
Arturo Moquillaza	Pontificia Universidad Católica del Perú, Peru
Alicia Mon	Universidad Nacional de La Matanza, Argentina
María Fernanda Montoya Vega	Monash University, Australia
Jaime Muñoz-Arteaga	Universidad Autónoma de Aguascalientes, Mexico
Luis Freddy Muñoz Sanabria	Fundación Universitaria de Popayán, Colombia
Elena Navarro	Universidad de Castilla - La Mancha, Spain
Sergio Ochoa	Universidad de Chile, Chile
João Soares de Oliveira Neto	Universidad Federal de Bahía, Brazil
Manuel Ortega Cantero	Universidad de Castilla - La Mancha, Spain
Patricia Paderewski Rodríguez	Universidad de Granada, Spain
Natalia Padilla Zea	Universidad Internacional de la Rioja, Spain
Phil Palanque	ICS-IRIT, University Toulouse III, France
Otto Parra González	Universidad de Cuenca, Ecuador
Manuel Alejandro Pastrana Pardo	Institución Universitaria Antonio José Camacho, Colombia
Víctor M. R. Penichet	Universidad de Castilla - La Mancha, Spain
Víctor Manuel Peñeñory	Universidad de San Buenaventura Cali, Colombia
Ivo Pérez Colo	Universidad Nacional del Centro de la Provincia de Buenos Aires, Argentina
Byron Pérez Gutiérrez	Universidad Militar Nueva Granada, Colombia
Maribel Ramos Hernández	Universidad de Playa Ancha, Chile
Miguel Ángel Redondo Duque	Universidad de Castilla - La Mancha, Spain
Oscar Revelo Sánchez	Universidad de Nariño, Colombia
Dewar Rico Bautista	Universidad Francisco de Paula Santander Ocaña, Colombia
Geraldina Roark	Universidad Nacional del Centro de la Provincia de Buenos Aires, Argentina
Andrés Rodríguez	Universidad Nacional de la Plata, Argentina
Beatriz E. Rodríguez Chinchilla	Universidad Francisco de Paula Santander Ocaña, Colombia
Raúl Eduardo Rodríguez Ibáñez	Universidad Simón Bolívar, Colombia

Contents

AI Agents for Heuristic Usability Evaluation: A Comparative Study with Human Experts

Holman Cabezas Mondragón[1](✉), Huizilopoztli Luna-García[1], Wilson J. Sarmiento[2], José M. Celaya Padilla[1], Claudia Acra Despradel[3], and Klinge O. Villalba Condor[4]

[1] Universidad Autónoma de Zacatecas, Zacatecas, Mexico
{holmanc,hlugar,jose.celaya}@uaz.edu.mx
[2] Universidad Militar Nueva Granada, Bogotá, Colombia
wilson.sarmiento@unimilitar.edu.co
[3] Universidad Nacional Pedro Henríquez Ureña, Santo Domingo, República Dominicana
c.acra@unphu.edu.do
[4] Universidad católica de Santa María, Arequipa, Peru
kvillalba@ucsm.edu.pe

Abstract. Heuristic usability evaluation is essential for identifying interaction issues in digital products, but traditional methods rely heavily on human expertise, making them costly, time-consuming, and often inconsistent across different evaluators. This study presents a comprehensive comparison between AI-driven heuristic evaluations and expert assessments, using Nielsen's heuristics as a benchmark framework. Controlled experiments were conducted on multiple digital platforms within the WebArena environment, including OpenStreetMap, GitLab, and OneStopShop. Results demonstrate that AI agents powered by Large Language Models can achieve substantial agreement with human evaluators (Cohen's Kappa values between 0.68–0.74) while significantly reducing subjectivity and evaluation time. The automated approach maintains consistency across evaluations and provides scalable solutions for usability testing. The findings highlight the potential of AI to enhance and complement traditional usability testing methodologies by providing cost-effective, consistent, and rapidly deployable assessments. This research contributes to the integration of AI-driven approaches in usability evaluation practices, optimizing the user experience assessment process for modern digital product development.

Keywords: Heuristic Usability Evaluation · Nielsen's Principles · Machine Learning · Large Language Models (LLMs) · Automated Agents · WebArena · BrowserGym · User Experience (UX)

1 Introduction

The usability of digital products plays a critical role in the success of web applications, mobile platforms, and interactive systems. Since its inception, the heuristic evaluation method proposed by Jakob Nielsen and Rolf Molich has been regarded as one of the

H. Luna-García et al. (Eds.): HCI-COLLAB 2025, CCIS 2850, pp. 1–15, 2027.
https://doi.org/10.1007/978-3-032-31223-5_1

most practical and influential approaches for detecting usability issues [1]. In particular, Nielsen established a series of guidelines—commonly known as "*usability heuristics*"—which have been widely adopted in the industry due to their simplicity and effectiveness in diagnosing user experience shortcomings [2].

However, the traditional application of heuristic evaluations relies strongly on the expertise of human evaluators—typically specialists in quality or user experience—who review an interface to identify inconsistencies with Nielsen's proposed principles [2]. While this method can be effective, it has certain drawbacks. First, the availability of evaluators with specialized training may be limited, especially in smaller organizations or rapidly evolving projects. Second, the process can become costly and time-consuming, as each expert must carefully analyze every part of the interface. In addition, findings often vary, because not all evaluators apply the criteria in the same way or assign the same level of importance to the different types of issues they uncover, this depends on the evaluators' experience and other subjective factors [3].

In recent years, some initiatives have explored partial automation of usability evaluations through machine learning [4–6]. These solutions aim to reduce both the cost, duration of evaluations and provide greater consistency in identifying problems by minimizing the inherent subjectivity of human inspection. With the advent of Large Language Models (LLMs) [7] and their ability to process and classify vast amounts of data, the prospect of developing automated agents that can detect usability flaws quickly —and at a level of precision comparable to expert reviewers— has grown more viable.

Some studies have focused on test implementations based on Nielsen's heuristics [8–13], even proposing specific attributes to be reviewed or updating the original principles to include more complex interaction scenarios. There are also proposals for agents that concentrate primarily on performing actions in web environment [14, 15], demonstrating a certain level of autonomy in basic tasks. However, there is still a gap when it comes to systematically applying a set of concrete items —derived from Nielsen's heuristics— in a fully automated agent and then directly comparing its performance to human-led inspection in a realistic web setting. Addressing this gap, the present work evaluates in an experimental setup the viability and potential benefits of incorporating automated heuristic evaluations in settings that closely mirror real-world industry practices.

In this context, Granollers lays out a specific set of items that extend Nielsen's heuristics, offering a more detailed guide for detecting usability issues [10], these items can serve as the foundation for both automated and manual evaluation processes. In this way, this work uses the items proposed by Granollers to build automated evaluation processes supported by intelligent agents, with the advantage that the same items can be used for comparison with traditional methods performed by human experts, defined in this work as a gold standard.

Moreover, in order to test these items in a realistic manner, this study looks to WebArena [16], a web interaction laboratory that integrates fully functional sites in common domains (e.g., e-commerce, discussion forums, or content management). WebArena provides an environment for assessing how well agents adhere to heuristic principles in scenarios that simulate typical user tasks.

The main goal of this work is to compare the performance of a specialized usability-testing agent against human evaluators. Specifically, it analyzes how accurately and efficiently both approaches identify usability problems, while looking at the time required for each assessment. The study aims to determine how closely the automated agent's results match those of experts, potentially reducing costs and subjectivity in the process. If these findings hold, they could pave the way for broader adoption of automated solutions within the industry, boosting the efficiency and quality of usability evaluations.

The paper is organized as follows, Section 2 shows a review of major contributions in the literature that underscore the relevance of heuristic evaluations and their benefits in digital product development. Section 3 describes the methodology for designing and implementing the AI agent, highlighting the metrics used to measure its precision and effectiveness. The results are discussed in Section 4, which presents the findings in terms of practical applicability. Finally, the last section presents the main conclusions of this work, study limitations, and potential directions for future research.

2 Related Works

This study is based on a simplified version of the Multivocal Literature Review (MLR) approach [17], aiming to identify advancements in usability evaluation and automated testing through artificial intelligence. The review included both academic literature and grey literature, capturing formal scientific knowledge as well as emerging practical insights from the industry. To structure the search, key databases and repositories were selected: Crossref, Semantic Scholar, and OpenAlex, which cover sources such as PubMed, arXiv, Web of Science, Scopus, and other specialized repositories. Inclusion criteria were established based on the following thematic areas:

- **Usability Evaluation and Heuristic Principles:** Methods for usability evaluation, Human-Computer Interaction (HCI), User-Centered Design (UCD), and Nielsen's heuristics.
- **Automation of Heuristic Evaluations and AI Testing:** Application of artificial intelligence and machine learning in heuristic evaluations, automated testing tools, large language models (LLMs), and intelligent agents applied to usability.
- **Interface Evaluation and User Experience (UX):** Studies on heuristics applied to interface design and the impact of automation on user experience.
- **Emerging Trends in Testing Automation:** Recent approaches in reinforcement learning, Robotic Process Automation (RPA), and AI-driven automated test generation.

A total of 72 keywords related to the selected topics, chosen based on the most commonly used terms in the literature, were defined for the initial search, identifying 98 relevant articles aligned with these criteria. Additionally, 22 grey literature sources were located, including specialized repositories particularly relevant to the review process. Among the sources found, some articles have been particularly influential in the development of this line of research, such as Github webarena [18], which provides a web testing environment; Github BrowserGym [19], an automation tool for browser testing; Github AgentLab [20], which facilitates the creation and testing of automated agents;

OpenAI API documentation [21], essential for understanding the use of OpenAI's language models; and langchain [22], a framework that allows integrating AI models into complex workflows. These works have been crucial in the evolution of this field.

Several repositories and resources were particularly valuable, including:

- **BrowserGym**: An ecosystem explicitly designed for evaluating and training intelligent web agents based on large language models (LLMs), offering a standardized benchmarking environment [23].
- **Mind2Web**: Demonstrated advances in creating generalist AI agents capable of navigating and interacting with the web through natural language understanding [15].
- **WebArena**: Provided realistic environments and standardized scenarios for building and assessing autonomous web navigation agents, enabling practical assessments of real-world tasks [16].
- **WebAgent Framework**: Highlighted the real-world application of web agents, combining planning, contextual understanding, and program synthesis for complex web-based tasks [24].
- **SteP**: Introduced a stacked policy approach to leverage multiple LLM-driven web agent actions, effectively enhancing automation and adaptability in dynamic web environments [25].

These repositories provided valuable information on emerging tools, experimental frameworks, and practical applications, effectively complementing the findings obtained from academic literature.

From this review, key works in the field of usability heuristics are highlighted. Particularly significant are Jakob Nielsen [1], which propose a set of heuristics widely adopted for their simplicity and effectiveness in identifying usability issues. These heuristics serve as foundational principles for current usability evaluations and have become an industry standard. Additionally, Granollers et al. [20] conducted a critical review of Nielsen's heuristics, proposing an alternative set with a broader and more adaptable approach for diverse types of interactive systems.

The integration of automation into heuristic evaluation has enabled Nielsen's classical heuristics and Granollers' adaptations to be effectively applied in more dynamic and scalable practical scenarios. Through the use of extended language models (LLMs), it is now possible to simulate complex human interactions and rapidly detect violations of these heuristics. This not only enhances the accuracy and speed of evaluations but also enables continuous, more consistent testing tailored to specific contexts, significantly increasing practical value in user experience improvement.

Moreover, recent studies demonstrate the increasing adoption of artificial intelligence techniques, particularly large language models (LLMs) [21], in automating certain heuristic evaluation tasks traditionally performed by humans. These advanced models enable rapid identification and prioritization of usability issues, significantly reducing manual evaluation time and improving consistency. Prominent examples include automated systems capable of simulating user interactions and identifying usability violations based on predefined heuristics, thus bridging the gap between theoretical frameworks and practical usability testing.

3 Methodology

This section describes the methodology employed to compare automated heuristic evaluations against assessments conducted by human usability experts. It details the methods, tools, metrics, and procedures used to ensure the validity and reliability of the study.

3.1 Experimental Design

To assess the viability and effectiveness of automating heuristic evaluation, an experimental design with the following characteristics was established:

- An automated agent based on Large Language Models (LLMs) was used to answer heuristic evaluation questions.
- Manual evaluations were conducted by usability experts.
- A cross-comparison design was implemented, wherein both the automated agent and human evaluators analyzed the same applications under identical conditions.
- Results obtained from both methods were analyzed using statistical techniques.

3.2 Evaluated Applications

Three applications within the WebArena environment were selected, deployed through an AWS instance (recommended type: t3a.xlarge, 1000GB EBS root volume, specific security group, and SSH key access) to guarantee a controlled and replicable evaluation environment. The selected applications included:

- **OpenStreetMap:** A collaborative online mapping platform.
- **GitLab:** A source code management and CI/CD system.
- **OneStopShop:** An e-commerce application with product search functionality.

These applications were chosen for representing diverse digital interaction domains, allowing the assessment of the automated evaluation method's applicability across varied contexts.

3.3 Evaluation Scenario: User Stories

To standardize the analysis, the following user story related to the search engine of each application was formulated:

"As a user, I want to use the application's search bar to find a specific item within its content."

Based on this user story, 15 specific heuristic items derived from Granollers' [26] guidelines were evaluated, with binary (Yes/No) answers (Table 1).

Table 1. Heuristic Evaluation Criteria

Heuristic	Evaluation Questions
H1 - Visibility and system state	● Does the application include a visible title page, section or site? ● Does the user always know where it is located? ● Does the user always know what the system or application is doing? ● Are the links clearly defined? ● Can all actions be visualized directly? (No other actions are required)
H2 - Connection between the system and the real world, metaphor usage and human objects	● Does information appear in a logical order for the user? ● Does the design of the icons correspond to everyday objects? ● Does every icon do the action that you expect? ● Does the system use phrases and concepts familiar to the user?
H3 - User control and freedom	● Is there a link to return to the initial state or homepage? ● Are the functions "undo" and "redo" implemented? ● Is it easy to return to an earlier state of the application?
H4 - Consistency and standards	● Do link labels have the same names as their destinations? ● Do the same actions always have the same results? ● Do the icons have the same meaning everywhere? ● Is the information displayed consistently on every page? ● Are the colors of the links standard? If not, are they suitable for their use? ● Do navigation elements follow the standards? (Buttons, checkboxes, etc.)

(*continued*)

Table 1. (*continued*)

Heuristic	Evaluation Questions
H5 - Recognition rather than memory, learning, and anticipation	● Is it easy to use the system for the first time? ● Is it easy to locate previously searched information? ● Can you use the system at all times without remembering previous screens? ● Is all content needed for navigation or tasks found on the current screen? ● Is the information organized according to logic familiar to the end user?
H6 - Flexibility and efficiency of use	● Are there keyboard shortcuts for common actions? ● If there are, is it clear how to use them? ● Is it possible to easily perform an action done earlier? ● Does the design adapt to screen resolution changes? ● Is the use of accelerators visible to the normal user? ● Does it always keep the user engaged? (Without unnecessary delays)
H7 - Help users recognize, diagnose, and recover from errors	● Does it display a message before taking irreversible actions? ● Are errors shown in real time? ● Is the error message easily interpretable? ● Is some code also used to reference the error?
H8 - Error prevention	● Does a confirmation message appear before taking the action? ● Is it clear what information needs to be entered in each form field? ● Does the search engine tolerate typos and spelling errors?
H9 - Aesthetic and minimalist design	● Is the design free from redundant information? ● Is the information short, concise, and accurate? ● Is each item of information distinct and not easily confused? ● Is the text well-organized, with short sentences that are quick to interpret?

(*continued*)

Table 1. (*continued*)

Heuristic	Evaluation Questions
H10 - Help and documentation	● Is there a "help" option? ● If so, is it visible and easy to access? ● Is the help section aimed at solving problems? ● Is there a section of frequently asked questions (FAQ)? ● Is the help documentation clear, with examples?
H11 - Save state and protect work	● Can users continue from a previous state (where they had previously been or from another device)? ● Is "Autosave" implemented? ● Does the system respond well to external failures? (Power outage, internet failure, etc.)
H12 - Color and readability	● Are the fonts of adequate size? ● Do the fonts use colors with sufficient contrast against the background? ● Do background images or patterns allow the content to be read clearly? ● Does it consider people with reduced vision?
H13 - Autonomy	● Does it keep the user informed of system status? ● Is the system status visible and updated? ● Can the user make their own decisions? (Personalization)
H14 - Defaults	● Does the system or device provide an option to return to factory settings? ● If so, does it clearly indicate the consequences of the action? ● Is the term "Default" used appropriately?
H15 - Latency reduction	● Is the execution of heavy tasks transparent to the user? ● While running heavy tasks, is remaining time or some animation shown?

Source: Own elaboration based on Granollers [26].

3.4 Automated Evaluation

The growing complexity of digital interfaces has led to an increasing demand for usability evaluation methods that are both scalable and efficient. Traditional heuristic evaluations, while effective, often require significant human effort and expertise, limiting their applicability in fast-paced development environments. To address these limitations, this study introduces an automated heuristic evaluation approach, leveraging GPT-4o within a structured evaluation pipeline. This approach enables the simulation of user interactions, the extraction of relevant interface data, and the automated assessment of usability principles, reducing the dependency on manual inspections while maintaining a high standard of accuracy.

The evaluation process is structured into five key phases (Fig. 1). The first phase, Input Data, requires the user to provide essential information, including: (1) a user story, which outlines the expected interaction flow; (2) the URL of the interface to be evaluated; and (3) a list of heuristic questions, derived from established usability principles. These elements serve as the foundation for guiding the automated assessment.

Following this, in the Navigation Automation phase, the agent utilizes Playwright to systematically explore the interface. The system identifies critical elements within the Document Object Model (DOM) and performs interactions based on the user story. The pre-configured setup ensures consistency in detecting interface components, executing user actions, and handling dynamic elements, making the evaluation process more reliable.

In the Information Extraction phase, the agent collects key data points from the interface, including visible text, user-generated events (such as clicks, input changes, and state transitions), and screenshots capturing significant moments during navigation. These data points are structured and processed to ensure they are well-formatted before being analyzed by the language model.

The LLM Query phase involves sending the structured data to GPT-4o, which then evaluates the interface against the heuristic questions. The model assesses various aspects of usability, such as content clarity, element positioning, accessibility, and overall user experience. To enhance efficiency, optimizations have been applied to reduce response latency and ensure the consistency of the model's evaluations.

Finally, in the Validation and Reporting phase, the agent consolidates the LLM's responses into a structured evaluation report. The report provides a comprehensive analysis of heuristic compliance, highlighting areas where usability improvements are necessary. Additionally, the system integrates AgentLab, a platform that facilitates automation and evaluation processes by providing a pre-configured environment for conducting heuristic assessments.

This automated approach introduces a scalable and replicable method for usability evaluation, reducing the subjectivity and resource constraints associated with human-led inspections. By leveraging GPT-4o and integrating automation tools, the study explores the potential of AI-driven heuristic evaluation as a viable alternative to traditional usability assessment techniques.

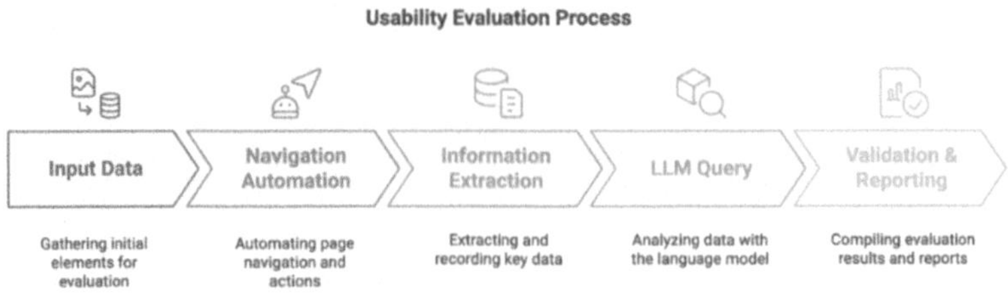

Fig. 1. Automated Heuristic Evaluation Process Using GPT-4o Source: Own elaboration

3.5 Human Evaluation

Twenty-one usability experts participated, selected based on their experience in software testing and interaction design.

3.5.1 Evaluators' Selection and Characteristics

Engineers holding a professional degree with more than four years of usability experience.

Predominantly between 36 and 55 years old, with 52% female participation.

Only 5% held formal certification in Nielsen's heuristics.

3.5.2 Human Evaluation Procedure

Each expert independently completed evaluations using the same heuristic questionnaire, without prior access to the automated agent's results to avoid bias.

3.5.3 Evaluation Metrics

Specific metrics were established to evaluate and compare both methods:

- Average execution time.
- Accuracy and coverage in identifying heuristic issues.
- Agreement between the automated agent and human evaluators, measured using Cohen's Kappa coefficient

3.5.4 Statistical Techniques Applied

Statistical methods were applied to compare the results of automated and human evaluations: Agreement and Variability Analysis: Cohen's Kappa coefficient was used to measure agreement adjusted for chance. Analyses were performed individually for each of the three evaluated platforms, ensuring accuracy and objectivity in the results obtained.

4 Results

This section presents the outcomes derived from the comparative analysis between automated heuristic evaluations performed by an agent based on a Large Language Model (LLM), specifically OpenAI's GPT-4o model, and manual evaluations conducted by usability experts on the three selected platforms: OpenStreetMap, GitLab, and OneStopShop.

Total Responses by Evaluator and Platform

Fig. 2 summarizes the total responses collected from both automated evaluators (Bot) and human evaluators (Expert), classified into affirmative (Yes) and negative (No) responses based on the 15 heuristic items assessed. The comparison is made between the same heuristics evaluated by the bot and the humans, with the results being directly compared, as the same heuristics are being assessed by both.

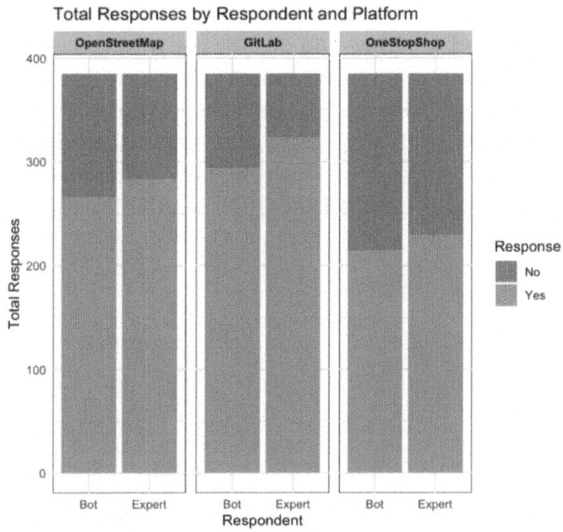

Fig. 2. Comparison of Bot and Expert Responses Across Platforms. Source: Own elaboration based on experimental data.

This chart compares "Yes" and "No" responses from bots and experts on OpenStreetMap, GitLab, and OneStopShop. Differences in response proportions highlight variations in agreement across platforms.

OpenStreetMap

On the OpenStreetMap platform, the automated agent provided a total of 267 affirmative responses (69.35%) and 118 negative responses (30.65%). In comparison, human experts recorded a slightly higher number of affirmative responses, totaling 284 (73.77%), with negative responses at 101 (26.23%). The distribution indicates that both approaches demonstrated similar judgment patterns, though human evaluators tended to assess heuristic compliance slightly more positively.

Inter-expert agreement analysis for OpenStreetMap revealed Cohen's Kappa values ranging from 0.17 to 0.65, demonstrating moderate agreement among human evaluators, with an average agreement of **0.38**.

Gitlab

On the GitLab platform, the automated agent generated 295 affirmative responses (76.62%) and 90 negative responses (23.38%), whereas human evaluators reported a total of 324 affirmative responses (84.16%) and 61 negative responses (15.84%). These results suggest that experts were more optimistic about usability performance, identifying fewer heuristic issues compared to the automated agent. Inter-expert agreement on GitLab showed high consistency, with Cohen's Kappa values ranging between 0.35 and 0.77, averaging at **0.62**, indicating a very substantial level of agreement among experts.

OneStopShop

For OneStopShop, the automated agent identified fewer heuristic compliance issues, with 215 affirmative responses (55.84%) and 170 negative responses (44.16%). Conversely, human evaluators registered a higher rate of affirmative responses, with 230 positive responses (59.74%) and fewer negative responses (155, representing 40.26%). This discrepancy highlights a moderate divergence between automated and manual evaluations, with human experts perceiving greater compliance with heuristic guidelines.

Inter-expert agreement analysis for OneStopShop yielded moderate to substantial Cohen's Kappa values ranging from 0.77 to 1.00, with an average of **0.88**, indicating moderate consistency among human evaluators.

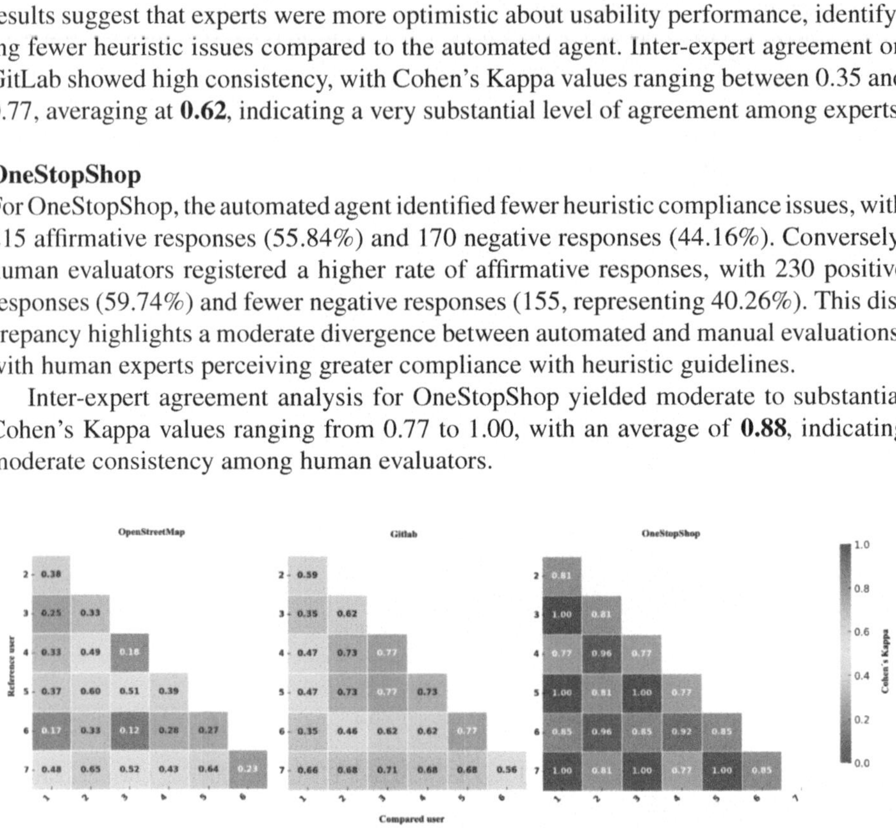

Fig. 3. User Agreement Matrix Based on Cohen's Kappa in OpenStreetMap, GitLab, and OneStopShop.
Source: Own elaboration based on experimental results.

Cohen's Kappa (Fig. 3) coefficient illustrates the consistency in classification between different user pairs across three platforms. Higher values (red) indicate stronger agreement, while lower values (blue) indicate weaker agreement.

Comparative Analysis and Agreement Metrics

To quantitatively assess the level of agreement between automated and manual evaluations, Cohen's Kappa coefficient was calculated individually for each platform:

OpenStreetMap: Cohen's Kappa = 0.74, indicating substantial agreement between automated and human evaluators.

GitLab: Cohen's Kappa = 0.68, representing an agreement level between moderate and substantial. **OneStopShop: Cohen's Kappa = 0.71,** demonstrating substantial agreement. These results highlight a high degree of consistency and reliability in automated heuristic evaluation methods compared to traditional manual evaluations, supporting the validity of automated approaches for practical usability assessments.

5 Conclusion

The results of this study demonstrate that automated heuristic evaluation based on Large Language Models (LLMs) can achieve a level of accuracy and consistency comparable to that of usability experts. By analyzing Cohen's Kappa agreement coefficients among human evaluators, it was found that the variability in their responses was not significantly different from the variability observed when comparing the automated agent with the experts. This suggests that discrepancies between automated and human evaluations fall within the natural variability range seen among usability specialists.

The analysis of the evaluated platforms—OpenStreetMap, GitLab, and OneStopShop—revealed that the agreement level between the automated system and the experts is within the same range observed in human-to-human evaluation. On average, the Kappa coefficient obtained when comparing the agent's assessments with those of human evaluators was similar to the average Kappa coefficient among experts themselves, indicating that the automated system's performance aligns with human variability patterns.

These findings have significant implications for the industry, as they suggest that automated systems can serve as a viable alternative to manual evaluations, reducing costs and time without compromising accuracy. While experts remain essential for identifying and prioritizing critical usability issues, incorporating automated agents can enhance process efficiency, particularly in scenarios where access to specialized evaluators is limited.

5.1 Limitations

One of the main limitations of this study is that the same user flow was selected for all evaluations. This approach was adopted to minimize navigation issues for the automated agent and focus exclusively on its ability to identify heuristic violations. However, this decision restricts the study's capacity to assess how agents handle more complex scenarios involving dynamic and varied interaction flows. Future studies could expand this evaluation by considering more diverse user flows and exploring ways to enhance the automated agents' navigation capabilities in more open-ended environments.

5.2 Future Work

Regarding future work, the aim is to establish a reference framework that standardizes usability test automation, not only in terms of heuristic evaluation but also in its application to various international standards. The goal is to develop an adaptive framework capable of optimizing the evaluation process and aligning with the specific requirements of regulations such as different ISO standards for usability and accessibility. This approach will enable automation to function not just as an evaluation tool but as a versatile system tailored to the needs of different contexts, strengthening the integration of artificial intelligence in user experience quality assurance.

Acknowledgments. The authors would like to express their sincere gratitude to the Autonomous University of Zacatecas for the financial support granted to Engineer Holman Cabezas Mondragón through CONACYT, with CVU number 1320292, under the Graduate Studies Scholarship Program. This support was essential in enabling the completion of the present research. The author, Wilson J. Sarmiento, a full-time professor at the Universidad Militar Nueva Granada (UMNG), acknowledges and recognizes the UMNG for its support of his research work.

References

1. Nielsen, J., Molich, R.: Heuristic evaluation of user interfaces. In: Proceedings of the SIGCHI Conference on Human Factors in Computing Systems, pp. 249–256. ACM, New York (1990)
2. Nielsen, J.: Usability inspection methods. In: Conference companion on Human factors in computing systems - CHI'94, pp. 413–414. ACM Press, Boston (1994)
3. Ling, C., Salvendy, G.: Effect of evaluators' cognitive style on heuristic evaluation: Field dependent and field independent evaluators. Int. J. Hum.-Comput. Stud. **67**(4), 382–393 (2009)
4. Kumar, B., et al.: A static machine learning based evaluation method for usability and security analysis in e-commerce website. IEEE Access. **11**, 40488–40510 (2023)
5. Wang, X., Hu, B.: Machine learning algorithms for improved product design user experience. IEEE Access. **12**, 112810–112821 (2024)
6. Abbas, A.M.H., Ghauth, K.I., Ting, C.-Y.: User experience design using machine learning: a systematic review. IEEE Access. **10**, 51501–51514 (2022)
7. Chang, Y., et al.: A survey on evaluation of large language models. ACM Trans. Intell. Syst. Technol. **15**(3), 39:1–39:45 (2024)
8. Tan, W.S., Liu, D., Bishu, R.R.: Web evaluation: heuristic evaluation vs. user testing. Int. J. Ind. Ergon. **39**(4), 621–627 (2009)
9. Alsumait, A., Al-Osaimi, A., AlFedaghi, H.: Use of survey techniques as usability evaluation for child e-learning programs. In: Proceedings of the International Conference on Computer Science and Software Engineering, pp. 325–330 (2008)
10. Dieber, J., Kirrane, S.: A novel model usability evaluation framework (MUsE) for explainable artificial intelligence. Inf. Fusion. **81**, 143–153 (2021)
11. Júnior, D.G.S., Hernández-Ramírez, R., Estima, J.O.: Investigating usability indicators for the adoption of AI models in heuristic evaluation. In: Springer Series in Design and Innovation, vol. 41, pp. 159–169. Springer, Cham (2023)
12. Damaševičius, R., Zailskaitė-Jakštė, L.: Usability and security testing of online links: a framework for click-through rate prediction using deep learning. Electronics. **11**(3), 400 (2022)
13. Grier, R.A., Bangor, A., Kortum, P., Peres, S.C.: The system usability scale: beyond standard usability testing. Proc. Hum. Factors Ergon. Soc. Annu. Meet. **57**(1), 187–191 (2013)
14. Yao, S., Chen, H., Yang, J., Narasimhan, K.: WebShop: towards scalable real-world web interaction with grounded language agents. Adv. Neural Inf. Process. Syst. **35**, 20744–20757 (2022)

15. Deng, X., et al.: Mind2Web: towards a generalist agent for the web. arXiv preprint https://arxiv.org/abs/2306.06070 (2023)
16. Zhou, S., et al.: WebArena: a realistic web environment for building autonomous agents. arXiv preprint https://arxiv.org/abs/2307.13854 (2023)
17. Garousi, V., Felderer, M., Mäntylä, M.V.: Guidelines for including grey literature and conducting multivocal literature reviews in software engineering. Inf. Softw. Technol. **106**, 101–121 (2019)
18. web-arena-x/webarena, https://github.com/web-arena-x/webarena (2025). Accessed 25 April 2025
19. ServiceNow/BrowserGym, https://github.com/ServiceNow/BrowserGym (2025). Accessed 25 April 2025
20. ServiceNow/AgentLab, https://github.com/ServiceNow/AgentLab (2025). Accessed 25 April 2025
21. OpenAI API Documentation., https://platform.openai.com (2025). Accessed 25 April 2025
22. LangChain., https://www.langchain.com (2025). Accessed 25 April 2025
23. Chezelles, T.L.S.D., et al.: The BrowserGym ecosystem for web agent research. arXiv preprint https://arxiv.org/abs/2412.05467 (2024)
24. Gur, I., et al.: A real-world webagent with planning, long context understanding, and program synthesis. arXiv preprint https://arxiv.org/abs/2307.12856 (2023)
25. Sodhi, P., Branavan, S., Artzi, Y., McDonald, R.: SteP: Stacked LLM policies for web actions. arXiv preprint https://arxiv.org/abs/2310.03720 (2023)
26. Granollers, T.: Usability evaluation with heuristics. New proposal from integrating two trusted sources. In: Marcus, A., Wang, W. (eds.) Design, User Experience, and Usability: Theory and Practice. DUXU 2018 Lecture Notes in Computer Science, vol. 10919, pp. 396–405. Springer, Cham (2018)

AI-Human Interaction Patterns: An Exploratory Study

Julio Ariel Hurtado Alegría[1](✉), Marta Cecilia Camacho Ojeda[2], María Clara Gómez Álvarez[3], María Lili Villegas[4], and César Alberto Collazos[1]

[1] Universidad del Cauca, Popayán, Colombia
{ahurtado,ccollazo}@unicauca.edu.co
[2] Colegio Mayor del Cauca, Popayán, Colombia
cecamacho@unimayor.edu.co
[3] Universidad Nacional de Colombia, Sede Medellín, Medellín, Colombia
mcgomez@unal.edu.co
[4] Universidad del Quindío, Armenia, Colombia
mlvillegas@uniquindio.edu.co

Abstract. Generative Artificial Intelligence (GenAI) has a significant potential to enhance productivity and quality, however, the adoption of Generative AI in real-world scenarios lacks the empirical studies. There is a limited understanding of how Large Language Models (LLMs) can be effectively applied, its impacts, and its potential limitations in software engineering activities. To address these issues, this study introduces a set of AI-human interaction patterns and evaluates it through two exploratory studies involving students and professional software engineers. The results show, as highly effective, the proposed patterns, with 90% of participants with intention of using them in future projects. These patterns were found to improve efficiency (80% agreement) and quality (75% agreement). The 85% of participants considered them easy to understand and apply. By providing empirical evidence on the application of these patterns, this work contributes to advancing in the responsible and effective use of GenAI in software engineering practices.

Keywords: Generative AI · Human-Computer Interaction · Human – Generative AI Interaction Patterns

1 Introduction

Integrating Generative Artificial Intelligence - GenAI, particularly Large Language Models - LLMs, like collaborative tools in software engineering, presents a significant research opportunity, enhancing human abilities with complementary capabilities. However, LLMs may struggle with ambiguous requirements, causing issues in real-world applications where precise behavior is crucial [1]. This work explores the potential of LLMs in software engineering area, facing some challenges by augmenting capabilities

H. Luna-García et al. (Eds.): HCI-COLLAB 2025, CCIS 2850, pp. 16–31, 2027.
https://doi.org/10.1007/978-3-032-31223-5_2

for problem-solving and achieve quality software products. As part for the evolution towards an Automated Software Engineering 2.0 [2], this paper proposes an iterative and collaborative approach that extends the principles of pair programming to incorporate GenAI since early phases of the software development lifecycle. In this model, GenAI participates as an agent, directly collaborate with human engineers to together drive productive processes including decision-making and problem-solving.

To formalize this approach, we define roles, tasks, artifacts, and a set of AI-human interaction patterns that guide the collaboration process. To validate the proposed approach, we conducted and reported an embedded study involving both students and professional software engineers from two Colombian regions: Cauca and Quindío. For evaluating the AI-assisted soft-ware engineering process and patterns, we used two user perception indicators: perceived usefulness and perceived ease of use [3].

2 Related Work

Hamza et al. [4] conducted an analysis about the use of ChatGPT in soft-ware engineering through a hands-on workshop. The study involving 22 professionals in software engineering. In a three-hour session, participants explored how AI-assisted development impacts productivity, the activities, and confidence. Their findings suggest that, although AI enhances efficiency in code generation and optimization, humans remains crucial for addressing different concerns and complex problem-solving. This study contributes to understanding as the AI evolves in the context of the software engineering and proposes key recommendations for its effective integration into software engineering practices, process and methods.

Abrahao et al. [5] analyze the role of AI-powered tools like GitHub Copilot in collaborative software engineering. They identify patterns such as: Co-creation Strategy, Human-Centered Refinement and Adaptive Artefacts. For example, improved designs according to experts or context changes. The proposed patterns emphasize the importance of balancing automation with human participation to avoid bias and incorporate non-systematizable human criteria. This balance ensures that AI systems complement human expertise rather than replacing it, allowing for more ethical and context-aware decision-making in software development.AI-based technologies, for instance avatars, chatbots, and virtual assistants, can be integrated into the software development lifecycles in order to increase efficiency, quality, and facilitate collaboration. These tools are usefulness for automating repetitive tasks, as techniques assistants, and as media of communication among team members. Furthermore, LLMs can be used for more advanced tasks, such as code generation and review, vulnerability analysis, and documentation, among others, become them in a valuable development toolkit [1, 6, 7].

Jiang et al. [8] studied relevant interactions in user centered development context. Including collaboration, competition, conflict, and symbiosis Human-AI, as well as the ways to enhance these interactions using IA tools. The Jiang et al. [8] work proves a comprehensive overview of current research and offering insights into how AI can strengthen human capabilities and foster harmonious human-AI relationships. Additionally, the work recommends the use of technology acceptance models, such as the Technology Acceptance Model (TAM) [3], for evaluating the potential user adoption of

AI technologies, emphasizing the importance of perceived usefulness and ease of use discovering user attitudes toward AI.

This model is used in this paper instrumentalized as a survey for evaluating our proposal. Treude and Gerosa [9] classify human-AI interactions into eleven types, including Auto-Complete Code Suggestions, Conversational Assistance, Selection-Based Enhancements, Command-Driven Actions, Contextual Recommendations Zhang et al. [7] provide a survey for studying how Large Language Models (LLMs) automate some software engineering tasks such as Code Generation and refactoring, Bug Detection and Fix and Quality attributes. Because the importance achieved by the AI role, several challenges must be considered:

- Trust and Reliability: Software engineers must often and critically question AI-generated outputs [4].
- Ethical: Bias in training data can affect AI reliability and effectivity [5].
- Complexity: looking for a suitable adoption of AI tools into existing methods, processes and practices [7].
- Explainability: becomes a significant challenge in AI. Understanding as decision-making works is a key concern in the development processes (Fig. 1).

Fig. 1. AI Paired Process Model. Authors own elaboration

3 Paired Human-AI Software Development Process

The Paired Human-AI Software Development Process extends the principles of pair programming and collaborative teams across multiple phases of software development, integrating AI tools as a knowledge-rich participant that works alongside human developers throughout the entire lifecycle. The process is iterative and incremental, refining both the software and the development strategies. Frequent and meaningful interactions between human engineers, AI tools, and stakeholders enrich the process, promoting fast feedback loops and client engagement, which are critical for adaptive and high-quality software solutions. Beyond automation, the AI-assisted development process serves as an accelerator for collaboration, enabling software teams to engage in strategic co-development. By formalizing roles, tasks, and artifacts; and establishing well-defined AI-human interaction patterns, this model enhances knowledge transfer, reduces cognitive load, and optimizes decision-making. The strengths of this approach are increasing productivity and activating collaborative strategies that drive software engineering toward a dynamic and shared knowledge-based process.

Through interaction patterns, AI becomes more than a tool—it becomes an active participant in an innovative development ecosystem. Specifically, in software development, some types of interaction be-tween AI and developers are also defined, which allows identifying critical areas such as trust, cognitive load, and customization that warrant further exploration and can help guide further research and tool development, e.g., to better orchestrate various interaction types throughout the development activities [9].

The roles of the process are described as follows:

–Business Analyst - Defines business requirements alignment with stake-holder needs.

–System Architect - Designs high-level abstraction structures for achieving specific quality attributes and trade-off among these.

–Developer - Implements software components.

–Tester - Validates system functionality and correctness.

–AI Assistant - Supports each role by generating, validating, and refining artefacts.

–Customer (with AI) - Uses AI tools to provide structured feedback and refine requirements.

The tasks of the process are described as follows:

–Requirement Elicitation - The Business Analyst and AI analyze domain knowledge and user needs.

–System Design - The Architect and AI collaborate on high-level architecture, modeling alternatives.

–Implementation - The programmer and the AI iteratively coding, testing and refactoring software components.

–Testing - The Tester and the AI generate test cases, automatizing tests, executes tests and analyze results.

–Deployment and Maintenance - AI aids to monitoring services, faults prevention, and suggest product improvements.

The artifacts of the process are described as a follow:

1. Requirements Artifacts
    a. Stakeholder Needs Document: structured list of user needs and goals. Co-created by the Business Analyst and AI.
    b. Domain Knowledge Base: repository of domain-specific information (e.g., regulations, industry standards). Structured by the AI and validated by the Business Analyst.

   c. Requirement Specification: formal document detailing functional and non-functional requirements. Human and AI discuss prioritization based on value generation, user impact, and feasibility.
   d. User Stories/Use Cases: descriptions of system interactions from the user's perspective. Generated collaboratively by the Business Analyst and AI.
2. Design Artifacts
   a. Architecture Diagram: Visual representation of the system's components, interactions, and data flow. Co-created by the Architect and AI.
   b. Design Alternatives Document: Comparison of different architectural approaches. AI and human provide pros, cons, and trade-offs for each option.
   c. Technology Stack Recommendation: List of tools, frameworks, and platforms. Suggested by the AI and validated by the Architect.
   d. System Constraints Document: Summary of technical and business constraints (e.g., scalability, security). Identified by the AI and refined by the Architect.
3. Implementation Artifacts:
   a. Source Code: AI assists in writing, refactoring, and optimizing code.
   b. Code Review Reports: Automated feedback from the AI on code quality, adherence to standards, and potential bugs.
   c. Refactoring Suggestions: List of improvements to the code. Generated by the AI and implemented by the Developer.
   d. Component Validation Logs: Records of automated tests and validations performed by the AI during development.
4. Testing Artifact

a. Test Cases: comprehensive set of test scenarios. Co-created by the Tester and AI, covering functional, non-functional, and boundary cases.
b. Test Execution Reports: results of automated tests run by the AI and reviewed by humans. Includes pass/fail status and performance metrics.
c. Defect Log: list of bugs or issues identified during testing. Prioritized by the AI based on severity and impact.
d. Test Coverage Report: summary of the percentage of code or functionality covered by tests. Generated by the AI.

5. Release Artifacts

a. Deployment Plan: step-by-step roadmap for deploying the system in hardware or virtual resources. Co-created by the Operations Team and AI.
b. Monitoring Dashboard: a view of system performance, health, and usage by specialized systems. Augmented by AI analytics.
c. Incident Reports: documentation of issues detected by the AI. Includes recommended solutions.
d. Maintenance Recommendations: list of improvements or optimizations suggested by the AI. Based on system usage and performance data and refined by humans.

4 Paired Human-AI Software Development Process

A Human-AI interaction pattern for software development is a replicable interaction way where humans and artificial intelligence systems collaborate to achieve a goal as part of a software construction activity [10]. Each pattern is defined by roles, responsibilities, and interaction traces among human and AI, aiming to enrich the interaction for maximizing efficiency, creativity, and effectiveness. It often resolves common contrary forces, such as balancing the human experience with AI's computational power, looking for AI trust outputs, and maintaining the context-awareness during the whole collaboration. Human-AI interaction patterns are particularly useful for designing systems where humans and AI work together, potentiating each capability, such as creating artefacts, running decision-making, problem-solving, or implementation of technical solutions activities [11]. They provide a structured approach showing strengths while mitigating their weaknesses.

4.1 AI Proposes, Human Discusses Interaction Pattern

Motivation: Developers often struggle with initial ideation and require inspiration to generate new concepts. AI can provide diverse suggestions, serving as a creative stimulus.

Forces: Creativity vs. Context Awareness, AI can generate novel ideas but may lack full context.

Problem: The human must balance leveraging AI-generated ideas while ensuring their relevance and feasibility.

Solution See the solution structure in Fig. 2.

1. AI generates multiple ideas or solutions based on an initial prompt.
2. Human evaluates, refines, and selects the most promising.
3. AI provides further refinements based on human feedback.

Example: A developer designing a software architecture asks ChatGPT for alternative modular designs and then refines them based on system constraints.

Known Uses: Conversational assistants like ChatGPT aiding software design brainstorming [9].

Pros: Accelerates ideation, reduces cognitive load.

Cons: AI-generated ideas may lack domain-specific knowledge.

Related Patterns: Conversational Co-Creation, AI Generates, Human Adjusts.

4.2 Human Proposes, AI Validates Interaction Pattern

Motivation: Ensuring the correctness and feasibility of human-generated solutions often requires additional validation, which AI can provide efficiently.

Forces: Accuracy vs. Creativity — AI ensures correctness but may constrain innovative solutions.

Problem: The AI must provide useful validation without discouraging creative risk taking.

Solution: See Fig. 3.

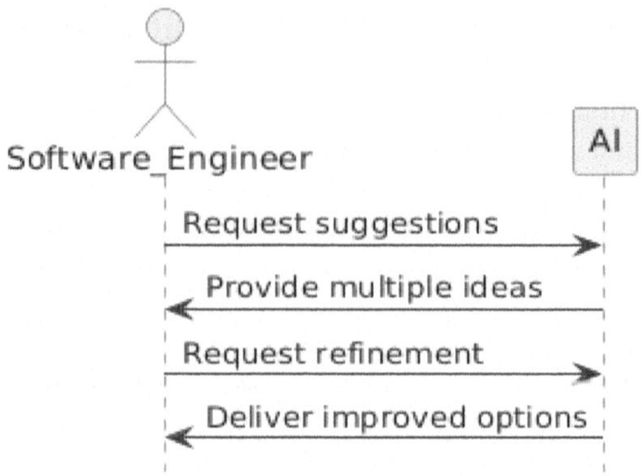

Fig. 2. AI Proposes, Human Discusses Pattern. Authors own elaboration

1. Human proposes a concept or solution.
2. AI evaluates feasibility, correctness, and potential improvements.
3. Human refines the solution based on AI feedback.

Example: A developer writes an SQL sentence and AI detects problems such as performance problems or vulnerabilities.

Known Uses: AI review code, like SonarQube, detecting vulnerabilities and refactoring suggestions [2].

Pros: Prevents logical errors for enhancing quality.

Cons: AI could enforce rigid conventions, limiting the innovation.

Related Patterns: AI Generates, Human Adjusts is just the complementary pattern for achieving am interaction cycle.

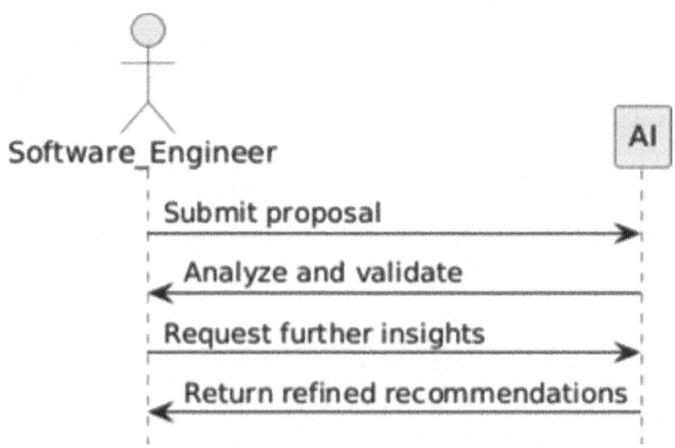

Fig. 3. Human Propose AI Validates Interaction Pattern. Authors own elaboration

4.3 Conversational Co-Creation Interaction Pattern

Motivation: Some tasks benefit from a dynamic exchange between human and AI, refining ideas iteratively.

Forces: Flexibility vs. Efficiency — Iteration enhances creativity but can pro-long decision-making.

Problem: Without structured feedback, AI may generate redundant responses.

Solution: See Fig. 4.

1. Human and AI engage in iterative question-answer exchanges.
2. Each iteration improves clarity, accuracy, or efficiency of the solution.
3. Process continues until a satisfactory outcome is reached.

Forces: Automation vs. Judgment, AI enhances review efficiency but may misinterpret intent.

Example: A team uses GitHub Copilot to progressively refine a machine learning pipeline.

Known Uses: GitHub Copilot assisting developers through incremental refinements [6].

Pros: Enhances collaboration, supports iterative improvement.

Cons: Risk of excessive loops, loss of context in extended interactions.

Related Patterns: AI Proposes, Human Discusses.

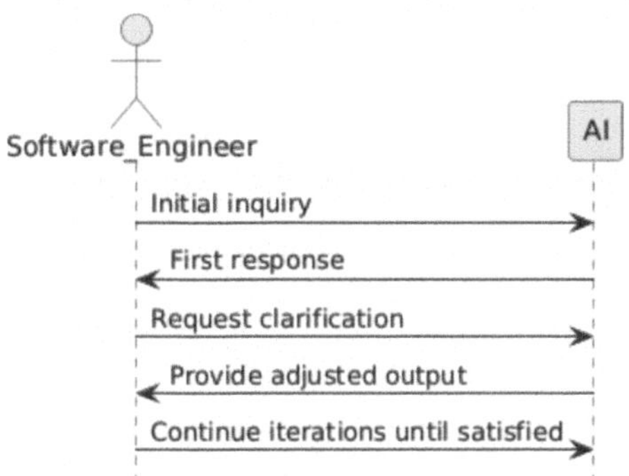

Fig. 4. Co-creation Interaction Pattern. Authors own elaboration

4.4 Human Resolve, AI Reviews Interaction Pattern

Motivation: AI can function as a secondary reviewer, ensuring quality control and catching potential issues before to delivery

Forces: Automation vs. Judgment — AI enhances review efficiency but may misinterpret intent.

Problem: AI suggestions must be assessed carefully to avoid unnecessary changes.

Solution: See Fig. 5.

1. Human proposes a solution.
2. AI analyzes for errors, optimizations, or security concerns.
3. Human incorporates relevant suggestions.

Example: AI-powered security scanners flag potential vulnerabilities in a web application.

Known Uses: AI-assisted code review tools like DeepCode [4].

Pros: Improves software quality, saves review

Cons: AI may misunderstand human intent.

Related Patterns: Human Proposes, AI Validates.

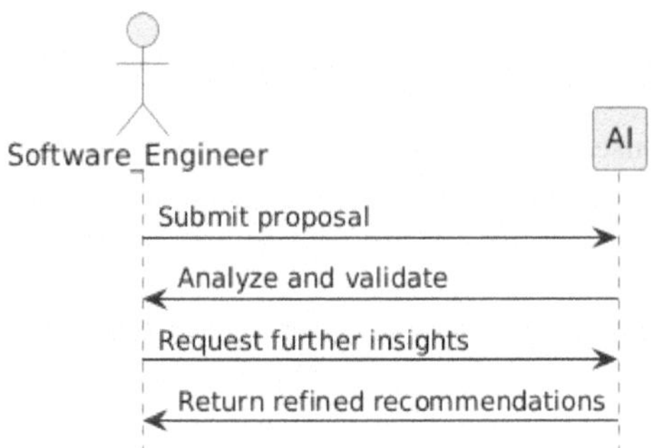

Fig. 5. Human resolve, AI Reviews Interaction Pattern. Authors own elaboration

4.5 AI Generates, Human Adjusts Interaction Pattern

Motivation: AI accelerates initial development by generating artifacts that humans refine for final use.

Forces: Automation vs. Control — AI speeds up development but requires human oversight.

Problem: AI-generated outputs often need fine-tuning to align with project needs.

Solution: See Fig. 6.

1. AI generates a draft solution (code, documentation, models, etc.).
2. Human reviews, refines, and adapts as needed.
3. AI suggests further refinements if prompted.

Example: A developer uses CodeT5 to generate function templates, refining them afterward.

Known Uses: Large language models like CodeT5 generating boilerplate code [7].

Pros: Increases efficiency, supports rapid prototyping.

Cons: AI output may require substantial revision.

Related Patterns: It is a refinement of AI Proposes, Human Discusses pattern.

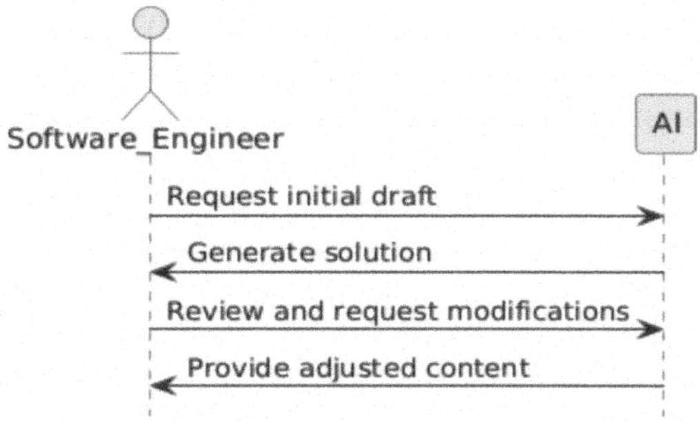

Fig. 6. AI Generates, Human Adjust Pattern. Authors own elaboration

5 Exploratory Studies

We conducted two embedded exploratory studies aimed at understanding the adoption potential of a proposed process and its interaction patterns in both industrial and academic settings [13]. The studies, following a proof-of-concept approach, as described by Neto et al. [14], were conducted in March 2025 within the context of two software engineering courses. The activities consisted of three main components: (1) a presentation introducing the proposed activities and interaction patterns, (2) a development workshop where participants applied these patterns using various AI tools, and (3) a survey to gather participants' perceptions regarding the utility of the AI interaction patterns. The goal of these studies was to assess the intention to adopt these patterns in both industrial and academic settings, as perceived by typical practitioners.

We formulated the research question to guide our study: Do AI-human interaction patterns have the potential to be adopted in industry? To address this question, we considered two key variables of adoption potential:

Usefulness: This variable aims to analyze practitioners' perceptions of the value of the process and the interaction patterns.

Ease of Use: This variable focuses on understanding how practitioners perceive the proposed process and the interaction patterns.

For gathering the information for measuring the above variables, we design a survey following the guidelines defined by Davis [3] and adapted by Marin et al. [15]. The studies included a workshop with the goal of building a Connect Four game using the AI-Paired Process Model and its interaction patterns. The activity emphasizes teamwork, AI-assisted problem-solving, and the creation of basic artifacts and provides a hands-on opportunity to explore the transformative potential of AI-assisted collaboration in software development.

5.1 Exploratory Study with Requirements Engineering Students

The study was conducted in collaboration with the Software Development Technology program at Colegio Mayor del Cauca institution (Unimayor) in Colombia. It involved twenty-four students enrolled in the second semester of a software engineering course within this program. The course was selected by opportunity and relevance of the subjects as potential software engineers.

Data Collection: The study took place on March 12th 2025, where the students, organized by teams, should define the functional and non-functional requirements of a videogame (course-project) using user stories and quality scenarios. In previous sections, most groups proposed the games they wanted to develop, taking into account their programming knowledge and skills and the project timeframe. The concepts of requirements, types of requirements, and the techniques to be applied to identify requirements were also previously explained, such as interviews, prototypes, and review of similar products. For the students, this exercise was their first experience with requirements specification. The study measures the use intention of the patterns in software engineering teams, as perceived by a typical practitioner. The students fill out a survey to know their perception of AI interaction patterns used in the requirements specification task.

Results and Analysis: The students selected which pattern to use in the exercise. The 70% of students selected AI proposes Human discusses pattern, 12.5% selected the pattern AI Generates, Human Adjust, and 16.7% selected the pattern Human make, AI reviews. The students selected the pattern according to each team's progress; those who had identified some requirements used AI to review this progress (See Fig. 6). This distribution suggests that the choice of interaction pattern is context-dependent and aligns with the team's progress in the project. The students considered that the human-IA interaction patterns help manage the project more efficiently, 29.2% totally agreed, 66.7% agreed and 4.1% considered that it did not affect the management. Such responses show the potential of the use of IA for improve the productivity in software engineering tasks. These results demonstrate the potential of AI interaction pat-terns to enhance productivity in software engineering tasks. The high percentage of agreement (95.9% combined) suggests that students found the patterns useful for developing a solution.

Fig. 7. Patterns used in the software engineering course in Unimayor. Authors own elaboration

The 50% of the students who participated in the exercise answered that they agree that the use of human-AI interaction patterns improves project results, and 16.7% totally agree with this statement. While 33.3% responded neutrally that the use of Human-AI interaction patterns does not affect the quality of the results (See Fig. 7). While a majority (66.7%) acknowledged the positive impact of AI patterns on quality, the relatively high percentage of neutral responses suggests that the influence of AI on quality may depend on factors such as the complexity of the task, the clarity of the AI's output, or the students' familiarity with the patterns. This finding highlights the need for further investigation into how AI can consistently contribute to quality improvement. The 83.3% of the students considered that the patterns are easy to understand and apply after performing the exercise, and 16.7% considered them neutral in this regard (See Fig. 8). This high level of agreement suggests that the patterns are intuitive and accessible, even for students who may not have prior experience with AI tools. The simplicity of the patterns likely contributed to their successful adoption in the exercise.

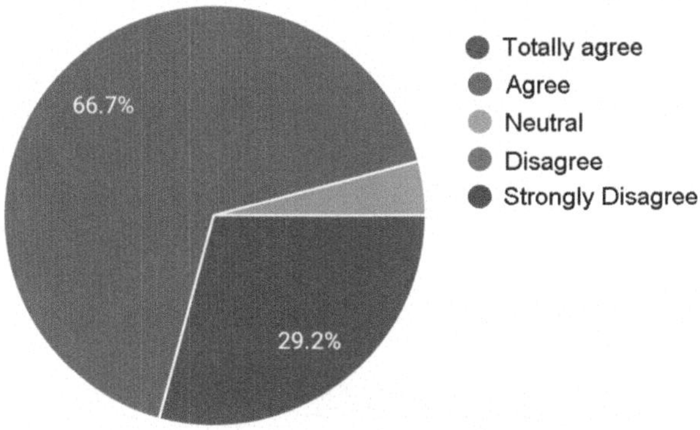

Fig. 8. Human-IA interaction patterns help to manage the project more efficiently? Authors own elaboration

The response with the greatest dispersion was the clarity and completeness of the instructions and documentation of the human-AI interaction patterns, although 62.46% considered that they were clear and complete, 29.2% were neutral and 8.33% thought that the instructions and documentation were not clear, so there is an opportunity to improve the proposal of human-IA interaction patterns. Although for the major part of students (37.5% combined) the indicated instructions are suitable, the study allows to identify some improvement opportunities because a significant percentage of neutral and negative responses (37.5% combined), see Fig. 9. For enhance the adoption and effectiveness of the AI interaction patterns is recommendable including examples and step-by-step guides.

5.2 Exploratory Study with Software Engineers

The second one study considered two stages: patterns and process presentation and the application with two teams of software engineers developing the connect four game, it was conducted with professionals in the context of the Master of Computation in the Quindío University - Colombia. The subjects were selected by opportunity and relevance as experimented software engineers.

Data collection: The study had the participation of seven male software engineers and one-woman engineer of the master with experience in the industry, including previous experiences working with the AI. Only five participants answered the survey. The activity

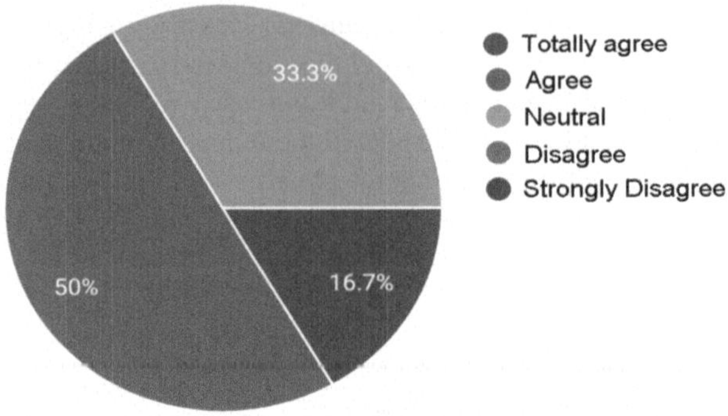

Fig. 9. Do human-AI interaction pat-terns improve the quality of project outcomes? Authors own elaboration

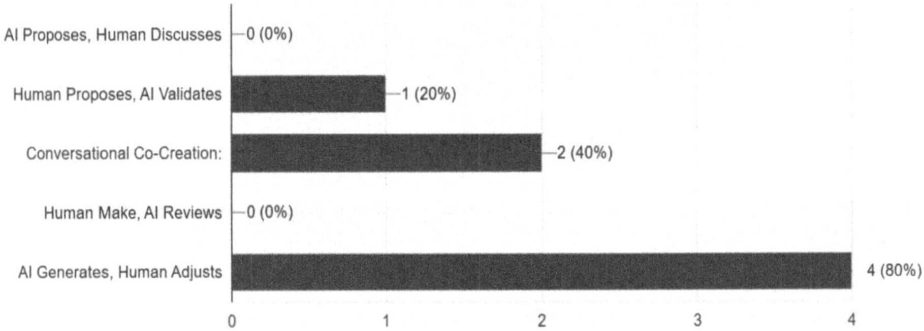

Fig. 10. Used Interaction Patterns by Software Engineers. Authors own elaboration

was structured in the workshop and we used a reflection session at the end and applied a survey for evaluating the perceived facility to use and usefulness.

Results and Analysis: The evaluation is based on participants' perceptions about the ease of use, and usefulness, as well as the challenges and lessons learned during its application:

1. **Participant Profile:** The participants include professionals with experience performing various roles in software development, such as analysts, developers, and testers. Their professional experience ranges from 1 to 12 years, providing a diverse perspective on the adoption of the process and its patterns. This diversity helps that the findings are representative of both novice and experienced practitioners.
2. **Tools:** The most frequently AI tools mentioned by participants include: Chat-GPT, Claude, Deep Seek, and Hugging Face. Study these tools in software engineering activities is a key area.
3. **Common interaction patterns:** As Fig. 10 shows, AI Generates, Human Adjusts and Conversational Co-Creation. The first one pattern is particularly useful in tasks where initial ideas or drafts are needed, such as code generation or documentation.

The second one is commonly used in scenarios requiring creative problem-solving or brainstorming.

The overall perception of the process and its patterns was positive, with the major part of participants expressing agreement or strong agreement in the following areas:

1. **Efficiency:** 80% of participants agreed that the process helps manage projects more efficiently. This indicates that the AI interaction patterns facilitate the work and reduce time spent on repetitive or complex tasks.
2. **Result Quality:** 75% of participants suggests that AI-assisted tasks, such as code generation and validation, contribute to higher-quality deliverables.
3. **Ease of Use:** 85% of the participants found the process easy to understand and apply. A good level of usability is critical for achieving the adoption of AI tools in software engineering.
4. **Intention to Use:** 90% of participants expressed intention to continue using the process and design patterns in future projects.

Challenges identified by participants:

1. It is necessary a clear specification of objectives to avoid deviations. This highlights the importance of well-defined prompts when working with AI.
2. The importance of constructing coherent and specific prompts to obtain effective results from AI. This suggests a need for training or elaborate a guideline on prompt engineering.
5. Technical debt as a factor that make difficult the adoption of the process. This indicates that integrating AI into existing activities may require addressing challenges such as to build considering legacy systems or refactoring code.

Learned Lessons:

1. The importance of conducting several iterations to refine the product. This iterative approach aligns with modern software development approached such as agile practices.
2. The importance of a role to coordinate the team tasks and artefacts. This role must coordinate the team according to the project goals. AI as a valuable tool for increasing productivity, but not as a replacement for human abilities such as collaboration and judgment.
3. Participants emphasized that it should complement, not replace, human skills such as collaboration, judgment, and creativity. Some suggestions include additional training on constructing effective prompts, the importance of maintaining a balance between AI use and human skills and the need for clear and comprehensive documentation to facilitate the process and interaction patterns adoption.

6 Conclusions, Limitations and Further Work

AI-Paired Process Model extends some principles from collaborative processes to every activity of software development process, considering the GenAI as a collaborative potential partner. The AI-Paired Process Model follows a transformative approach from software engineering, given the strengths of LLMs to augment human capabilities. By formalizing process elements (roles, artefacts, tasks, collaboration patterns), the process provides a structured definition, as Wang et al. propose too [16]. However, more research is needed to refine the approach, address ethical and technical concerns, and focusing on how AI complements rather than replaces human expertise.

The development process is not only driven by technical expertise but also influenced by the soft skills of engineers, such as effective communication, collaborative teamwork, critical thinking, and decision-making. Engineers can complement their skills with GenAI capabilities to improve efficiency and quality, through the well-defined human-AI interaction patterns, such as collaboration on complex tasks or the delegation decision. The findings demonstrate the potential of GenAI interaction patterns to enhance software engineering practices by improving efficiency, quality, and usability. However, their successful adoption depends on addressing challenges such as prompt engineering, technical debt, and the need for clear documentation. By leveraging the strengths of these patterns and incorporating participant feedback, educators and practitioners can further integrate AI into software development activities to achieve better outcomes. Some future research directions, includes the need for more diverse user groups, varied AI roles, and complex tasks, as well as the integration of multi-disciplinary and collaborative teams.

Acknowledgments. This study has been partially funded and supported by the Ibero-American Science and Technology for Development Program (CYTED), through RIPAISC - Ibero-American Network for the Advancement of Quantum Software Engineering (525RT0174).

References

1. Hou, X., et al.: Large language models for software engineering: a systematic literature review. ACM Trans. Softw. Eng. Methodol. **33**(8) (2024). https://doi.org/10.1145/3695988
2. He, J., Treude, C., Lo, D.: LLM-based multi-agent systems for software engineering: literature review, vision and the road ahead. ACM Trans. Softw. Eng. Methodol. (2025). https://doi.org/10.1145/3712003
3. Davis, F.D.: Perceived usefulness, perceived ease of use, and user acceptance of information technology. MIS Quarterly. **13**(3), 319–340 (1989). https://doi.org/10.2307/249008
4. Hamza, M., Siemon, D., Akbar, M.A., Rahman, T.: Human-AI collaboration in software engineering: lessons learned from a hands-on workshop. In: Proceedings of the 7th ACM/IEEE International Workshop on Software-Intensive Business, IWSiB'24, pp. 7–14. Association for Computing Machinery, New York, NY, USA (2024). https://doi.org/10.1145/3643690.3648236
5. Abrahao, S., Grundy, J., Pezze, M., Storey, M.A., Andrew Tamburri, D.: Soft-ware engineering by and for humans in an AI era. ACM Trans. Softw. Eng. Methodol. (2025). https://doi.org/10.1145/3715111

6. Barke, S., James, M.B., Polikarpova, N.: Grounded copilot: How programmers interact with code-generating models. Proc. ACM Program. Lang. **7**, 85–111 (2023)
7. Zhang, Q., et al.: A survey on large language models for software engineering. Sci. China Inf. Sci. **69**, 141102 (2026). https://doi.org/10.1007/s11432-025-4670-0
8. Jiang, T., Sun, Z., Fu, S., Lv, Y.: Human-AI interaction research agenda: a user-centered perspective. Data Inf. Manage. **8**, 100078 (2024). https://doi.org/10.1016/j.dim.2024.100078
9. Treude, C., Gerosa, M.: How developers interact with AI: a taxonomy of human-AI collaboration in software engineering. In: Proceedings 2025 IEEE ACM 2nd International Conference on AI Foundation Models and Software Engineering Forge 2025. IEEE (2025). https://doi.org/10.1109/Forge66646.2025.00033
10. Amershi, S., et al.: Guidelines for human-AI interaction. In: Proceedings of thc 2019 CHI Conference on Human Factors in Computing Systems, CHI'19, pp. 1–13. Association for Computing Machinery, New York, NY, USA (2019). https://doi.org/10.1145/3290605.3300233
11. Bansal, G., Wu, T., Zhu, J., Fussell, S.: Up next: human-AI interaction in the context of creative work. Proc. ACM Hum.-Comput. Interaction. **5**(CSCW1), 1–23 (2021)
12. Zhang, Y., Liu, Y., Chen, X.: Enhancing software quality assurance with AI-powered chatbots and virtual assistants. In: International Conference on Software Engineering (ICSE), pp. 123–135. IEEE (2023)
13. Wohlin, C., Runeson, P., Host, M., Ohlsson, M.C., Regnell, B., Wesslen, A.: Experimentation in software engineering. Springer Sci. Busi. Media. (2012). https://doi.org/10.1007/978-3-642-29044-2
14. Neto, A.J.R., Borges, M.M., Roque, L.: A preliminary study of proof of concept practices and their connection with information systems and information science. In: Proceedings of the Sixth International Conference on Technological Ecosystems for Enhancing Multiculturality, pp. 270–275. ACM, New York, NY, USA (2018)
15. Marin, J., Hurtado, J., Bastarrica, M., Silvestre, L.: Tailoring hybrid soft-ware processes in a medium-size software company. In: Proceedings of the 38th ACM/SIGAPP Symposium on Applied Computing, SAC'23, pp. 1042–1050. Association for Computing Machinery, New York, NY, USA (2023). https://doi.org/10.1145/3555776.3577709
16. Wang, H., Yang, Z., Li, L.: Applications of large language models in software development: A survey. J. Software Eng. Res. Dev. **11**(2), 45–60 (2023)

Assessment of Collaborative Performance in Learning Scenarios - An Empirical Study in Engineering Courses

Oscar Revelo Sánchez(✉), Manuel Bolaños González, and Alexander Barón Salazar

Universidad de Nariño, San Juan de Pasto, Colombia
{orevelo,mbolanos,abaron_98}@udenar.edu.co

Abstract. This study presents an empirical analysis of the assessment of collaborative performance in learning scenarios in engineering courses. For this purpose, an instrument based on a previously developed questionnaire measuring collaborative performance through seven operational processes was validated and applied. The research was carried out with 251 students from different courses, divided into experimental groups formed according to personality traits and a control group formed according to student preference. The results show that group formation based on personality traits influences collaborative performance, with variations depending on the type of group formation. The homogeneous and mixed formations, which prioritised emotional stability (N), scored higher on leadership and collaboration, while the heterogeneous formation scored lower than the control group. In addition, the conflict management process was identified as the most problematic in all groups, highlighting the need for specific conflict management strategies. From a methodological perspective, the validated instrument showed high reliability (Cronbach's $\alpha > 0.9$), consolidating itself as a robust tool for assessing collaborative dynamics in academic environments. It is concluded that strategic team building based on personality criteria can optimise certain collaborative work processes, but its impact varies according to the combination of traits considered. These insights are highly relevant to Human-Computer Interaction (HCI), as they inform the design of educational tools that support adaptive group formation and real-time feedback in collaborative learning platforms.

Keywords: Collaborative Performance · Group Formation · Engineering Education · Teamwork

1 Introduction

Instrument validation is a critical process in research that ensures the reliability and validity of measurement tools [1]. This process involves a series of methodological steps designed to confirm that an instrument accurately measures what it is intended to assess. The use of qualitative and quantitative methods to analyse various aspects of any measurement tool is fundamental. This rigorousness is especially relevant in contexts where data accuracy directly influences decision-making.

H. Luna-García et al. (Eds.): HCI-COLLAB 2025, CCIS 2850, pp. 32–47, 2027.
https://doi.org/10.1007/978-3-032-31223-5_3

In higher education, and particularly in engineering courses, the assessment of collaborative performance has become an essential component for the development of interpersonal and professional competences. The quality of team building and the accurate measurement of its effectiveness allows the identification of both strengths and areas for improvement, which in turn favours the optimisation of pedagogical strategies and the promotion of active learning [2].

Based on the importance of having validated measurement tools, this study focuses on the assessment of collaborative performance, recognising that the tool used must faithfully reflect the dynamics and processes of interaction in work teams. Despite the existence of numerous instruments for assessing collaboration, the integration of methodologies that consider criteria based on personality traits represents an innovative and necessary proposal. Recent research has shown that group formation using models that incorporate dimensions of the Big Five model can positively influence team dynamics and collaborative performance [3, 4]. This approach, when contrasted with traditional methods based on student preference, offers a broader perspective for identifying effective strategies for team formation and coordination.

This study aims to validate a collaborative performance assessment instrument adapted to engineering contexts, and to analyse the impact of group formation based on personality traits versus formation based on student preference. The aim is to provide empirical evidence to guide decision making in the organisation of collaborative activities, thereby strengthening both educational practice and the development of essential competences for future professionals.

The remainder of this paper is structured as follows: Section 2 describes the proposed evaluation strategy; Section 3 presents the research design; Section 4 describes the study's findings, and finally, Sections 5 and 6, discussion, conclusions and future work.

2 Assessing Collaborative Performance

According to Cavique and Ramos [5], the evaluation of collaborative performance in academic environments involves the evaluation of both the process and the product of group activities. Process evaluation focuses on the dynamics of teamwork, while product evaluation emphasises the accuracy and quality of the final result. As described below, this study focused on process evaluation.

2.1 Instrument Used

Identifying the critical characteristics of the collaborative process and developing effective assessment tools for these characteristics are major challenges [6]. Various methods and approaches for assessing the quality of collaboration in both academic and organisational settings have been proposed in the literature. However, these studies are often presented without rigorous validation [7]. Chebil et al. [8] point out that the assessment is generally done by identifying specific metrics and their subsequent measurement, as described in research by Dascalu et al. [9], Chounta and Avouris [10] and D'Angelo et al. [11]; and by designing questionnaires that capture and assess relevant aspects, as in the work of Meier et al. [6], Diez et al. [12], Marek et al. [13] and Herro et al. [14].

For this study, we chose to select and adapt the questionnaire-type tool developed by Diez et al. [12], considering its completeness and systematic ease of use, as well as its specific focus and validation in educational contexts. This choice is also due to the fact that, as an instrument designed for self- and co-assessment, it does not represent an additional workload for the teacher. Collaborative performance is assessed using seven indicators that the authors refer to as operational processes (see Fig. 1). These processes describe the functions and interactions that occur during group work and how they are managed to carry out the tasks assigned to the group. These operational processes are directly or indirectly aligned with the criteria or dimensions of group performance assessment considered relevant in collaborative work settings, as mentioned in some of the studies included in Section 2.1.

Fig. 1. Operational processes of collaborative performance. Adapted from [12]

It is important to note that the proposal by Diez et al. [12] conceives the assessment of collaborative performance as an integral and multidimensional process, where one of its facets is specifically collaboration, subdivided into the sub-dimensions of cooperation and coordination. However, these are better understood as individual student competencies or skills rather than the overall process of collaboration itself.

The instrument consists of a questionnaire that assesses the level of collaborative performance (see Appendix 1), and a document that allows students to interpret the score they receive and provides them with guidelines for improvement (see Appendix 2). This tool has been implemented as a 'Survey' type activity for Moodle™, which can be imported into any course or academic space available in the Moodle™ LMS. The implementation of the activity can be downloaded from www.galeras.net/ors/val_des_col.xml.

2.2 Likert Scale Processing

Considering that the 24 items of the Collaborative Performance Assessment Instrument are scored on a Likert scale, the following procedure was used to obtain the results of the instrument:

The sum of the scores given to the 24 items by each of the participating students was obtained, both globally and by grouping the items corresponding to each operational process. The lowest possible sum is 0 in all cases and the highest is 96 in the global case;

12 for the processes of *participation/decision making*, *internal communication/mutual respect/trust* and *collaboration/cooperation/coordination*; 8 for the processes of *conflict management*, *problem resolution* and *leadership*; and 32 for the process of *external communication/feedback*.

For better understanding, the sums obtained in the previous step were normalized on a scale from 0.0 to 5.0 using min-max normalization [15], where the new minimum is considered as 0.0 and the new maximum as 5.0.

2.3 Instrument Reliability Test

Before applying the instrument, the reliability of the results (consistency of the answers) was verified by calculating Cronbach's α in a pilot test with 32 completed instruments, obtaining an overall value of 0.9105 and, for each of the operational processes included in the instrument by Diez et al. [12], the values shown in Table 1.

Table 1. Cronbach's α by operational process. Own elaboration

Operational process	Cronbach's α
Participation/Decision Making	0.8227
Conflict management	0.5511
Problem resolution	0.6058
Internal Communication/Mutual Respect/Trust	0.6713
External Communication/Feedback	0.7762
Collaboration/Cooperation/Coordination	0.9243
Leadership	0.9767

It can be observed that the overall internal consistency is very high, above 0.9, and all the operational processes can be considered consistent, except for *conflict management*, whose value is considered fair [16]. When analysing the possible improvement of the consistency of some of the items, the results were not significant. Overall, these values support the reliability of the results presented.

For confirmation, Cronbach's α was applied to all results (251 completed instruments), yielding an overall value of 0.9009 and, for each of the operational processes, the values shown in Table 2.

The overall internal consistency remains very high at 0.9 and all operational processes can be considered consistent, except for *conflict management*, which is still considered fair.

However, knowing Cronbach's alpha alone does not prove the validity of the instrument used. The conceptual coherence of the instrument was validated by observing whether the results it provided were consistent with the theory of collaborative work. Specifically, and as will be seen below, for each of the types of grouping (homogeneous, heterogeneous and mixed), a contrast was made between the experimental groups and

Table 2. Cronbach's α by operational process (verification). Own elaboration

Operational process	Cronbach's α
Participation/Decision Making	0.6994
Conflict management	0.5585
Problem resolution	0.7093
Internal Communication/Mutual Respect/Trust	0.7515
External Communication/Feedback	0.8610
Collaboration/Cooperation/Coordination	0.8276
Leadership	0.9464

the control group (grouping by student preference), both globally and for each of the operational processes.

According to Hernández Sampieri et al. [16], Cronbach's α values above 0.9 are considered excellent, values above 0.8 are good, and values above 0.7 are acceptable. In this context, the instrument demonstrated excellent internal consistency globally ($\alpha > 0.9$), and acceptable consistency for most dimensions, except for conflict management, which showed fair reliability ($\alpha \approx 0.55$).

3 Method

The research process of the main study was structured on the basis of a quasi-experimental empirical design [16], as illustrated in Fig. 2. This design involved a collaborative activity in which a group formation model based on participants' personality traits was applied [17], with the purpose of testing the following hypotheses: H_0, which states that students' collaborative performance does not improve when considering their personality traits for the formation of work groups; and H_1, which postulates that collaborative performance does improve when integrating these traits in the group formation process.

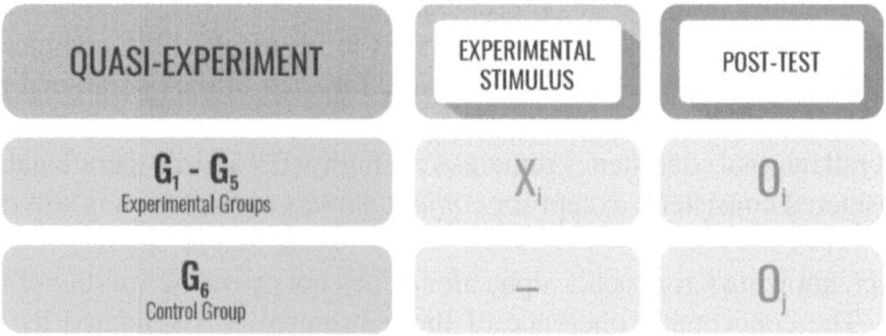

Fig. 2. Experimental design of the main study. Own elaboration

The collaborative activity served as a basis for validating, in parallel, the coherence and applicability of the instrument described in Section 2.1. To this end, a methodological approach to instrument validation was adopted that aimed to fairly assess the quality of the instrument, with emphasis on quantitative validation through a reliability test and content validity through a pilot test, in accordance with the guidelines proposed by Soriano Rodríguez [18].

The experiment, which consisted in carrying out a collaborative learning activity, was carried out with 251 students from 16 courses belonging to the academic programmes of the Faculty of Engineering of the University of Nariño, in San Juan de Pasto - Colombia, in the academic semesters A-2023 and B-2023. Table 3 summarizes the characterization of the courses.

Courses indexed 1 to 11 were the experimental groups to which the experimental treatment (X_i) was applied: homogeneous, heterogeneous and mixed formation of the groups required for the collaborative activity, using the group formation strategy based on personality traits. Indexed courses 12 to 16 formed the control group, to which the experimental treatment was not applied; the groups required for the activity were formed according to the students' preferences. O_i and O_j, on the other hand, were the post-tests applied at the end of the experiment to both the experimental and control groups, consisting in the individual completion of the instrument described in section 2.1, to determine the impact of the experimental treatment on the collaborative performance of the participants.

In the context of mixed group formations, the functional validation of group formation strategies is achieved through the consideration of one dimension of the Big-Five model in each instance, with the remaining dimensions being allocated to either homogeneity or heterogeneity. The dimensions selected for homogeneity were openness (O), neuroticism (N) and conscientiousness (C). The choice of these dimensions was informed by prior studies demonstrating their significant correlation with academic performance and collaborative behaviours in technical domains [19–21]. Openness is associated with creativity and idea generation, while conscientiousness relates to task completion and reliability. Emotional stability influences conflict tolerance and emotional regulation, key for sustained group engagement.

To strengthen the rigor of the study and increase replicability, an analysis of potential validity threats is presented below.

- *Internal Validity*: Although random assignment was not feasible, the use of control groups and statistical contrasts mitigates potential confounding variables. However, variations in the teaching staff and class dynamics could influence the results.
- *External Validity*: Since the study was conducted exclusively in engineering programs at a single institution, the generalization to other disciplines or institutions should be approached with caution.
- *Construct Validity*: The instrument was validated through Cronbach's α and conceptual alignment with existing theories. Nevertheless, biases may exist due to self-reported data, which can be affected by social desirability.

Future studies should consider longitudinal designs and cross-institutional samples to increase generalizability.

Table 3. Characterization of experimental groups, Own elaboration

Course	Semester	Number of students	Group	Grouping type
1. Programming I - Group 1	A-2023	11	E_1	Mix (O)
2. Programming I - Group 2	A-2023	18	E_2	Mix (N)
3. Operations Research - Group 1	A-2023	21	E_2	Mix (N)
12. Operations Research - Group 2	A-2023	19	C	S.P.
4. Introduction to engineering	A-2023	35	E_3	Heterogeneous
5. Numerical methods - Group 1	A-2023	16	E_4	Homogeneous
6. Numerical methods - Group 2	A-2023	21	E_5	Mix (C)
13. Research Project I	A-2023	13	C	S.P.
7. Audit and IT security	B-2023	13	E_5	Mix (C)
8. Programming II - Group 1	B-2023	16	E_3	Heterogeneous
9. Programming II - Group 2	B-2023	13	E_1	Mix (O)
10. Numerical methods - Group 1	B-2023	8	E_4	Homogeneous
14. Numerical methods - Group 2	B-2023	13	C	S.P.
15. Operations Research - Group 1	B-2023	13	C	S.P.
11. Operations Research - Group 2	B-2023	11	E_3	Heterogeneous
16. Computer graphics	B-2023	10	C	S.P.
Total		**251**		

4 Results

4.1 General Statistical Contrast

As mentioned in Section 4, post-tests (O_i and O_j) were administered to the study groups at the end of the experiment to determine the impact of the experimental treatment. These post-tests consisted of the individual completion of the instrument described in Section 2.1. The post-tests made it possible to compare the experimental groups with the control group to determine whether there was an improvement in the collaborative performance of the students by applying the proposed model of group formation based on personality traits, as opposed to the formation based on student preference, which is traditionally used by teachers when developing collaborative activities.

Figure 3 shows the contrast between the mean scores obtained in each of the groupings considered (experimental groups) and the grouping by student preference (control group). The results show that, on average, the scores obtained in the post-tests by the experimental groups are apparently different from those obtained by the control group.

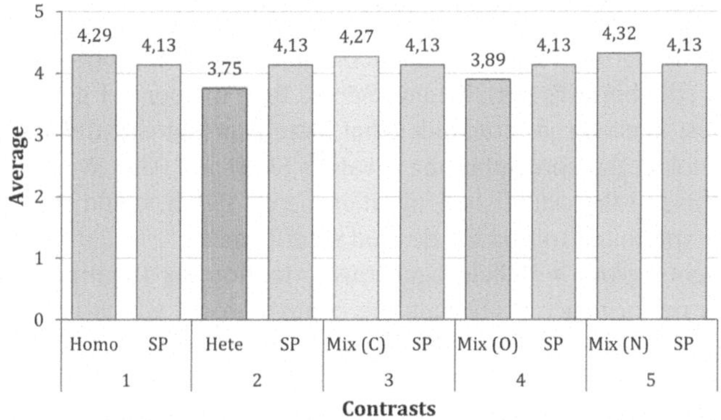

Fig. 3. Contrast of experimental versus control groups. Own elaboration

To provide a statistically sound conclusion regarding the proposed experimental treatment, a statistical analysis was carried out using the Mann-Whitney U test. This test was used to statistically confirm the difference between the scores obtained by the experimental groups compared to those obtained by the control group. It was used to ascertain the general difference in the collaborative performance achieved by the students in the specific subject matter of each of the courses. The decision to use this test was taken because the collaborative performance scores of the students do not follow a normal distribution.

The results of the application of the Mann-Whitney U test for each of the contrasts are presented in Table 4, Table 5, Table 6, Table 7 and Table 8, obtained using SPSS™ at a 95% confidence level and considering the following hypotheses: H_0, The means of the students' post-test scores are similar; H_1, The means of the students' post-test scores are different.

Table 4. U-test for homogeneous grouping vs. student preference grouping. Own elaboration

Variable	Group Type		Z	U	p
	Experimental (G_1) n = 24	Control (G_6) n = 68			
	Average range	Average range			
Scores CP	54.98	43.51	−1.810	612.5	.070

A *p*-value of.070 was obtained when the experimental group G_1 was compared with the control group G_6. As this value is greater than.05, there is no statistical evidence to reject the null hypothesis (H_0) or to accept the alternative hypothesis (H_1). There is insufficient evidence at a significance level of 5% that the mean scores obtained by students with homogeneous group formation and those obtained by those with formation by their preference are statistically different.

Other contrasts can be consulted at http://www.galeras.net/ors/appendices_4.pdf.

All these results allow us to highlight the following:

- The experimental groups with homogeneous and mixed (C) formation have slightly higher mean collaborative performance scores than the control group. Although the hypothesis test in each case concludes that there is no statistically significant difference, if we look at the corresponding *p*-values (.070 and.087), we can see that these values are close to the established significance of 5%. It would therefore be worth refining the experiment to find the desired significance.
- The experimental group with heterogeneous formation has a significantly lower mean collaborative performance score than the control group, which is confirmed by the hypothesis test and the effect size. This result allows us to conclude that heterogeneous grouping based on personality traits does not seem to be the most appropriate strategy in engineering courses if the aim is to improve the collaborative performance of the participants.
- The experimental group with mixed (O) formation is, according to the hypothesis test, the one with the most similar average collaborative performance score to the control group. This result allows us to conclude that mixed grouping based on personality traits, where the openness (O) dimension is favoured for homogeneity and the other dimensions for heterogeneity, produces very similar collaborative performance results compared to grouping by student preference in engineering courses.
- In summary, the suggested formations to achieve an overall improvement in the collaborative performance of the participants, in order of score would be: Mixed (N), Homogeneous and Mixed (C).

4.2 Statistical Contrasts by Operational Processes

As showed in Table 9, the subsequent discussion will present the overall results of the students. The objective of this presentation is to provide a summary of the findings for all participants. However, it should be noted that presenting the results at a general level does not offer any meaningful insight. In practice, the most interesting aspect of the experience is the particular analysis of each group and its subsequent feedback. However, this aspect is beyond the scope of this paper.

However, with respect to the aggregate results of the students, it can be discerned that operational processes 4 and 6 are the ones that obtain the highest average scores, which implies that *internal communication* is adequate and effective, and that *collaboration* is present among the students to achieve the objectives that have been established. Conversely, operational process 2 exhibited the lowest score, a salient factor in the management of collaborative work groups, irrespective of their composition. This is primarily due to the fact that conflicts have been shown to diminish the performance of work groups, particularly when personal elements are involved [22, 23]. Additionally, there is notable uniformity in the behaviour across groups, as evidenced by the minimal variability in the data.

Table 9. General descriptives of students' scores on operational processes. Own elaboration.

	Operational Process	Mean	SD	Mode	Min	Max
1	Participation/Decision Making	4.20	0.90	5.00	0.83	5.00
2	Conflict management	3.21	1.64	5.00	.00	5.00
3	Problem resolution	4.12	0.94	5.00	.00	5.00
4	Internal Communication	4.51	0.75	5.00	.00	5.00
5	External Communication	4.29	0.72	5.00	.00	5.00
6	Collaboration	4.31	0.88	5.00	.00	5.00
7	Leadership	3.89	1.43	5.00	.00	5.00

As showed in Table 10, the mean scores of the experimental and control groups in each of the operational processes are summarised. This is followed by the corresponding statistical traces and contrasts.

Table 10. Average scores of the experimental groups by type of formation. Own elaboration.

Operational Process	Experimentals					Control
	Hom	Het	Mix (C)	Mix (O)	Mix (N)	
Participation/Decision Making	4.20	4.00	4.26	4.08	4.50	4.24
Conflict management	3.44	2.63	3.84	2.71	3.53	3.33
Problem resolution	4.38	3.57	4.36	4.01	4.41	4.29
Internal Communication	4.57	4.43	4.50	4.17	4.66	4.61
External Communication	4.49	3.92	4.47	4.02	4.50	4.45
Collaboration	4.36	4.06	4.33	4.05	4.63	4.43
Leadership	4.60	3.68	4.12	4.20	4.02	3.55
Average score	**4.29**	**3.75**	**4.27**	**3.89**	**4.32**	**4.13**

In order to provide statistically sound conclusions regarding the proposed experimental treatment, a statistical analysis was carried out using the Mann Whitney U test, seeking to statistically confirm the difference between the scores obtained by the experimental groups compared to those obtained by the control group in each of the operational processes, i.e. a specific difference in the collaborative performance achieved by the students in the subject matter of each of the courses. This test was used considering that the collaborative performance scores of the students by operational process do not follow a normal distribution either.

Thus, the results of the application of the Mann Whitney U test for each of the contrasts are shown in Table 11, Table 12, Table 13, Table 14 and Table 15, which were obtained using SPSS™, with a confidence level of 95% and considering the following hypotheses: H_0, the means of the scores obtained by the students in a specific operational process are similar; H_1, the means of the scores obtained by the students in a specific operational process are different.

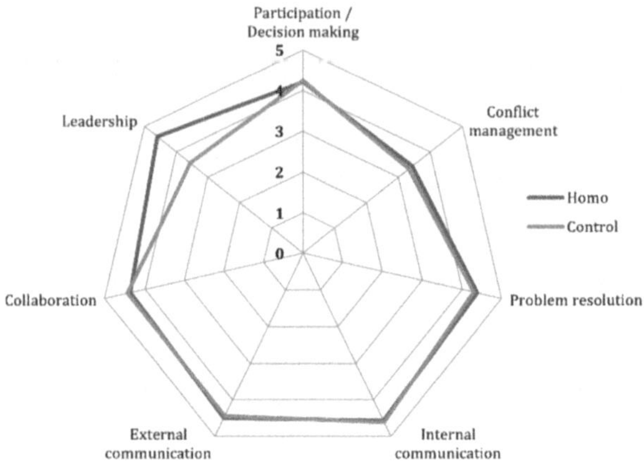

Fig. 4. Trace of the homogeneous grouping versus the control group. Own elaboration.

Table 11. U-tests for homogeneous grouping vs. grouping by student preference. Own elaboration.

Variable	Group Type		Z	U	p	g
	Experimental (G_1) n = 24	Control (G_6) n = 68				
	Average range	Average range				
Participation/Decision Making	45.15	46.98	−0.299	783.5	0.765	–
Conflict management	47.40	46.18	−0.194	794.5	0.846	–
Problem resolution	49.88	45.31	−0.756	735.0	0.450	–
Internal Communication	47.67	46.09	−0.272	788.0	0.786	–
External Communication	45.92	46.71	−0.127	802.0	0.899	–
Collaboration	47.44	46.17	−0.211	793.5	0.833	–
Leadership	57.75	42.53	−2.489	546.0	.013	0.674

Figure 4 shows a very similar behaviour in the operational processes between the experimental group with homogeneous formation and the control group, with the exception of the *leadership* process. This is confirmed by the calculation of the U-tests for each of the processes, which are shown in Table 11. It can be seen that all processes, except leadership, have *p*-values greater than.05, which means that there is insufficient evidence at a 5% significance level that the scores in these processes are statistically different. For *leadership*, as the *p*-value is less than.05, it is accepted that there is a statistically significant difference in favour of the experimental group. For this case, the effect size (g) was also calculated, obtaining a value of 0.674 which is considered to be medium, implying that there is a statistically significant difference between the results obtained by the experimental group and those obtained by the control group in the *leadership* process that is not due to chance.

Other contrasts can be consulted at http://www.galeras.net/ors/appendices_4.pdf.

All these behaviours highlight the following:

- Those groups whose formation has been pre-established by the teachers (experimental) through the proposed model, have had, in general, a better collaborative performance than the groups with formation by student preference (control), except in the case of heterogeneous formation. The homogeneous and mixed (N) formations were the highest scoring.
- The lowest rated process in all relationships is conflict management. This is an area for improvement regardless of the type of grouping, as conflict within the group can affect its performance [23].
- *Internal communication* is the process that always stands out in control groups. Allowing students to choose their peers or group members makes them feel more comfortable and motivated to work, allowing communication within and outside the group to flow better [24].
- The mixed formations that privilege the dimension of conscientiousness (C) and emotional stability (N) share the best average score for all operational processes. This confirms the findings of some studies that state that these dimensions of the Big-Five model are among the most representative, both in their individual and group work [20, 21, 25–27].
- On the other hand, as mentioned above, the mixed formation that privileges the dimension of openness (O) was the one that obtained the lowest mean score, ratifying, in the same way, what has been exposed in some related studies [20, 25–29].
- Based on the corresponding statistical contrast, it can be noted that homogeneous group formation based on personality traits enhances the *leadership* process in the students and thus in the working groups, as opposed to group formation based on their preference.
- Based on the corresponding statistical contrast, it could be highlighted that mixed group formation, in which the dimension of conscientiousness (C) is privileged, could enhance the processes of *conflict management* and *leadership* in the students and therefore in the working groups, as opposed to the formation of groups by their preference, refining the corresponding experimentation process.
- Based on the corresponding statistical contrast, it could be highlighted that the mixed group formation, in which the dimension of openness (O) is privileged, could enhance

the processes of *conflict management* and *external communication* in the students and therefore in the working groups, as opposed to the formation of groups by their preference, refining the corresponding experimentation process.

- Based on the corresponding statistical contrast, it could be highlighted that mixed group formation, in which the dimension of emotional stability (N) is privileged, could enhance the processes of *participation/decision making* and *collaboration* in the students and thus in the working groups, as opposed to the formation of groups by their preference, refining the corresponding experimentation process.

5 Discussion

The findings obtained in this study provide relevant elements to understand how the evaluation of collaborative performance may be influenced by the group formation strategy based on personality traits. In general, it was observed that experimental groups, formed by criteria such as homogeneity or mixed combinations, tend to present similar or even higher collaborative performance than groups formed by student preference. However, it is important to note that the heterogeneous formation showed significantly lower scores, suggesting that trait diversity, in this context, could hinder effective team integration and coordination.

The use of the validated instrument, proposed by Diez et al. [12], made it possible to identify strengths and areas for improvement in different operational processes. For example, the *leadership* process was notably enhanced in the group with homogeneous formation, which shows the potential of this approach to develop management and coordination competencies in collaborative work teams. Likewise, the results obtained in the mixed group that favoured the dimension of emotional stability (N) support the hypothesis that certain personality traits can favour key aspects such as *participation, decision-making* and *collaboration*, in accordance with recent studies [20, 27].

Another relevant aspect is the performance in *conflict management*, which was consistently ranked as the subdimension with the lowest scores in all the groups evaluated. This finding is consistent with the literature that points out the negative impact that conflicts can have on the effectiveness of teamwork [22, 23], and highlights the need to incorporate specific formation strategies for the proper management of these situations in collaborative learning contexts.

The high internal consistency of the instrument, reflected in Cronbach's α values above 0.9, reinforces the reliability of the tool to capture important nuances of collaborative performance. This aspect not only guarantees the validity of the results but also allows teachers and students to have useful information to provide feedback and adjust group dynamics, thus promoting continuous improvement in the quality of collaborative work.

The results suggest that the incorporation of personality trait-based criteria for group formation may contribute to optimising certain operational processes, especially in areas such as *leadership* and *collaboration*. However, the heterogeneous formation strategy may require further refinement, as its implementation did not result in significant improvements and, in some cases, showed lower performance than groups formed by student preference. These findings invite further research in this field, exploring adjustments in the experimental design and the integration of specific interventions for conflict management, in order to comprehensively enhance collaborative performance in learning scenarios.

6 Conclusions and Future Work

The results obtained in this study show the importance of the evaluation of collaborative performance in learning activities in engineering courses. It was found that the formation of groups based on personality traits has an impact on the dynamics of teamwork, influencing various operational processes such as *communication*, *conflict management* and *leadership*. In general terms, groups formed with homogeneous and mixed criteria (favouring dimensions such as emotional stability and conscientiousness) performed better than those formed by student preference. However, heterogeneous formation showed less favourable results, suggesting that extreme diversity of traits may generate difficulties in team integration and coordination.

The use of the validated evaluation instrument allowed the identification of strengths and areas for improvement in the collaborative process. *Conflict management* was found to be the aspect with the lowest score in all groups, which underlines the need to implement specific strategies for conflict management in educational settings. It was also observed that homogeneous formation enhanced *leadership* in the teams, while mixed formation based on emotional stability favoured *decision-making* and *collaboration*, which reinforces the idea that certain personality traits can play a key role in the optimisation of teamwork.

In terms of future work, there is a need for further studies to refine the group formation process, exploring more detailed combinations of personality traits and their impact on collaborative performance. In addition, it would be valuable to incorporate intervention strategies for the development of key competencies in conflict management, promoting more balanced and effective learning. Another relevant line of research would be the application of automated methodologies, such as the use of machine learning algorithms, to optimise group formation and more accurately predict collaborative performance. Finally, it is recommended to extend the study to other educational contexts and disciplines to assess the generalisability of the findings and their applicability in different collaborative learning environments.

References

1. Boateng, G.O., Neilands, T.B., Frongillo, E.A., Melgar-Quiñonez, H.R., Young, S.L.: Best practices for developing and validating scales for health, social, and behavioral research: a primer. Front. Public Health. **6**, 149 (2018). https://doi.org/10.3389/fpubh.2018.00149
2. Revelo Sánchez, O., Collazos, C.A., Redondo, M.A.: A strategy based on genetic algorithms for forming optimal collaborative learning groups: an empirical study. Electronics. **10**, 463 (2021). https://doi.org/10.3390/electronics10040463
3. Mertz, P.S., Sherrer, S.M., Bowers, G.M.: Teaching and assessing undergraduate collaboration skills scaffolded through the biochemistry curriculum using collaboration rubrics and student learning contracts. Biochem. Mol. Biol. Educ. **51**, 499–507 (2023). https://doi.org/10.1002/bmb.21760

4. Wicaksono, S.R.: Impact of collaborative learning in higher education environment. Sustain. J. Kaji. Mutu Pendidik. **7**, 53–58 (2024). https://doi.org/10.32923/kjmp.v7i1.4069
5. Cavique, L., Ramos, M.R.: Assessment in collaborative learning: a mediation Analysis approach. Rev. Educ. Distancia RED. **24** (2024). https://doi.org/10.6018/red.606551
6. Meier, A., Spada, H., Rummel, N.: A rating scheme for assessing the quality of computer-supported collaboration processes. Int. J. Comput.-Support. Collab. Learn. **2**, 63–86 (2007). https://doi.org/10.1007/s11412-006-9005-x
7. Steves, M.P., Scholtz, J.: A framework for evaluating collaborative systems in the real world. In: 38th Annual Hawaii International Conference on System Sciences (HICSS 2005), pp. 1–9. IEEE, Big Island, HI, USA (2005). https://doi.org/10.1109/HICSS.2005.15
8. Chebil, R., Chaari, W.L., Cerri, S.A., Ghedira, K.: A causal graph based method to evaluate e-collaboration scenarios. In: Workshops on Enabling Technologies: Infrastructure for Collaborative Enterprises (WETICE 2013), pp. 225–230. IEEE, Hammamet, Tunisia (2013). https://doi.org/10.1109/WETICE.2013.10
9. Dascalu, M., Trausan-Matu, S., McNamara, D.S., Dessus, P.: ReaderBench: automated evaluation of collaboration based on cohesion and dialogism. Int. J. Comput.-Support. Collab. Learn. **10**, 395–423 (2015). https://doi.org/10.1007/s11412-015-9226-y
10. Chounta, I.-A., Avouris, N.: Towards the real-time evaluation of collaborative activities: Integration of an automatic rater of collaboration quality in the classroom from the teacher's perspective. Educ. Inf. Technol. **21**, 815–835 (2016). https://doi.org/10.1007/s10639-014-9355-3
11. D'Angelo, C.M., Smith, J., Alozie, N., Tsiartas, A., Richey, C., Bratt, H.: Mapping individual to group level collaboration indicators using speech data. In: 13th International Conference on Computer Supported Collaborative Learning (CSCL 2019), pp. 628–631. International Society of the Learning Sciences (ISLS), Lyon, France (2019)
12. Diez, E.V., Zárraga-Rodríguez, M., García, C.J.: Tool to assess teamwork performance in higher education. Intang. Cap. **9**, 281–304 (2013). https://doi.org/10.3926/ic.399
13. Marek, L.I., Brock, D.-J.P., Savla, J.: Evaluating collaboration for effectiveness. Am. J. Eval. **36**, 67–85 (2015). https://doi.org/10.1177/1098214014531068
14. Herro, D., Quigley, C., Andrews, J., Delacruz, G.: Co-measure: developing an assessment for student collaboration in STEAM activities. Int. J. STEM Educ. **4**, 1–12 (2017). https://doi.org/10.1186/s40594-017-0094-z
15. Han, J., Kamber, M.: Data Mining: Concepts and Techniques. Elsevier Inc., San Francisco, CA, USA (2006)
16. Hernández Sampieri, R., Fernández Collado, C., Baptista Lucio, P.: Metodología de la investigación. México D. F., México, McGraw-Hill Education (2014)
17. Revelo Sánchez, O., Collazos, C.A., Redondo, M.A.: Automatic group organization for collaborative learning applying genetic algorithm Techniques and the big five model. Mathematics. **9**, 1578 (2021). https://doi.org/10.3390/math9131578
18. Soriano Rodríguez, A.M.: Diseño y validación de instrumentos de medición. Diá-Logos. **19–40** (2015). https://doi.org/10.5377/dialogos.v0i14.2202
19. De Raad, B., Schouwenburg, H.C.: Personality in learning and education: a review. Eur. J. Personal. **10**, 303–336 (1996). https://doi.org/10.1002/(SICI)1099-0984(199612)10:5%3C303::AID-PER262%3E3.0.CO;2-2
20. Amin, A., Rehman, M., Akbar, R., Basri, S., Hassan, M.F.: Trait-based personality profile of software programmers: a study on Pakistan's software industry. In: 8th International Conference on Intelligent Systems, Modelling and Simulation (ISMS 2018), pp. 90–94. IEEE, Kuala Lumpur, Malaysia (2018). https://doi.org/10.1109/ISMS.2018.00026
21. Karimi, Z., Baraani-Dastjerdi, A., Ghasem-Aghaee, N., Wagner, S.: Using personality traits to understand the influence of personality on computer programming. J. Cases Inf. Technol. **18**, 28–48 (2016). https://doi.org/10.4018/JCIT.2016010103

22. De Dreu, C.K.W., Weingart, L.R.: Task versus relationship conflict, team performance, and team member satisfaction: A meta-analysis. J. Appl. Psychol. **88**, 741–749 (2003). https://doi.org/10.1037/0021-9010.88.4.741
23. Kozlowski, S.W.J., Ilgen, D.R.: Enhancing the effectiveness of work groups and teams. Psychol. Sci. Public Interest. **7**, 77–124 (2006). https://doi.org/10.1111/j.1529-1006.2006.00030.x
24. Barkley, E.F., Major, C.H., Cross, K.P.: Collaborative Learning Techniques: A Handbook for College Faculty. Jossey-Bass, San Francisco, CA, USA (2014)
25. Anvari, F., Richards, D.: Using personality traits and a spatial ability test to identify talented aspiring designers in user-centred design methodologies. In: In: 10th International Conference on Evaluation of Novel Approaches to Software Engineering, pp. 90–101. SCITEPRESS-Science and Technology Publications, Barcelona, Spain (2015). https://doi.org/10.5220/0005366600900101
26. Karimi, Z., Baraani-Dastjerdi, A., Ghasem-Aghaee, N., Wagner, S.: Links between the personalities, styles and performance in computer programming. J. Syst. Softw. **111**, 228–241 (2016). https://doi.org/10.1016/j.jss.2015.09.011
27. Rehman, M., Safdar, S., Mahmood, A.K., Amin, A., Salleh, R.: Personality traits and knowledge sharing behavior of software engineers. In: 8th International Conference on Information Technology (ICIT 2017), pp. 6–11. IEEE, Amman, Jordan (2017). https://doi.org/10.1109/ICITECH.2017.8079908
28. Aqeel Iqbal, M., Aldaihani, A.R., Shah, A.: Big-five personality traits mapped with software development tasks to find most productive software development teams. Int. J. Innov. Technol. Explor. Eng. **8**, 965–971 (2019). https://doi.org/10.35940/ijitee.J9755.1081219
29. Toala-Sánchez, G., Cachero, C., Meliá, S.: Evaluating the effect of developers' personality and productivity on their intention to use model-driven web engineering techniques: an exploratory observational study. J. Web Eng. **17**, 483–526 (2019). https://doi.org/10.13052/jwe1540-9589.17674

Calibration Protocol for Integrating the OptiTrack Motion Capture System with Meta Oculus Quest

Sergio Díaz, Javier A. Torres Marin, and Wilson J. Sarmiento(✉)

Grupo de Investigación en Multimedia, Universidad Militar Nueva Granada, Bogotá, Colombia
{est.sergiod.diaz,javier.torres,
wilson.sarmiento}@unimilitar.edu.co

Abstract. To achieve adequate user experience in an immersive system, maximizing the sense of presence is directly related to the mechanisms and devices designed to enhance immersion. One example is the inclusion of real elements within a virtual environment that users can naturally manipulate in a mixed-reality system. These systems can be developed by integrating motion capture technologies, ranging from built-in tracking systems in virtual reality head-mounted displays to high-precision tracking laboratories. This paper presents a calibration protocol aimed at integrating two optical tracking systems to work together and enhance the user's sense of presence within a virtual environment. The first system is a high-precision tracking system for interactive objects. The second system is a low-cost tracking system embedded in a commercial head-mounted display for tracking the user's fingers and hands. The paper details the stages of the protocol through its application in a virtual environment and discusses the results of the subjective evaluation conducted with users.

Keywords: Head-mounted display · Motion capture · Tracking

1 Introduction

The main goal of any immersive virtual environment is to break the barrier between physical and virtual spaces for the user, creating an interactive experience where proximity to an environment surpasses the senses, enabling higher levels of presence. In recent years, technology has undergone rapid expansion; in immersive technology, this growth is reflected in the increasing availability of more accessible head-mounted displays (HMDs) with operational improvements, focusing on generating compelling spatial presence experiences.

The application of optical motion capture systems has enabled the development of various tools for virtual and extended reality environments. Based on stereography and optical triangulation, these systems use cameras and markers to assign three-dimensional coordinates to a group of points captured from different directions [1]. Passive optical

H. Luna-García et al. (Eds.): HCI-COLLAB 2025, CCIS 2850, pp. 48–60, 2027.
https://doi.org/10.1007/978-3-032-31223-5_4

systems employ retroreflective markers tracked by a set of infrared cameras [1]. Moreover, current advances allow some HMDs to integrate optical motion capture, as seen in the Apple Vision Pro, the Meta Oculus Quest series, and the VIVE Focus series.

On the other end of the spectrum, there is high-precision optical motion capture; one such system is OptiTrack, which has been widely applied in biomechanical studies focusing on gait data analysis due to its fine accuracy. However, due to the distance between the cameras and the user, effectively tracking finger positions in interactive applications remains challenging. It is crucial to highlight that a user's sense of proprioception is fundamental for achieving an adequate level of presence, and accurate tracking of limbs and fingers is essential in this regard.

Therefore, it is natural to consider a solution that integrates two systems: a high-precision system for tracking interactive objects and a low-cost system for tracking users' fingers and hands. However, a significant technical challenge lies in the integrated calibration of both tracking systems. This paper presents an approach to address this issue through a four-stage interaction calibration protocol.

The remainder of this document is structured as follows. Sect. 3 presents the materials and methods, describing the virtual environment used to test the calibration protocol and describing each of its stages. Sect. 4 discusses the results of subjective evaluations conducted with several users, and final section presents conclusions and future work reflections.

2 Related Work

The integration of motion capture systems with Virtual, Mixed, or Extended Reality has shown significant advantages and applications. For example, Simonetto et al. propose a virtual reality system integrated with a motion capture system applied to occupational safety, enabling interaction between individuals and their virtual and real environments [2]. The system demonstrated effective interaction in various scenes with both virtual and real objects [2]. Another application of this integration has been in audiovisual production. The CoMRMoCap Mixed Reality (MR) system assists actors by overlaying digital content onto the real set. Actors can visualize digital characters and scene elements in real time using a Video See-Through Head Mounted Display (VST-HMD). The system supports collaboration, allowing multiple actors to wear MoCap suits and VST-HMDs simultaneously [3]. One of these integrations' most widely expanded applications is in video game development and understanding. The work by Xu et al. demonstrated that the integration of virtual reality provides a highly immersive gaming experience by enabling interaction with virtual and real objects across different scenes [4].

However, this integration presents significant challenges, particularly in the joint calibration of systems. Xu et al. applied Kalman filters to reduce noise from capture devices, improving data accuracy [4]. Liu et al. propose a fast and accurate initialization method between a MoCap system and inertial sensors.

Their approach introduces a novel observation vector construction scheme based on MoCap to determine the initial rotation matrix quickly. Additionally, they propose a joint optimization scheme based on a new state model to estimate the system's pose, velocity, and errors, enhancing initialization accuracy [5]. Romeiro et al. highlights the calibration challenge in audiovisual production and analyze the development of 3D VR environments suitable for real-time motion capture. Their goal is to reduce recording time per scene by utilizing pre-recorded performances within MoCap software. Their approach aims to prevent performance issues in the virtual environment displayed in the HMD while also considering the ergonomic challenges of the process [6].

3 Materials and Methods

3.1 Virtual Immersive Experience

The virtual environment (Fig. 1) used to propose and test this protocol is a bar where the user can experiment with two different experiences. The first is a diner roll, where the user can ask for a drink while interacting with a bartender (NPC). The second experience allows the user to live the experience as a bartender, now offering and serving a drink to a diner (NPC). The experiences are supported by predesigned animations triggered by human-mediated interactions [7–9].

Fig. 1. Virtual and real scene (*Source: Own elaboration).*

Hardware

Hardware equipment that supports immersive experience is a motion capture system that allows real-time tracking of body and physical objects and a head-mounted display (HMD) that provides an immersive visualization experience. The motion capture consists of a room of 7 × 10 × 3 *m* with 16 high-speed IR cameras. Each camera has a resolution of 1280 × 1024 (1.3 MP) with a maximum frame rate of 240, providing sub-millimeter accuracy and a range of about 12 m. The HMD is an Oculus Quest 2 that integrates four cam- eras (for real-time hand/finger tracking) and inertial sensors that provide six degrees of freedom (6DOF) head tracking to compensate for both angular and linear displacement of the head. A high-speed gigabit Ethernet switch connects the motion capture system to a workstation with CPU/GPU support to deliver high-quality virtual reality experiences.

Oculus Quest 2, with four integrated cameras, manages to provide six degrees of freedom (6DOF) head tracking and compensates for both angular and linear head displacement of the head, as well as the integration of a real-time hand tracking system. The device exploits the hardware of an external computer (CPU, graphics card, and RAM) to deliver high-quality virtual reality experiences [10].

Physical interactive props

A set of physical props was built to generate a suitable grade of immersion, i.e., two bars (drink preparing bar and diner bar), a chair, a menu, and three glasses of liquor (wine, shot and whisky). The process of interactive objects (menu and glasses) must be built to generate haptic feedback in the interaction process (Fig. 1). The glasses were 3D modeled independently, keeping the real dimensions and proportions of every object on scene and at the same scale rate on the virtual scene. The following steps were performed to replicate the 3D objects and create interactive props in the real space.

1. Making the 3D model: A 3D model is made according to interaction requirements; a digital replica must be modeled with the same reference dimensions, considering that one unit equals one meter.
2. Making a polygonal reduction: For this modeling process, we need to reduce and simplify the vectors of interactive models as much as possible to expand them to individual pieces.
3. Unfolding model for paper: Once we have simplified models, we use Pepakura Designer Software to do the unfolding process, defining the model's dimensions and the printing paper size, taking each piece to be printed to assemble each object.
4. Making a cardboard model: Each piece is printed on paper, cut on cardboard, and assembled to make the cardboard models [11].
5. Making final assembly: When each interactable object is jet assembled in cardboard, it is necessary to make a wood structure to connect an OptiTrack marker and assign it an id in Motive, so each object will be transmitted through a pivot to a virtual environment, where a 3d model will be assigned to each marker.

When each object of the interaction is assembled, we are completely covered in tape so that the marker remains still, avoiding possible miscalibrations. Figure 2 shows the building process for the wine glass interactive prop.

Software

The virtual environment was developed in Unity game engine that integrates a custom rendering engine with the nVidia PhysX physics engine and Mono (*C#*) interpreter.

The Oculus SDK software allows the Air Link and Link Cable process to connect the *Oculus Quest 2* device to a compatible computer. The *Oculus Developer Hub* software enables the *"Developer Mode"*, the debugging in real-time and checks the correct implementation of XR compatible framework to run ap- plications on the Oculus device.

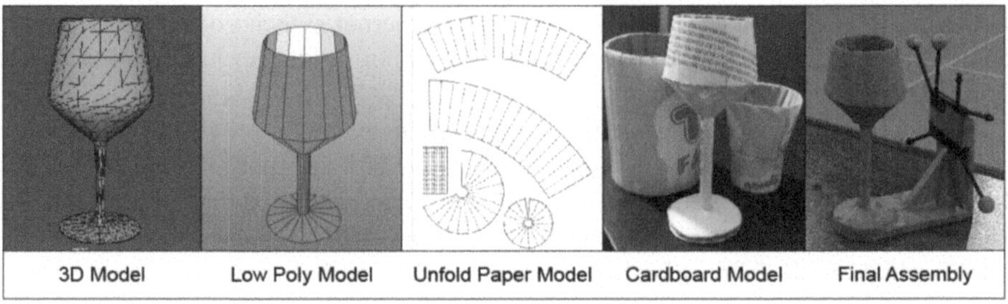

Fig. 2. Props Assembly Process. Left to right: making the 3D model, making a polygonal reduction, unfolding model for paper, making a cardboard model and making final assembly (*Source: Own elaboration)*

The motion capture system is managed by *Motive Tracker* licensed engineering-grade software, which allows the orchestration of physical props tracking through passive markers; in this way, it can compute the position of detected continuous cartesian coordinates and rotation in real-time. The OptiTrack Unity 3D plugin performs the connection between Motive Tracker software and the virtual environment developed by UDP protocol in NatNet proprietary messages.

In the virtual space, we define a parent object having all the static objects as children, this parent object will update its position according to the middle point between the markers.

In the experiment, the static real object was a table with two markers placed in the corners; the center of the real table will correspond to the center of the virtual table (the parent object of all the virtual objects in the interaction) to adjust the scene in position and scale, only the table will be modified until its virtual limits correspond to the limits of the markers.

3.2 Interaction Calibration Protocol

Figure 3 illustrates the proposed calibration protocol. This procedure comprises a four-step sequence involving manual operator input, structured as an interactive calibration framework, i.e. Initial adjustments, Axis coordination between virtual spaces, Interactive props calibration and Avatar calibration. Each phase of the protocol is detailed in the following sections.

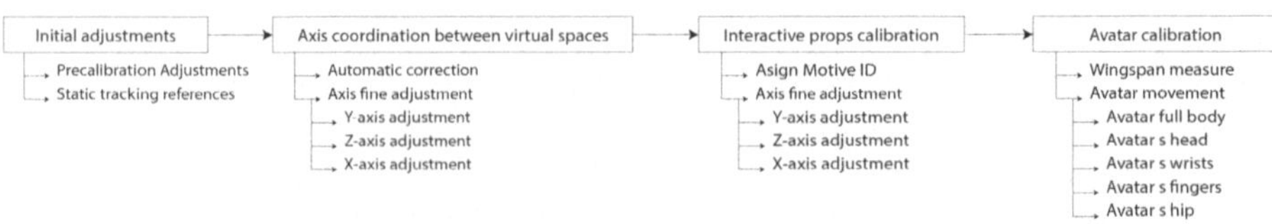

Fig. 3. Calibration protocol *(Source: Own elaboration).*

3.3 Initial Adjustments

3.3.1 Precalibration Adjustments

To begin the calibration process, we must define a precalibrate state start point to generate a safe-stable condition. In this way, the first is to set up the origin point in the workspace that will correspond to the origin point of the virtual spaces; the second is to define a north direction of the user reference. For this, Motive software requires a camera calibration process to be carried out.

The goal is to get an optimal tracking space between the infrared cameras, where each manages to sample at least 15.000 uniformly distributed data. After, the software allows defining the level and direction of the ground; in this way, the origin point is set up.

The next is to define the guardian system on the Oculus Quest 2, a safe physical space for user interaction. For this, the user must be placed on the point demarcated as the origin, wearing HMD and looking towards the positive Z axis of motion capture space. At this moment, the user must confirm the guardian system in the Oculus, checking that the center of the virtual space corresponds to the origin point of the defined work area, thus, the north direction of the user set up.

3.3.2 Static Tracking References

For the interaction we are using physical references to mark off the interaction limits, a pair of bars where all non-static object events will occur. The closer the region of action of the user to the origin of the virtual and real spaces, the lower the chances of having gaps between devices in the interaction.

When making a virtual and real correspondence space, it is necessary to define the interactable elements for the user, checking which will remain static on the whole interaction, objects such as a table or a shelf.

Those static objects will be the referents to carry out the calibration process; being static objects, we will be able to place at least two markers, and, knowing the distance between them, we will be able to compare the position and dimensions between the virtual and the real space.

3.4 Axis Coordination Between Virtual Spaces

It is necessary to remember that in a virtual reality environment, the calibration will primarily rely on the headset's (HMD) coordinates. Therefore, the next step is to convert the coordinates from the OptiTrack virtual space to the coordinates used by the Oculus Quest 2.

In the virtual scene where we join both systems, we will keep separately the objects in charge of the Oculus Quest 2 and the objects in charge of receiving and assigning the OptiTrack markers to be able to manipulate them independently and make it easy to calibrate.

With the right scale level correspondence, it is time to calibrate the position of the virtual scene with a two-stage method: a mathematical calibration to reduce the error between the virtual spaces and a manual calibration that will adjust virtual space to real space.

3.4.1 Automatic Correction

Once the first debugging is done, there is a possibility of doing a fine adjustment of the coordinate axes of the HMD and the OptiTrack. Why the coordinate systems are pointing in different directions, so it is necessary to make a rotation correction of those spaces in each axis points in the same direction in virtual and in real space.

3.4.2 Axis Fine Adjustment

At this point, we should have the coordinate systems adjusted and the static objects' correspondence size (between virtual and real space); the next step is to be able to run a scene with all the elements to see the position and rotation of the HMD and the hands on the runtime screen.

We will put the user in contact with one of the static objects, in our case, in front of a table, by placing his hands on it. In the virtual scene hierarchy, we select the object in charge of tracking the OptiTrack system and move it close to the Oculus hands, keep in mind that we will generate a coincidence of the position of the real and the virtual table.

We ask the user to perform a series of movements to be able to adjust each of the axes in position, each action involves the identification and adjusting of the boundaries of an object on each axis.

3.4.3 Y-axis Adjustment

The subject with the HMD extends his hands on the physical table in front of him, Fig. 4 shows this step; meanwhile, in virtual space, a mediator translates the y-axis value of the OptiTrack tracking object until the surface of the virtual table collides with the visible hands of the Oculus.

Fig. 4. Y-axis adjustment *(Source: Own elaboration)*

3.4.4 Z-axis Adjustment

The subject with the HMD places his hands on the front and back limits of the physical table; it is possible to see this in Fig. 5; in virtual space, a mediator translates the z-axis value of the OptiTrack tracking object until the limits of the virtual table are located between the two visible hands of the Oculus.

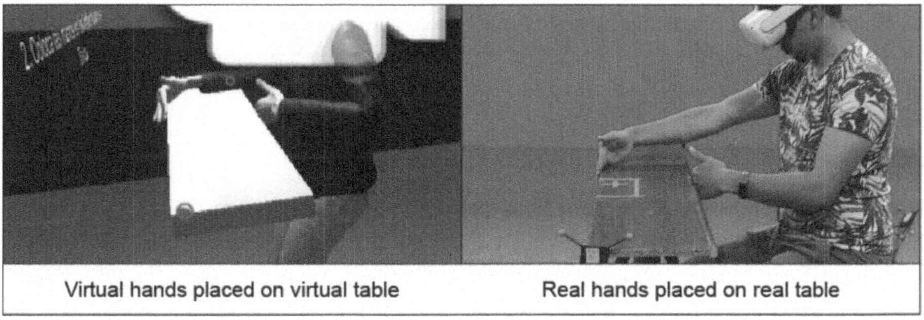

Fig. 5. Z-axis adjustment *(Source: Own elaboration)*

3.4.5 X-axis Adjustment

An OptiTrack marker is given to the user with the HMD, who is asked to place the marker between both hands; in virtual space, a mediator must be able to see the marker in the scene and translate the x-axis value of the OptiTrack tracking object until the virtual marker is located between the two visible hands of the Oculus.

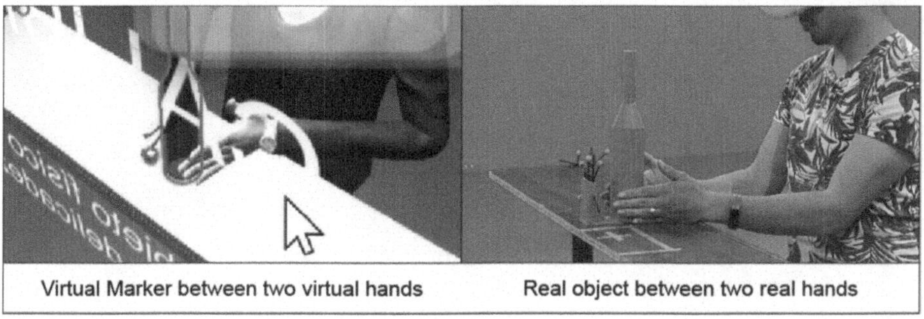

Fig. 6. X-axis adjustment *(Source: Own elaboration)*

The user with HMD must manipulate the marker in different directions to verify the correct adjustment of the virtual spaces; Fig. 6 shows this process.

We have adjusted the position of the OptiTrack tracking object while the virtual scene is running. To save these modifications, we will select the OptiTrack tracking object; in the inspector window, look for the transform component in the three points on the right side of the component and save the calibration setup to run the virtual environment in the production stage.

3.5 Interactive Props Calibration

Having proportions of the real objects correspond to the virtual ones; it is necessary to calibrate each object pivot, keeping in mind that each one has a marker attached to some part of its wood structure (not precisely located in the center of the object).

Just as the scene was calibrated in each axe, a similar process must be carried out with each non-static object. By analyzing collisions between the objects in the scene, the pivot displacement of each object will be adjusted.

3.5.1 Assigning Motive ID

In the motion capture console, an ID is assigned to each object marker to transmit its position and rotation variation. In the virtual environment, we create a key object that will be each pivot, and in the hierarchy, as a child of the pivot, we place one of the interactable objects. On the pivot object, we assign a tracking point script in the inspector to write the ID that was established in Motive; now, we can update the position and rotation of every non-static object.

3.5.2 Axis Fine Adjustment

Each prop requires precise alignment along all axes; this fine-tuning process is depicted in Fig. 7 and further elaborated upon below.

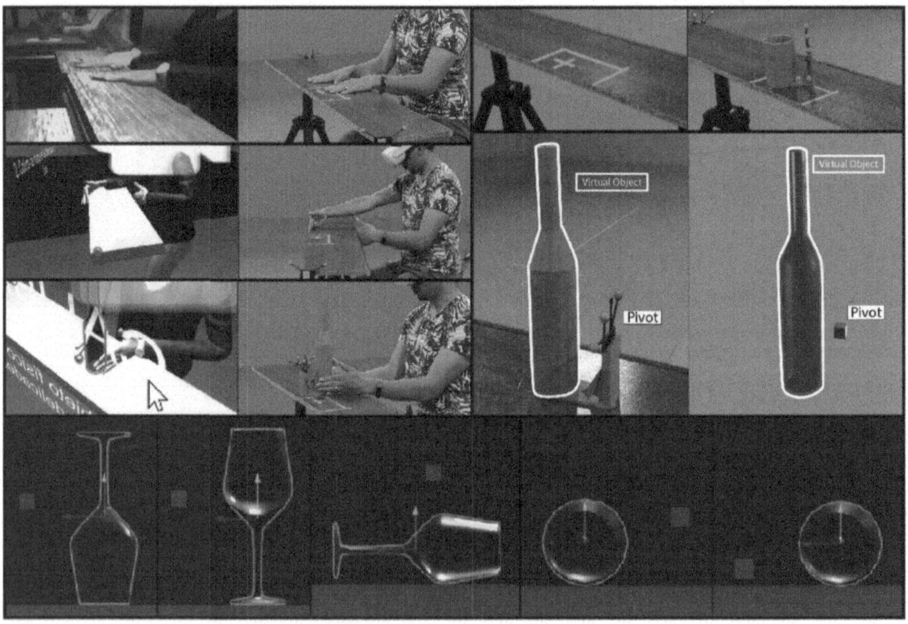

Fig. 7. Axis fine adjustment of each prop *(Source: Own elaboration.*

3.5.3 Y-axis Adjustment

The physical object is placed on a calibrated static surface; in a virtual environment, a mediator translates the height of the pivot child object until it is positioned correctly, then places the object upside down to verify the height calibration.

3.5.4 Z-axis Adjustment

Rotate the physical object, leaving the marker facing upwards, and place it on a static surface already calibrated; in a virtual environment, a mediator translates the position of the pivot child object until it is positioned correctly, then rotates the physical object 180° to verify the calibration.

X-axis adjustment. Rotate the physical object with the marker looking to the side and place it on a static surface already calibrated; in a virtual environment, a mediator moves the position of the pivoted child object until it is positioned correctly, then rotates the physical object to verify the calibration.

This process must be carried out with each non-static interactable object for the user; if the limits of the virtual and the real object do not correspond, it is advisable to verify each size and dimension.

We have adjusted the position of non-static objects while the virtual scene is running. To save these modifications, look for the transform component in the inspector window. In the three points on the right side of the component, click on *"Copy Component"*, stop the execution of the scene, and, in the same three points of the object, click on *"Paste Component Values"* that is how to save the coordinates that have been adjusted.

3.6 Avatar Calibration

If the interaction integrates an avatar, it is necessary to establish a connection between the avatar model's skeleton and the user's movement, simulating the motion of the head, hips, wrists, and fingers. Additionally, the subject's wingspan must be measured and adjusted to match the avatar's size to ensure proper reach and alignment of the virtual body.

In the graphical debugging tools provided by the game engine, the position and rotation of the HMD and the user's hands can be inspected, along with the movement of each finger. Based on this, the following methods for transferring motion data to the avatar's body are proposed.

3.6.1 Avatar Full Body

During development, an average-height avatar is generated for both male and female users. The Oculus automatic system adjusts the camera height to match the user's stature. However, this automatic adjustment can cause issues when using a full-body avatar. Using the camera position provided by the HMD to scale the avatar using a simple proportional rule is recommended.

3.6.2 Avatar's Wrists

The position and rotation of the wrists are crucial for accurate user interaction with the avatar, as they determine the kinematic movement and rotation of the arm bones. For this reason, during the development stage, adding an extra quaternion adjustment is necessary to correct the orientation of each hand.

3.6.3 Avatar's Fingers

During the development stage, the finger bone rotations of the Oculus hand model in Unity are mapped to the bones of the avatar's hands. In some cases, no additional calibration is needed, but if there are significant differences between the user's fingers and the avatar's, a scaling adjustment must be performed to ensure proper correspondence.

3.6.4 Avatar's Head and Hips

In some cases, a fixed-head avatar is used. In this case, the head rotation follows the HMD camera, and the same rotation is applied to the hips. However, this approach becomes problematic for an avatar with a free-moving head, as it results in more natural movement, allowing the avatar to move its head independently of the torso. This protocol proposes handling the hip rotation independently of the avatar's camera direction using two possible approaches. The first is a vector pointing toward the midpoint between the avatar's wrists. The second is a vector orthogonal to the avatar's shoulder line.

If several avatars or NPCs that use the same bone hierarchy are going to be used, it is necessary to classify the bones of each avatar inside a virtual environment.

3.7 Switching Virtual and Interactable Objects in Virtual Environment

Depending on the proposed interaction, some NPCs may have to manipulate non-static objects, that's why we need two types of visually similar non-static objects in the scene, the one previously created with the pivot, and one that contains the animations corresponding to the actions of the NPC.

The animations of the non-static complementary objects should be created in the same way that the NPCs animations, if there is a sequence of actions of the NPC with the complementary object, both must coincide in duration and the trigger time. In the interaction the NPC is going to modify the position of the object with the animations, object that is going to be delivered to the HMD user, and when the user takes it, a mediator disable the complementary object and enable the non-static object with the pivot, that's why is very important that the appearance place of one is the same disappearance place of the other. To improve the switching of these objects, a series of demarcations are made in real space indicating the final position of the animated object, so that the mediator can see where to place the non-static object, preventing the user from noticing the switching.

4 Subjective Validation

The protocol was executed with 20 users of different body types. Thirty-five percent of the participants were women, while the remaining were men. Each user selected an avatar according to their gender preference.

Once the calibration protocol was completed, interaction tests were con- ducted, including free movement within the environment and moving objects from the service bar to the customer counter. Users' movements were observed as they picked up and placed objects, and a field diary was kept. An unstructured interview was conducted at the end of the test, including a discussion about the perceived accuracy of the object arrangement and the sensations of agency and embodiment generated by the avatar.

Most users initially exhibited hesitant movements when picking up objects and navigating the space. However, as the interaction progressed, they became more confident, and the process went smoothly. One key observation was that users' first instinct was to place their hands on the front counter, confirming the table's position. Precise movements were observed when grasping and releasing objects.

Users reported a positive experience and expressed that using real objects enhanced their sense of immersion. They also stated that their avatar corresponded to their body and accurately represented their movements, indicating a strong sense of embodiment. Additionally, they affirmed that their body movements felt precise and appropriate, aligning with the concept of agency.

It can be concluded that the developed protocol enabled adequate user interaction, and the reported sensations of presence align with previous state-of- the-art experiments [12], where interaction with physical objects enhances user immersion.

5 Final Remarks and Future Work

This paper presents a calibration protocol designed to integrate two optical track- ing systems to work together, ensuring an adequate sense of user presence within a virtual environment. The protocol's stages are detailed through its application in a virtual setting. The proposed protocol was successfully implemented in an environment where a user and an avatar interact simultaneously with various complex objects distributed throughout the virtual space, identifying their positions, translations, rotations, and dimensions while embodying an avatar, recognizing the physical limits of interaction and the area where their actions take place.

The virtual environment was tested with twenty different users, each with varying body scales, demonstrating an increased sense of agency and embodiment when applying the calibration protocol in all cases. Future work will expand the protocol's implementation in developing extended and mixed reality systems, incorporating real complex objects into different environments and automating the manual steps of the proposed protocol.

Acknowledgements. The author, Wilson J. Sarmiento, a full-time professor at the Universidad Militar Nueva Granada (UMNG), acknowledges and recognizes the UMNG for its support of his research work.

References

1. Ameler, T., et al.: A comparative evaluation of steamvr tracking and the optitrack system for medical device tracking. In: 2019 41st annual international conference of the IEEE engineering in medicine and biology society (EMBC), pp. 1465–1470. IEEE (2019)
2. Simonetto, M., Arena, S., Peron, M.: A methodological framework to integrate mo- tion capture system and virtual reality for assembly system 4.0 workplace design. Saf. Sci. **146**, 105561 (2022)

3. Cannavò, A., Bottino, F., Lamberti, F.: Supporting motion-capture acting with collaborative mixed reality. Comput. Graph. **124**, 104090 (2024)
4. Xu, L., Zhang, F.: A MoCap system for real-time entertainment interaction. In: Lu, H., Guna, J., Li, Y. (eds.) International Symposium on Artificial Intelligence and Robotics 2020, vol. 11574, p. 115740M. International Society for Optics and Photonics, SPIE (2020)
5. Liu, M., Xie, L., Wang, W., Yan, Y., Yin, E.: A fast and accurate initialization method for mocap-inertial navigation system. IEEE Sensors J. **24**(6), 8390–8402 (2024)
6. Romeiro, N.C., Salomão, A., Zanini, L.M.F., Vieira, M.L.H.: Practices to mocap real-time streaming to vr. In: De Paolis, L.T., Arpaia, P., Sacco, M. (eds.) Extended Reality, pp. 61–73. Springer Nature Switzerland, Cham (2024)
7. Cheng, L.P., et al.: Turkdeck: Physical virtual reality based on people. In: Proceedings of the 28th Annual ACM Symposium on User Interface Software & Technology, UIST'15, pp. 417–426. Association for Computing Machinery, New York, NY, USA (2015)
8. Cheng, L.P., Marwecki, S., Baudisch, P.: Mutual human actuation. In: Proceedings of the 30th Annual ACM Symposium on User Interface Software and Technology, UIST'17, pp. 797–805. Association for Computing Machinery, New York, NY, USA (2017)
9. Casanova, N., et al.: Touch & live. an immersive experience for acting in others' bodies. In: 2020 IEEE Conference on Virtual Reality and 3D User Interfaces Abstracts and Workshops (VRW). pp. 507–508 (2020)
10. Monica, R., Aleotti, J.: Evaluation of the oculus rift s tracking system in room scale virtual reality. Virtual Reality, 1–11 (2022)
11. Frens, J.: Cardboard modeling studio: a designerly exploration tool for rich and embodied interaction. In: Proceedings of the fifth international conference on Tangible, embedded, and embodied interaction. pp. 365–368 (2010)
12. Usoh, M., et al.: Walking > walking-in-place > flying, in virtual environments. In: Proceedings of the 26th Annual Conference on Computer Graphics and Interactive Techniques, SIGGRAPH'99, pp. 359–364. ACM Press/Addison-Wesley Publishing Co., USA (1999)

Designing for Neurodiversity: A Usability and Accessibility Evaluation for ASD

Valéria Farinazzo Martins[1](✉), Flávio Hergersheimer Navikas[1], Fernanda Dreux Miranda Fernandes[2], and Cibelle Albuquerque de la Higuera Amato[3]

[1] Programa de Pós-Graduação em Computação Aplicada, Universidade Presbiteriana Mackenzie, São Paulo, Brasil
valeria.farinazzo@mackenzie.br

[2] Faculdade de Médica da Universidade de São Paulo, São Paulo, Brasil
fernandadreux@usp.br

[3] Programa de Pós-Graduação em Ciências do Desenvolvimento Humano, Universidade Presbiteriana Mackenzie, São Paulo, Brasil
cibelleamato@mackenzie.br

Abstract. Digital accessibility is essential for ensuring inclusive interactive experiences for diverse user profiles, particularly for individuals with Autism Spectrum Disorder (ASD), who often face barriers when interacting with computational systems. However, traditional guidelines, such as the Web Content Accessibility Guidelines (WCAG), do not fully address the specific needs of this audience, highlighting the necessity for more specialized methodologies. In this context, this study proposes and validates a heuristic evaluation model focused on the usability and accessibility of interactive systems for ASD users. The model was developed based on existing guidelines, a systematic literature review, and expert interviews, consolidating a set of heuristics tailored to the cognitive and sensory characteristics of ASD individuals. To validate the methodology, the model was applied in the evaluation of the digital game "Sago Mini Forest Adventure", which is commonly used in therapy sessions for children with ASD. The results showed that 54.2% of the accessibility criteria were met, indicating a reasonable level of compliance while also revealing challenges, particularly in support documentation and interface flexibility. The findings suggest that the proposed approach contributes to advancing accessibility evaluation methodologies by providing an objective tool for improving inclusive digital experiences tailored to the needs of neurodivergent users.

Keywords: Digital Accessibility · Usability · Autism Spectrum Disorder · Human-Computer Interaction · Heuristic Evaluation

1 Introduction

The field of Human-Computer Interaction (HCI) aims to develop methodologies that create meaningful digital experiences, bridging user needs with technological solutions. This interdisciplinary approach integrates knowledge from Computer Science, Psychology, Cognitive Science, and Visual Design [1]. Within this context, the adoption of

H. Luna-García et al. (Eds.): HCI-COLLAB 2025, CCIS 2850, pp. 61–74, 2027.
https://doi.org/10.1007/978-3-032-31223-5_5

User-Centered Design (UCD) has demonstrated a significant impact on usability and accessibility, leading to higher user engagement and satisfaction [2]. Although UCD has been recently embraced by the industry, companies are increasingly incorporating user-centered research from the early stages of development, aligning their business models with real user needs [3].

When developing interactive systems, usability and accessibility are fundamental aspects. Usability assesses the quality of user experience, covering both objective performance metrics and subjective satisfaction [4]. Accessibility, on the other hand, ensures that all users, regardless of their conditions or disabilities, can interact with a system under equal conditions [5]. To standardize digital accessibility, guidelines such as the Web Content Accessibility Guidelines (WCAG), developed by the World Wide Web Consortium (W3C), provide principles for building accessible systems. However, these guidelines are broad in scope, making it difficult to interpret and apply specific accessibility criteria [6].

Among the key accessibility challenges is the inclusion of individuals with Autism Spectrum Disorder (ASD). ASD involves difficulties in communication, social interaction, and repetitive behaviors, as well as sensory sensitivities [7, 8]. Technology plays a crucial role in promoting inclusion and developing skills for people with ASD, making it essential to understand their needs to design accessible interactive systems. However, existing accessibility evaluation methods do not fully address the specific challenges of ASD, as they are often too general and primarily focus on motor and visual impairments.

Given this scenario, this study proposes the development and validation of a heuristic evaluation methodology that incorporates usability and accessibility criteria adapted for ASD. The approach integrates Technology and Health, exploring existing accessibility resources and expanding beyond W3C guidelines to create a more inclusive and participatory evaluation framework. To validate the methodology, the model was applied in the assessment of the digital game "Sago Mini Forest Adventure", which is commonly used in therapy sessions for children with ASD. The results showed that, while the game offers a moderate level of accessibility, there is room for improvement in areas such as support documentation and user interaction customization.

This study aims to contribute to the expansion of digital accessibility research for ASD, providing an objective tool for evaluating interactive systems. By proposing a specialized heuristic evaluation model, it seeks to support developers and designers in creating more accessible, intuitive, and adaptive digital experiences, ultimately promoting greater autonomy and inclusion for individuals with ASD in the digital environment.

2 Background

2.1 Accessibility and Digital Inclusion

Accessibility is a fundamental principle to ensure that all individuals, regardless of their physical, cognitive, or social conditions, can fully participate in society. This concept involves removing barriers and creating suitable conditions for inclusion in various contexts, such as services, products, and environments. In addition to being an essential right, accessibility requires a governmental commitment to ensure that society adapts and meets demands equitably [9].

According to Sassaki [10], accessibility unfolds into various dimensions, addressing the elimination of barriers in learning, socialization, and participation in leisure, work, and education activities. He categorizes accessibility into seven main dimensions: architectural, attitudinal, communicational, instrumental, methodological, natural, and pragmatic. Recently, digital accessibility has been added to this classification, referring to technological solutions that enable autonomous and independent web navigation. This approach seeks to ensure that anyone, regardless of their abilities, can access and use the materials available on the internet.

[11] highlights that digital accessibility and the use of interactive computing systems are directly related to citizenship. This implies harmonizing users' capabilities with the characteristics of digital environments, products, or services according to established standards and norms. In software development, the Web Accessibility Initiative (WAI) defines web accessibility as the practice of designing websites, tools, and technologies to be usable by people with disabilities [12]. Thus, web accessibility allows users with visual, auditory, motor, cognitive, or neurological disabilities to perceive, understand, navigate, and interact with online content [13]. To meet this need, assistive technologies (AT) are employed, having been applied for years in mobility, learning, work, and interaction contexts. The goal of AT is to enhance or provide functional abilities for people with disabilities, promoting a more independent and inclusive life [14].

Another emerging concept in the field of accessibility is Inclusive Design (ID). According to Silva [15], ID seeks to understand users' real needs and ensure that applications and products are accessible to everyone, regardless of age, gender, or disability [16]. adds that this concept applies to creating products that require hardware and software adaptations to serve users with specific limitations. Thus, ID expands the concepts of usability, accessibility, and comfort, benefiting society as a whole. In software development, both usability and accessibility are considered non-functional requirements, depending on users' characteristics, skills, and limitations, as well as the context of use [17].

Digital accessibility impacts all audiences but is especially essential for people with disabilities, allowing them to perform online activities independently. In Brazil, the Brazilian Inclusion Law [18] aims to ensure accessibility and inclusion for people with disabilities in various sectors. However, a study conducted by the Movimento Web Para Todos in partnership with BigData Corp revealed that in 2020, less than 1% of Brazilian websites were fully accessible to this audience. More recent data from 2024 indicates a decline in website accessibility in Brazil, with only 2.9% of websites passing accessibility tests. This demonstrates that, despite legislative advances, significant challenges remain to achieving a truly inclusive internet.

2.2 Autism

What is now referred to as Autism Spectrum Disorder (ASD) was first described based on a group of 11 children by an Austrian psychiatrist working in the United States in the 1940s [19]. Over the decades, an increasing number of studies have been conducted to identify the origin, characteristics, and, most importantly, the best therapeutic and educational approaches for autistic individuals.

For the past eight decades, the search for clearer criteria to identify autism has been accompanied by efforts to determine causal factors and effective treatments. However, despite the involvement of numerous researchers from various fields, no definitive answers have been found. There is no single gene responsible for autism, no clearly identified neurological specialization mechanism explaining the condition, and no universal educational or therapeutic method that is effective for all autistic individuals.

The most recent publications from the American Psychiatric Association [20] and the World Health Organization [21] introduced a bidimensional model for the autism spectrum, considering both the severity of symptoms and the varying levels of environmental support and adaptation required. There was also a significant shift in how diagnostic criteria are structured. DSM-5 now considers only two main symptom groups: Deficits in social communication and social interaction, regarded as the most critical features of autism. And restricted and/or repetitive interests and behaviors, along with sensory integration differences.

It has become increasingly evident that the core traits shared by all autistic individuals involve difficulties in interpersonal relationships and social communication skills, that is, the functional aspects of language in both verbal and nonverbal communication. While autistic individuals may have different formal language abilities (such as vocabulary, phonetics, and grammar), they consistently face challenges in functional language use. It is crucial to recognize that autistic individuals can have varied levels of intelligence, different health conditions, diverse learning styles, and specific sensory processing strengths or difficulties.

The advancement of digital technologies has led to the frequent development of applications designed to enhance everyday life. When well-designed, these digital solutions can be used for various purposes and made accessible to all individuals, regardless of their characteristics or limitations. Since the early 2000s, Digital Information and Communication Technologies have been increasingly used to assist autistic individuals, as well as their parents, therapists, and teachers. Computational tools have been employed to support social skills, memory, communication, vocabulary acquisition, and literacy [22].

Several studies indicate that autistic children often have a strong interest in using computers, tablets, and smartphones [23–26]. However, these digital devices must be designed with specific features to ensure their effective use for achieving learning and communication goals. Otherwise, they may create interaction barriers, limiting an autistic individual's ability to use technology autonomously.

2.3 Guidelines for Accessible Interfaces for People with Autism (GAIA)

GAIA [22] is a proposed Web accessibility guidelines document focused on autism-related aspects. The author aimed to describe these recommendations in a more intelligible and detailed manner for psychologists, educators, and computing professionals, so they can be implemented with a clear understanding of the benefits children with autism will gain when interacting with an application. Although this guide primarily targets web applications, most recommendations have been generalized to allow adaptation to other interaction contexts. The guide is divided into 10 sections, detailed below:

- Visual and Textual Vocabulary: Provides information on text structure, language, verbal and pictorial communication, reading flow, and color contrast. For example, one recommendation states: *"Use simple visual and textual language, avoiding jargon, spelling errors, metaphors, abbreviations, and acronyms, and using terms, expressions, names, and symbols familiar to the users' context."*
- Customization: Offers guidelines to allow users to adapt interface elements according to their needs. One example is: *"Allow customization of colors, text size, and fonts used in page elements."*
- Engagement: Presents guidelines on focus, attention, and strategies to help users interact with the system. An example of such a strategy is: *"Design simple interfaces with few elements, containing only the necessary functionalities and content for the current task."*
- Redundant Representations: Refers to using multiple formats to present information (text, image, or audio). An example is: *"Symbols, pictograms, and icons should have a nearby textual equivalent to facilitate understanding and contribute to vocabulary enrichment."*
- Multimedia: Expanding on the previous category, these recommendations focus on the appropriate use of multimedia resources in web interfaces to support memory, attention, visual and textual comprehension, and sensory integration for individuals with ASD. An example is: *"Avoid using disruptive or explosive sounds, such as sirens and fireworks."*
- System Status Visibility: Focuses on how to inform users about task progress, including error messages, help prompts, and status updates of elements. An example is: *"Allow critical actions to be reversed, canceled, undone, or confirmed."*
- Affordance: Recommendations related to users identifying interface elements in terms of their functionality, thus reducing cognitive load. An example is: *"Use larger icons, buttons, and form controls that provide an adequate click/touch area and ensure they appear clickable."*
- Navigability: Web interface recommendations include: a) promoting simplified navigation; b) providing consistent location indicators; and c) designing sequential navigation when applicable. An example is: *"Avoid automatically redirecting pages or setting task expiration times, as the user should control navigation and task completion time."*
- Response to Actions: Providing complete feedback for user actions is important for everyone, regardless of their characteristics. For individuals with ASD, it is crucial for guiding them in task execution and understanding application behavior. An example is: *"Provide feedback confirming correct actions or alerting users to potential errors, using audio, text, and images to convey messages while avoiding icons with emotions or facial expressions."*
- Touchscreen Interaction: These recommendations are important because touchscreen devices involve direct manipulation of interface elements, and individuals with ASD tend to interact better with these devices. A recommendation for these devices is: *"Touchscreen interaction should have appropriate sensitivity and prevent errors from accidental selections and unintended touches on screen elements."*.

2.4 AASPIRE (Academic Autistic Spectrum Partnership in Research and Education)

A resource aimed at improving accessibility for individuals with Autism Spectrum Disorder (ASD) is the Academic Autistic Spectrum Partnership in Research and Education (AASPIRE), developed by Portland State University [27]. Founded in 2006, AASPIRE brings together the academic community, the autistic community, and professionals who provide support and services for autistic individuals to conduct research projects that address the needs of adults on the autism spectrum.

Unlike GAIA [28], AASPIRE [27] is specifically designed for adults with ASD and has distinct areas of application. While GAIA [28] was developed with a focus on interactive system design, AASPIRE [27] operates within the healthcare field, separate from technology. Its primary goal is to provide information, recommendations, and guidelines for preventive primary care, offering support not only to individuals with ASD but also to caregivers and professionals, functioning as a bidirectional resource. This platform also compiles a set of practical recommendations for conducting professional follow-up sessions for adults with ASD. In addition to its recommendations, AASPIRE allows for the creation of personalized reports in a checklist format, generating documents for guidance, tracking, or structured workflows.

Despite the significant increase in research on autism, there has been little focus on improving the lives of autistic adults. Adults on the spectrum are often not included as resources or partners in autism research, despite having a wealth of knowledge, experiences, insights, and skills to contribute [27].

3 Methods

To achieve the objectives of this case study, the methodology used in the research is described here, ensuring the integrity of the results and maximizing the efficient use of resources. The study was conducted in multiple stages, covering different contexts and areas of study, ultimately leading to the development of a heuristic evaluation model based on usability and accessibility criteria for individuals with Autism Spectrum Disorder (ASD).

The research adopted a mixed-methods approach, combining both qualitative and quantitative methods. The qualitative component involved exploring literature and resources within the context of ASD and HCI, while the quantitative aspect focused on the analysis and processing of collected data.

The methodology was structured into two main phases, comprising a total of nine stages. These phases were divided into the development of the heuristic evaluation model and its assessment phase. During the development phase, interactions with ASD specialists were conducted to validate the model. This model integrates usability evaluation based on Granollers (2018) and aligns with the GAIA and AASPIRE models.

In the evaluation phase, a game commonly used by specialists working with children with ASD was selected. Usability and accessibility experts then applied the heuristic evaluation model, and a final score was generated based on the assessments.

4 Case Study

4.1 Contextualization

This case study is derived from a master's program in Computing at a private university in São Paulo, Brazil. The research aims to address digital accessibility aspects related to the inclusion of individuals with ASD. The dissertation focuses on the usability and accessibility evaluation of interactive systems, proposing a heuristic evaluation model based on the study of the relationship between ASD and technology.

The research aims to develop and validate a heuristic evaluation methodology focused on usability and accessibility criteria tailored for individuals with ASD. There is a recognized gap in assessment resources for ASD within HCI literature, which justifies the need for specialized evaluation methodologies. The methodology includes:

- A systematic mapping to explore the state of the art and identify gaps in the current literature related to accessibility evaluation [29].
- Interviews with two ASD specialists to gain insights into the relationship between ASD and technology from expert perspectives. The interviews were semi-structured and aimed to gain more knowledge about ASD and the technological gaps in the evaluation of software designed for the autistic population.
- A literature review covering medical, educational, and technological perspectives on ASD.
- The development of evaluation criteria, integrating existing guidelines such as GAIA and AASPIRE, adapted for heuristic evaluation and usability aspects [30].

The proposed model is tested through practical application in a real interactive system and reviewed by HCI specialists. The research highlights the importance of creating inclusive digital experiences for individuals with ASD, proposing a comprehensive heuristic evaluation model. This model is built from a multidisciplinary approach, combining systematic mapping, expert interviews, and an in-depth review of existing literature and guidelines.

The final outcome is a validated evaluation framework designed to improve the usability and accessibility of interactive systems for individuals with ASD. To achieve this, the "Sago Mini Forest Adventure" game was selected as the target for heuristic evaluation using this model, assessed by four usability and accessibility experts.

4.2 Results

The results obtained from the application of the aforementioned methodology present the complete model, described in this section. The model underwent a review by HCI specialists, who provided valuable feedback for final adjustments. The review focused on the clarity and applicability of the evaluation criteria, leading to significant improvements.

The final version of the model was consolidated into a spreadsheet template, ready to be used in practical accessibility and usability evaluations. The proposed final model consists of 15 heuristics (numbered H1 to H15) and a total of 63 evaluation questions. Below, the 15 heuristics are described, along with comments on the content and purpose of the evaluation questions. The process of this methodology can be obtained in [29].

H1 -Visibility and System Status:

1. Visual elements that blink or flash on the screen.
2. User progress tracking in long usage journeys.
3. Illustrations, diagrams, and icons that are contextually aligned with the informative content, with clear captions.
4. User preference selection for media type.
5. Alerts regarding sound usage.
6. Possibility of undoing actions and confirming critical actions.
7. Estimated usage time of the resource.

H2 -Connection Between the System and the Real World, Use of Metaphors, and Human Objects:

8. Visual elements should have easily recognizable symbols, avoiding complex metaphors and incorporating familiar real-world elements.
9. Use of personas and digital assistants to represent humans.

H3 -User Control and Freedom.

10. Customization of color (including contrast), font, and sound responses (including the ability to enable/disable them), as well as simplification of screen components.
11. For uncommon symbols, a description must accompany the element.
12. Application compatibility with assistive software/hardware for individuals with disabilities or impairments (e.g., screen readers, text-to-Braille converters).

H4 -Consistency and Standards.

13. Proper use of a color palette suitable for individuals with hypo- or hypersensitivity to visual stimuli.
14. Screens should have clearly separated sections using colors or other means of distinction.
15. Use of multiple media formats to convey content and information.
16. Short paragraphs that are sufficiently descriptive.
17. Screen quality should remain intact when zooming in or out.
18. Activities should be presented in an orderly and clearly structured manner.
19. Clear layout distinction between primary and secondary content.
20. Predictability in functionalities, behaviors, and screen layouts.
21. The layout should clearly indicate clickable or interactive elements.

H5 -Recognition Rather Than Recall, Learning, and Anticipation.

22. Screen identification (ensuring users can recognize where they are).
23. Clear information on screen location and navigation history.

H6 -Flexibility and Efficiency of Use.

24. Using simple and easily understandable language, avoiding jargon.
25. Avoiding the use of abbreviations, acronyms, and metaphors.
26. Avoiding distracting elements near high-attention areas.
27. Facilitating comparison and association of ideas between text and images clearly.

28. Providing explanations for the use of jargon, symbols, or specific vocabulary when necessary.
29. Ensuring easy fundamental navigation, such as back, exit, and help options on all screens.
30. Providing sufficient time to complete activities.
31. Disabling or avoiding timed/clocked activities or allowing customization of timers.
32. Offering pauses for users to confirm whether they are ready to proceed.

H7 -Helping Users Recognize, Diagnose, and Recover from Errors.

33. Providing immediate feedback and alert messages after an action to prevent user rework.

H8 -Error Prevention.

34. Offering preventive and corrective guidance when the user does not interact as expected with key elements.
35. Auditory feedback for common interactions, such as button presses or page transitions.
36. Clear and precise alerts when an error occurs due to user or system actions.
37. Ensuring predictability in functionalities, behaviors, and layouts, even when errors occur.

H9 -Aesthetic and Minimalist Design.

38. Maintaining a minimalist design on screens.
39. Using larger and more prominent visual elements than typically used.
40. Avoiding figures, icons, or shapes that represent emotions as feedback.

H10 -Help and Documentation.

41. Providing clear instructions, guiding the user through warning boxes, interactive step-by-step instructions, index tables (when applicable), and captions (when applicable).
42. Offering introductory explanations for long or complex processes.
43. Providing tutorials for long journeys, especially to help users understand and recover from errors.

H11 -Save Progress and Protect Work.

44. Clearly informing users about their progress within an activity.

H12 -Color and Readability.

45. Ensuring sufficient contrast between multiple elements for proper navigation and screen exploration, particularly for individuals with hypo- or hypersensitivity to visual stimuli.
46. Using a color palette with soft tones.
47. Providing adequate spacing between words to enhance readability.
48. Aligning text consistently to the right, avoiding centered alignment.
49. Avoiding uppercase text (all caps).
50. Maintaining a consistent reading hierarchy, ensuring that no words or phrases appear significantly larger than others within the same paragraph.

51. Using a comfortable sans-serif font for reading.
52. Ensuring adequate contrast in images, avoiding excessive visual strain, bright flashes, and highly vibrant colors.

H13 -Autonomy.

53. Providing native options to increase font size and adjust other screen elements.
54. Enabling/disabling sounds, music, narrations, alerts, auditory feedback, and video captions.
55. Allowing appropriate time for users to orient themselves, identify, and understand the presented information.
56. Providing native volume adjustment for emitted sounds.

H14 -Standards.

57. Ensuring that actions, interaction modes, and response patterns are familiar to users.
58. Making links easily identifiable.
59. Notifying users before opening external links.
60. Ensuring touch/click areas are larger than the dimensions of buttons, icons, and links in the interface.

H15 -Reducing Delays.

61. Avoiding unnecessary redirects.
62. Preventing tasks, processes, or sessions from expiring unexpectedly.
63. Supporting the completion of tasks or activities without unnecessary interruptions.

4.3 Application of the Evaluation Model in a Game

The proposed heuristic evaluation model was applied to a selected interactive game to assess its usability and accessibility for individuals with Autism Spectrum Disorder (ASD). The objective was to analyze how well the game aligns with the established heuristics (H1 to H15) and to identify areas for potential improvement.

To test the model's effectiveness, it was applied in the evaluation of the digital game "Sago Mini Forest Adventure" (free downloaded from app stores), which is commonly used in therapies for children with ASD, available on all market platforms. The evaluation lasted six days. All interactions, including screens, functions, user journeys, and menus, were explored. Four HCI specialists conducted the evaluation, navigating through all game interactions and responding to the model's assessment questions. On the final day, the results were analyzed and consolidated, presenting the heuristic evaluation outcome.

The evaluation results revealed that the game met 54.2% of the assessment criteria, achieving an average score of 83.5 out of 154. This suggests that, although the game provides a reasonable user experience, there are significant areas for improvement, particularly in help and documentation, which received lower scores.

The evaluation process provided valuable insights into the game's strengths and weaknesses, especially regarding interface design, user control, feedback mechanisms, and accessibility features. Specific aspects such as visual contrast, navigation structure, interaction predictability, and error prevention were carefully analyzed.

These findings contribute to a better understanding of accessibility barriers in interactive systems and serve as a guideline for future improvements in game design, ensuring inclusive digital experiences for individuals with ASD.

5 Discussion

The results of this study indicate that evaluating the accessibility and usability of interactive systems designed for individuals with Autism Spectrum Disorder (ASD) requires specialized and adapted approaches that address their specific needs. The proposed methodology, based on a structured heuristic evaluation derived from Granollers' heuristics [30] and complemented by alternative guidelines such as GAIA [28] and AASPIRE [27], has proven to be an effective strategy for expanding accessibility assessments beyond conventional W3C standards.

The application of this methodology in an interactive game revealed that 54.2% of the accessibility criteria were met, indicating that while the system provides a reasonable level of accessibility, there are still significant gaps that could affect the user experience for individuals with ASD. Among the most problematic aspects, the lack of adapted support and documentation was a key issue, making navigation and interaction understanding more difficult. Additionally, problems related to interface personalization, sensory stimulus control, and clarity of information were identified as critical areas impacting user experience.

A relevant observation from the results is that WCAG (Web Content Accessibility Guidelines), which are frequently used as the standard for digital accessibility, present limitations when applied to ASD. As highlighted by [31], the generic approach of WCAG can lead to superficial evaluations, failing to consider specific aspects such as hyper- and hyposensitivity to sensory stimuli, communication difficulties, and the need for structured and predictable interfaces. This finding reinforces the importance of developing more targeted and customized evaluation models, such as the one proposed in this study.

Another significant point concerns the expert evaluations, which emphasized the need for refinement in certain heuristics, particularly those related to flexibility and efficiency of use. The recommendations suggest that interactive systems designed for ASD users should allow for greater personalization, including adjustments to color, font, animation speed, and control over sounds and visual stimuli. Moreover, the predictability of interactions and the reduction of distracting elements were identified as essential aspects for ensuring a more comfortable and intuitive experience.

The findings of this study reinforce the need to expand accessibility assessment criteria beyond conventional standards, considering the cognitive and sensory specificities of ASD. Additionally, they highlight the importance of developing more robust evaluation tools and methodologies that can provide detailed insights for designers and developers. Adopting more specialized models can significantly contribute to the creation of more inclusive digital experiences, promoting greater autonomy and comfort for individuals with ASD.

Based on the results, future research should explore the application of the model across different contexts and platforms, assessing its effectiveness in various types of interactive systems. Furthermore, directly involving individuals with ASD in accessibility testing could provide even more precise insights for refining evaluation methodologies. The integration of assistive technologies and the development of ASD-specific accessibility guidelines are promising directions for strengthening digital accessibility and ensuring truly inclusive systems.

6 Conclusion and Future Work

This research has made a significant contribution to the field of Human-Computer Interaction (HCI) by proposing a heuristic evaluation model focused on the accessibility and usability of interactive systems for individuals with Autism Spectrum Disorder (ASD). Given the lack of assessment methodologies specifically tailored to this audience, the study addresses a critical gap by integrating digital accessibility references and criteria adapted to the specific needs often associated with ASD.

The proposed model was developed using a multidisciplinary approach, combining a systematic literature review, interviews with ASD specialists, a review of accessibility guidelines, and the adaptation of existing models such as GAIA and AASPIRE. Furthermore, the research validated its methodology through the evaluation of a digital game, demonstrating the feasibility and practical applicability of the model. The results indicated that while the evaluated game presented a reasonable level of accessibility, critical areas require improvement, particularly regarding the presence of support documentation and adaptable usability elements.

The primary contribution of this work lies in the development of a structured heuristic model applicable to various interactive contexts. The model provides designers and software developers with an objective tool to identify accessibility barriers and implement adjustments to make their solutions more inclusive. Additionally, by moving beyond exclusive reliance on W3C guidelines, the study offers an alternative evaluation approach that can be used at different stages of interactive system development.

However, some limitations were identified. The model's application was conducted in a single context, with a limited number of specialists and evaluators. To further validate its effectiveness and broaden its impact, future studies should involve more diverse user samples, including individuals with different ASD profiles. Moreover, future research could explore the integration of the model with automated tools, enhancing its adoption by development teams. Another future work could include other types of computational applications beyond games, as well as a usability and accessibility evaluation with the autistic population.

Ultimately, this study reinforces the importance of digital accessibility as an essential factor in ensuring equitable interactive experiences. Advancing research in this field is crucial to building a more inclusive, intuitive, and adaptable digital environment, promoting greater autonomy and participation for individuals with ASD in the digital society.

Acknowledgments. The authors acknowledge the use of ChatGPT4.0 for assisting in organizing ideas and coherence of the manuscript in English.

Disclosure of Interests The authors have no competing interests to declare that are relevant to the content of this article.

References

1. Mads, S., Dam, F.: Using multitouch collaboration technology to enhance social interaction of children with high-functioning autism. Interact. Des. Found. **1**(3), 21–25 (2014)
2. Norman, D.A.: Human-centered design considered harmful. Interactions. **12**(4), 14–19 (2005)
3. Kronschnabl, A., Vieira, B.: Bridging another digital divide: accessibility for blind and low-vision consumers. McKinsey Digital. (2023)
4. Sauer, J., et al.: Usability, user experience and accessibility: towards an integrative approach. Int. J. Hum.-Comput. Stud. **139**, 102432 (2020)
5. Henry, S.L.: Introduction to web accessibility. W3C Web Accessibility Initiative (WAI) (2020)
6. Abuaddous, H.Y., et al.: Web accessibility challenges. Int. J. Adv. Comput. Sci. Appl. **7**(10) (2016)
7. Lord, C., et al.: Autism spectrum disorder. Nat. Rev. Dis. Primers. **6**(1), 1–23 (2020)
8. Virnes, M., et al.: Benefits of multi-touch technology in special needs education: A review. Procedia Comput. Sci. **67**, 169–178 (2015)
9. Kraemer, G.M., Thoma, A.S. da: Acessibilidade como condição de acesso, participação, desenvolvimento e aprendizagem de alunos com deficiência. Psicol. Ciênc. Prof. 38(3), 554–563 (2018). doi:https://doi.org/10.1590/1982-3703000202011
10. Sassaki, R.K.: As sete dimensões da acessibilidade. Larvatus Prodeo, São Paulo (2019)
11. Melo, A.M.: Acessibilidade e inclusão digital. In: *Livro dos Tutoriais do XIII Simpósio Brasileiro sobre Fatores Humanos em Sistemas Computacionais*, pp. 29–54 (2014)
12. Martins, V.F., Souza, A.G., Sette, G.A., Ribeiro, G.R., de la Amato, C.A.H.: Material digital acessível adaptado a partir de um livro didático físico: Relato de experiência. Rev. Ibér. Sist. Tecnol. Inf. **E26**, 514–527 (2020)
13. Rutter, R., et al.: Web Accessibility: Web Standards and Regulatory Compliance. Apress, Berkeley (2007)
14. Rodrigues, P.R., Alves, L.R.G.: Tecnologia assistiva: Uma revisão do tema. Holos. **6**, 170–180 (2013)
15. Silva, C.S.M.R.: Design de produto para crianças autistas. Universidade Técnica de Lisboa, Portugal, Tese de Doutorado (2011)
16. Cruz, V.C.D.S.: Projecto e desenvolvimento de uma ajuda técnica numa perspetiva de design inclusivo. Universidade da Beira Interior, Portugal, Tese de Doutorado (2010)
17. Lucian, B.O., Stumpf, A.: Análise de aplicativos destinados ao aprendizado de crianças com transtorno do espectro autista. Des. Tecnol. **9**(19), 43–65 (2019)
18. Brasil: Lei n. 13.146, de 6 de julho de 2015. Institui a Lei Brasileira de Inclusão da Pessoa com Deficiência (Estatuto da Pessoa com Deficiência). http://www.planalto.gov.br/ccivil_03/_ato 2015-2018/2015/lei/l13146.htm (2015)
19. de la Amato, C.A.H.: O que se sabe sobre autismo. In: Fernandes, F.D.M. (ed.) Orientações para famílias de crianças no espectro do autismo: fonoaudiologia baseada em evidências, pp. xx–xx. Pró-Fono, Barueri (2019)
20. American Psychiatric Association: Diagnostic and Statistical Manual of Mental Disorders (DSM-5), 5th edn. Artmed, Porto Alegre (2014)
21. World Health Organization: ICD-11: International Classification of Diseases for Mortality and Morbidity Statistics, 11th rev. https://icd.who.int (2022).
22. Britto, T.C.P.: GAIA: uma proposta de guia de recomendações de acessibilidade web com foco em aspectos do autismo. Dissertação de Mestrado. (2016)
23. Kagohara, D.M., Sigafoos, J., Green, V.A., O'Reilly, M.F., Didden, R., Lancioni, G.E.: Using iPods® and iPads® in teaching programs for individuals with developmental disabilities: A systematic review. Res. Dev. Disabil. **34**(1), 147–156 (2013). https://doi.org/10.1016/j.ridd.2012.07.027

24. Boucenna, S., et al.: Interactive technologies for autistic children: A review. Cogn. Comput. **6**(4), 722–740 (2014). https://doi.org/10.1007/s12559-014-9276-x
25. Kumm, A.J., Viljoen, M., de Vries, P.J.: The digital divide in technologies for autism: Feasibility considerations for low- and middle-income countries. J. Autism Dev. Disord. **52**, 2300–2313 (2022). https://doi.org/10.1007/s10803-021-05178-1
26. Fernandes, M., Nohama, P.: Jogos digitais para pessoas com transtornos do espectro do autismo (TEA): Uma revisão sistemática. Rev. Iberoam. Tecnol. Educ. Educ. Tecnol. **26**, 72–80 (2020)
27. Nicolaidis, C., et al.: The development and evaluation of an online healthcare toolkit for autistic adults and their primary care providers. J. Gen. Intern. Med. **31**, 1180–1189 (2016)
28. Pagani, T.: Sites inclusivos a pessoas com autismo. https://gaia.wiki.br/ (2016)
29. Navikas, F.H.: Avaliação de usabilidade e acessibilidade de sistemas interativos com foco em indivíduos com TEA. Programa de Pós-Graduação em Computação Aplicada, Universidade Presbiteriana Mackenzie, São Paulo, Dissertação de Mestrado (2024) Disponível em: https://dspace.mackenzie.br/items/b8d684fa-d5a3-418f-80cf-d6b9e4bc31f4
30. Granollers, T.: Usability evaluation with heuristics: new proposal from integrating two trusted sources. In: Design, User Experience, and Usability: Theory and Practice. DUXU 2018. LNCS, vol. xxxx, pp. 396–405. Springer, Cham (2018)
31. Power, C., et al.: Guidelines are only half of the story: Accessibility problems encountered by blind users on the web. In: Proceedings of the SIGCHI Conference on Human Factors in Computing Systems, pp. 433–442. ACM, New York, NY, USA (2012)

Designing with Purpose: Merging UCD, Soft Skills and Sustainability in a Computer Science Curriculum

Valéria Farinazzo Martins(✉) and Ismar Frango Silveira

Programa de Pós-Graduação em Computação Aplicada, Universidade Presbiteriana Mackenzie, São Paulo, Brasil
{valeria.farinazzo,ismar.silveira}@mackenzie.br

Abstract. This paper explores the integration of User-Centered Design (UCD), Soft Skills and sustainability principles into Human-Computer Interaction (HCI) education, emphasizing the need to prepare future technologists for inclusive, and environmentally conscious innovation. As computational systems increasingly shape societal interactions, the paper argues that HCI must adopt an interdisciplinary framework—bridging computer science, psychology, design, and soft skills — to address complex challenges like accessibility, cultural diversity, and climate change. Through a case study of undergraduate students in São Paulo, Brazil, the research examines how active learning methodologies (e.g., Project-Based Learning) and UCD practices—such as iterative prototyping, usability testing, and user feedback—equip students to design solutions aligned with the UN Sustainable Development Goals (SDGs). By prioritizing social responsibility and environmental conscience, this approach not only enhances technical proficiency but also cultivates a generation of designers and engineers capable of creating technologies that respect human dignity, promote equity, and mitigate ecological harm. The paper concludes that embedding UCD and sustainability into HCI curriculum is essential for nurturing professionals who can balance innovation with ethical accountability in an increasingly digitized world.

Keywords: Human-Computer Interaction (HCI) · User-Centered Design (UCD) · Sustainability Education · Soft Skills · Interdisciplinary Learning

1 Introduction

Technology can play a transformative role in supporting environment-based teaching by creating immersive, interactive, and data-driven learning experiences that connect students to ecological concepts, sustainability challenges, and real-world environmental issues [1]. It bridges the gap between theoretical environmental concepts and actionable, real-world learning. By integrating tools like Extended Reality (XR), simulations, real-time data platforms, and collaborative online spaces, educators can cultivate a generation of environmentally literate, technologically adept, and socially responsible problem-solvers. This approach not only enhances academic outcomes but also prepares students to tackle the pressing environmental challenges of the 21st century [2].

H. Luna-García et al. (Eds.): HCI-COLLAB 2025, CCIS 2850, pp. 75–89, 2027.
https://doi.org/10.1007/978-3-032-31223-5_6

Between many learning outcomes, the following could be mentioned:

- Engagement: Interactive technologies make abstract environmental concepts tangible and relatable.
- Critical Thinking: Simulations and real-world data encourage problem-solving and systems thinking.
- Empowerment: Students see themselves as agents of change through projects that address local/global sustainability goals (e.g., UN SDGs).

In the field of Computer Science (CS), it is possible to develop systems that not only promote environmental education for children [3] but also process data from environmental sensors to identify desirable patterns [4, 5] and integrate IoT sensors with the environment [6–8]. CS plays a crucial role in addressing environmental challenges, making technological advancements essential for a sustainable future.

CS and Environmental Sciences (ES) intersect in many exciting ways, enabling innovative solutions for sustainability and ecological challenges. In this context, the course of Human-Computer Interaction (HCI) is fundamental in the education of Computer Science students, equipping them to design accessible, intuitive, and efficient digital interfaces. HCI courses can significantly enhance ES by equipping students with the skills to design, develop, and evaluate technologies that promote sustainability, environmental awareness, and data-driven decision-making.

In HCI courses, during their undergraduate studies, students explore both theoretical and practical aspects of human-computer interaction, including usability, user experience (UX), accessibility, and interface evaluation. With the growing digitization of services, user-centered system development has become essential for creating effective and socially responsible technological [9].

Given its extensive interconnection with other fields of knowledge, HCI is considered a cross-cutting area, establishing links with Artificial Intelligence, Graphics and Interactive Techniques, Software Development Fundamentals, Software Engineering, and Society [10]. This integration strengthens HCI's relevance in developing innovative and socially responsible solutions, directly influencing how we interact with technology in daily life.

Teaching HCI requires approaches that transcend theory, emphasizing active and practical methodologies that encourage experimentation and real-world problem-solving [11]. Techniques such as Project-Based Learning (PBL) [12, 13] foster the development of essential skills by allowing students to design and implement interactive interfaces. This approach makes learning more dynamic and engaging, stimulates collaboration among students, and strengthens critical thinking in building user-oriented solutions.

The intersection of technology, user experience, and sustainable development has become essential for advancing computing and digital innovation. Well-designed interfaces can play a key role in raising awareness and promoting sustainable practices, encouraging users to adopt more responsible behaviors. In academia, integrating environmental challenges into HCI education enables students to develop technological applications that support the UN's (United Nations) Sustainable Development Goals (SDGs), such as smart cities, sustainable consumption, and climate change solutions.

This interdisciplinary approach broadens students' perspectives on computing's societal and environmental impact, preparing them to design technologies with positive outcomes.

Thus, the central objective of this article is to present a case study with students from a university in São Paulo, Brazil, within an HCI course. It highlights active learning and practical methodologies in HCI learning, emphasizing the relevance of User-Centered Design (UCD) in student formation.

2 Background

2.1 Human-Computer Interaction in Computing Education

HCI is an essentially interdisciplinary field focused on designing, evaluating, and implementing interactive computing systems that prioritize human needs, behaviors, and experiences [9]. At its core, HCI integrates principles from computer science, cognitive psychology, design, and social sciences to bridge the gap between technology and users. It emphasizes creating intuitive, accessible, and inclusive interfaces while addressing usability [14], UX, and soft skills [15]. In undergraduate programs, HCI equips students with the tools to critically analyze how technology shapes—and is shaped by—human actions, fostering a holistic understanding of systems that are both functional and socially responsible.

The inclusion of HCI in CS curriculum is important for preparing students to address real-world challenges in an increasingly digitized world [16]. As technology permeates every aspect of life, from education to healthcare and environmental sustainability, graduates must design solutions that align with diverse user needs and values. HCI teaches students to adopt user-centered methodologies, such as iterative prototyping, usability testing, and participatory design, ensuring technologies are not only efficient but also equitable. This approach cultivates empathy, critical thinking, and problem-solving skills, enabling future professionals to create systems that respect human dignity, promote accessibility, and mitigate unintended societal or environmental harms. Moreover, HCI education plays a pivotal role in advancing sustainable and ethical innovation, under the umbrella that was named Sustainable HCI (SHCI) [2, 17]. It is a research area within HCI that focuses on designing and evaluating digital systems to promote environmental, social, and economic sustainability. It explores how technology can mitigate environmental impact, encourage sustainable behaviors, and support long-term ecological balance. SHCI encompasses various topics, such as energy-efficient computing, e-waste reduction, sustainable design practices, and persuasive technologies that influence user behavior toward sustainability. Researchers in this field also examine the ethical implications of digital sustainability, addressing concerns like digital obsolescence and the carbon footprint of data centers. By integrating sustainability principles into system design, SHCI aims to create technologies that contribute positively to both human and planetary well-being.

By integrating topics like environmental impact assessments, and inclusive design, HCI courses encourage students to view technology through a lens of social responsibility. For instance, projects aligned with the UN SDGs—such as designing apps for climate action or tools for accessible education—highlight HCI's potential to drive positive global change. Ultimately, embedding HCI into undergraduate programs ensures that emerging technologists are not only skilled in coding and algorithms but also committed to developing human-centric solutions that prioritize well-being, equity, and sustainability in a rapidly evolving digital landscape.

Among the key challenges in Teaching and Learning HCI Concepts are the interdisciplinary complexity and the need to bridge theory and practice - applying HCI fundamentals to real-world projects poses challenges. Students often lack opportunities to engage with actual users for testing and feedback, leading to designs that prioritize aesthetics over functionality. Limited access to interdisciplinary collaboration (e.g., working with developers or stakeholders) further complicates the learning process.

Besides, the rapid evolution of design tools (e.g., AI-driven prototyping, XR interfaces) and industry trends (e.g., voice UIs, micro-interactions) creates pressure to constantly update curriculum. Students may feel disconnected from current practices if courses focus solely on static principles without addressing emerging technologies. Similarly, the subjective nature of design critiques—where feedback can vary widely based on cultural or contextual factors—adds uncertainty for learners seeking clear guidelines.

Designing for diverse audiences—spanning abilities, cultural backgrounds, and technological literacy—is a core HCI challenge. Students often lack exposure to marginalized user groups (e.g., people with disabilities, non-native speakers), leading to oversights in accessibility (e.g., screen reader compatibility, color contrast). Teaching inclusive design requires navigating complex ethical and practical considerations, which can be difficult to convey in theory-only environments.

As technology's impact on mental health, privacy, and equity grows, educators face the challenge of integrating ethical discussions into HCI education. Concepts like dark patterns, data exploitation, or algorithmic bias require critical thinking that students may not naturally associate with design. Balancing business objectives with user well-being adds another layer of complexity to decision-making frameworks.

To overcome these barriers, educators can adopt PBL, partner with industry for real-world case studies, and emphasize iterative design processes. Tools like user personas can help students navigate complexity while fostering empathy and responsibility.

2.2 User Centered Design and Project Based Learning to Foster Soft Skills

UCD is a cornerstone of Human-Computer Interaction (HCI) [18], providing a structured framework for developing interactive systems that align with the expectations and needs of end-users. Integrating UCD into academic training enables students to understand the importance of designing efficient, intuitive, and inclusive interfaces, ensuring a positive experience for diverse user profiles. Furthermore, teaching UCD reinforces the necessity of iterative testing, usability evaluation, and continuous adaptation of solutions based on real user feedback, preparing students for the challenges of the technology market [19].

Computational systems not only solve problems but also foster social connectivity and support a wide range of human activities. As such, they must operate efficiently while respecting individual dignity, social justice, and human values. HCI adopts an interdisciplinary perspective, combining computer science, psychology, business strategy, and design to ensure that interactions between humans and systems are optimized.

Every user is unique, and from the HCI perspective, the design of any system must anticipate and respect this diversity [20]. This includes not only accessibility but also cultural and social norms, neurodiversity, multiple interaction modalities, and the emotional responses that systems evoke in users. An effective computational system should inspire trust, treat users fairly, ensure privacy and security, and adhere to ethical principles in its development and application.

To achieve these goals, adopting a design-centered engineering approach is essential. This begins with a clear intention and an understanding that design is an iterative process. It involves continuous usability evaluations and analyses of user impact, ensuring systems are constantly refined. Moreover, technology influences the user experience not only through its functionality but also through how it perceives and communicates with users, demanding empathetic and inclusive design.

The intersection between Computer Science and Environmental Sciences has become increasingly important for developing innovative solutions focused on sustainability (Ling et al., 2024). Interdisciplinary collaboration enables technology and environmental experts to combine their knowledge to create computational systems that assist in ecosystem monitoring, natural resource management, and public awareness of sustainable practices. HCI techniques, such as UCD, can be applied to make these solutions more accessible, intuitive, and effective, ensuring that the developed technologies meet the needs of diverse audiences and drive behavioral change toward more conscious and sustainable consumption.

In an educational context, integrating Computer Science and Environmental Sciences allows students to develop a critical perspective on the impact of technology on the environment while enhancing their technical skills [21]. Interdisciplinary projects can range from the development of applications for air and water quality monitoring to the creation of environmental awareness platforms with interactive and gamified interfaces. Additionally, collaboration between students and researchers from these fields fosters experimentation with new computational approaches, such as artificial intelligence applied to environmental analysis, smart sensors for real-time data collection, and decision-support systems for environmental policies, expanding the potential positive impact of the solutions developed.

PBL is an educational methodology that actively engages students in their own learning process, focusing on solving relevant problems. This approach can be applied across various courses and disciplines, encouraging students, as active participants in their learning journey, to develop problem-solving strategies and acquire disciplinary skills in an autonomous and collaborative manner.

In PBL, students identify what they already know and what they need to learn, confronting problems without having sufficient prior knowledge. Instructors present challenging situations, and student groups analyze the problems, conduct research, and develop well-founded solutions or recommendations [22–25].

3 Applied Teaching Methodology

3.1 Course Structure

For many years, HCI has played a crucial role across various disciplines. It is a central concern in the design of computer systems and an essential component of the design process [26, 27]. From this perspective, HCI encompasses the design, implementation, and evaluation of interactive systems within the context of user-performed tasks.

The course content covers both end users and computational systems, considering cultural, social, organizational, and cognitive aspects. The course in which this project was developed is taught in the sixth semester of the undergraduate Computer Science program. The syllabus includes fundamental concepts of interaction, the distinction between interface and interaction, types of interactive systems, interaction metaphors, requirement identification and modeling (mental models, scenarios, task analysis, personas, interview techniques), interaction design, prototyping, usability and user experience, usability evaluation methods, usability metrics (effectiveness, efficiency, and user satisfaction), and data analysis. One of the main challenges of the course is covering all the content while ensuring that students gain hands-on experience in software interface projects, which is particularly important.

One of the key challenges of the course is covering all the content while ensuring that students gain hands-on experience. In this regard, actively engaging students in the development of software interface projects is a fundamental aspect of the course.

The growing concern for sustainability and global environmental challenges has driven the need for innovative technological solutions that promote the conscious use of natural resources. In this context, the HCI course plays a fundamental role in equipping students with the skills to design user-centered interactive systems that consider not only usability and user experience but also the environmental impact of the applications they develop. Integrating environmental themes into HCI education aligns with the United Nations Sustainable Development Goals (SDGs) (Hansson et al., 2021), particularly SDG 4 (Quality Education), SDG 11 (Sustainable Cities and Communities), SDG 12 (Responsible Consumption and Production), and SDG 13 (Climate Action). By developing sustainability-focused projects, students apply User-Centered Design (UCD) principles to create interfaces and applications that promote environmental awareness, resource monitoring, and societal engagement in more sustainable practices.

Furthermore, this interdisciplinary approach not only broadens students' perspectives on the impact of computing on society but also prepares them to tackle real-world challenges in a job market where socio-environmental responsibility is becoming an increasingly relevant factor in digital product and service development. By incorporating real-world environmental issues into course projects, students have the opportunity to develop prototypes of sustainability-focused applications, such as educational platforms, waste management apps, environmental monitoring systems, and interfaces that encourage eco-friendly behaviors in users' daily lives.

3.2 Practical Projects

The course implemented PBL in combination with the development of software focused on an environmental theme, which served as the semester's central project. The PBL methodology was applied from the first class, with students organized into groups of up to three members and encouraged to find solutions for a given problem. This semester, the topic was the environment, aligned with the United Nations Sustainable Development Goals (SDGs). Another key aspect was the integration of soft skills throughout the phases of PBL.

The classes were structured so that groups could apply HCI concepts throughout the project, from problem definition to implementation and testing. Below are the ten stages carried out in this project, based on [25]:

- Stage I: Problem Definition and Understanding. Groups were formed to develop software on an environmental topic for any platform (desktop, mobile, etc.) and for any target age group.
- Stage II: Brainstorming and Project Validation.

Students conducted a brainstorming session to define the product, target audience, and development platform. They then presented their project idea to the professor, who validated the topic's relevance and its feasibility within the available timeframe (4 months). At this stage, the activities also aimed to develop soft skills such as teamwork, organization, leadership, and creativity.

- Stage III: Solution Proposal.

Based on their prior knowledge of prototyping, students proposed solutions to address the problem, with a particular focus on environmental solution. At this stage, the activities also aimed to develop soft skills such as teamwork, organization, leadership, creativity, and learning.

- Stage IV: User Profile and Requirements Definition.

Groups defined the characteristics of their target audience (age, educational level, familiarity with apps, etc.) and the objective of the software. They also investigated the complexity of development and the need to incorporate usability principles. At this stage, the activities also aimed to develop soft skills such as teamwork, organization, and learning.

- Stage V: Task Planning and Assignment.

Based on the problem and the new knowledge acquired, groups assigned individual responsibilities and planned the game's features, including mechanics, scoring criteria, and other elements. At this stage, the activities also aim to develop soft skills such as teamwork, organization, and leadership.

- Stage VI: Independent Study and Course Progress.

Each student studied the assigned topics as planned, in parallel with the course content. At this stage, the activities also aimed to develop soft skills such as organization, and learning.

- Stage VII: Knowledge Integration.

Groups met to share their learning and refine their project development. At this stage, the activities also aimed to develop soft skills such as teamwork, organization, and learning.

- Stage VIII: Prototyping and Documentation.

Initially, students submitted prototype documentation, including user profiles, personas, requirement lists, UML diagrams, screen prototypes, and scenarios. Later, they coded the game in the chosen programming language, designed the user manual, and wrote the implementation report. At this stage, the activities also aimed to develop soft skills such as teamwork and learning.

- Stage IX: Prototype Evaluation and User Testing.

Groups presented their prototypes to the professor, who provided feedback on potential improvements. They then tested their prototypes with a group of potential users, collected data, and calculated effectiveness, efficiency, and user satisfaction metrics. Additionally, a heuristic evaluation was conducted by usability experts, generating a report detailing identified issues, their severity, and suggested improvements. At this stage, the activities also aimed to develop soft skills such as teamwork and learning.

- Stage X: Final Assessments.

Various evaluations were conducted, including the professor's assessment of group performance and prototype quality, an informal self-assessment by students about the course, peer evaluation, and a reflection on the soft skills developed during the process. At this stage, the activities also aimed to develop soft skills such as creativity and learning.

4 Case Study / Conducted Experiments

The study took place in the second semester of 2024 at a private Brazilian university located in São Paulo, Brazil, within the Computer Science program. The Human-Computer Interaction course is offered in the sixth semester of the program and consists of both theoretical and practical classes, with a total workload of 4 h per week—2 h in person and 2 h online. The classes were conducted in rooms equipped with one laptop per student. The class consisted of 36 students, who were divided into groups of 2 or 3, forming 16 different projects.

4.1 Resulting Projects

The theme of each project was freely chosen within the environmental context, resulting in a wide variety of topics. In total, 16 projects were developed by students, who were divided into groups of up to three members. The most common themes included the following:

- A service to inform about water quality and beach characteristics along the coast of Rio de Janeiro, Brazil.
- Assistance in helping people understand how their daily actions impact the environment.

- Software to promote sustainability and material reuse, facilitating the creation of useful and creative items.
- Location tracking of recycling collection points.
- Raising user awareness about the environmental impact of household appliances and encouraging the adoption of more sustainable practices (EcoImpact Software).
- Encouragement of plant cultivation.
- Development of an innovative simulator designed to calculate, monitor, and compare an individual's environmental impact based on daily energy, gas, transportation, and recycling habits.
- An interactive digital platform focused on environmental education, designed to teach children about environmental preservation in an engaging and practical way (EcoImpacto Platform).
- An online platform offering accessible and educational tools for individuals interested in monitoring and reducing their carbon footprint.
- An application to educate users on the correct disposal of asbestos.
- Among other topics.

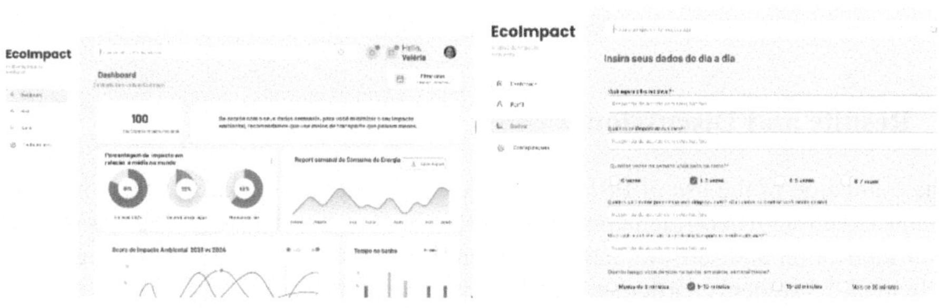

Fig. 1. Screens of the EcoImpact platform – awareness on energy conservation (in Portuguese). Source: Authors

The project, which lasted throughout the semester, was divided into four deliverables:

1. Initial project idea – validated by the professor to ensure students could proceed with the project. Adjustments were required if the professor deemed the topic or its complexity unsuitable.
2. Documentation – including a detailed description of the application, functional and non-functional requirements, scenarios, personas, and interviews with the potential target audience.
3. Prototype – created using software such as Figma.
4. Implementation – the project was developed using a platform and/or programming language of the group's choice, followed by an in-class presentation where all students provided feedback.
5. Usability testing – conducted by potential target audience members to evaluate the project's effectiveness.

Figures 1 and 2 present examples of screens from the software developed by the groups. Figure 1 presents a system called EcoImpact, which allows users to input data related to their daily consumption and generates a dashboard with comparative graphs displaying consumption in various scenarios. Figure 2 showcases the EcoImpacto platform's home screen, featuring options such as Minigames, Quiz, and Learn More, along with screens from two games — one focused on recycling and another on water conservation.

Fig. 2. A figure caption is always placed below the illustration. Short captions are centered, while long ones are justified. The macro button chooses the correct format automatically. Source: Authors

5 Results and Discussion

The evaluation of the use of PBL and the development of soft skills in the course was conducted through questionnaires answered by the students. The objective was to assess their motivation and self-evaluation regarding soft skills, as highlighted in Figs. 3 and 4. In total, 23 students participated in this assessment.

Fig. 3. Self-assessment of soft skills: communication, teamwork, organization, leadership, learning, and creativity. Source: Authors

Based on the presented chart (Fig. 3), most students rated themselves as "Good" or "Very Good" in the majority of soft skills, particularly in Communication, Organization, Leadership, and Learning, suggesting that the course contributed to their development. Learning and Organization stood out with a higher number of positive ratings, indicating that students felt they improved in these areas throughout the semester.

However, Leadership and Creativity showed more variation, with some students rating themselves as "Poor" or "Neutral." This may suggest that not all students had sufficient opportunities to develop leadership skills or that they lacked confidence in this area. Creativity also presented a more balanced distribution, indicating that its development varied among students.

Teamwork received predominantly positive ratings, with very few students marking it as "Very Poor" or "Poor," which suggests that the course dynamics encouraged collaboration. On the other hand, Communication, despite having several positive evaluations, also had a significant number of "Neutral" and "Poor" ratings, indicating that this skill might require additional encouragement or structured activities to support its development.

To further enhance student learning, the course could implement more activities that stimulate creativity, communication, and leadership, ensuring that all students feel more confident in these areas. Strategies such as group dynamics, presentations, and creative challenges could be incorporated to strengthen these skills and provide more engagement opportunities.

The results from the chart (Fig. 4) indicate that the majority of students (52.2%) feel more motivated using PBL, suggesting that project-based methodologies were well received and contributed to greater engagement on the course. Additionally, a significant portion of students (34.8%) expressed a preference for a combination of PBL and traditional exams, highlighting the importance of balancing different assessment methods to cater to various learning styles.

Only a small percentage (8.7%) reported feeling more motivated when taking exams, reinforcing the idea that PBL tends to be more effective in sustaining student motivation compared to purely exam-based assessments. Moreover, very few students indicated that they do not feel motivated by either approach or see no difference between the methods, suggesting that the course structure was generally successful in maintaining student engagement.

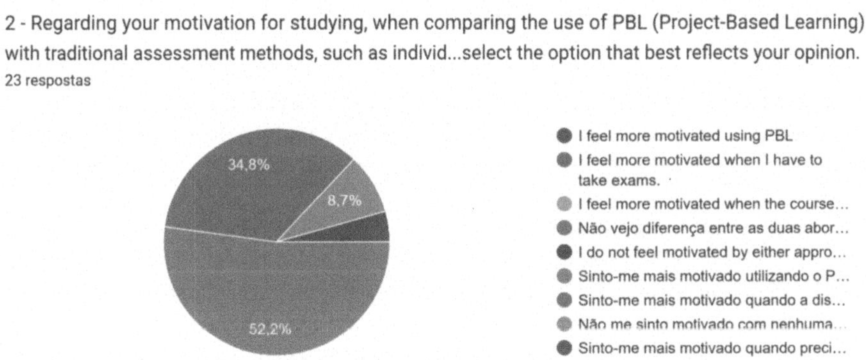

Fig. 4. Question on the use of PBL in the Course. Source: Authors

Given these findings, maintaining or further refining project-based methodologies while integrating some traditional assessment methods could be beneficial. Since a portion of students still value structured evaluations, incorporating periodic assessments, quizzes, or complementary evaluation strategies alongside PBL could help meet their needs. The overall high motivation levels indicate that the course design is effective, but additional refinements, such as real-world project applications, clearer assessment criteria, or gamified learning elements, could further enhance student engagement and learning outcomes.

Regarding students' perceptions of the methodology applied in the course, their feedback provided meaningful insights into the use of PBL for the development of interactive systems focused on the SDGs and the enhancement of soft skills. Among the most frequently mentioned advantages were the motivational nature of practical development and the value of collaborative work as a key factor in promoting knowledge exchange and strengthening teamwork abilities.

Despite the positive outcomes, some challenges were also identified. The most common concern was the limited time available to complete a project of considerable complexity, particularly in relation to conducting tests with real users. Students also reported difficulties in identifying and engaging target audience representatives who would be available to test the systems within the course schedule (even though this step was optional due to these constraints).

These observations suggest that the instructional strategy was effective in fostering student engagement and raising awareness of SDG-related topics. However, for future applications, it would be beneficial to allow more time for project development — for instance, by integrating this approach into capstone or final graduation projects — and to provide institutional support to enable more active participation of end users in the evaluation phase. It is also important to note that involving real users would require prior approval from a Research Ethics Committee, which could be an additional limitation given the tight timelines of regular academic courses.

6 Conclusion and Future Work

The paper discusses integrating User-Centered Design and sustainability into Human-Computer Interaction education, emphasizing Project-Based Learning as a key methodology. It argues that teaching HCI through practical, real-world environmental challenges enhances students' ability to design ethical, inclusive, and sustainable technology solutions.

Historically, HCI has been taught through theoretical lectures, case studies, and usability principles. These traditional methods often focus on predefined design heuristics rather than hands-on experimentation. In this case, there is a challenge in bridging theory with real-world application, particularly regarding sustainability.

On the other hand, PBL encourages active student participation by applying HCI concepts to real-world problems, such as environmental sustainability. In this study, students worked on sustainability-driven projects aligned with the UN SDGs. The methodology involved iterative design, usability testing, and integrating user feedback to refine solutions, based on UCD. UCD ensures that interactive systems consider accessibility, usability, and soft skills.

The case study presented in this research accentuates the effectiveness of integrating UCD and sustainability principles into HCI education through active learning methodologies. By engaging undergraduate students in real-world, sustainability-focused projects, the study demonstrated that PBL fosters both technical and soft skills development. The research highlights the importance of designing technology that promotes sustainable behavior, such as environmental monitoring apps and waste management platforms. Ethical design practices encourage students to create solutions that are socially responsible and environmentally friendly.

The students' projects, which addressed environmental issues aligned with the UN SDGs, demonstrate their ability to apply UCD principles — such as iterative prototyping and usability testing — to create meaningful and impactful digital solutions. The results indicate that this pedagogical approach not only enhances students' proficiency in HCI but also instills a sense of ethical responsibility and environmental awareness.

The paper allows us to reach several key conclusions about the integration of sustainability into HCI education through UCD and PBL: first, traditional HCI teaching methods often fail to bridge theory and practice, particularly in sustainability. PBL, by engaging students in real-world projects, strengthens their ability to design ethical, inclusive, and sustainable technology solutions. UCD plays a pivotal role in ensuring accessibility, usability, and ethical considerations in interactive systems.

The paper also emphasizes the intersection of HCI with environmental sciences, cognitive psychology, and design. It suggests that interdisciplinary collaboration enhances students' understanding of how technology impacts ecological and societal systems. By incorporating user feedback and iterative testing, students develop more effective sustainability-driven technologies. Designing solutions such as shown demonstrates how HCI can actively contribute to sustainability efforts.

Moving forward, further research could explore long-term impacts on students' careers, industry collaborations, and the role of emerging technologies, such as AI and data-driven approaches, in strengthening sustainability-driven HCI education. Further works include the expansion of empirical studies on UCD and SHCI, the creation of Open Educational Resources (OER) for SHCI and exploring AI and Data-Driven Approaches in SHCI Education. Overall, the paper advocates for a shift in HCI education towards a more applied, sustainability-conscious approach that prepares students to develop responsible and impactful technological solutions. Finally, as other future work, additional experiments could be conducted involving data collection through questionnaires or comparative evaluation instruments to assess the impact on students' experience

Acknowledgments. The authors acknowledge the use of ChatGPT4.0, Qwen2.5-Max, and DeepSeek for assisting in organizing ideas, suggesting titles and enhancing the clarity and coherence of the manuscript in English.

Disclosure of Interests The authors have no competing interests to declare that are relevant to the content of this article.

References

1. Gomes, C.P.: Computational sustainability: computational methods for a sustainable environment, economy, and society. In: Frontiers of Engineering: Reports on Leading-Edge Engineering from the 2009 Symposium, pp. 27–40. National Academies Press (2010)
2. Hajj-Hassan, M., Chaker, R., Cederqvist, A.-M.: Environmental education: a systematic review on the use of digital tools for fostering sustainability awareness. Sustainability. **16**(9), 3733 (2024). https://doi.org/10.3390/su16093733
3. Valderrama-Hernández, R., Alcántara, L., Limón, D.: The complexity of environmental education: teaching ideas and strategies from teachers. Procedia Soc. Behav. Sci. **237**, 968–974 (2017)
4. Zhong, S., et al.: Machine learning: new ideas and tools in environmental science and engineering. Environ. Sci. Technol. **55**(19), 12741–12754 (2021)
5. Zhu, J., Luo, Z., Liu, Y., Tong, H., Yin, K.: Environmental perspectives for food loss reduction via smart sensors: a global life cycle assessment. J. Clean. Prod. **374**, 133852 (2022)
6. Ferdoush, S., Li, X.: Wireless sensor network system design using Raspberry Pi and Arduino for environmental monitoring applications. Procedia Comput. Sci. **34**, 103–110 (2014)
7. Mois, G., Folea, S., Sanislav, T.: Analysis of three IoT-based wireless sensors for environmental monitoring. IEEE Trans. Instrum. Meas. **66**(8), 2056–2064 (2017)
8. Maraveas, C., Piromalis, D., Arvanitis, K.G., Bartzanas, T., Loukatos, D.: Applications of IoT for optimized greenhouse environment and resources management. Comput. Electron. Agric. **198**, 106993 (2022)
9. Rogers, Y., Sharp, H., Preece, J.: Design de Interação. Bookman Editora (2013)
10. ACM/IEEE-CS: Computer Science Curricula 2023: Curriculum Guidelines for Undergraduate Degree Programs in Computer Science. Association for Computing Machinery (ACM) (2023) https://dl.acm.org/doi/book/10.1145/3664191
11. Giacummo, A.V.H., Silva, L.B., Martins, V.F.: EcoTrashers: Un Juego Serio para Mejorar la Conciencia sobre el Reciclaje y la Educación Ambiental. Rev. Asoc. Interacc. Pers.-Orden. (AIPO). **5**(2), 33–44 (2024)
12. Simanjuntak, M.P., Hutahaean, J., Marpaung, N., Ramadhani, D.: Effectiveness of problem-based learning combined with computer simulation on students' problem-solving and creative thinking skills. Int. J. Instr. **14**(3), 519–534 (2021)
13. Ribeiro, L.R.C.: Aprendizagem baseada em problemas (PBL) na educação em engenharia. Rev. Ensino Eng. **27**, 23–32 (2008)
14. Ghosh, S., Dubey, S.: The field of usability and user experience (UX) design. In: Correia, A. (ed.) Navigating Usability and User Experience in a Multi-platform World, pp. 117–154. IGI Global (2025)
15. Rodney, R.: From empathy to ethics: uncovering user experience implications. J. Inf. Ethics. **32**(2), 56–69 (2023)
16. Yardi, S., Krolikowski, P., Marshall, T., Bruckman, A.: An HCI approach to computing in the real world. J. Educ. Resour. Comput. (JERIC). **8**(3), 1–20 (2008)
17. Bremer, C., Knowles, B., Friday, A.: Have we taken on too much? A critical review of the sustainable HCI landscape. In: Proceedings of the 2022 CHI Conference on Human Factors in Computing Systems, pp. 1–11 (2022)
18. Vredenburg, K., Mao, J.Y., Smith, P.W., Carey, T.: A survey of user-centered design practice. In: Proceedings of the SIGCHI Conference on Human Factors in Computing Systems, pp. 471–478 (2002)
19. Al-Sa'di, A., McPhee, C.C.A.: User-centred design in educational applications: a systematic literature review. In: 2021 International Conference on Engineering Technologies and Computer Science (EnT), pp. 105–111. IEEE (2021)

20. Dankwa, N.K., Draude, C.: Setting diversity at the core of HCI. In: Antona, M., Stephanidis, C. (eds.) International Conference on Human-Computer Interaction, pp. 39–52. Springer, Cham (2021)
21. Gordon, N.: Education for sustainable development in Computer Science. Innov. Teach. Learn. Inf. Comput. Sci. **9**(2), 1–6 (2010)
22. Hung, W.: All PBL starts here: the problem. Interdiscip. J. Probl.-Based Learn. **10**(2) (2016). https://doi.org/10.7771/1541-5015.1604
23. Constantinou, C.S., Nicolaou, S.A.: Motivation, challenges, support (MCS) cycle model for the development of PBL tutors. Qual. Res. Educ. **7**(1), 1–35 (2018). https://doi.org/10.17583/qre.2018.3064
24. Pletsch, M., Souza, F., Orleans, L.A.: A diferenciação curricular e o desenho universal na aprendizagem como princípios para a inclusão escolar. Rev. Educ. Cult. Contemp. **14**(16) (2017)
25. Martins, V.F., de Almeida Souza Concilio, I., de Paiva Guimarães, M.: Problem-based learning associated with the development of games for programming teaching. Comput. Appl. Eng. Educ. **26**(5), 1577–1589 (2018)
26. Hewett, T., et al.: ACM SIGCHI Curricula for Human-Computer Interaction. Technical Report. ACM Press, New York, NY, USA (1992)
27. Dix, A., Finlay, J.E., Abowd, G.D., Beale, R.: Human-Computer Interaction, 3rd edn. Pearson Education, Harlow (2004)

Developing an Educational Game for Financial Education Using Design Thinking and Co-design

Lucas Ellery Viana, Guilherme Crosera Lobo, and Maria Amelia Eliseo(✉)

Mackenzie Presbyterian University, São Paulo SP 01239-001, Brazil
{10323504,10381446}@mackenzista.com.br,
mariaamelia.eliseo@mackenzie.br

Abstract. This study explores the needs and expectations of Brazilian youth regarding the use of technology to support Financial Education. By adopting a User-Centered Design approach and employing Design Thinking and Co-design methodologies, an educational game prototype was developed to simulate real-life financial challenges and foster learning through gamification. The initial concept was tested during a Design Thinking session involving nine students from different undergraduate programs. The results confirmed that gamification is an effective approach for supporting Financial Education. Based on the insights obtained, low-fidelity prototypes were developed. Subsequently, a Co-design session was conducted with ten volunteer students enrolled in Computing programs, who evaluated the validity of the game's development progress and provided suggestions for improvements and additional features. The process involved the active engagement of potential users throughout requirement elicitation, prototyping, and iterative validation. As a contribution, this research offers insights to support the development of technological solutions aimed at assisting young individuals in financial management and promoting informed economic decision-making.

Keywords: Financial Education · Serious Game · Co-design · Design Thinking · User-Centered Design

1 Introduction

Financial education is "the process by which financial consumers/investors improve their understanding of financial products, concepts and risks" [1]. By acquiring knowledge, receiving guidance, and developing financial management skills, individuals become better equipped to identify risks and opportunities, ultimately improving their financial well-being and decision-making. Given the growing significance of money in contemporary society, financial education has become an essential skill. Financial education should begin early, involving children and adolescents in learning fundamental concepts such as budgeting, expense control, saving, and investing. Developing these skills from an early age fosters responsible financial management in adulthood [2].

Technology serves as a promising tool in addressing gaps in financial literacy, offering innovative solutions that make financial education more accessible and engaging

H. Luna-García et al. (Eds.): HCI-COLLAB 2025, CCIS 2850, pp. 90–105, 2027.
https://doi.org/10.1007/978-3-032-31223-5_7

for young people [3]. Accordingly, technology has already been leveraged to support financial education, as demonstrated by Silveira and Passos [4], who analyzed the use of financial management applications such as Guiabolso, Wallet, Mobills, and Organizze among university students. However, despite the availability of such solutions, financial literacy challenges persist. This raises important questions: Are these technological tools truly effective and efficient in practice? Do their features genuinely meet users' needs and enhance their financial management skills?

Therefore, the main objective is to analyze the needs and expectations of young Brazilians in using technology to support Financial Education, based on User-Centered Design. Specific objectives include planning and conducting Design Thinking sessions with potential users to validate the idea and gather application requirements, planning and conducting co-design sessions for the joint construction of the application prototype with users and developing a prototype to support Financial Education based on the results of the Design Thinking and Co-design sessions. Based on these analyses, the research presents a prototype of a game to support Financial Education built from insights obtained from users, using the User-Centered Design approach, combined with Design Thinking and Co-design.

The design thinking methodology, which is widely used in product development, is a tool that allows for a deeper analysis of the problem with a user-centered perspective. The Design Thinking approach for Educators prescribes the design process to generate and enhance solutions for various types of challenges, allowing freedom to make mistakes and learn from them, generating new ideas, receiving feedback from collaborators, and recycling the entire process [5].

Co-design refers to collaborative design that corroborates the development of a product that aligns with users' desires. Thus, both methodologies, design thinking and co-design, are characterized by being user-centered, presenting an open dialogue and always willing to do what is efficient for user satisfaction [5].

Therefore, the methodological process consists of organizing a design thinking session to validate the idea and co-design sessions to ensure that the solution development meets users' expectations. The design thinking session includes questionnaires to profile and measure the financial knowledge of potential users, as well as group dynamics and brainstorming to collect their opinions. Subsequently, in the co-design session, the progress of the game prototype development will be validated, with volunteers interacting with the solution and generating insights. Thus, the aim is to obtain subsidies for the construction of an effective technological tool to support the financial education of young Brazilians.

This article is divided into five sections, in addition to this Introduction. Section 2 presents the theoretical framework addressing topics such as financial education, design thinking, co-design, and analysis of related works. Section 3 presents the work methodology, with a detailed description of how the researchers applied the studied methodologies. Section 4 discusses the results obtained at each stage of the research and its outcome. Finally, Section 5 presents the final considerations and future work that can be carried out based on this research.

2 Theoretical Framework

2.1 Financial Education

Financial education is a human science that balances "being" and "having," involving the psychological effort to control money flow in pursuit of personal goals [6]. Saving money is integral to good financial education, while investing optimally allocates saved capital. Therefore, saving and investing are complementary concepts, with saving focusing on consumption control and requiring mental balance in spending decisions.

Financial education is related to personal money management, enabling individuals to critically understand their financial choices [7]. This aligns with the Brazilian Constitution, which connects education to individual development and civic participation, making financial education crucial for understanding both personal and national finances.

Thus, financial education fosters financial prevention and protection, enabling citizens to manage their finances and make informed decisions. The Brazilian government has attempted to address the personal finance education gap, with significant initiatives like the Education of Young and Adults (EJA), focusing on workers who handle finances daily [8].

Furthermore, the lack of financial knowledge exacerbates personal well-being concerns, as rising delinquency rates and financial insecurity contribute to stress, anxiety, and poor mental health [9]. This underscores the link between financial education and emotional well-being, where poor financial management leads to impulsive decisions with detrimental effects on mental health.

2.2 Design Thinking

Design Thinking is a flexible framework for problem-solving, using methodologies associated with design to identify, frame, and address challenges across various domains [10]. It is not a method but an approach that emphasizes empathy, collaboration, and experimentation, encouraging innovation by integrating diverse perspectives. Three core mindsets in Design Thinking are: human-centeredness, abductive reasoning, and learning through failure. They stress the importance of focusing on people to solve human-centered problems, challenging existing knowledge to explore alternatives, and framing failure as a valuable learning opportunity [11].

This iterative, user-centered process begins with the Empathy phase, where designers seek to understand users' needs through observation, interviews, and immersion. The Definition phase consolidates insights to clearly define the problem, followed by Ideation, where various solutions are generated. In the Prototyping phase, selected ideas are transformed into tangible prototypes for practical evaluation. The Testing phase involves presenting prototypes to users for real feedback, fostering continuous improvement [12].

2.3 Co-design

Co-design is a specific form of co-creation, where designers and non-designers collaborate throughout the design process [13]. It as a joint effort between people from diverse knowledge areas, aiming to find solutions that satisfy all participants [14]. Collaborative design is not limited to the design field, as collaboration is fundamental to human processes.

Co-design is also a team-based approach where the designer guides the process, incorporating community, collaborative, and cooperative design principles [15]. Non-designers actively participate in design decisions, making co-design similar to Participatory Design but with a more active user role. Co-design is a user-centered methodology that treats users as experts in their own experiences [13]. Effective co-design relies on user engagement, which can vary in intensity at different stages. Participatory activities help gather valuable information, improve product quality, clarify real requirements, reduce costly additions, and ensure better user acceptance and utilization [16].

Co-design is grounded in the principle that those impacted by design decisions should participate in the decision-making process, particularly in political contexts, where affected individuals should contribute to solving their own problems. This approach is based on equality, recognizing everyone's creative abilities and encouraging universal participation in change [17]. By valuing individuals' life experiences, co-design empowers users to shape their future, contrasting with traditional approaches where experts impose solutions without considering the affected individuals' insights [17].

2.4 Related Works

Kenny et al. [18] presents a study that applied Design Thinking and Co-design to develop an agricultural app, aiming to address the needs of farmers, consultants, and inspectors in collaboration with researchers, developers, and the national agricultural authority. Following Design Thinking phases, the study began with Empathy, using stakeholder mapping, interviews, and focus groups to identify user concerns. In the Definition phase, interdisciplinary reflection refined insights, while Ideation facilitated validation and co-creation with stakeholders. The Co-design phase focused on solution development through workshops, emphasizing real-time support and accessibility. The study concluded that the app should enhance information flow, mutual understanding, and accountability, with an intuitive interface and clear data visualization, ensuring alignment with users' needs and technological capabilities.

Adikari et al. [19] applied a co-design approach inspired by design thinking to develop and evaluate an Information System for the artist community. Over five weeks, a multidisciplinary team engaged in facilitated ideation sessions to explore artistic concepts, engagement barriers, and system functionalities. Selected ideas were evaluated based on commercial value, feasibility, and desirability. Through iterative redesign, prototyping, and continuous collaboration, the study produced design solutions and prototypes aligned with the community's needs.

Fariyanto et al. [20] developed an app for village leader elections in Indonesia using the UX Design Thinking method to facilitate voting for citizens abroad. The research incorporated usability testing and the System Usability Scale (SUS) to assess prototype effectiveness. By following the phases of Empathy, Definition, Ideation, Prototyping, and Testing, the app improved accessibility, convenience, and inclusivity for overseas voters, eliminating the need for physical travel and enhancing the voting experience.

Usability testing yielded a score of 77, indicating good usability, while the User Experience Questionnaire (UEQ) revealed positive user feedback on attractiveness, clarity, efficiency, precision, stimulation, and recency.

These studies are relevant to this research as they demonstrate the application of design thinking and co-design in the development of technological solutions across diverse sectors, including agriculture, the arts, and electoral processes, areas similarly addressed in this work. However, this project diverges by focusing on a youth demographic and financial education, aiming to develop an effective technological solution for the financial literacy of Brazilian young people.

3 Methodology

The research employs both quantitative and qualitative approaches. Data were statistically analyzed based on questionnaire responses, and a descriptive analysis was also conducted, detailing participants' actions observed during the Design Thinking and Co-design sessions.

Initially, literature reviews were conducted on financial education, design thinking, and co-design. For financial education, the reviews explored online course curricula on personal finance, investor profile questionnaires, and types of investments in Brazil, along with their associated risks. In the context of design thinking and co-design, the reviews aimed to understand how to apply these methodologies and identify the key concepts necessary for correctly implementing user-centered design.

Given the involvement of human participants in the experiment, this project received approval from the Research Ethics Committee on April 30, 2024, under opinion number 6.796.222 and CAAE 77657824.4.0000.0084. All ethical principles were fully respected.

3.1 Planning the Design Thinking Session

For the Design Thinking session, the researchers organized an in-person activity with university students to gather insights for the ideation phase of the technological solution and to identify its requirements and functionalities. Prior to user interaction, the researchers conducted a requirements gathering session and a pilot test to evaluate the dynamics, execution time, activity alignment, and the potential to address the raised questions. During the pilot test, several necessary adjustments were identified, such as modifying the advantages of certain assets that had low realism.

At the beginning of the activity, participants completed a pre-test questionnaire to assess their profiles and prior knowledge in financial education. Before the activity, volunteers were asked to collectively estimate the monthly costs for utilities, including water, electricity, internet/phone/TV/cell phone plans, rent, food, transportation, and health insurance, for an individual living alone. This step aimed to assess their understanding of fixed monthly expenses.

Subsequently, a physical game designed by the researchers was introduced, simulating everyday financial decisions through a series of rounds. In each round, participants were faced with bills to pay, investment options, bank loans, and advantages they could acquire. The goal was to balance their finances and make strategic decisions to maximize their end balance. At the start of each round, participants received a salary of 3,000 reais and a random event card that simulated life's unpredictability, which could result in either a gain or a loss. As detailed in Table 1, the random event cards included titles and descriptions, specifying the amount gained or lost, as well as a number for easy identification by the researchers.

Table 1. Random events

Title	Description	Amount	Number
Found Money	While walking down the street, you found a bill on the ground.	+$50.00	1
Winning Sports Bet	Your bet on a sports event was successful.	+$100.00	2–5
Raffle Prize	You decided to buy a ticket for a local raffle, and to your surprise, your number was drawn.	+150.00	6–7
Year-End Bonus	Your company granted a year-end bonus to all employees.	+250.00	8–9
Unexpected Inheritance	You received an inheritance from a distant relative.	+500.00	10
Appliance Breakdown	Your appliance broke down and needs to be replaced.	−$100.00	11
Helping a Relative	A close relative needed financial help, and you decided to assist them.	−150.00	12−13
Veterinary Expenses	Your pet required unexpected veterinary treatment.	−$200.00	14–16
Traffic Fine	You received a traffic ticket for parking in a restricted area.	−$250.00	17–20
Late Payment Penalty	You forgot to pay an important bill and were penalized.	−$300.00	21–24
Medical Emergency	You faced a medical emergency and received hospital treatment.	−$400.00	25
Stolen Credit Card	Your credit card was stolen and used for fraudulent purchases.	−$500.00	26–27
Car Accident	You were involved in a car accident, causing damage to your vehicle.	−$700.00	28–29
Residential Fire	A fire partially destroyed your home, and you had to cover the damages.	−1,000.00	30

To generate additional income, as shown in Table 2, participants could invest their money in three different options, each with varying success rates and return percentages.

If successful, the return percentage was added to the initial investment; if unsuccessful, it was deducted. A roulette was used by the researchers to determine the success of the investments each round.

Table 2. Investments

Type	Chance of Success	Rate of Return
Treasury Bonds	90%	10% of the invested amount
Stocks	70%	30% of the invested amount
Cryptocurrencies	50%	50% of the invested amount

Participants were then presented with various financial management options, including the management of fixed expenses. In each round, they could choose to pay or defer these monthly expenses, which would be deducted from their salaries. If expenses were unpaid, interest was applied to the owed amount. The expenses are listed in Table 3, which shows the expense name and the amount to be paid each round.

Table 3. Fixed expenses

Expenses	Amount
Water	$50.00
Electricity	$50.00
Internet/Phone/TV/Mobile Plan	$300.00
Rent	$1,150.00
Food	$400.00
Transportation	$200.00
Health Insurance	$150.00
Total	$2,300.00

Participants could take out loans at any time for immediate cash, with interest rates set at 12.5%, 15%, and 17.5% per round for the first, second, and third loans, respectively, applied to the outstanding balance. Additionally, each round allowed participants to purchase assets offering strategic advantages, as shown in Table 4, which details the asset names, descriptions, and acquisition costs.

During the activity, the researchers divided their tasks, with one facilitating the session and addressing volunteers' questions, while the other observed and recorded participants' behaviors, questions, and suggestions. This was followed by a brainstorming session, where participants were asked for their overall opinions of the game and suggestions for improvement, encouraging all groups to contribute ideas for enhancing the application.

Table 4. Acquisition of assets

Name	Description	Value
Education	Increases investment success rate by 10%.	$2,000.00
Start a Business	Increases salary by $1,000.00.	$2,000.00
Buy a Property	Eliminates rent expense.	$3,000.00
Insurance	Covers 50% of the cost when receiving a random event card.	$100.00
Investment Consulting	Increases investment return percentage by 10%	$2,000.00
Bank Partnership	Reduces interest rates by 33%.	$2,000.00
Buy a Bicycle	Eliminates transportation expense.	$500.00

3.2 Development of the Game Prototype

Following the Design Thinking session, the results were analyzed, leading to the identification of a gamified solution. Based on these insights, low-fidelity prototyping began using Figma software. To support the development process, a Game Design Document, sequence diagram, game requirements, and the Figma prototype were created and made available on GitHub at the following link: https://github.com/lucasviana20/Aventura-Financeira-Rumo-Riqueza.

3.3 Planning the Co-design Session

For the co-design session, a face-to-face interaction with the prototype was planned for the youth participants. To understand user needs and actions, the researchers employed three different approaches. The first involved navigating the prototype developed in Figma, providing data on its navigability, design, and educational value. After this task, users interacted with a new version of the prototype developed in Pygame (a cross-platform game library used with the Python programming language), which incorporated input and output values. Finally, the participants were guided to interact with printed screens of the prototype, where they were asked to use a pen to suggest changes. During this process, the researchers closely observed the users and took notes on their behaviors and suggestions during each interaction.

After implementing the co-design session, the researchers collected data that provided the necessary insights for developing design recommendations for creating applications suitable for young people. Additionally, the requirements document was updated based on the necessary changes identified by the researchers. However, due to time constraints, the research was unable to implement the changes in the prototype.

4 Results and Discussion

4.1 Design Thinking Session

In the Design Thinking session, nine students from different undergraduate courses (economics, technology, engineering, business administration, and advertising) participated in a convenience sample. The selection of students from different courses was intentional to diversify opinions. Initially, participants were asked to complete a pre-test questionnaire, divided into two parts. The first part aimed to profile the users. Based on the collected responses, 77.8% of participants were between 18 and 24 years old, 100% used technological devices for more than 5 h daily, 66.7% had not yet achieved financial independence, and 77.8% had some familiarity with investments, mainly low-risk ones, and were willing to seek information on how to proceed with financial education. The analysis revealed that participants had a strong affinity with technology and were striving for financial independence. The second part of the questionnaire aimed to measure the participants' financial knowledge level, with questions formulated based on recognized financial education course curricula, identifying a good basic understanding of finance. Table 5 presents the questions, correct answers, and the accuracy rate.

There was good engagement from the participants in the activity, which was initially planned to last one hour but extended by an additional half hour, totaling one and a half hours. During this time, the planned activity using paper and pen, as described in Subsection 3.1, was conducted. The participants' insights were crucial for decision-making regarding the design and gameplay of the product.

Based on the activity and participant feedback, the researchers concluded that it had the potential to become an engaging educational game for young people. During the session, competitiveness and the exchange of experiences were identified as key motivators, with participants constantly observing each other's behavior and adjusting strategies based on others' successes or failures. Consequently, the researchers decided to introduce an in-game newspaper feature, providing subtle financial education tips and updates on other players' performances. Another participant suggestion was incorporating more realistic elements, leading to the inclusion of a Score system, inspired by Serasa, a Brazilian company specializing in credit decision analytics and information. Additionally, following the participants' input, the game was adapted to allow long-term investments, reflecting participants' investment habits. Other suggestions, such as developing a mobile version of the game, led to the creation of mobile screen prototypes, and the inclusion of more educational content was also incorporated.

4.2 Prototype Development

Based on the insights and suggestions provided by the users, a low-fidelity screen prototype was developed using the Figma software. To preserve the element of competitiveness and interaction among users, the researchers conceptualized the game's home screen to resemble a table, mirroring the physical setup of the Design Thinking session where participants were gathered around a table, as illustrated in Fig. 1. The game was developed for Brazilian students, hence the screens display text in Portuguese. The menu bar on the left presents the following commands in order from top to bottom: Investments,

Assets, Loans, Expenses, and News. In the upper right corner, there is a green button labeled "End Round"

Upon accessing the Investment menu from the sidebar, the user will encounter the following options, previously suggested by participants in the Design Thinking session: Treasury Bonds, Stocks, Cryptocurrencies, and Long-Term Investments. After selecting Long-Term Investments, the user is directed to the available investment options within this category, as shown in Fig. 2(a) and (b). By accessing the sidebar once more and selecting "Assets," the user will be directed to the game's assets screen (Fig. 3), where they can purchase various assets, each offering distinct advantages within the game, as outlined in Table 4.

As previously noted, the Score system was suggested by participants in the design thinking session; therefore, it was implemented on the Loan screen, which can be

Table 5. Financial knowledge identification questionnaire

Question	Correct Answer	Accuracy Rate
1. How would you calculate your monthly available budget?	Subtracting all your expenses from your salary	77.8%
2. Why is it important to track your spending regularly?	To ensure you never exceed your budget and to identify areas where you can save	100%
3. Why is it important to understand the interest rate when taking out a loan?	To assess the total cost of the loan and make informed decisions	77.8%
4. How would you evaluate the decision to take out a loan?	Consider whether the purchase is really necessary and if there is the ability to repay the loan	100%
5. What is an effective strategy for dealing with accumulated debt?	Create a repayment plan prioritizing the debts with the highest interest rates	77.8%
6. What is the difference between good debt and bad debt?	Good debt is used to invest or acquire assets that can increase your wealth, while bad debt creates liabilities	77.8%
7. How can diversifying assets help reduce risk in investments?	Investing in different types of assets reduces the impact of poor performance in a specific area	55.6%
8. What is the difference between a fixed-income investment and a variable-income investment?	In a fixed-income investment, the investor receives a guaranteed fixed return, while in a variable-income investment, the returns are not guaranteed and may fluctuate based on market performance	100%

(*continued*)

Table 5. (*continued*)

Question	Correct Answer	Accuracy Rate
9. Imagine you receive a gift of R$1,000 that you can only spend in one year, and the annual inflation rate is 1%. In one year, with the same amount, you will be able to buy the same things you could buy today.	False	100%
10. Anna saves R$500 per year for 10 years and then stops saving additional money. Charlie saves nothing for 10 years but later receives a gift of R$5,000. If both Anna and Charlie earn a return of 5% per year, who will have more savings after 20 years?	Anna	88.9%

Fig. 1. Game home screen (Source: Authors)

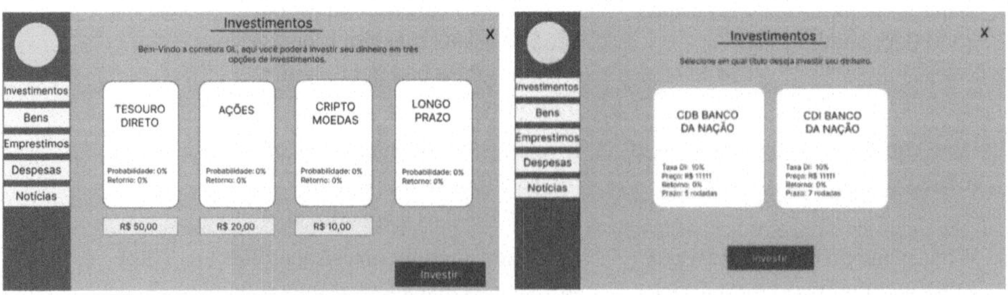

Fig. 2. (a) Investment screen (Source: Authors) and (b) Long-term investment screen (Source: Authors)

accessed via the sidebar by clicking the 'Loans' button. Additionally, this screen allows the player to take out loans, view the interest rate, and repay their bank debts, as shown in

Fig. 4(a). The Fixed Expenses screen, corresponding to the "Expenses" button (Fig. 4b), allows the player to pay their monthly expenses each round and view their debts if any expenses remain unpaid.

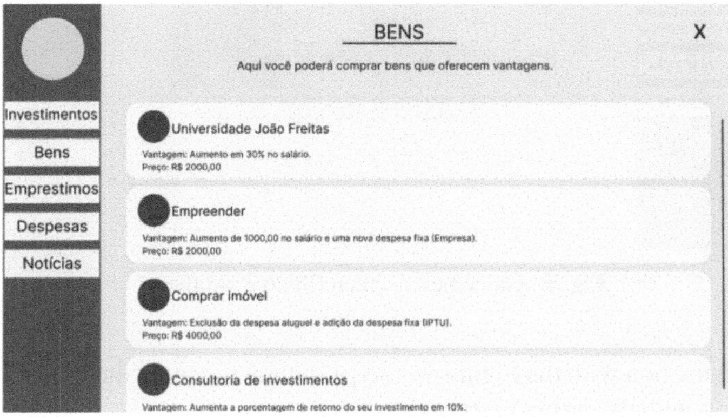

Fig. 3. Game assets (advantages) screen (Source: Authors)

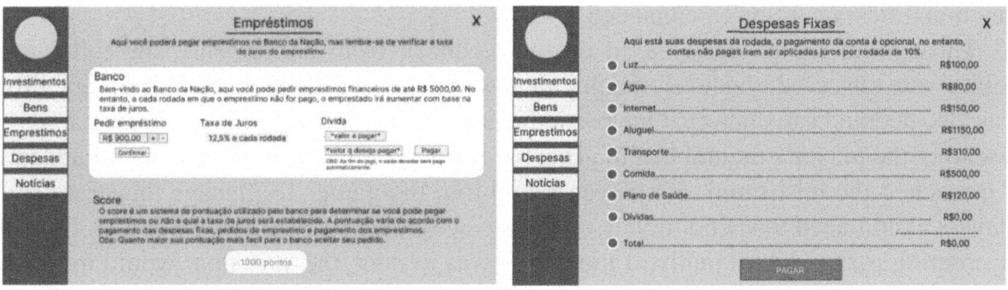

Fig. 4. (a) Game loan screen (Source: Authors) and (b) Game fixed expenses screen (Source: Authors)

To include more explanatory elements with an educational character, as requested by the volunteers in the Design Thinking session, the "News" menu was created. Each round, the player receives a newspaper intended to tell a short story with subtle tips on financial education and the actions of other players (Fig. 5).

4.3 Co-design Session

After the development of the screens, several questions were raised, such as the ideal name for the game, the need to add icons to the screens, which user actions would require confirmation screens, and whether the usability of the screens was effective and efficient for the user. To address these issues and generate new ideas, a co-design session was organized. This session included 10 volunteers, students from Computing programs, who were divided into three groups. The groups rotated through three interactions with the

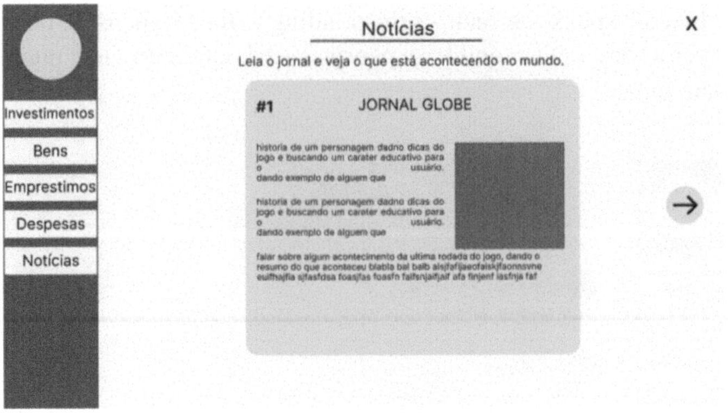

Fig. 5. Game news screen (Source: Authors)

prototype: interaction with the Figma prototype, interaction with the Pygame prototype, and interaction with the printed screens.

The Figma activity addressed issues related to navigability and screen design, leading to improvements such as redesigned buttons, added icons, vertical navigation between news sections, and a popup for entering the investment amount. The Pygame prototype provided a more representative gameplay evaluation due to the implementation of game functionalities, resulting in enhanced screens.

Throughout the process, based on the feedback from participants, the following points were observed: the level of enjoyment was rated as excellent, and the navigability was also deemed satisfactory. One participant suggested incorporating a stress bar, representing the player's mental health. This bar would gradually increase each round, and if it reached the maximum, the player would lose the game. To manage the stress bar, players would need to spend money on leisure activities, such as going out with friends or ordering pizza. Additionally, if the player was in debt, the stress bar would increase more rapidly each round. Another suggestion involved the possibility of bankruptcy; if the player accumulated a certain amount of debt, they would lose the game.

Finally, the participants were invited to make adjustments using printed versions of the game screens and a pen. The goal was to ensure that the adopted design was acceptable to users. Throughout the activity, they made several suggestions: highlighting the debts and total in the Expenses section, reducing the explanatory text about the Score in the Loans section; rounding the buttons, changing the font of the text, and creating a more engaging background; adding icons representing assets and providing information about investments in the corresponding section; including a tutorial to guide players during their first interaction with the game; replacing the direct explanatory text with a question mark icon next to items, which would expand the explanation upon being clicked; replacing the exit button with a back arrow icon; and changing the button color in the active menu to improve its visibility. Additionally, all participants were asked to choose the name of the game from the suggestions, with "*Aventura Financeira: Rumo à Riqueza* (Financial Adventure: Towards Wealth)" being selected.

5 Final Considerations and Future Work

This study aimed to explore the needs and expectations of university students regarding a technological solution to support Financial Education. To achieve this, a user-centered approach was adopted, incorporating Design Thinking sessions to validate the concept and Co-design sessions to refine the solution.

Initially, a financial management game was conceptualized to simulate real-life financial situations. This idea was tested in a Design Thinking session, and the results confirmed that gamification is an effective approach to supporting Financial Education. Based on the insights gathered, low-fidelity prototypes were developed. Subsequently, a Co-design session was conducted, allowing users to validate the progress of the game's development and suggest improvements and additional features.

As a contribution, this research provides an analysis of the needs and expectations of Brazilian youth regarding the use of technology for Financial Education, along with a prototype of a serious game. The prototype was developed to assist young people who are beginning their financial independence and was designed to be used by users of different knowledge levels or fields of expertise. The findings indicate that young people are keen to acquire financial knowledge, as demonstrated by their engagement during the Design Thinking session and their responses to the questionnaire. Additionally, feedback from the Co-design session suggests that the target audience values a more dynamic and interactive learning experience that blends education with entertainment.

As limitations of this study, although the game encourages players to reflect on investment opportunities, it could further reinforce other key personal finance concepts, such as the importance of building an emergency fund. The game does not include accessibility guidelines, as the intention was to focus on developing features that meet user expectations. Another limitation concerns the refinement of the interface layouts, as certain design principles could be further explored; however, this aspect was beyond the scope of this research. Furthermore, the Design Thinking and Co-design sessions involved only students from University, which may have introduced bias into the collected data.

For future work, it is recommended to enhance the prototype by incorporating accessibility features and the suggestions from the Co-design session, conduct usability testing on the improved version, refine the interface design, and fully implement the game. Following these steps, the game could be deployed in public and private schools or made available in app stores, such as the Play Store and App Store, providing young people with an engaging tool for learning and improving their financial management skills.

Disclosure of Interests.. The authors have no competing interests to declare that are relevant to the content of this article.

References

1. OECD (Organisation for Economic Co-operation and Development): Recommendation of the Council on Principles and Good Practices for Financial Education and Awareness. OECD (2020) https://legalinstruments.oecd.org/en/instruments/OECD-LEGAL-0338
2. Detoni, D.J., Lima, M.S.: Educação financeira para crianças e adolescentes. In: VIII Simpósio de Excelência em Gestão e Tecnologia, pp. 1–8. Paraná (2011). https://www.aedb.br/seget/arquivos/artigos11/35114357.pdf
3. Abar, C., Branco, A., Araújo, J.: Estudo de pesquisas sobre educação financeira com a utilização de tecnologias. TANGRAM – Rev. Educ. Mat. **1**(4), 87–107 (2018). https://doi.org/10.30612/tangram.v1i4.8807
4. Silveira, N., Passos, M.: O uso de dispositivos de controle financeiro-econômico no desenvolvimento da educação financeira em jovens universitários. State University of Goiás (2021) http://aprender.posse.ueg.br:8081/jspui/handle/123456789/289
5. Pereira, I.L., Guimarães, A.J., Nascimento, J.S., Neto, S.J.C., de Souza, R.A.C.: Aplicação do design thinking para educadores no desenvolvimento de uma solução inovadora / Application of design thinking for educators in the development of an innovative solution. Braz. J. Dev. **5**(7), 7676–7686 (2019). https://doi.org/10.34117/bjdv5n7-009
6. Domingos, R.: Educação financeira uma ciência comportamental. RECIMA21 - Rev. Cient. Multidiscip. **3**(4), e341217 (2022). https://doi.org/10.47820/recima21.v3i4.1217
7. Cordeiro, N.J.N., Costa, M.G.V., da Silva, M.N.: Educação financeira no Brasil: uma perspectiva panorâmica. Ensino Mat. Debate. **5**(1), 69–84 (2018) https://revistas.pucsp.br/index.php/emd/article/view/36841
8. Hurtado, A.P.G., Freitas, C.C.G.: A importância da educação financeira na educação de jovens e adultos. Rev. Educ. Popul. **19**(3), 56–76 (2020). https://doi.org/10.14393/REP-2020-52731
9. Ferreira, J.C.: A importância da educação financeira pessoal para a qualidade de vida. Cad. Adm. **11**(1), 1–17 (2017) https://revistas.pucsp.br/index.php/caadm/article/view/33268
10. Alt, L.: O que é design thinking. Rev. Coach. Bras. **213**, 14–17 (2017) https://mamtra.com.br/wp-content/uploads/2017/08/Coaching-e-Thinking-Desing.pdf
11. Nakata, C., Hwang, J.: Design thinking for innovation: composition, consequence, and contingency. J. Bus. Res. **118**, 117–128 (2020). https://doi.org/10.1016/j.jbusres.2020.06.038
12. Dam, R.F., Siang, T.Y.: What is design thinking and why is it so popular? Interaction Design Foundation. https://www.interaction-design.org/literature/article/what-is-design-thinking-and-why-is-it-so-popular (2024). Accessed 26 Mar 2024
13. Sanders, E.B.N., Stappers, P.J.: Co-creation and the new landscapes of design. CoDesign. **4**(1), 5–18 (2008). https://doi.org/10.1080/15710880701875068
14. Fontana, I.M., Heemann, A., Gomes, M.G.F.: Design colaborativo: fatores críticos para o sucesso do co-design. In: Anais do 4° Congresso Sul-Americano de Design de Interação, pp. 371–382. Blucher, São Paulo (2012)
15. Baranauskas, M.C.C., Martins, M.C., Valente, J.A.: Codesign de Redes Digitais: tecnologia e educação a serviço da inclusão social. Penso Editora, Porto Alegre (2013)
16. Caixeta, M., Camelo, G., Fabricio, M.: Codesign e arquitetura para a saúde. Rio Books, Rio de Janeiro (2021)
17. Blomkamp, E.: The promise of co-design for public policy. In: Routledge Handbook of Policy Design, pp. 59–73. Routledge (2018)
18. Kenny, U., Regan, Á., Hearne, D., O'Meara, C.: Empathising, defining and ideating with the farming community to develop a geotagged photo app for smart devices: a design thinking approach. Agric. Syst. **194**, 1–22 (2021). https://doi.org/10.1016/j.agsy.2021.103248

19. Adikari, S., Keighran, H., Sarbazhosseini, H.: Embed design thinking in co-design for rapid innovation of design solutions. In: Marcus, A. (ed.) Design, User Experience, and Usability: Design Thinking and Methods. DUXU 2016. Lecture Notes in Computer Science, vol. 9746, pp. 1–13. Springer, Cham (2016). https://doi.org/10.1007/978-3-319-40409-7_1
20. Fariyanto, F., Suaidah, S., Ulum, F.: Perancangan aplikasi pemilihan kepala desa dengan metode UX design thinking (studi kasus: Kampung Kuripan). J. Teknol. dan Sist. Inf. (JTSI). **2**(2), 52–60 (2021) http://jim.teknokrat.ac.id/index.php/JTSI

Development of a Wearable Device and Architecture for Monitoring Hamstring Muscle Activity

Filipe Costa Pereira(✉) and Bruno da Silva Rodrigues

Computing and Informatics Department, Mackenzie Presbyterian University, São Paulo SP 01302907, Brazil
costapfilipe@gmail.com, bruno.rodrigues@mackenzie.br

Abstract. Hamstring injuries are among the most frequent musculoskeletal problems in sports, and the literature indicates that multiple factors contribute to their occurrence, with muscle fatigue being one of the most relevant. In this context, IoT-based wearable technologies have emerged as promising tools for continuous monitoring of muscle activity, enabling early identification of fatigue and supporting injury prevention strategies. This study presents the development of a real-time monitoring system that uses a wearable device to assess hamstring muscle activity and detect signs of fatigue. The proposed prototype captures surface electromyographic signals and performs fatigue detection through frequency-domain analysis, in which a reduction in median frequency relative to a baseline is interpreted as the onset of fatigue. Experimental evaluations conducted during hip lift exercises demonstrated the system's ability to identify fatigue-related patterns in muscle activation. Furthermore, the system architecture was designed for scalability, allowing the simultaneous monitoring of multiple users. This characteristic makes the solution applicable in different contexts and suitable for both professional athletes and recreational users.

Keywords: IoT · Wearable Device · Hamstrings · Muscle Activity · Muscle Fatigue · Injury Prevention

1 Introduction

Muscles are formed by specialized cells which contract and relax in response to different stimuli, functions that are essential for body support, locomotion, and maintenance of body shape [1]. In this context, the issue of muscle injuries emerges, which are recurrent in sports activities and cause loss of time for athletes in training and competitions [2], as well as for non-professional physical activity practitioners.

Among the various muscle injuries that affect both amateur practitioners and professional athletes, it is evident that hamstring muscle injury is one of the most common in sports [3]. Injury to this muscle group is frequently observed in soccer, but also occurs commonly in sports such as American football, Australian football, track and field, and

H. Luna-García et al. (Eds.): HCI-COLLAB 2025, CCIS 2850, pp. 106–118, 2027.
https://doi.org/10.1007/978-3-032-31223-5_8

water skiing. It is worth noting that this injury presents the highest recurrence rate when compared to other types of injuries [4].

Among the various factors that can trigger hamstring injury, muscle fatigue stands out [5], which is characterized by a reduction in the capacity to produce force during muscle contractions, limiting individual performance [6]. At the end of European soccer matches, a high number of hamstring injuries are observed, suggesting muscle fatigue as a risk factor for these injuries [7].

In this regard, the development of non-conventional interaction devices that allow collecting and processing information from an individual's muscles, and the interpretation of this data to assist in real-time decision-making, can benefit both high-performance athletes, by measuring muscle performance and fatigue, helping to optimize training, prevent injuries and improve these athletes' performance, as well as amateur athletes, by improving muscle recovery or optimizing training in gyms.

The identification and assessment of muscle fatigue is of paramount importance and can be performed by monitoring the muscle using the electromyography (EMG) technique during muscle activity [8]. Electromyography can be applied non-invasively, known as surface electromyography (sEMG). This technique uses surface electrodes on the skin to measure the electrical activities of muscles [9]. Thus, sEMG is an important ally for collecting and monitoring muscle data in wearable devices.

Therefore, the objective of this work is to develop a system that uses wearable technology to monitor hamstring muscle activity in real-time through sEMG and assess fatigue aiming to prevent injury to this muscle group. For this purpose, a system composed of wearable devices and software will be used to monitor the hamstring muscles in real-time and analyze the data collected during physical activities. Thus, it is expected that in the future this system may assist in identifying muscle fatigue and contribute to the prevention of hamstring injury.

To present this work, the article is organized as follows: Section 2 presents the theoretical foundations, which aids in understanding the other sections; Section 3 addresses the materials and methods of the project, as well as describes the system architecture; Section 4 details the prototype development, explaining each element of the architecture; Section 5 presents the results and discussions about the use of the system; and Section 6 brings the conclusions of the work.

2 Theoretical Foundations

2.1 Muscles and Hamstring Muscles

The human muscular system is composed of three distinct varieties of tissue: skeletal, cardiac, and smooth. Skeletal muscles are mostly connected to the bone structure of the body. This connection allows these muscles to play a fundamental role in controlling and executing body movements [10].

A skeletal muscle is composed of a group of muscle cells, also called muscle fibers [10]. These specialized cells contract and relax in response to stimuli, functions that are essential for body support, locomotion, and maintenance of body shape [1].

Among the muscles of the human body is the hamstring muscle group, which is composed of three individual muscles: semitendinosus, semimembranosus, and biceps femoris [4]. The biceps femoris has two heads: short and long [11].

All muscles that make up the hamstrings originate at the ischial tuberosity, except for the short head of the biceps femoris, which originates at the linea aspera of the femur. Additionally, all insert into the tibia and, specifically the biceps femoris, also inserts into the fibula. Innervation is provided by the tibial nerve, except for the short head of the biceps femoris, which is innervated by the common fibular nerve. All these muscles are supplied by perforating branches of the deep femoral artery [12]. Figure 1 presents the anatomy of the posterior thigh region, where the hamstrings are located.

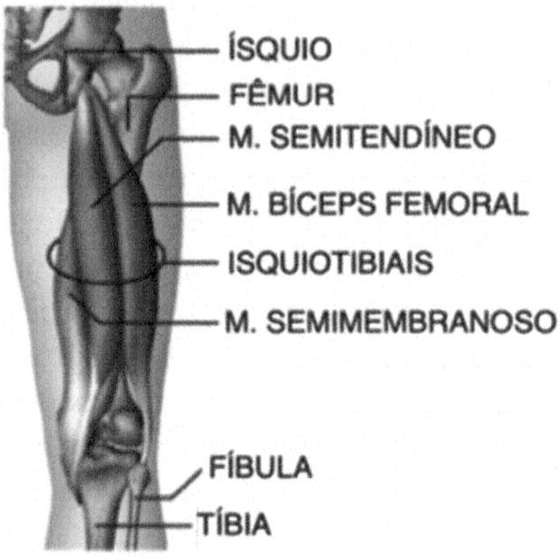

Fig. 1. Anatomy of the posterior thigh region. Source: Anderson Luiz de Oliveira

The hamstring muscles act in knee flexion, medial rotation, and hip extension movements [4]. The biceps femoris, with its short and long heads, is responsible for knee flexion and lateral rotation of the tibia. The long head also contributes to hip extension. The semitendinosus and semimembranosus share similar functions, performing knee flexion, hip extension, and medial rotation of the tibia with knee flexion [12].

2.2 Hamstring Muscle Injury

Muscle injuries are common in sports [2] and can be caused by contusion, strain, or laceration [14]. Most sports injuries are contusions or strains, with contusions resulting from external compressive force and strains resulting from excessive internal tensional force [15].

Various characteristics can be considered for the classification of injuries, such as: time, severity, and type. Regarding time, an injury can be acute or chronic, with the former referring to injuries that evolved in less than three weeks. Concerning severity, injuries can be categorized as: stretching, partial rupture, or total rupture of muscle fibers. In addition, injuries can result from extrinsic or intrinsic factors, with extrinsic ones caused by external factors and intrinsic ones by problems in the muscle structure [16].

Hamstring muscle injury is one of the most common in sports [3] and has the highest recurrence rate when compared to other injuries. For athletes, the recurrence of injury to this muscle group after returning to sports remains the main complication [4].

One of the risk factors for hamstring injury is muscle fatigue which compromises the athlete's biomechanics, as well as neuromuscular control and the ability to produce force [5]. This is evidenced at the end of European soccer matches, where a high number of hamstring injuries are observed [7]. It is worth noting that muscle fatigue is considered one of the main factors that contributes to the triggering of different musculoskeletal injuries [17].

2.3 Electromyography

Electromyography (EMG) is a technique used for measuring myoelectric signals originating from motor neurons that compose the central nervous system. The EMG signal has various applications, such as the diagnosis of muscle injuries [18] and the identification and assessment of muscle fatigue [8].

EMG can be applied non-invasively, known as surface electromyography (sEMG), through the positioning of electrodes on the skin [9]. The electrodes can be gel-based or dry and are capable of identifying changes between the skin and muscle surface through an electrolytic conduction process [18].

This technique enables the analysis of muscle activity during movement, as well as the quantification of energy expended for performing a particular muscle contraction [19].

2.4 Wearable Devices

Wearable devices can be incorporated into the body, allowing constant monitoring of a person's activities and ensuring free movement of the user [20]. Generally, these devices have a reduced size and enable real-time data monitoring [21].

A possible application of wearable devices is in identifying abnormalities in the health condition of individuals, alerting about the need for specialized care [22]. In this context, the development of biosensors plays a crucial role, as it provides real-time health monitoring with an emphasis on prevention and personalized medicine [23].

In recent years, wearable devices have been widely adopted for monitoring and preventing sports injuries [21]. With the advancement of wearable technologies, various opportunities for data collection arise, enabling the monitoring of multiple athletes simultaneously, without the need for invasive techniques [24].

3 Related Works

Zadeh et al. [25] conducted a study with United States military cadets, analyzing the use of wearable technologies as tools to predict and prevent injuries during sports practices. The results showed that these devices allowed instructors to collect important information to personalize exercises according to the physical characteristics of each participant, reducing the risk of injuries. In conclusion, the researchers highlighted that these technologies have potential for predicting sports injuries.

Liu et al. [21] conducted research in which wearable devices were used to monitor muscle activation in a group of 20 cyclists, seeking to identify signs of fatigue during exercises. The researchers employed electromyography (EMG), through which they analyzed the amplitude of muscle signals to quantify contractions, in addition to applying a signal analysis technique to evaluate muscle condition. In summary, the results indicated that the equipment created proved to be effective for monitoring muscle fatigue levels during physical exercise.

Costa et al. [26] conducted a comparative study between muscle fatigue indices among cyclists and non-cyclists, using spectral analysis of the EMG signal with Fourier (FFT) and wavelet (WT) transforms. During an incremental maximum power test, parameters such as median frequency and fatigue indices for different muscles were analyzed. In summary, the results demonstrated that WT may be suitable for dynamic tasks and that both methods – FFT and WT – produced similar median frequency values and fatigue indices, with no statistically significant differences between the analyses.

4 Methodology

Regarding the methodology employed in this work, initially an exploratory research was conducted in databases such as PubMed and IEEE via Periódico Capes, to find scientific research, articles, and publications aiming to understand the issue of hamstring muscle injury, identify techniques with potential to assist in injury prevention, and analyze the state of the art related to the topic. From this exploratory research, it was identified that the electromyography technique could be applied to detect the development of fatigue and, therefore, assist in the prevention of injuries in the hamstring muscles. Furthermore, it was found that spectral analysis of the EMG signal, with Fourier (FFT) and wavelet (WT) transforms, enables an assessment of muscle fatigue.

Based on this definition, a low-cost architecture was developed consisting of a wearable device with an electromyography sensor to monitor muscle activity, as well as a platform for real-time processing and monitoring of data collected by the wearable device. Figure 2 presents the architecture of the system developed in this work.

In the architecture proposed in Fig. 2, it is possible to observe that in addition to the wearable device, a gateway was implemented and configured to receive the data collected by the wearable device and display them in real-time through an interface. Built from a Raspberry Pi 4, the data visualization interface was implemented in Javascript using the React library and Python using the Flask library. The entire application was containerized with Docker to isolate and customize execution environments.

In addition to allowing real-time monitoring of individuals' muscle activity, the gateway will connect the wearable device to a local server. The local server will be used to host the following microservices: a microservice for management of collected data; a microservice for muscle fatigue calculation; a worker for asynchronous processing of collected data; and a dashboard for data visualization.

It is worth noting that the system was integrated with third-party company services, including: Auth0's login and user management; AWS's file storage and queue control; and MongoDB Atlas's non-relational database storage.

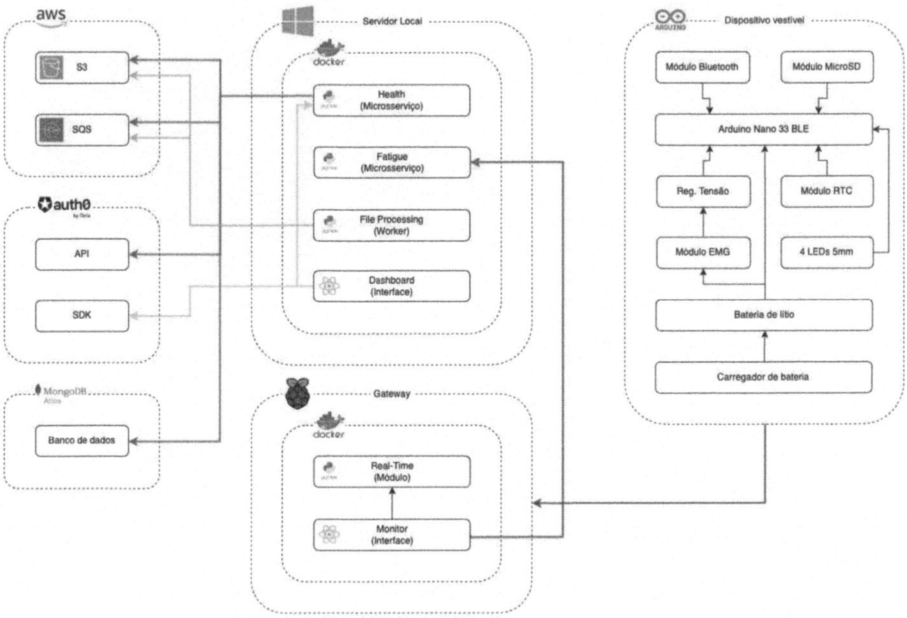

Fig. 2. Architecture of the system. Source: Authors

5 Results and Discussion

5.1 Wearable Device

As presented in Fig. 2, for the development of the low-cost wearable device, the open-source Arduino prototyping platform was chosen, using the Arduino Nano 33 BLE (Bluetooth Low Energy) board. In addition to this board, the circuit consists of: a BLE module whose model is the JDY-24; a micro SD (Secure Digital) memory card module; an RTC (Real Time Clock) module; a module with EMG sensor; a voltage regulator from 5 V to 3.3 V; 4 LEDs of 5 mm; an 8.4 V and 3000mAh lithium battery; and an 8.4 V battery charger. The developed wearable device was fitted with a case modeled and printed using a 3D printer to protect the circuit during testing. Figure 3 presents the prototype of the wearable device.

In order to facilitate user interaction with the device, 4 LEDs were installed and are visible on the case. As shown in Fig. 3(a), from left to right, the LEDs represent: power, data, memory card, and bluetooth. Table 1 presents the operation of the LEDs in the wearable device.

Regarding the operation of the circuit, the data collection process is initiated when the wearable device receives a START command from the gateway via Bluetooth. With this, a file in CSV format is created on the memory card of the wearable device, where the EMG module simultaneously records the individual's muscle activity, date, and time, which are obtained through the RTC module. On the Arduino board, these data are formatted and saved in a buffer, storing a volume of data which, in this case, is 1000 data points. When the buffer reaches maximum capacity, the data are sent by the BLE module

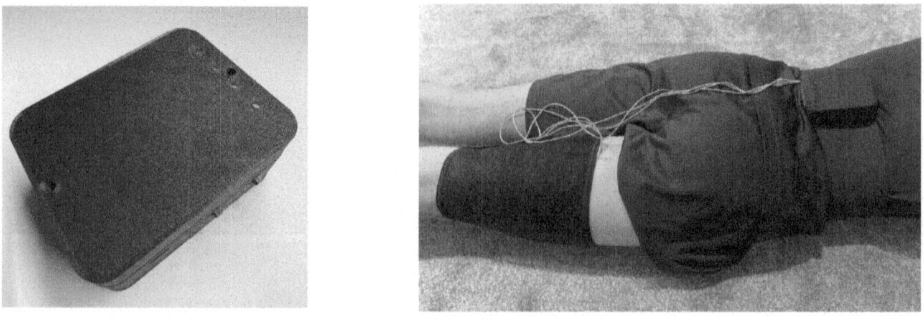

(A) (B)

Fig. 3. Prototype of the wearable device case turned on (a) and device worn by system user (b). Source: Authors

Table 1. Operation of LEDs in the wearable device. Source: Authors

LED Function	Action	Meaning
Power LED	On	Device turned on
	Off	Device turned off
Data LED	Flashing intermittently	Data set being collected
Memory card LED	Flashes once	Data set is persisted
	Flashing intermittently	Signaling a problem with the SD card
Bluetooth LED	Flashes once	Data set is sent to the gateway
	Flashing intermittently	Signaling a connection problem

and saved in the CSV file, and the buffer is reset. This process is iteratively repeated until the wearable device receives a STOP command from the gateway via Bluetooth, forcing the buffer data to be saved to the CSV file and ending data collection. Figure 4 presents a diagram with the data processing steps in the wearable device.

5.2 Gateway Application

The gateway allows real-time monitoring of muscle activity by receiving, via Bluetooth communication, data sent by the wearable device. For this purpose, the application interface is divided into tabs, which include: Monitoring tab and Devices tab.

The Devices tab (Fig. 5) allows the user to search for and pair Bluetooth devices with the gateway. In this interface, the Scan button was implemented, responsible for identifying and listing nearby Bluetooth devices, and a button to connect or disconnect devices, completing the pairing process between the wearable device and the application. Figure 5 presents the Devices tab of the gateway interface.

The Monitoring tab of the interface was developed to make it possible to track muscle activity through a graph, updated in real-time, of the electromyography signal as a function of time. This graph provides a direct and objective visualization of the

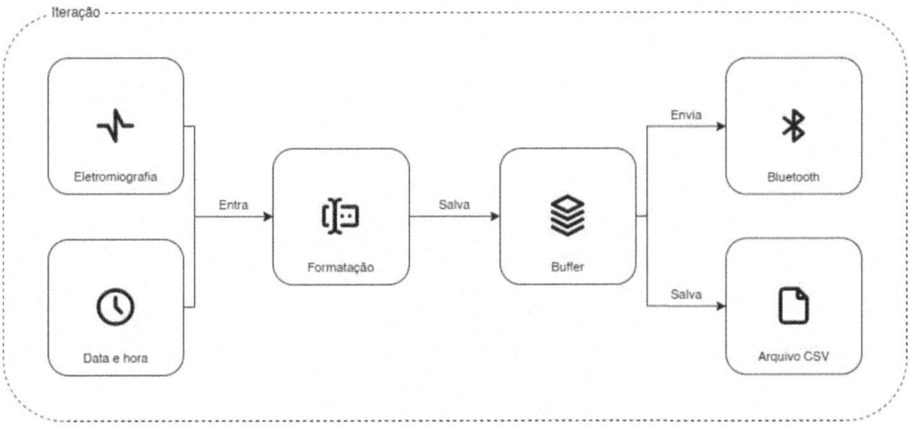

Fig. 4. Data processing steps in the wearable device. Source: Authors

Fig. 5. Interface of the devices tab of the application gateway. Source: Authors

collected data. Additionally, the interface has a button to start monitoring, which allows the user to activate the capture of muscle signals and a fatigue alert icon. Figure 6 presents the interface created for real-time monitoring of muscle activity.

5.3 Local Server

The local server presented in the system architecture (Fig. 2) was developed using a microservices architecture, where two microservices were implemented, in addition to a worker and a dashboard.

The "Health" microservice offers an HTTP API for communication which allows the sending of CSV files and data management. Regarding functionality, when a new file is received by the microservice, the system sends it to AWS and processing is performed by the worker asynchronously. Through the API, it is possible to insert, view, update, or remove activity data.

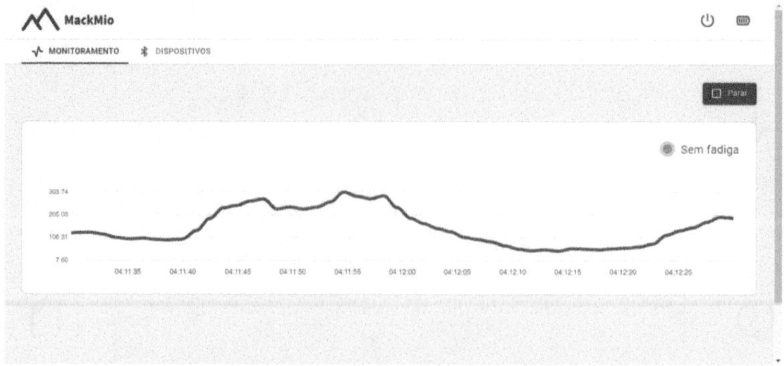

Fig. 6. Interface of the monitoring tab of the application gateway. Source: Authors

The worker continuously monitors a queue of files to be processed. While there are files in the queue, the worker obtains the information from this file and processes it. In this processing, the system captures the start and end of the recorded activity and pre-formats the data points of the electromyography time series. Then, the worker communicates with the "Health" microservice through the API to create a section and insert the time series data.

The dashboard communicates with the "Health" microservice API for data visualization and management, consisting of 3 pages: home, activities, and integration. Figure 7 presents the dashboard's home page.

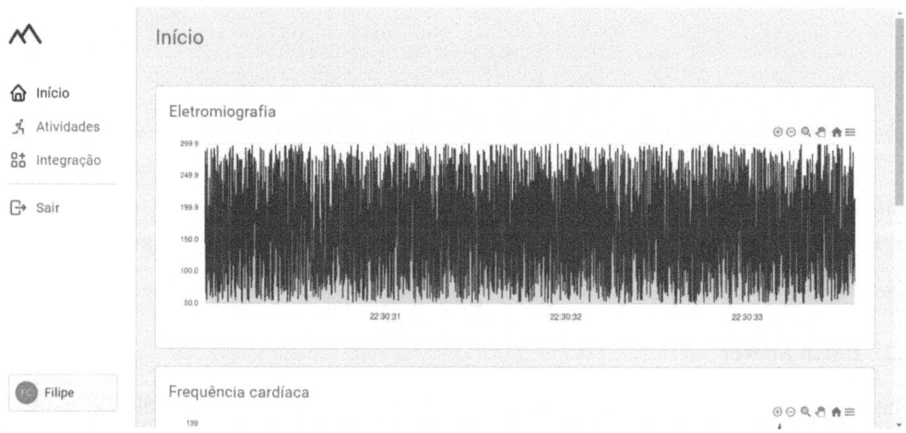

Fig. 7. Dashboard home page with electromyography graph. Source: Authors

The microservice used for fatigue calculation offers an HTTP API for communication and connects to the gateway via WebSocket protocol to receive electromyography data updated in real-time, with this data being saved in a circular array. For each new set of data received, pre-processing occurs, applying a Butterworth bandpass filter with a lower cutoff frequency of 20 Hz and an upper cutoff of 150 Hz, considering that the highest concentration of electromyography information occurs in this interval [27]. Figure 8(a) presents a filtered electromyography signal of the hamstrings during the hip lift exercise, where 4 repetitions with isometry were performed.

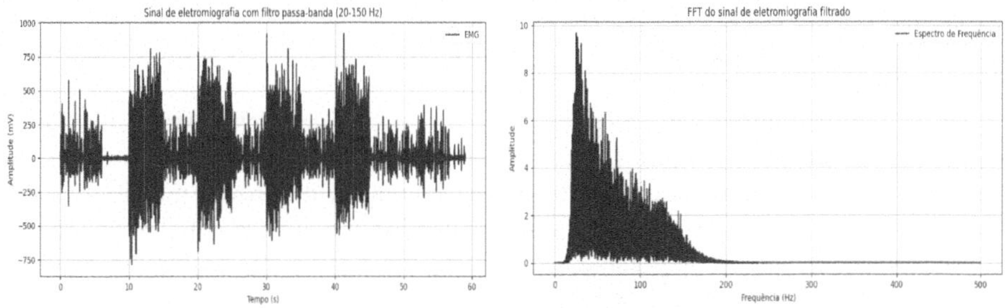

(a) (b)

Fig. 8. Electromyography signal with bandpass filter (20–150 Hz) (a) and Fast Fourier Transform of the filtered electromyography signal (b). Source: Authors

After pre-processing the signal, the Fast Fourier Transform (FFT) is applied to obtain the frequency spectrum of the signal (Fig. 8b). Next, the Power Spectral Density (PSD) is obtained, which represents the distribution of signal power among frequencies. From the PSD, the median frequency (MDF) calculation is performed [28], storing the result of this calculation in an array of median frequencies. When the array of median frequencies has at least 2 elements, then: the last median frequency is compared with the first recorded and, if there is a decrease of at least 10% relative to the first [29], muscle fatigue is considered to be present; and the slope calculation is applied [21] which represents the rate of change of MDF over time, storing this data. The lower the slope value, the greater the indication of muscle fatigue. It is worth noting that the microservice makes the slope information and fatigue detection available through the API. Figure 9 presents the trend of MDF and slope over time.

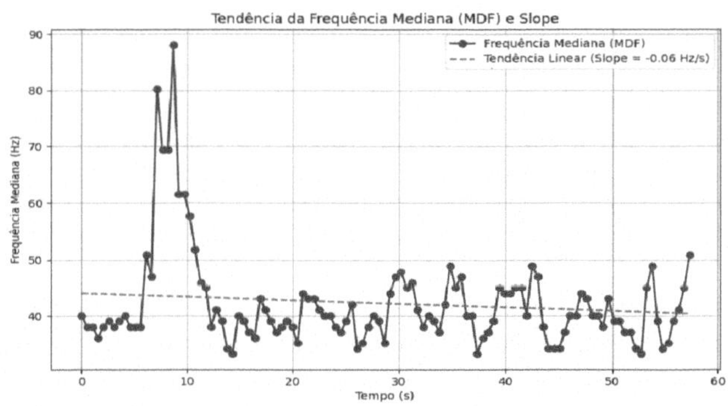

Fig. 9. Median frequency and slope over time. Source: Authors

6 Conclusion

Hamstring muscle injury is considered one of the most recurrent in sports, with muscle fatigue being one of the risk factors. In view of this, the present work presented a system based on wearable devices for real-time muscle monitoring and fatigue analysis aiming at the prevention of hamstring injury. Thus, it is emphasized that the project intends to benefit both individuals who practice physical activities professionally and recreationally.

The system was conceived and implemented based on decades of scientific studies on the problem of muscle injuries, more specifically of the hamstrings. That said, the application of electromyography stands out, a technique with proven potential for the evaluation of muscle activity and, furthermore, the use of validated calculations for the identification of fatigue. Also notable is the composition of various technologies which work together to maximize user experience.

It is worth highlighting some relevant characteristics of the system: scalability, since it allows integrating data from multiple users; methodology, which can be adapted to prevent injuries in other muscles, not just in the hamstrings; and architecture, which enables the incorporation of additional sensors to collect other types of data.

As future work, tests with athletes will be conducted to obtain a larger volume of data and evaluate the system's performance in a sports environment. An artificial intelligence model will also be introduced to identify patterns in the data, working together with already defined algorithms. And, furthermore, new features will be added, such as the integration of the system with services from companies in the healthcare market.

Therefore, it is expected that the project will proceed to a new stage with the purpose of being improved and, subsequently, intended for the end user, providing safety during the practice of physical activities and providing opportunities for data analysis to improve physical conditioning.

References

1. da Silva, F., Diniz, G.: Anatomia e fisiologia humana, vol. 3. Difusão, São Caetano do Sul (2021)
2. Pollock, N., James, S.L.J., Lee, J.C., Chakraverty, R.: British athletics muscle injury classification: a new grading system. Br. J. Sports Med. **48**(18), 1347–1351 (2014). https://doi.org/10.1136/bjsports-2013-093302
3. Kerin, F., Walsh, S., O'Donoghue, G., Delahunt, E.: Intramuscular tendon injuries of the hamstring muscles: a more severe variant? A narrative review. Sports Med. Open. **9**(1), 75 (2023). https://doi.org/10.1186/s40798-023-00621-4
4. Ernlund, L., Vieira, L.A.: Hamstring injuries: update article. Rev. Bras. Ortop. (Engl. Ed.). **52**(4), 373–382 (2017). https://doi.org/10.1016/j.rboe.2017.05.005
5. Buckthorpe, M., et al.: Recommendations for hamstring injury prevention in elite football: translating research into practice. Br. J. Sports Med. **53**(7), 449–456 (2019). https://doi.org/10.1136/bjsports-2018-099616
6. Wan, J., Qin, Z., Wang, P., Sun, Y., Liu, X.: Muscle fatigue: general understanding and treatment. Exp. Mol. Med. **49**(10), e384–e384 (2017). https://doi.org/10.1038/emm.2017.194

7. Mendiguchia, J., Alentorn-Geli, E., Brughelli, M.: Hamstring strain injuries: are we heading in the right direction? Br. J. Sports Med. **46**(2), 81–85 (2012). https://doi.org/10.1136/bjsm.2010.081695
8. Noda, D., Marchetti, P.H., Junior, G.: A Eletromiografia de superfície em estudos relativos à produção de força. Rev. CPAQV–Centro de Pesquisas Avançadas em Qualidade de Vida. **6(3)**(2) (2014).
9. Alcan, V., Zinnuroğlu, M.: Current developments in surface electromyography. Turk. J. Med. Sci. **53**(5), 1019–1031 (2023). https://doi.org/10.55730/1300-0144.5667
10. Silverthorn, D.U.: Fisiologia Humana: Uma Abordagem Integrada, 7th edn. Artmed Editora, Porto Alegre (2017)
11. Silvers-Granelli, H.J., Cammack, B., Kocher, M., Mandelbaum, B.R.: Hamstring muscle injury in the athlete: state of the art. J. ISAKOS. **6**(3), 170–181 (2021). https://doi.org/10.1136/jisakos-2017-000145
12. Rodgers, C.D., Raja, A.: Anatomy, bony pelvis and lower limb, hamstring muscle. In: StatPearls. StatPearls Publishing, Treasure Island, FL (2024)
13. de Oliveira, A.L.: Lesão dos músculos posteriores da coxa (isquiotibiais). https://www.andersonluizdeoliveira.com.br/lesao-dos-musculos-posteriores-da-coxa-isquiotibiais/
14. Santanna, J.P.C., et al.: Lesão muscular: Fisiopatologia, diagnóstico e tratamento. Rev. Bras. Ortop. **57**(1), 001–013 (2022). https://doi.org/10.1055/s-0041-1731417
15. Järvinen, T.A., Järvinen, M., Kalimo, H.: Regeneration of injured skeletal muscle after the injury. Muscles Ligaments Tendons J. **3**(4), 337–345 (2013)
16. Barroso, G.C., Thiele, E.S.: Lesão muscular nos atletas. Rev. Bras. Ortop. **46**(4), 354–358 (2011). https://doi.org/10.1590/S0102-36162011000400002
17. Marshall, P.W.M., Lovell, R., Jeppesen, G.K., Andersen, K., Siegler, J.C.: Hamstring muscle fatigue and central motor output during a simulated soccer match. PLoS One. **9**(7), e102753 (2014). https://doi.org/10.1371/journal.pone.0102753
18. Gohel, V., Mehendale, N.: Review on electromyography signal acquisition and processing. Biophys. Rev. **12**(6), 1361–1367 (2020). https://doi.org/10.1007/s12551-020-00770-w
19. Ocarino, J.M., Silva, P.L.P., Vaz, D.V., Aquino, C.F., Brício, R.S., Fonseca, S.T.: Eletromiografia: interpretação e aplicações nas ciências da reabilitação. Fisioter. Bras. **6**(4), 305–310 (2005). https://doi.org/10.33233/fb.v6i4.2012
20. Gao, W., et al.: Fully integrated wearable sensor arrays for multiplexed in situ perspiration analysis. Nature. **529**(7587), 509–514 (2016). https://doi.org/10.1038/nature16521
21. Liu, S., Wang, Y., Yang, D., Ou, Y., Zhao, Y., Zhao, J.: An EMG patch for the real-time monitoring of muscle-fatigue conditions during exercise. Sensors. **19**(14), 3108 (2019). https://doi.org/10.3390/s19143108
22. Khan, Y., Ostfeld, A.E., Lochner, C.M., Pierre, A., Arias, A.C.: Monitoring of vital signs with flexible and wearable medical devices. Adv. Mater. **28**(22), 4373–4395 (2016). https://doi.org/10.1002/adma.201504366
23. Guk, K., et al.: Evolution of wearable devices with real-time disease monitoring for personalized healthcare. Nano. **9**(6), 813 (2019). https://doi.org/10.3390/nano9060813
24. Preatoni, E., Nodari, S., Lopomo, N.F.: The use of wearable sensors for preventing, assessing, and informing recovery from sport-related musculoskeletal injuries: a systematic scoping review. Sensors. **22**(9), 3225 (2022). https://doi.org/10.3390/s22093225
25. Zadeh, A., Khazaee, A., Ahmad, R., Iakovidis, D.K.: Predicting sports injuries with wearable technology and data analysis. Inf. Syst. Front. **23**(4), 1023–1037 (2020)
26. Costa, M.V., et al.: Análise espectral do sinal EMG de exercício incremental em ciclistas e não ciclistas usando as transformadas de Fourier e Wavelet. Rev. Bras. Cineantropom. Desempenho Hum. **14**(6), 660–671 (2012). https://doi.org/10.1590/1980-0037.2012v14n6p660

27. Abbaspour, S., Fallah, A.A.: A combination method for electrocardiogram rejection from surface electromyogram. Open Biomed. Eng. J. **8**(1), 13–19 (2014). https://doi.org/10.2174/1874120701408010013
28. Chen, S., et al.: A real-time fatigue monitoring and analysis system for lower extremity muscles with cycling movement. Sensors. **14**(7), 12410–12424 (2014). https://doi.org/10.3390/s140712410
29. Dimitrov, G.V., Arabadzhiev, T.I., Mileva, K.N., Bowtell, J.L., Crichton, N., Dimitrova, N.A.: Muscle fatigue during dynamic contractions assessed by new spectral indices. Med. Sci. Sports Exerc. **38**(11), 1971–1979 (2006). https://doi.org/10.1249/01.mss.0000233794.31659.6d

Enhancing Elderly Care with Empathetic Technologies: Insights from Human-Computer Interaction

André Luiz Satoshi Kawamoto[1](✉), Alberto Hitos García[2], Patricia Paderewski Rodríguez[2], and Francisco Luís Gutiérrez Vela[2]

[1] Universidade Tecnológica Federal do Paraná, via Rosalina Maria dos Santos 1233, Campo Mourão 87301-899, Brazil
kawamoto@utfpr.edu.br

[2] Universidad de Granada, C. Periodista Daniel Saucedo Aranda S/N, 18071, Granada, Spain
{albertohitos,patricia,fgutierr}@ugr.es

Abstract. Empathetic technologies transform elderly care by enhancing emotional well-being, autonomy, and social engagement. This paper examines integrating assistive technologies (ATs) with empathy-driven principles to support older adults. We conduct a structured narrative literature review, categorizing existing studies based on key themes such as emotional recognition, adaptive interaction, and user-centered design. The findings highlight the potential benefits of AI-driven virtual agents, wearable health monitoring devices, and accessible user interfaces in mitigating age-related challenges. However, barriers such as usability, digital literacy, ethical concerns, and privacy risks must be addressed for broader adoption. Human-Computer Interaction (HCI) insight provides valuable guidance in designing effective ATs, incorporating user-centered approaches, co-design methodologies, and affective computing techniques. This paper also identifies critical research gaps, including the need for experimental validation, improved emotion recognition models, and strategies to ensure ethical implementation. Future research should focus on refining AI frameworks, enhancing accessibility, and promoting transparency in data usage to foster greater acceptance and effectiveness of empathetic assistive technologies. By addressing these challenges, ATs can better support aging populations, improving their quality of life and social inclusion.

Keywords: Empathetic Technologies · Assistive Technology · Human-Computer Interaction · Older Adults

1 Introduction

Population aging is inevitable due to increased life expectancy and declining birth rates worldwide. According to the World Health Organization (WHO), most people today can expect to reach their 60 s or beyond, a particularly evident trend in both developed and developing nations [27]. While this demographic transition marks a significant public

H. Luna-García et al. (Eds.): HCI-COLLAB 2025, CCIS 2850, pp. 119–132, 2027.
https://doi.org/10.1007/978-3-032-31223-5_9

health achievement, it also raises concerns about the sustainability of healthcare systems, social security, and the well-being of older adults [26]. Key challenges associated with aging include functional decline, cognitive impairments, and emotional vulnerabilities, all of which can compromise independence and quality of life. Functional limitations, often linked to chronic diseases and reduced mobility, increase the demand for long-term care services [27]. Moreover, mental health conditions such as depression, anxiety, and dementia are becoming increasingly prevalent among older populations, necessitating innovative intervention approaches [26].

In this context, Assistive Technology has been recognized as an effective tool for mitigating aging-related challenges and enhancing the quality of life. The WHO's global strategy for aging and health highlights the potential of technology to maintain functionality, improve autonomy, and support the emotional well-being of older individuals [26].

These technologies encompass mobility aids, digital interfaces tailored for older users, artificial intelligence-based virtual assistants, and remote health monitoring solutions. While assistive technologies offer viable solutions to address the physical, cognitive, and emotional challenges of aging, their adoption requires strategies to ensure accessibility, usability, and acceptance among older users and caregivers.

In this sense, empathetic technologies, which integrate principles of emotional recognition and adaptive interaction, present promising avenues for enhancing elderly care. Empathetic technologies are digital tools and systems designed to recognize, respond to, and simulate human emotions to foster meaningful and affective interactions between users and technological systems. These technologies rely on AI, affective computing, and human-centered design to create emotionally intelligent systems.

Although this work presents a narrative literature review, it aims to provide actionable insights for researchers and designers in the HCI field, particularly those working on AI and aging. By aligning theoretical findings with practical frameworks, the main contribution lies in the promotion of human-centered and ethically aware technological innovations.

Thus, this paper explores how Human-Computer Interaction (HCI) can influence the design of technologies, ensuring they are practical and culturally sensitive. The main objective is to provide a comprehensive understanding of the role empathetic technologies can play in enhancing elderly care and how insights from HCI can guide the development of these technologies. By examining the challenges that ageing population faces and presenting innovative solutions, the authors highlight the potential for empathetic technologies to significantly improve the quality of life for older adults while ensuring cultural sensitivity and usability.

2 Empathetic Technology Foundations and Applications

Empathetic technologies are digital tools and techniques designed to foster empathetic encounters and understanding between users and systems. These technologies are characterized by their ability to create relational and emergent experiences where digital and material elements interact dynamically. The concept emphasizes a processual view of digital materiality, suggesting that empathetic understanding emerges from user interaction and technology [21].

These technologies leverage artificial intelligence (AI), machine learning, and affective computing advancements to recognize and respond to users' emotional states. For example, robotic companions can use AI to engage older adults in cognitive activities and social interactions, thereby reducing feelings of loneliness [2]. Similarly, wearable devices with biosensors can monitor physiological signals, such as heart rate variability, to detect stress and suggest interventions, such as guided breathing exercises [23].

These technologies are designed to address older adults' functional needs and emotional and social well-being and can significantly enhance the quality of life for seniors by providing personalized support and companionship. Empathetic systems can adapt to users' unique preferences and behaviors, offering a more tailored and practical experience. Key principles of empathetic design include:

- **Emotional Recognition** – use of AI to analyze facial expressions, voice tones and behavioral patterns. This allows the system to detect and interpret the emotional states of users, enabling more responsive and sensitive interactions.
- **Adaptive Interaction** – alter responses based on individual preferences and cultural contexts. This principle involves recognizing and respecting cultural differences and providing care that is not only effective but also culturally sensitive.

The integration of empathetic technologies in elderly care has the additional potential advantage to alleviate the burden on caregivers. By providing consistent and reliable support, these technologies can assist caregivers in managing the daily needs of older adults, reducing stress and allowing for better focus on more complex care tasks.

Empathetic technologies represent a promising frontier in the enhancement of aging population care. By combining advanced AI capabilities with a deep understanding of human emotions and cultural nuances, these technologies offer a comprehensive approach to addressing the multifaceted needs of older adults.

3 Methodology

This study is a narrative literature review aimed at synthesizing significant findings on applying empathetic technologies in elderly care. It provides a comprehensive topic overview, incorporating relevant studies and theories and helps to contextualize the existing research, highlighting gaps and proposing future research directions. Various academic databases were consulted to identify publications related to the subject:

- IEEE Xplore
- ACM Digital Library
- Springer Link
- Web of Science
- AI-based literature discovery tools, such as Consensus and Semantic Scholar

The search was performed using Boolean operators (AND/OR), combining keywords to refine the results. Searches were also conducted with individual keywords to ensure broader coverage. The following keywords were used:

```
"empathic technology", "empathetic technology" "empa-
thy", "elderly", "older adults", "elderly care", "assis-
tive technology"}
```

To ensure the relevance and quality of the selected studies, inclusion and exclusion criteria were applied. Inclusion criteria were:

IC1. Peer-reviewed articles.
IC2. Publications in English.
IC3. Studies focusing on assistive technologies and empathy in the context of elderly care.
IC4. Articles published in the last five years.

The exclusion criteria were:

EC1. Non-peer-reviewed works (e.g., non-reviewed conference papers, white papers).
EC2. Studies not directly related to the intersection of assistive technology and empathy.

The analysis was conducted by reviewing the abstracts and conclusions of the selected articles to extract key findings. Then, researchers performed a more in-depth reading to understand the studies better. In total, 157 articles were identified. After applying the exclusion criteria, 42 articles were retained for detailed analysis. The articles were then categorized based on identified challenges, opportunities, and practical applications of empathetic technologies for elderly care.

4 Challenges and Barriers in the Adoption of Empathetic Assistive Technologies

Implementing ATs for older adults faces complex challenges, ranging from practical adoption difficulties to ethical and social barriers. The acceptance of these technologies depends on accessibility, usability, and adaptation to users' needs. Additionally, issues such as privacy, stigmatization, and difficulties in computationally modelling empathy affect the feasibility of these solutions.

This section examines the main difficulties in adopting empathetic ATs for older adults. First, we discuss the general challenges in elderly care and how technology can help overcome them. Then, we address specific issues related to implementing empathy in these systems, including technical limitations, risks of social isolation, and the need for user-centered design.

4.1 Key Challenges in Elderly Care and the Role of Technology

Caring for seniors is an ever-evolving domain that presents numerous challenges, particularly empathy, access to healthcare, and ageism. These challenges affect the quality of life for seniors and highlight the critical role that technology can play in bridging gaps and improving care. This section examines the intricate relationship between these obstacles and the transformative potential of technological advancements in enhancing elderly care.

Empathy, the ability to understand the thoughts and feelings of others, is a key capability that impacts the quality of relationships among older adults. This ability involves both cognitive components (understanding others' feelings) and emotional components (feeling similar emotions or compassion) [1, 4] Compared to younger individuals, seniors may exhibit lower levels of cognitive empathy, which can lead to greater isolation and difficulty in maintaining interpersonal relationships [1].

Accessing healthcare services poses another challenge for many older adults, particularly in low-income countries. Additionally, healthcare services may not be designed to meet the specific needs of seniors, further complicating their access to appropriate care [26]. Ageism can exacerbate these issues, leading to social exclusion, financial difficulties, and a lack of access to technology and other resources. Discrimination based on age can also influence how healthcare professionals treat older adults, often resulting in suboptimal care [26].

Adopting technology offers numerous opportunities to improve the lives of older adults. However, a 'digital divide' exists between the aging population and younger generations, partly attributed to ageism. Older adults might internalize stereotypes suggesting they are incapable of mastering technology, which can hinder their ability to benefit from technological advancements [26].

Despite these issues, the development and implementation of empathetic technologies offer a promising solution to enhance the quality of life for older adults [16]. By combining artificial intelligence with user-centered interfaces, these technologies can effectively address many of these issues and encompass a variety of applications, including:

- **Avatars and Virtual Agents** able to perform social interaction and emotional support for older adults, reducing loneliness and promoting positive emotions. These avatars can recognize emotions through facial expressions and voice sentiment analysis, adapting responses based on the user's emotional state.
- **Remote Monitoring Systems**, i.e. wearable devices to monitor physical and mental health, allowing for closer monitoring of well-being and enabling quicker responses to health issues or falls.
- **Personalization of User Experience**, the adoption of empathetic systems designed to offer activities and interactions catering to individual preferences and needs.
- **User-Friendly and Accessible Interfaces** designed to be intuitive and easy for seniors, with features like voice recognition, natural language processing (NLP), and customization options such as font size and color contrast.
- **Promotion of Autonomy and Independence**, allowing older users to stay connected with the community and carry out daily activities even with some loss of capacity.

4.2 Barriers to Integrating Empathy into Assistive Technologies

Adopting empathy in assistive technologies for older adults faces significant ethical and technological issues ranging from privacy and autonomy concerns to practical challenges related to designing and implementing systems that genuinely understand and respond to the emotional needs of this audience [1, 27].

Ethical barriers are related to Privacy and Autonomy, Stigmatization and Exclusion, Risks of Social Isolation and the need to Extend instead or Replacing human needs for social contact.

Using technologies to monitor and respond to seniors' emotions raises questions about Privacy and Autonomy. Collecting data on emotional states and behavior can be seen as intrusive, especially if there is no adequate informed consent and clear understanding of how this data will be used and protected. There is also the concern that these technologies may limit the freedom of movement and independence of the aging population [27].

Stigmatization and Exclusion refers to the possibility of discrimination and exclusion of certain groups of people due to the classification and organization of assistive technologies [9]. If technologies are organized according to their ability to improve physical, intellectual, or social abilities, those who cannot afford such technologies may be marginalized. Assistive technology may symbolize vulnerability and stigma, affecting users' self-esteem and mental well-being [8].

Although technology can reduce physical and emotional distance, there is also the Risks of Social Isolation, especially when seniors try replacing real human contact with virtual interactions [27]. Thus, assistive technologies must be very clear to state that they are designed to complement the basic human needs for social contact, rather than replacing them (Extend instead of Replacing) [27]

From a technological perspective, one can mention several barriers that might hinder the effective implementation of empathetic assistive technologies. The design of assistive technology often fails by not considering older adults' emotional and social needs. Many devices are designed with a primary focus on functionality without considering users' aesthetic, emotional, and cognitive preferences [8]. This raises the need to adopt User-Centered Design and Co-design approaches, where seniors are involved from the beginning of the design process to ensure that products meet their real needs [8, 22].

The complexity of empathy represents another technological barrier. Fulfilling the empathy requirements in AI systems is a challenging task, as machines cannot feel human emotions and may struggle to emulate emotional nuances and respond genuinely [1].

Another technical challenge overcome is to provide accuracy in emotion detection, particularly in older people. Difficulties in emotion detection through voice analysis and facial expressions still present limitations, especially concerning mature individuals [4, 24]. Systems may misinterpret emotions, leading to inadequate responses and a lack of trust in technology [4].

Many older adults may not be familiar with digital technologies, making the development of intuitive interfaces a challenge [10, 24]. This audience requires intuitive interfaces and accessibility features that minimize the learning curve and consider potential sensory, cognitive, and motor limitations [19, 22, 24].

Assistive technology must meet each user's individual needs. Personalization consists of adjusting the system interface and the virtual agent's responses to individual preferences and emotional particularities [27].

Finally, the needs and abilities of seniors change over time. Adaptation to Changes is crucial, meaning that assistive technology must flexibly accommodate different levels of decline and disability [8, 22]. However, implementing this characteristic is challenging.

Addressing these barriers requires structured design approaches that ensure assistive technologies are both functionally effective and emotionally supportive. HCI provides various frameworks to guide the development of empathetic assistive technologies, helping designers create solutions that prioritize usability, personalization, and emotional adaptation. The following section explores key HCI frameworks that address the challenges identified, including User-Centered Design, Co-design, and Affective Computing. These approaches help ensure that assistive technologies meet the functional needs of older adults and foster engagement and trust by considering their emotional and cognitive characteristics.

5 Insights from Human-Computer Interaction

HCI offers various perspectives on developing empathetic technologies for older adults, focusing on enhancing their emotional and social well-being. A fundamental principle is a user-centered approach, which recommends actively involving seniors in the design process considering their needs, abilities, preferences, and emotional states when developing technologies tailored to their specific requirements [6]. This is achieved through engaging aged individuals in continuous testing, allowing them to interact with simulated systems or prototypes to gather valuable insights for future improvements [16].

Designing interfaces for the aging population must balance functionality and usability, ensuring that sophisticated systems are both effective and accessible [24]. Interfaces should also accommodate a wide range of older users, considering different levels of technological literacy, needs, and abilities [16].

Likewise, empathetic technologies play a crucial role in addressing social isolation and loneliness, which significantly impacts the mental and physical health of older adults [16, 27]. A key component of these systems is emotion analysis, a subfield of computer science that focuses on recognizing, analyzing, and interpreting human emotions through various inputs such as text, speech, facial expressions, and physiological signals.

Regarding design preferences, studies indicate that older adults prefer virtual agents with female voices and visual representations [6, 7]. Additionally, agents with expressive voices and distinct personalities are generally well received [7]. While the system's response speed and potential errors in text or speech can be issues, users tend to be more tolerant of technical problems when they know they are interacting with an artificial agent [16].

5.1 HCI Frameworks Applicable to the Design of ATs

Various HCI frameworks have been developed to translate theoretical insights into practical design principles for empathetic assistive technologies. User-Centered Design (UCD), Co-design, and Affective Computing are examples of models that enable ATs to integrate adaptive emotional responses and promote greater acceptance among older adults. By connecting theoretical insights with concrete methodological approaches, these frameworks help develop technologies that not only meet functional needs but also respect the social and emotional dimensions of the user experience. The studies referenced in this section were drawn both from the narrative literature review and from complementary sources considered highly relevant to illustrate practical applications of the discussed frameworks.

User-Centered Design (UCD). User-Centered Design (UCD) is a philosophy and a design process that places the user at the center of the development process. The main objective of UCD is to create products and services that are easy to use, effective, and satisfying for end users [14, 15].

UCD involves deeply understanding users' needs, desires, and limitations and using this information to guide design decisions. This includes analyzing the context of use, users' cognitive and physical abilities, and their emotional needs [15].

Applying UCD principles in developing assistive technologies for seniors is essential to ensure the usability and acceptance of devices [15]. For example, considering the location of controls, text size, color contrast, and clarity of instructions are important for effective technology use [25].

UCD also emphasizes the importance of iterative evaluation, where designers test prototypes with users and adjust based on the feedback received. This framework requires empathic qualitative approaches to inform and inspire designers to understand the user's personal experience and private context [15].

Co-design with Seniors. Co-design is a participatory approach that involves users in the design process. Rather than designing "for" seniors, Co-design seeks to design "with" them, recognizing them as experts in their own needs and experiences [8].

This collaboration technique allows mature adults to contribute creatively to the solution and problem formulation, which can lead to more relevant and effective solutions. This approach can be crucial when the needs of older adults are not evident at the beginning of the design process [8].

Co-design also creates opportunities for users to interact with each other, share ideas, and test new concepts, promoting a sense of belonging and empowerment. For example, co-design has been successfully applied in developing touchscreen applications for people with dementia [8].

Using storyboards, sketches, prototyping, and participatory workshops may help engage older adults in the design process [12].

Affective Computing. Affective Computing is an HCI field aimed at equipping systems with the ability to recognize, interpret, and respond to human emotions. The ability to recognize emotions can enable assistive technologies to become more personalized and adaptable to the needs of older adults [20].

In affective computing, emotion recognition can be performed by analyzing facial expressions, voice, and other physiological signals. For example, cameras capture facial images, and voice processing can recognize the user's emotional state [16, 20].

This information can be used to adapt technology's behavior, providing emotional support when needed and making the interaction more natural and intuitive [16].

Emotion detection is fundamental in offering personalized and practical support. Affective computing is being used to develop empathetic virtual agents that can respond to the emotions of older adults, increasing their engagement and well-being [24].

Other Important Concepts. Inclusive Design, which considers the diversity of needs and capabilities, ensuring that products are accessible and usable by the broadest possible range of people, including older adults [8].

Usability, a critical feature in developing assistive technologies, especially for older adults, due to potential physical and cognitive changes that may hinder interaction with devices. Usability includes various factors such as ease of learning, efficiency, ease of memorization, and user satisfaction [14, 15, 22].

Empathy-Driven Design, an approach that seeks to create products that not only meet functional needs but also evoke positive emotions in users, considering the social and cultural context [25]

Materiality, the study of the relationship between people and objects, can influence the perception and acceptance of assistive technologies, emphasizing that technology should be naturally integrated into the daily lives of older adults [8].

It is important to consider the context of use, including where and how the product will be used, as well as potential distractions and other variables that may affect device performance [15].

In summary, designing effective assistive technologies for older adults requires a holistic approach that combines HCI knowledge with the inclusion of UCD principles, co-design, affective computing, inclusive design, and an understanding of the importance of usability, empathy, and materiality. By applying these frameworks and principles, it is possible to create technologies that enhance the quality of life and promote the autonomy and well-being of older adults.

6 Case Studies and Practical Applications

This section presents some projects and approaches in designing assistive technologies (AT) for seniors, focusing on human-computer interaction (HCI) and empathy.

The COMODAL Project explored the consumer market for assistive technology products (ATP) for individuals with ages varying from 50 to 70 years [25]. Using mixed methods such as literature reviews, market analyses, interviews, and co-creation workshops, it developed a characteristics matrix to assist designers and companies. High rates of non-use and abandonment of ATPs were found due to factors such as aesthetic appeal and stigma, revealing that younger mature individuals prefer products that holistically support their independence and health.

Another example is the MATUROLIFE Project, which used advanced material science to develop wearable and furniture products for older adults [17]. This project involved interviews and co-creation workshops in nine European countries. Prototypes made with selectively metallized fabrics and integrated sensors were tested to provide personalized services, highlighting the importance of considering user behavior in the design phase.

In developing a Wheelchair Stability Assessment System, an innovative methodology was created to assess the stability of wheelchairs [18]. The approach included online research, interviews, focus groups with healthcare professionals, and sketch models to explore design aspects. The question "How would the system be if designed by Apple?" guided the final products' visual simplicity and high perceived value.

The 'Ommetje' Walking App aimed to motivate mature adults to become more physically active by using walking as the main activity [5]. Participants used the app for four months and shared their experiences in group sessions, revealing that the quality of walks was more motivating than the quantity.

Exploring platforms for collaborative sharing of vision and hearing, the CollectiveEyes and CollectiveEars Project analyzed them from the perspectives of socio-materiality and pleasure [11]. The analysis highlighted the importance of the hedonic perspective for design, opening new opportunities for the CollectiveEars platform.

In the EMPATHIC-VC Project, the interaction with virtual coaching agents was investigated using a Wizard of Oz (WebWOZ) platform [16]. The platform was extended with audio/video functions to simulate interactions based on the GROW model, focusing on nutrition and social engagement. A pilot study showed that older audiences preferred female virtual agents, personalizing EMPATHIC-VC for the target population.

The projects analyzed emphasize the importance of user-centered design and co-creation, ensuring that assistive technologies holistically meet the needs of seniors. Usability, aesthetic appeal, and ease of use are critical for adopting such technologies. Considering emotional and social aspects in the design can open new opportunities for the development of innovations. Adopting new technologies, such as VR, AI, and IoT sensors, should include continuous evaluations to ensure the effectiveness and acceptance of services offered to mature audiences.

Another relevant initiative is the PERGAMEX Project (PERvasive GAming EXperiences for @ll), which focuses on designing personalized pervasive gaming experiences for older adults [3]. The project was conducted by research groups from several Spanish universities to promote active aging by enhancing social interactions, particularly intergenerational connections, and improving overall well-being. Throughout the development of gaming experiences, co-creation techniques and affective user experience evaluation methods were applied. Ethical, gender-sensitive, and value-sensitive design aspects were considered during all stages, from study and design to implementation and deployment.

The project provided design and evaluation guidelines for games and resulted in the development of various pervasive gaming experiences, some specifically targeting older adults and others fostering intergenerational socialization. The technologies involved ranged from traditional mobile devices, tablets, and personal computers to more advanced systems such as interactive tables (tangible interaction), Kinect sensors (gesture interaction), virtual assistants (voice interaction), wearables (affective interaction), and social robots.

7 General Design Recommendations for Empathetic Assistive Technology

This section organizes design recommendations into three dimensions: Usability and Accessibility, Personalization and Adaptation, and Ethical and Social Considerations.

The Usability and Accessibility dimension suggests that interfaces should follow universal design principles, ensuring that senior individuals with varying levels of digital literacy can use them efficiently. Additionally, providing support for different forms of interaction, including voice commands, touch, and gestures, might facilitate the use by persons with motor or visual limitations. Minimizing cognitive load by avoiding overloaded interfaces and complex menus is crucial. Instead, the design should prioritize simplified layouts and guided processes.

Personalization and Adaptation, in its turn, recommends adapting to individual preferences. Systems should be configurable, allowing adjustments in parameters such as response speed, tone of voice, and complexity level of interactions. Furthermore, empathetic assistive technologies should learn from user behavior over time, adjusting responses and interactions to become more natural and relevant. They should also be able to integrate with existing devices, as many elderly individuals already use smartphones or smart speakers. Compatibility with these devices can facilitate adoption and acceptance.

Regarding the Ethical and Social Considerations dimension, the recommendations mainly concern privacy and data transparency. Empathetic technologies should clearly explain data collection and processing, with control options for users. Another important recommendation is to avoid replacing human contact. The design should always emphasize that technology complements, rather than replaces, the support of caregivers and family members. This can be achieved by encouraging human interactions whenever possible. Finally, it is essential to reduce technological stigma through the appearance and language used by systems, which should be designed to be friendly and encouraging, avoiding reinforcing stereotypes about aging and technological difficulties.

8 Conclusion

This article explored the role of empathetic assistive technologies in elderly care, highlighting challenges, opportunities, and design principles derived from Human-Computer Interaction research. The analysis pointed out that such technologies can significantly improve the quality of life for seniors by providing emotional and functional support. However, technological and ethical barriers still need to be overcome to ensure greater acceptance and effectiveness of these technologies. The involvement of older adults in the design process through co-design and user-centered design approaches is essential for creating solutions that are better suited to their needs.

Considering the identified gaps, several directions for future research are proposed. First, researchers should conduct experimental studies to evaluate the impact of empathetic technologies on older adults' emotional health and well-being. Second, developing more precise computational models of empathy for emotion recognition and real-time response adaptation is necessary. Third, ensuring transparency in using emotional data and protecting user autonomy through security and privacy strategies in empathetic assistants is required. Fourth, investigating ways to make assistive technologies more accessible to elderly individuals with different levels of digital literacy can promote digital accessibility and social inclusion.

The suggested research directions will allow a more significant positive impact of empathetic technologies in the context of aging, promoting greater autonomy, emotional support, and quality of life for seniors. There is a growing recognition of the importance of empathy in the design of assistive technologies for mature audiences. Including empathetic and personalized responses can increase acceptance and engagement. Older adults must participate in all project stages, from conception to final development. The co-design approach can ensure that technological solutions are relevant, usable, and acceptable to users.

Collaboration between designers, engineers, healthcare professionals, and social scientists is essential to overcome ethical and technical barriers. Studies combining qualitative and quantitative methods are needed to understand user experience and measure the impact of technologies.

Beyond literature synthesis, future work should focus on developing and testing concrete prototypes of empathetic assistive technologies. Practical evaluations in real or simulated environments are essential to validate the proposed frameworks and assess their usability and emotional impact in elderly care contexts. Integrating empathy into assistive technologies for older adults presents both opportunities and challenges. A careful, multidisciplinary approach is required to address ethical and technological barriers while ensuring user-centered design. By advancing research in emotion recognition, personalization, and accessibility, empathetic assistive technologies can significantly enhance aging populations' quality of life and emotional well-being.

Acknowledgments. This work has been supported by the PLEISAR-Social project, Ref. PID2022-136779OB-C33, funded by the Ministry of Science and Innovation of Spain (MCIN/AEI/10.13039/501100011033, EU), and the C-ING-179-UGR23 project, funded by the Regional Ministry of Universities, Research and Innovation and the FEDER Andalucía 2021-2027 Programme.

Disclosure of Interests The authors have no competing interests to declare that are relevant to the content of this article.

References

1. Beadle, J.N., de la Vega, C.E.: Impact of aging on empathy: review of psychological and neural mechanisms. Front. Psych. **10**, 331 (2019). https://doi.org/10.3389/fpsyt.2019.00331
2. Broadbent, E., et al.: ElliQ, an AI-driven social robot to alleviate loneliness: progress and lessons learned. J. Aging Res. Lifestyle. **13**, 22–28 (2024). https://doi.org/10.14283/jarlife.2024.2
3. Cerezo Bagdasari, E.M., Gutiérrez Vela, F.L., Perales López, F.J.: Projecte pergamex: jocs pervasius per a tothom. Anu. Envell. Illes Balears. **2023**, 406–429 (2023)
4. De Carolis, B.N., Palestra, G., Castellano, G.: Exploring the role of empathy in designing social robots for elderly people. In: Adjunct Proceedings of the 32nd ACM Conference on User Modeling, Adaptation and Personalization (UMAP Adjunct '24), pp. 120–125. ACM, New York (2024). https://doi.org/10.1145/3631700.3664887
5. den Haan, M.C., Brankaert, R.G.A., Lu, Y.: Applying design methods to promote older adults' walking activities based on their hobbies and personal interests. In: Woodcock, A., Moody, L., McDonagh, D., Jain, A., Jain, L. (eds.) Design of Assistive Technology for Ageing Populations. Intelligent Systems Reference Library, vol. 167, pp. 257–273. Springer, Cham (2020). https://doi.org/10.1007/978-3-030-26292-1_14
6. Esposito, A., et al.: The dependability of voice on elders' acceptance of humanoid agents. In: 20th Annual Conference of the International Speech Communication Association (Interspeech 2019), pp. 31–35. ISCA (2019). https://doi.org/10.21437/Interspeech.2019-1734
7. Esposito, A., et al.: Elder user's attitude toward assistive virtual agents: the role of voice and gender. J. Ambient. Intell. Humaniz. Comput. **12**, 4429–4436 (2021). https://doi.org/10.1007/s12652-019-01423-x
8. Guerrero, G., Silva, F.J.M.D., Pereira, A., Fernández-Caballero, A.: A proposal for a taxonomy of augmented humanity based on current needs, topics and challenges. In: Novais, P., et al. (eds.) Ambient Intelligence – Software and Applications – 14th International Symposium on Ambient Intelligence. ISAmI 2023. Lecture Notes in Networks and Systems, vol. 770, pp. 74–83. Springer, Cham (2023). https://doi.org/10.1007/978-3-031-43461-7_8

9. Justo, R., et al.: Analysis of the interaction between elderly people and a simulated virtual coach. J. Ambient. Intell. Humaniz. Comput. **11**, 6125–6140 (2020). https://doi.org/10.1007/s12652-020-01983-3
10. Karaca Şalgamcıoğlu, B.: Future older adults and mobile applications for health. In: Woodcock, A., Moody, L., McDonagh, D., Jain, A., Jain, L. (eds.) Design of Assistive Technology for Ageing Populations. Intelligent Systems Reference Library, vol. 167, pp. 275–292. Springer, Cham (2020). https://doi.org/10.1007/978-3-030-26292-1_15
11. Kimura, R., Nakajima, T.: Sharing human seeing and hearing and their annotated portfolio. In: Novais, P., et al. (eds.) Ambient Intelligence – Software and Applications – 14th International Symposium on Ambient Intelligence. ISAmI 2023. Lecture Notes in Networks and Systems, vol. 770, pp. 3–12. Springer, Cham (2023). https://doi.org/10.1007/978-3-031-43461-7_1
12. Knight, J., Ross, E., Gibbons, C., McEwan, T.: Unlocking service flow—fast and frugal digital healthcare design. In: Woodcock, A., Moody, L., McDonagh, D., Jain, A., Jain, L. (eds.) Design of Assistive Technology for Ageing Populations. Intelligent Systems Reference Library, vol. 167, pp. 171–187. Springer, Cham (2020). https://doi.org/10.1007/978-3-030-26292-1_9
13. Langley, J., Wheeler, G., Partridge, R., Bec, R., Wolstenholme, D., Sproson, L.: Designing with and for older people. In: Woodcock, A., Moody, L., McDonagh, D., Jain, A., Jain, L. (eds.) Design of Assistive Technology for Ageing Populations. Intelligent Systems Reference Library, vol. 167, pp. 3–19. Springer, Cham (2020). https://doi.org/10.1007/978-3-030-26292-1_1
14. Mayas, C., Krömker, H.: Mobility information services for older people. In: Woodcock, A., Moody, L., McDonagh, D., Jain, A., Jain, L. (eds.) Design of Assistive Technology for Ageing Populations. Intelligent Systems Reference Library, vol. 167, pp. 293–307. Springer, Cham (2020). https://doi.org/10.1007/978-3-030-26292-1_16
15. McCarthy, A.D., Moody, L.: Assistive technology (AT) usability and adoption: future drivers. In: Woodcock, A., Moody, L., McDonagh, D., Jain, A., Jain, L. (eds.) Design of Assistive Technology for Ageing Populations. Intelligent Systems Reference Library, vol. 167, pp. 105–125. Springer, Cham (2020). https://doi.org/10.1007/978-3-030-26292-1_6
16. Mendes, C., Pereira, R., Ribeiro, J., Rodrigues, N., Pereira, A.: Chatto: An emotionally intelligent avatar for elderly care in ambient assisted living. In: Novais, P., et al. (eds.) Ambient Intelligence – Software and Applications – 14th International Symposium on Ambient Intelligence. ISAmI 2023. Lecture Notes in Networks and Systems, vol. 770, pp. 93–102. Springer, Cham (2023). https://doi.org/10.1007/978-3-031-43461-7_10
17. Moody, L., Cobley, A.J.: MATUROLIFE: Using advanced material science to develop the future of assistive technology. In: Woodcock, A., Moody, L., McDonagh, D., Jain, A., Jain, L. (eds.) Design of Assistive Technology for Ageing Populations. Intelligent Systems Reference Library, vol. 167, pp. 189–202. Springer, Cham (2020). https://doi.org/10.1007/978-3-030-26292-1_10
18. Moody, L., Magee, P., Stefanov, D.: Development of a wheelchair stability assessment system: design tools and approaches. In: Woodcock, A., Moody, L., McDonagh, D., Jain, A., Jain, L. (eds.) Design of Assistive Technology for Ageing Populations. Intelligent Systems Reference Library, vol. 167, pp. 235–256. Springer, Cham (2020). https://doi.org/10.1007/978-3-030-26292-1_13
19. Nayer, K., Coxon, S.: Improving the quality of life of individuals with dementia using personal digital media. In: Woodcock, A., Moody, L., McDonagh, D., Jain, A., Jain, L. (eds.) Design of Assistive Technology for Ageing Populations. Intelligent Systems Reference Library, vol. 167, pp. 311–334. Springer, Cham (2020). https://doi.org/10.1007/978-3-030-26292-1_17
20. Pereira, R., Mendes, C., Ribeiro, R., Ribeiro, J., Pereira, A.: Human-in-the-loop AAL approach to emotion capture and classification. In: Novais, P., et al. (eds.) Ambient Intelligence – Software and Applications – 14th International Symposium on Ambient Intelligence. ISAmI

2023. Lecture Notes in Networks and Systems, vol. 770, pp. 123–132. Springer, Cham (2023). https://doi.org/10.1007/978-3-031-43461-7_13
21. Pink, S., Sumartojo, S., Bond, C.H.L.: Empathetic technologies: digital materiality and video ethnography. Vis. Stud. **32**, 371–381 (2017). https://doi.org/10.1080/1472586X.2017.1396192
22. Spinelli, G. et al.: Contemporary themes in the design of AT for the ageing population: materiality, co-design and cultural influences. In: Woodcock, A., Moody, L., McDonagh, D., Jain, A., Jain, L. (eds.) Design of Assistive Technology for Ageing Populations. Intelligent Systems Reference Library, vol. 167, pp. 41–58. Springer, Cham (2020). https://doi.org/10.1007/978-3-030-26292-1_3
23. Talaat, F.M., El-Balka, R.M.: Stress monitoring using wearable sensors: IoT techniques in medical field. Neural Comput. Appl. **35**, 18571–18584 (2023). https://doi.org/10.1007/s00521-023-08681-z
24. Wiczorek, R., Bayles, M.A., Rogers, W.A.: Domestic robots for older adults: design approaches and recommendations. In: Woodcock, A., Moody, L., McDonagh, D., Jain, A., Jain, L. (eds.) Design of Assistive Technology for Ageing Populations. Intelligent Systems Reference Library, vol. 167, pp. 203–219. Springer, Cham (2020). https://doi.org/10.1007/978-3-030-26292-1_11
25. Woodcock, A., McDonagh, D., Magee, P., Tovey, M.: The value and place for empathy in designing for older people. In: Woodcock, A., Moody, L., McDonagh, D., Jain, A., Jain, L. (eds.) Design of Assistive Technology for Ageing Populations. Intelligent Systems Reference Library, vol. 167, pp. 59–77. Springer, Cham (2020). https://doi.org/10.1007/978-3-030-26292-1_4
26. World Health Organization: Global Strategy and Action Plan on Ageing and Health. UN, Geneva (2017) https://iris.who.int/handle/10665/329960
27. World Health Organization: World Report on Ageing and Health. UN, Luxembourg (2015) https://www.who.int/publications/i/item/9789241565042

Evaluating the Uncanny Valley in AI-Generated Digital Characters: A Perceptual and Visual Quality Analysis of Synthetic Video Content

Alexander Rozo-Torres[1](✉), Huizilopoztli Luna-García[1], and Wilson J. Sarmiento[2]

[1] Laboratory of Interactive Technologies and User Experience (LITUX), Universidad Autónoma de Zacatecas, Zacatecas, México
{omar.rozo.torres,hlugar}@uaz.edu.mx
[2] Multimedia Research Group (GIM), Universidad Militar Nueva Granada, Bogotá, Colombia
wilson.sarmiento@unimilitar.edu.co

Abstract. The Uncanny Valley effect describes the discomfort or eeriness experienced by humans when encountering highly realistic yet subtly imperfect digital characters, has been a long-standing challenge in computer graphics and artificial intelligence. With the recent advancements in generative artificial intelligence, particularly in text-to-video models, the creation of lifelike digital characters has become more accessible and sophisticated. However, these artificial intelligence-generated characters often exhibit subtle artifacts in motion, facial expressions, and realism, potentially amplifying the uncanny valley. This work explores the extent to which the uncanny valley is perceived in videos generated by text-to-video models. We begin by outlining key concepts related to digital character generation, the uncanny valley theory, and the impact of generative artificial intelligence on human perception. We then conduct an experimental evaluation where participants assess videos based on realism, emotional response, and perceived eeriness. The dataset consists of synthetic videos produced by various text-to-video models, including models trained on diverse datasets with differing levels of animation fidelity. Through qualitative and quantitative analyses, our results highlight significant variations in uncanny valley perception across models, revealing common weaknesses in facial consistency, eye movement, and expression dynamics that contribute to the uncanny sensation. Our findings offer insights into the factors exacerbating the uncanny valley in digital characters created by generative artificial intelligence and provide guidelines for improving the naturalness of synthetic characters in text-to-video applications. This research contributes to the ongoing discourse on human-artificial intelligence interaction, shedding light on the psychological barriers to adopting generative artificial intelligence for realistic digital humans.

Keywords: Uncanny Valley · Generative Artificial Intelligence · Perceptual Assessment · Digital Humans

H. Luna-García et al. (Eds.): HCI-COLLAB 2025, CCIS 2850, pp. 133–147, 2027.
https://doi.org/10.1007/978-3-032-31223-5_10

1 Introduction

The Uncanny Valley (UV) theory describes the discomfort or eerie sensation humans experience when interacting with artificial representations that, despite their high level of realism, exhibit subtle imperfections that disrupt their perceived naturalness. This effect applies to any synthetic or artificial human representation, including robotics, prosthetics, CGI characters, digital avatars, and AI-generated human figures [1, 2]. Over the past decades, this concept has been extensively studied in digital animation, robotics, video games, and Virtual Reality (VR), where imperfect realism has generated adverse reactions among users [3].

Advances in generative artificial intelligence (Generative AI, GenAI) have led to the development of text-to-video (Text-to-Video, T2V) models, enabling the automated creation of highly realistic digital characters. However, recent studies have shown that visual quality (VQ) alone is insufficient to ensure audience acceptance, as factors such as movement coherence, facial expressiveness, and speech synchronization significantly influence UV perception [4]. Furthermore, growing anxiety about Artificial Intelligence (AI) and its increasing integration into digital environments highlights the need to understand how humans process and interpret these visual representations [5].

Scientific literature has identified several factors that intensify the uncanny sensation in digital characters. For example, research has found that UV perception is more pronounced in hyperrealistic avatars compared to stylized representations, as minor anomalies in their expressions or movements create cognitive dissonance for viewers [6]. Other studies have explored the impact of meta-humans on user acceptance, indicating that while these figures have overcome some UV barriers in appearance, they still present challenges in the naturalness of their interactions [7].

UV has also been studied in the context of VR and video games, where immersion and interactivity can amplify the perception of eeriness [8]. Recent research has analyzed how the perceived realism of digital avatars affects users' relationships with these entities, finding that inadequate expressiveness and stiffness in movements contribute to a sense of unease [9]. Additionally, studies have shown that UV is more pronounced when avatars are presented in VR social networking platforms, suggesting that familiarity with the digital environment does not fully mitigate the negative response [10].

One of the main challenges in researching UV in GenAI-generated videos is the lack of standardized metrics to evaluate audience perception. Various studies have proposed assessment models based on emotional responses and psychophysiological measures to quantify the intensity of UV [11]. Furthermore, experimental methodologies utilizing eye-tracking and facial expression analysis have been identified to evaluate user responses to digitally generated avatars [8]. However, discrepancies remain regarding the optimal way to measure and mitigate this effect in GenAI models [12].

Given the growing adoption of Large Multimodal Models (LMM) technologies and their applications in entertainment, education, and digital communication, it is crucial to understand how audiences perceive these contents and what strategies can be employed to minimize the impact of UV. This study investigates the perception of the UV in videos generated using various GenAI tools from T2V models, analyzing differences in emotional responses and evaluating the influence of factors such as visual realism, movement fluidity, and facial expressiveness.

The paper is structured as follows: Sect. 2 reviews the state of the art on UV perception in digital media and GenAI models, including works in digital animation, digital humans, and immersive systems. Section 3 describes the methodology used for data collection and analysis, including the assessment of different GenAI-generated video platforms. Section 4 presents the empirical results derived from the perceptual assessment with domain experts and general users, discussing the theoretical and practical implications of these findings alongside strategies to mitigate the UV effect in T2V workflows. Finally, Sect. 5 outlines the conclusions and future research directions.

2 Related Work

The Uncanny Valley (UV), first introduced by Mori (1970), describes the discomfort or eerie sensation humans experience when interacting with artificial representations that appear almost human but exhibit subtle imperfections [1, 2]. Initially studied in robotics, this concept has gained prominence in digital animation [13], film [14], games [15], and computer-generated imagery (CGI), where advances in technology have enabled the creation of increasingly realistic virtual characters [16].

Over the years, digital animation has become a crucial area for UV studying. Research indicates that hyperrealistic animated characters often elicit mixed reactions due to inconsistencies in facial expressiveness, speech synchronization, and movement fluidity. Consequently, when these elements lack coherence, the audience perceives the character as unnatural, intensifying the UV effect [15].

Moreover, studies have shown that UV in 3D animation is not just a visual issue, but also a matter of movement consistency. According to Maldonado [17], characters that attempt hyperrealism without achieving smooth transitions and natural gestures tend to evoke unease [17]. Similarly, de Andrade Araujo et al. [23] observed that the density of hyperrealistic characters in VR environments can amplify the UV perception, as audiences feel more discomfort in densely populated digital spaces [19, 23].

In the realm of cinema, CGI has revolutionized character creation, but it has also introduced significant challenges related to UV. From early experiments in hyperrealistic animation, such as Final Fantasy: The Spirits Within (2001), to more recent productions like Alita: Battle Angel (2019), filmmakers have struggled to meet audience expectations of realism [20]. As a result, CGI characters often face greater scrutiny compared to animated or stylized figures.

Furthermore, research suggests that prolonged screen time for CGI characters increases the likelihood that viewers will detect subtle flaws, intensifying the uncanny effect. In this regard, Tucker (2014) found that Avatar (2009) successfully mitigated UV by blending human and alien traits, suggesting that stylization is an effective strategy to reduce the phenomenon [14]. Furthermore, Zibrek (2015) emphasizes that UV can be assessed using the implicit association test, and that video quality assessment (VQA) plays a significant role in evaluating CGI animation [21].

Given these challenges, researchers have proposed various strategies to reduce the impact of UV in digital media. On the one hand, Tinwell (2014) argues that opting for stylized rather than hyperrealistic character designs can significantly lower eerie perception in animation and video games [15]. On the other hand, recent studies suggest that enhancing facial expressions and body movements can make digital characters appear more natural and relatable [22]. In addition, in the film industry, motion capture technology combined with digital refinement has improved the realism of CGI characters. Nevertheless, Manaf et al. (2019) highlight that audiences continue to compare digital faces with real human standards, making UV a persistent challenge [20]. To address this issue, Maldonado (2022) proposes the integration of AI-driven techniques to refine animation fluidity and expressive coherence, offering a promising solution for future productions [17].

The VQA is crucial to content generated with GenAI, animation, and CGI, usually divided into subjective and objective methods. Subjective assessments, considered the gold standard, rely on human perception, evaluating aspects like realism, aesthetic appeal, and temporal coherence [23] through metrics such as Mean Opinion Score (MOS) and Difference Mean Opinion Score (DMOS) [24]. However, these methods are time-consuming, leading to the development of objective evaluation models that automate analysis using computational techniques [25].

Moreover, some key subjective criteria include visual realism that significantly impacts user experience (UX) [26]. Videos with unnatural motion, inconsistent lighting, or distortions can disrupt immersion and lead to negative evaluations. Another critical factor is temporal consistency, which refers to how smoothly objects and characters move between frames. Lack of consistency can make animations appear jittery or artificial movement [27]. Likewise, naturalness and aesthetic appeal enhance viewer engagement [28]. Additionally, the alignment between content and user expectations significantly impacts subjective evaluation. If a video contains elements that contradict physical reality, such as unnatural object interactions, awkward character expressions, or gravity-defying physics, it is likely to be perceived as unnatural or unsettling [18].

To ensure consistency, subjective evaluations are conducted in controlled environments, with standardized conditions like screen resolution, frame rate, and lighting. Datasets such as T2V Eval-Bench have been designed to structure the assessment of videos generated with GenAI [26].

On the other hand, objective VQA methods employ computational models, categorized as Full-Reference (FR), which compare generated content with a high-quality reference using Structural Similarity Index (SSIM) and Peak Signal-to-Noise Ratio (PSNR) [25]; Reduced-Reference (RR), which partially reference original content while maintaining efficiency [25]; and No-Reference (NR), which uses deep learning and statistical features to estimate perceptual quality [29].

Recent developments integrate multimodal AI-based models, analyzing spatiotemporal coherence, object stability, and perceptual realism to enhance accuracy [30]. Action Quality Assessment (AQA) has also emerged as a key metric, evaluating physical plausibility, structural correctness, and logical coherence in movements and interactions [27]. Additionally, the Scene Consistency Index (SCI) assesses the integration of characters and objects within their environments, ensuring alignment of lighting, shadows, and motion with real-world physics [26]. Meanwhile, the Temporal Stability Index (TSI) identifies flickering, sudden jumps, and frame inconsistencies that disrupt immersion [25].

Despite these advancements, challenges persist. Subjective evaluations, while highly reliable, are resource-intensive, whereas objective models, though efficient, struggle to capture human perception nuances. Hybrid approaches that combine human assessments with AI predictions are essential to bridge this gap [25].

As GenAI content grows more complex, evaluation methods must evolve. Self-supervised learning models capable of adapting to diverse video types, alongside metrics that assess emotional engagement and cognitive load, could provide a deeper understanding of user perception [30]. Ultimately, as GenAI content expands in entertainment, VR, and digital media, developing robust assessment frameworks will be essential to maintaining high visual fidelity and UX standards.

In recent years, GenAI has revolutionized the creation of digital humans, avatars, and hyperrealist images and videos. By leveraging deep learning models such as Generative Adversarial Networks (GANs), Large Language Models (LLMs), Diffusion and Large Multimodal Models (LMMs), can generate synthetic humans that closely resemble real people. However, as GenAI becomes increasingly realistic, it also intensifies the UV effect, where near-human representations evoke discomfort in viewers [31].

Moreover, photorealism in content generated by GenAI has become a major research focus. Peng et al. (2024) highlights that modern multimodal models have refined image generation to the point where users often cannot distinguish them from real photographs. Their study of 30,824 AI-generated images on social media found that most exhibit hyperrealistic stylization, making them nearly indistinguishable from authentic photos [31]. Moreira et al. (2024) attribute this hyperrealism to advances in digital synthesis and deep learning, enabling AI to replicate textures, lighting, and human details with remarkable accuracy [32].

Furthermore, digital avatars have evolved from simple stylized figures to metahumans. However, the absence of subtle human imperfections in these synthetic beings often leads to an emotional disconnect, thereby intensifying the UV effect [14, 20]. Experiments show that users respond more positively to stylized animated characters than to hyperrealistic figures with slight inconsistencies in facial expressions or gaze.

Beyond entertainment, the realism of GenAI models impacts perceptions of authenticity, challenging the boundaries between synthetic media and digital content created by humans. Söffner (2025) introduces the concept of virtualism, suggesting that AI is blurring the boundaries between reality and simulation [33]. In this context, the proliferation of deep-fakes and the increasing difficulty in distinguishing genuine images from GenAI ones raise ethical concerns and threaten information credibility [31]. Therefore, evaluating the UV in GenAI is essential, Engel-Hermann et al. (2024) warn about *"naïve realism"*, where users assume hyperrealistic content is authentic without questioning its origin. Establishing metrics to assess emotional and perceptual responses to generated media will enhance the design of digital avatars and synthetic video tools, ultimately mitigating the negative effects of the UV [34].

3 Methodology

The proposed methodology has been structured into four stages, focusing on the generation and assessment of hyperrealistic audiovisual sequences using GenAI. Figure 1 provides an overview of the methodology. First, the **Prompt Input Description Character** is clearly established, defining the initial concept by specifying the main action of the character, fundamental characteristics, and the scenic context. Subsequently, the text **Prompt Refinement** is carried out using T2T models, aiming to optimize precision, detail, and descriptive clarity in the narrative content. Next, audiovisual **Video Generation** is conducted using multiple multimodal T2V models, with supervised iterations to ensure diversity and select the most hyperrealistic and coherent sequence in relation to the original prompt. Finally, a comprehensive **Perceptual Assessment** of the T2V outputs is performed, combining expert analysis with the VP of a diverse group of evaluators. This stage specifically examines the VQ of the sequences, the perceived level of realism, narrative coherence, and the impact of the UV.

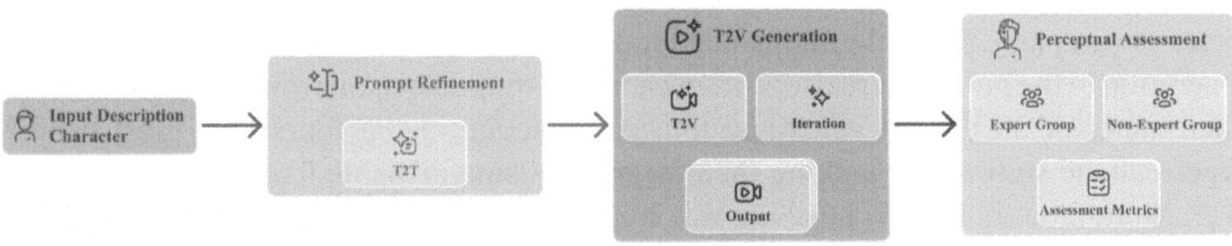

Fig. 1. Methodology used for T2V assessment, including character description, prompt refinement, video generation, and perceptual assessment.
Source: The authors.

Input Description Character. In this initial phase, the process begins by defining the conceptual framework of the video. This includes identifying the genre or theme, the main action to be performed, and the key elements of the sequence. Additionally, the character's physical and behavioral traits, as well as the environmental characteristics, are specified to establish a coherent visual and narrative structure.

Prompt Refinement (Text Input). Once the description is established, the text prompt is created and refined. An initial draft outlines the character's actions, physical attributes, expressive features, and environmental details. T2T models are then used to enhance specificity, coherence, and descriptive richness, incorporating details such as lighting, atmosphere, textures, and gestural interactions to improve the quality of the output video.

T2V Generation. The refined prompt is input into T2V models, which generate audiovisual content based on textual descriptions. Each model is configured with standardized parameters (resolution, duration, visual style) to ensure comparability. Multiple iterations are conducted per model, evaluating VQ, motion fluidity, and fidelity to the original description. During this phase, supervised adjustments are made to correct inconsistencies in gestures, facial expressions, scene transitions, enhancing realism and coherence.

Perceptual Assessment of Output Videos. Finally, the final sequences undergo a two-stage assessment: (1) Expert assessment by professionals in animation, CGI, and audiovisual design, and (2) General user feedback from participants without specialized training. The assessment measures perceived realism, narrative coherence, and the UV using both qualitative and quantitative methods. A comparative analysis is conducted across models to identify strengths, weaknesses, and areas for improvement in T2V.

4 Results

The following section presents the results obtained after applying the proposed methodology, generating and evaluating hyperrealistic audiovisual sequences using multimodal T2V models. The findings outlined here provide a clear assessment of which T2V models demonstrate the highest capability in producing realistic and coherent videos that align with the initial description, while minimizing the occurrence of the UV. Figure 2 shows the GenAI tools video outputs comparison.

Furthermore, the results derived from this experiment serve as an empirical basis for assessing the audience's VP at different levels of realism. This provides both objective and subjective criteria for measuring and analyzing VQ, as well as evaluating the psychological impact of the UV in the generated sequences.

In the **Input Description Character** stage, the character's scene was conceptualized and described, establishing the foundation for the generation of the detailed prompt. During this process, the character's main action was envisioned, considering the initial posture and the movements and expression. Subsequently, in the **Prompt Refinement** phase, the initial scene description was optimized using ChatGPT-o1,[1] applying prompting strategies to enhance clarity, detail, and coherence. The goal of this refinement was to provide a more descriptive and structured prompt, ensuring that T2V models accurately interpreted the character's main action and environment. To achieve this, an iterative approach was used, where ChatGPT was prompted to expand on the initial scene, incorporating details about facial expressions, lighting, atmosphere, and movement fluidity. Additionally, the language was adjusted to ensure greater semantic precision and to avoid ambiguities that could affect the coherence of the T2V. The following presents the improved prompt generated in this stage and the refinement resulted in a more detailed description, ensuring that T2V models had sufficient information to depict the action with greater fidelity and realism in the next T2V phase.

User: *"A young man sits at a table with a cup of coffee and a slight smile. After a brief pause, he calmly stands up and walks away from the table, leaving the scene."*

ChatGPT: *"**[Technical Context]** A Cinematic close-up to medium shot, 4K, 60fps, photorealistic lighting with natural global illumination, sharp focus, masterfully color graded, high temporal consistency. **[Digital Human Specs]** A young man with highly detailed skin textures, visible pores, and realistic facial hair. He has expressive eyes with natural moisture and subtle blinking, showing a slight, warm smile with realistic cheeks and lip movement. **[Action & Physics]** The man sits at a rustic wooden table with*

[1] ChatGPT-o1, OpenAI, https://openai.com/o1/

a steaming cup of coffee. After a brief, thoughtful pause, he executes a fluid, weight-balanced transition to stand up. He walks away from the table with a natural human gait, maintaining correct foot-planting and physical interaction with the floor. ***[Environment & Context]*** *Cozy cafe interior, rustic wooden table textures, steam rising from the cup, natural light coming from a window, consistent shadows, depth of field.* ***[Negative Prompt]*** *Deformed anatomy, extra fingers, distorted facial features, dead eyes, empty stare, robotic movement, flickering textures, jittery motion, sliding feet, character floating, disappearing coffee cup, warping table, low resolution, motion blur, watermarks, text."*

Consequently, in the **T2V Generation** phase, the prompt was used as text input in various T2V tools. Currently, multiple models specialize in generating audiovisual content from textual descriptions. Among these, the following were selected: Adobe Firefly,[2] Kling AI,[3] Meta AI,[4] Pika AI,[5] Runway Gen-3,[6] and Sora.[7] These platforms were employed to generate the visual representation of the character and its action, ensuring a comparative analysis across different models.

Since T2V models differ in their interpretation and visual synthesis, three iterations were performed for each tool, resulting in a total of three videos per model. Subsequently, the video from each tool that best met the following VQ and realism criteria was selected: fidelity to the prompt, visual realism, motion fluidity, spatial and environmental coherence, and emotional evocation. In Fig. 3, the selected output videos are presented after multiple iterations of generation using T2V tools, with the refined prompt as input.

To analyze VP and VQ in videos generated using GenAI, a structured survey was conducted with two distinct groups of participants: visual production experts and general users. The paper included 32 evaluators, divided into two groups:

- **Expert Group:** This group included 4 professionals with extensive experience in fields relevant to digital character creation and evaluation, including 3D animation, computer-generated imagery (CGI), graphic design, video game development, audiovisual production, film, and human-computer interaction (HCI) design. Their professional experience ranged from 10 to 32 years, and their ages spanned 35 to 60 years. The specific areas of expertise are illustrated in Fig. 4, providing a visual breakdown of their backgrounds.
- **General User Group:** This group consisted of 28 participants from diverse academic and professional backgrounds, aged between 18 and 42 years. Unlike the experts, they did not have specialized training in audiovisual technologies but were familiar with digital media and content generated by GenAI to varying degrees.

Participants were asked about their level of exposure to visual content generated by GenAI tools, including images, videos, 3D assets and synthetic avatars, to contextualize their familiarity with this type of technology. The results indicated that among

[2] Adobe Firefly, Adobe Inc., https://www.adobe.com/products/firefly.html
[3] Kling AI, Kling AI Labs, https://www.kling.ai
[4] Meta AI, Meta Platforms, https://www.meta.ai/ai-video-generator/
[5] Pika AI, Pika Labs, https://pika.art
[6] Runway Gen-3, Runway, https://runwayml.com/gen3
[7] Sora, OpenAI, https://openai.com/sora

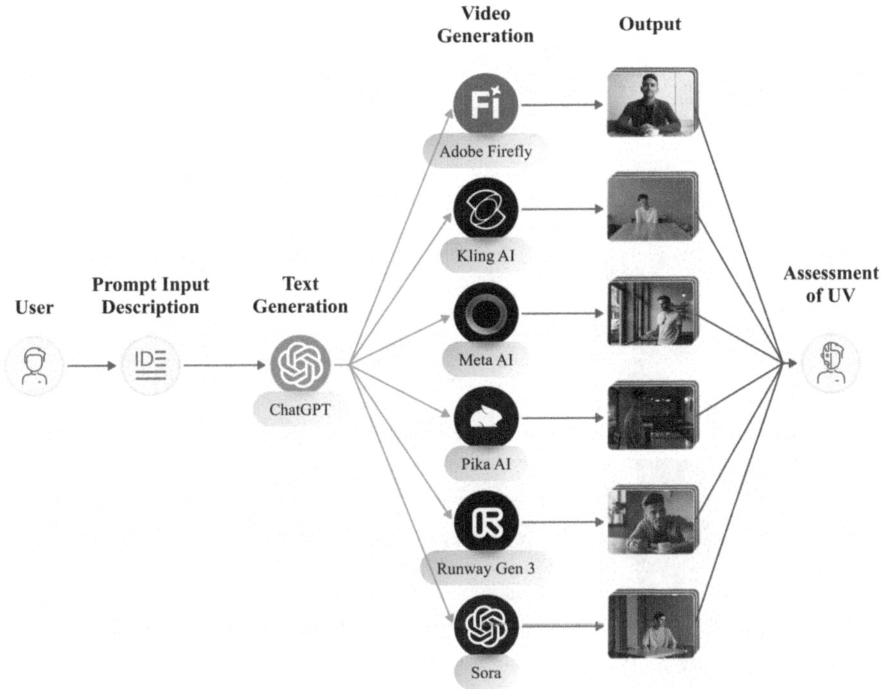

Fig. 2. Workflow of the T2V generation and assessment protocol. *Source*: The authors.

experts, 25% (1 of 4) reported being frequently exposed through their work or research. Oppositely, general users showed a more varied distribution: 35.7% reported occasional exposure, 35.7% indicated frequent exposure, and 28.6% stated they were very frequently exposed.

Subsequently, each participant watched the six generated videos and answered the corresponding questions for each one. First, the perception of the character's realism and naturalness was measured by asking: *Q1: How realistic and natural do you perceive the character?*. To assess the impact of the UV, participants were asked: *Q2: How comfortable or uncomfortable does the character make you feel?*. Figure 5 shows the distribution of responses for these questions. The results indicate that perceived realism remained close to or below the midpoint of the scale, with marked differences between experts and general users, suggesting that the characters did not fully achieve a natural appearance. Meanwhile, the impact of the UV effect remained neutral, with participants neither strongly rejecting nor fully accepting the generated characters.

Consequently, various technical and visual aspects of the video were evaluated using a Likert scale from 1 to 5, where 1 represented *"very low"* and 5 *"very high"*. The questions included: *Q3: Does the video have good image quality (sharpness, lighting, and details)?*, *Q4: How convincing and well-executed does the video seem overall?*, *Q5 Are the movements fluid and natural?*, *Q6: Do the facial expressions and gestures appear realistic?*, *Q7: Does the video accurately represent the action or concept described in the text? and Q8: Does the video seem realistic and credible within its context?*.

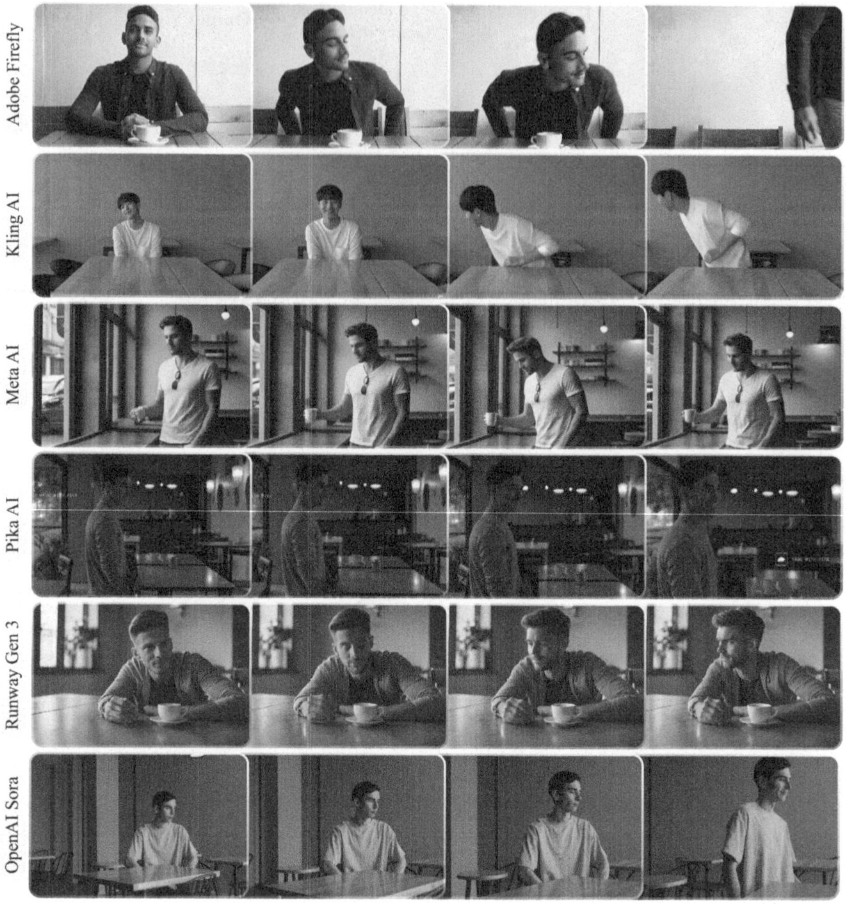

Fig. 3. Comparison of output video sequences using different T2V models, showcasing variations with the input prompt.
Source: The authors.

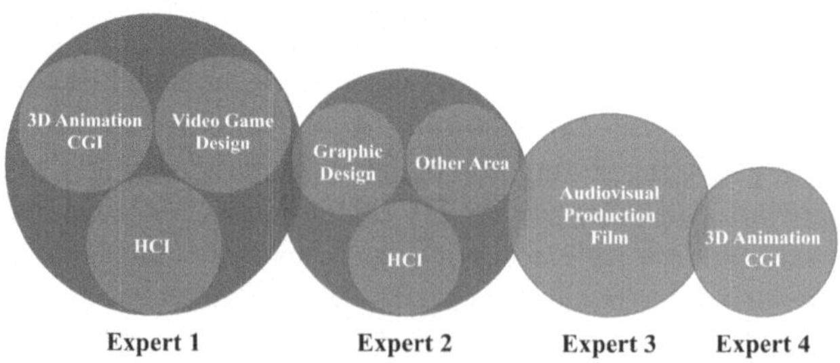

Fig. 4. Distribution of the expert group, covering areas such as 3D animation, CGI, audiovisual production, graphic design, videogames, and HCI design.
Source: The authors.

The Fig. 6 presents a detailed breakdown of these evaluations, where results indicate that the video generated by Kling AI achieved the highest scores across multiple criteria, consistently approaching the maximum scale of 5 in aspects such as image quality, movement fluidity, and facial expressivity. This indicates that Kling AI achieved superior perceptual realism and technical consistency across evaluated dimensions. By contrast, the video generated by Meta AI received the lowest ratings, particularly in motion naturalness and facial expressions, highlighting noticeable limitations in maintaining realism and avoiding the UV.

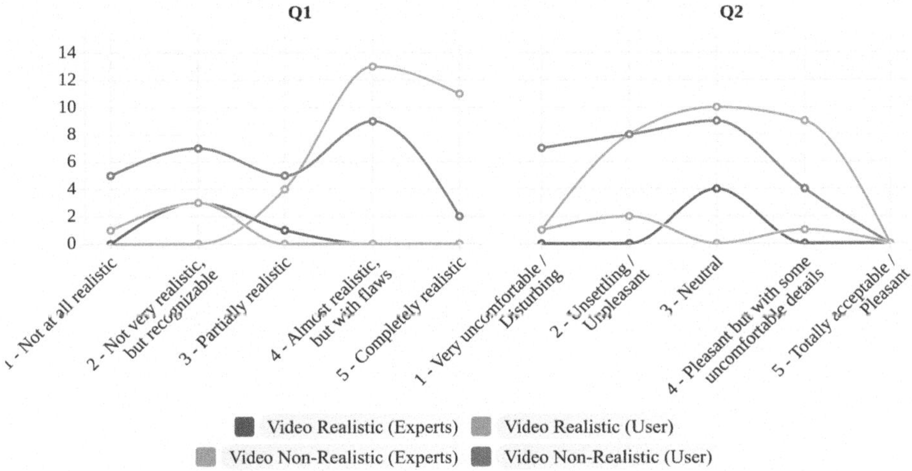

Fig. 5. Distribution of responses for Q1 and Q2. *Source:* The authors.

After assessing realism, VQ, consistency and coherence of the content, two additional questions were asked to identify potential deficiencies in video generation and its integration with the environment. These questions allowed participants to highlight specific aspects that could affect credibility and immersion in the scene: *Q9: Are there noticeable visual errors (distortions, blurriness, incorrect lighting)?* and *Q10: Is the integration of the characters with the environment believable?*

Kling AI received the lowest number of reported visual errors, with multiple participants indicating no noticeable issues, and it also had the highest coherence in character-environment integration. However, Videos Meta AI, Runway Gen 3, and Sora exhibited the highest frequency of severe visual errors, often rated as "*many*" distortions or inconsistencies. Additionally, these videos were also perceived as *"very artificial"* in terms of integration, reinforcing the UV. Adobe Firefly and Pika AI showed moderate results, with some inconsistencies in both visual quality and integration.

These findings suggest that while some GenAI models achieve higher visual fidelity, others struggle with motion coherence and realistic environmental blending, impacting overall immersion and perceived authenticity.

To complement the quantitative assessment a series of qualitative questions were included at the end of the questionnaire. These questions allowed participants to express their subjective impressions, identify key elements that influenced their perception of realism or artificiality, and suggest improvements to enhance the quality of the videos.

The results indicate a clear preference for Kling AI, which was selected as the best overall by 25 out of 32 participants 78.1% (25/32). Pika AI received 12.5% (4/32), and Adobe Firefly received 9.4% (3/32). This suggests that Kling AI stood out in terms of realism and visual coherence. Participants identified more natural facial expressions 78.1% (25/32) and smoother movements 71.9% (23/32) as the primary improvements needed to enhance the realism of the videos. Additionally, other aspects mentioned included lighting and shadow correction 25.0% (8/32), reduction of visual artifacts 15.6% (5/32), and narrative details, such as the absence of expected objects in the scene (*"the coffee cup is missing"*). These findings indicate that while hyperrealism has been achieved in some aspects, imperfections in expressions and movements remain the main obstacles to overcoming the UV.

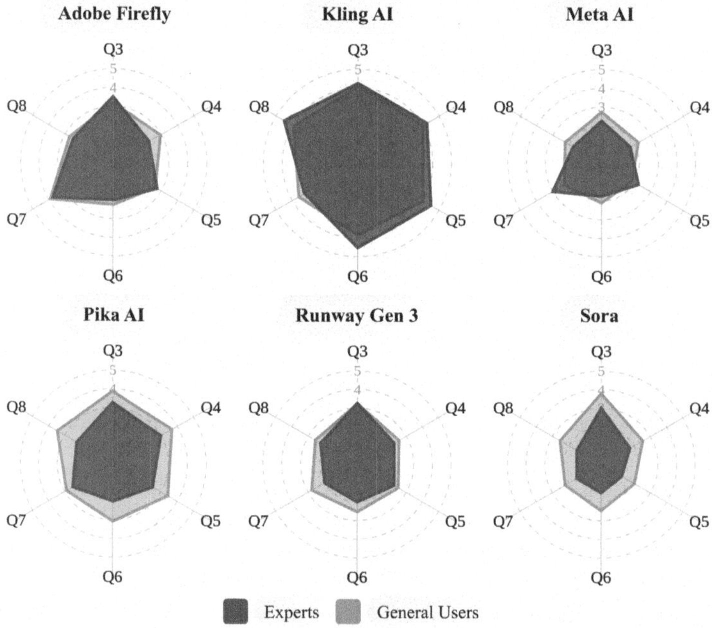

Fig. 6. Comparative analysis of output videos based on Q3 to Q8, evaluating visual and technical aspects.
Source: The authors.

The perception was reflected in multiple responses, where participants described the videos as *"uncomfortable"*, *"strange"*, or *"displeasing"*. Specifically, issues were identified in final movements, forced expressions, and a lack of synchronization in actions. Some comments highlighted the absence of emotions in characters, figure distortions in certain frames, and disconnect between gestures and facial expressions. One participant noted that *"the errors were so noticeable that they distracted from the overall context of the video"*, reinforcing the importance of visual and narrative cohesion in the perception of realism. The elements that contributed to making a video appear more believable were fluid and coherent movements, precise facial synchronization, and realistic lighting. On the other hand, the main factors that made the videos appear unreal included rigid facial expressions, unnatural movements, and empty stares. Additionally, errors in textures, lighting, and character morphology (such as the appearance of extra fingers or facial distortions) were key elements that led participants to notice the artificiality in the videos.

5 Conclusions and Future Work

The findings underscore the critical role of GenAI realism in shaping user perception and the persistence of the UV in hyperrealistic digital characters. The perceptual assessment demonstrated that higher realism does not always guarantee a positive reception, as even minor inconsistencies in facial expressions, motion fluidity, or environmental integration can provoke discomfort. Among the tested T2V models, Kling AI achieved the highest ratings, excelling in image quality, movement naturalness, and character-environment coherence, whereas Meta AI exhibited the lowest performance, particularly struggling with fluid motion and integration. These findings reveal that while GenAI has made significant strides in generating photorealistic content, the challenge remains in seamlessly embedding digital humans into believable environments without triggering perceptual dissonance.

Furthermore, differences between expert and general user assessment provided insightful contrasts. Professionals in 3D animation, CGI, game design, HCI, and audiovisual production were more sensitive to visual artifacts, inconsistencies, and the nuances of digital character animation, whereas general users displayed more varied responses, influenced by their level of prior exposure to T2V content. This suggests that future AI advancements must not only enhance technical fidelity but also account for cognitive and perceptual biases in human interaction with synthetic media. While this work primarily focused on digital humans generated via T2V models, its implications extend far beyond this domain. The challenges identified are highly relevant to the development of AI-driven avatars in virtual assistants, gaming, the Metaverse, and XR experiences, as well as real-time GenAI content for live broadcasting.

Several ongoing projects are already pushing the boundaries of hyperrealistic interactive avatars, making this paper a valuable contribution toward understanding user perception. Ultimately, this work provides a foundational methodology for the perceptual assessment of digital humans generated by GenAI, offering insights extendable to broader applications in synthetic media. As technology evolves, future research must focus not only on achieving visual fidelity but also on fostering intuitive, natural, and human-like interactions in digital environments.

Acknowledgments. The authors would like to express their sincere gratitude to the *"Secretaría de Ciencia, Humanidades, Tecnología e Innovación (SECIHTI)"* for the financial support granted to Engineer Alexander Rozo-Torres through the Postgraduate Studies Scholarship, under CVU number 2059278. This support was essential in enabling the completion of the present research. The author, Wilson J. Sarmiento, a full-time professor at the Universidad Militar Nueva Granada (UMNG), acknowledges and recognizes the UMNG for its support of his research work.

References

1. Mori, M., MacDorman, K.F., Kageki, N.: The uncanny valley [from the field]. IEEE Robot. Autom. Mag. **19**(2), 98–100 (2012). https://doi.org/10.1109/MRA.2012.2192811
2. MacDorman, K.F.: Does mind perception explain the uncanny valley effect? A meta-regression analysis and (de) humanization experiment. Comput. Hum. Behav.: Artif. Hum. **2**(1), 100065 (2024). https://doi.org/10.1016/j.chbah.2024.100065
3. Seyama, J.I., Nagayama, R.S.: The uncanny valley: effect of realism on the impression of artificial human faces. Presence Teleop. Virt. **16**(4), 337–351 (2007). https://doi.org/10.1162/pres.16.4.337
4. Hepperle, D., Purps, C.F., Deuchler, J., Wölfel, M.: Aspects of visual avatar appearance: self-representation, display type, and uncanny valley. Vis. Comput. **38**(4), 1227–1244 (2022). https://doi.org/10.1007/s00371-021-02151-0
5. Rodríguez, C.G.: Anxiety in the face of artificial intelligence. between pragmatic fears and uncanny terrors. Studies. Psychology. **45**(1), 123–144 (2024). https://doi.org/10.1177/02109395241241386
6. Shin, M., Kim, S.J., Biocca, F.: The uncanny valley: no need for any further judgments when an avatar looks eerie. Comput. Hum. Behav. **94**, 100–109 (2019). https://doi.org/10.1016/j.chb.2019.01.016
7. Bae, S., Jung, T., Cho, J., Kwon, O.: Effects of meta-human characteristics on user acceptance: from the perspective of uncanny valley theory. Behav. Inform. Technol. **44**(4), 731–748 (2024). https://doi.org/10.1080/0144929X.2024.2338408
8. Higgins, D., Egan, D., Fribourg, R., Cowan, B., McDonnell, R.: Ascending from the valley: can state-of-the-art photorealism avoid the uncanny? ACM Symp. Appl. Percept. **2021**, 1–5 (2021). https://doi.org/10.1145/3474451.3476242
9. Frampton-Clerk, A., Oyekoya, O.: Investigating the perceived realism of the other user's look-alike avatars. In: Proceedings of the 28th ACM Symposium on Virtual Reality Software and Technology, pp. 1–5 (2022). https://doi.org/10.1145/3562939.3565636
10. Aguilar, R.G.: Más allá del Uncanny Valley: forma de lo humano, mímesis y expresión. Bajo palabra Rev. filos. **28**, 176–197 (2021). https://doi.org/10.15366/bp2021.28.008
11. Ho, C.C., MacDorman, K. F.: Measuring the uncanny valley effect: refinements to indices for perceived humanness, attractiveness, and eeriness. Int. J. Soc. Robot. **9**, 129–139 (2017). https://doi.org/10.1007/s12369-016-0380-9
12. Mäkäräinen, M., Kätsyri, J., Förger, K., Takala, T. The funcanny valley: a study of positive emotional reactions to strangeness. In: Proceedings of the 19th International Academic Mindtrek Conference, pp. 175–181 (2015). https://doi.org/10.1145/2818187.2818292
13. Bancroft, T.: Creating Characters with Personality. Watson-Guptill, New York (2006)
14. Tucker, A.: Avatar in the uncanny valley: the Na'vi and us, the machinic audience. In: Interfacing with the Internet in Popular Cinema, pp. 73–103. Palgrave Macmillan US, New York (2014). https://doi.org/10.1057/9781137386694_4
15. Tinwell, A.: The Uncanny Valley in Games and Animation. CRC press (2014). https://doi.org/10.1201/b17830
16. Broad, T., Leymarie, F. F., Grierson, M. Amplifying the uncanny. (2020). https://doi.org/10.48550/arXiv.2002.06890
17. Maldonado Nolivos, V.D.: El valle inquietante, su ejecución y cómo evitarlo en animaciones 3D. Rev. Odigos. **3**(3), 9–26 (2022). https://doi.org/10.35290/ro.v3n3.2022.675
18. Araújo, V., Dalmoro, B., Geiss, R. C., Pinho, M. S., Musse, S.: How do we perceive characters? An analysis of human perception in still images, animations and VR scenarios. In: Proceedings of Brazilian Symposium on Games and Digital Entertainment (2022). https://doi.org/10.5753/sbgames_estendido.2022.225436

19. Seymour, M., Riemer, K., Kay, J.: Interactive realistic digital avatars-revisiting the uncanny valley. In: Proceedings of the Annual Hawaii International Conference on System Sciences, pp. 547–556 (2017). https://doi.org/10.24251/HICSS.2017.067
20. Manaf, A.A.A., Ismail, S.N.F., Arshad, M.R.: Perceived visual CGI familiarity towards uncanny valley theory in film. Int. J. Appl. Creat. Arts. **2**(1), 7–16 (2019). https://doi.org/10.33736/ijaca.1575.2019
21. Zibrek, K., McDonnell, R.: Evaluating the Uncanny valley with the implicit association test. In: Proceedings of the ACM SIGGRAPH Symposium on Applied Perception, pp. 135–135 (2015). https://doi.org/10.1145/2804408.2814179
22. Stark, L.: Animation and artificial intelligence. In: Proceedings of the 2024 ACM Conference on Fairness, Accountability, and Transparency, pp. 1663–1671 (2024). https://doi.org/10.1145/3630106.3658995
23. de Andrade Araujo, V. F., Costa, A. B., Musse, S. R.: Evaluating the uncanny valley effect in dark colored skin virtual humans. In: 2023 36th SIBGRAPI Conference on Graphics, Patterns and Images (SIBGRAPI), pp. 1–6. IEEE (2023). https://doi.org/10.48550/arXiv.2312.06790
24. Singam, A. K.: A review on recent approaches, methods of video quality assessment. Authorea preprints (2023). https://doi.org/10.22541/au.167907537.73274988/v1
25. Zheng, Q., et al.: Video quality assessment: a comprehensive survey (2024). https://doi.org/10.48550/arXiv.2412.04508
26. Qi, Z., Shi, P., Wang, S., Zhang, Z., Ying, Z., Pan, D.: Comprehensive subjective and objective evaluation method for text-generated video (2025). https://doi.org/10.48550/arXiv.2501.08545
27. Chen, Z., et al.: Rethinking action quality assessment for AI-generated videos. Adv. Neural Inf. Proces. Syst. **37**, 40111–40144 (2024). https://doi.org/10.48550/arXiv.2406.06087
28. Chivileva, I., Lynch, P., Ward, T.E., Smeaton, A.F.: A dataset of text prompts, videos and video quality metrics from generative text-to-video AI models. Data Brief. **54**, 110514 (2024). https://doi.org/10.1016/j.dib.2024.110514
29. Ghildyal, A., Chen, Y., Zadtootaghaj, S., Barman, N., Bovik, A. C.: Quality prediction of AI generated images and videos: emerging trends and opportunities. pp. 1–16 (2024). https://doi.org/10.48550/arXiv.2410.08534
30. Liu, X., et al.: A survey of AI-generated video evaluation (2024). https://doi.org/10.48550/arXiv.2410.19884
31. Peng, Q., Lu, Y., Peng, Y., Qian, S., Liu, X., Shen, C.: Crafting synthetic realities: examining visual realism and misinformation potential of photorealistic AI-generated images (2024). https://doi.org/10.48550/arXiv.2409.17484
32. Moreira, D., Marcel, S., Rocha, A.: Synthetic realities and artificial intelligence-generated contents. IEEE Secur. Priv. **22**(3), 7–10 (2024). https://doi.org/10.1109/MSEC.2024.3388244
33. Söffner, J.: Virtualism: how AI replaces reality. AI & Soc. **40**, 1389–1401 (2025). https://doi.org/10.1007/s00146-024-01999-9
34. Engel-Hermann, P., Skulmowski, A.: Appealing, but misleading: a warning against a naive AI realism. AI Ethics. **5**, 3407–3413 (2024). https://doi.org/10.1007/s43681-024-00587-3

Evaluation of the Technological Maturity of the Internet of Things in Industrial Companies: Applying ATLANTIS in the Buenos Aires Metropolitan Area - Argentina

Andrés Felipe Solis Pino[1,2](✉), Pablo H. Ruiz[2], Alicia Mon[3], and César Alberto Collazos[2]

[1] Corporación Universitaria Comfacauca – Unicomfacauca, Cl 4 No. 8-30 Centro Histórico, Popayán 190001, Cauca, Colombia
asolis@unicomfacauca.edu.co

[2] Universidad del Cauca, Calle 5 No. 4-70, Popayán 190003, Cauca, Colombia
{phruiz,ccollazo}@unicauca.edu.co

[3] Universidad Nacional de La Matanza, Florencio Varela 1903 (B1754JEC), San Justo 1754, Buenos Aires, Argentina

Abstract. The Internet of Things has significant potential to transform industrial operations. However, its adoption faces challenges related to organizational readiness and limited empirical evidence in Latin America. This research explicitly investigates Argentina's Buenos Aires Metropolitan Area, where industrial companies are pivotal to the national economy. Maturity models for the Internet of Things often lack contextualization, thus hindering practical assessment in industrial settings. Thus, this study assessed 37 industrial organizations using the ATLANTIS maturity model, which considers technological, organizational, and human dimensions, as well as multiple subcomponents. Data were collected through a structured questionnaire, and statistical analyses were performed to determine the levels of the organizations. The results show a difference in overall Internet of Things maturity between large enterprises and small and medium-sized enterprises, with the former showing higher scores on several dimensions. Large enterprises demonstrated notable strengths in device management and connectivity, while both groups showed higher scores in enterprise integration and relatively low scores in compliance and contextualization. A strong correlation was found between technology and organizational maturity scores, suggesting their interdependence. The study highlights the heterogeneous landscape of Internet of Things adoption, with large enterprises significantly more advanced than small and medium-sized organizations. This highlights the need for tailored strategies to support small and medium-sized enterprises in improving their technological infrastructure and organizational readiness to adopt the Internet of Things in the region successfully.

Keywords: Technological Maturity · Argentina · Industrial Companies

H. Luna-García et al. (Eds.): HCI-COLLAB 2025, CCIS 2850, pp. 148–161, 2027.
https://doi.org/10.1007/978-3-032-31223-5_11

1 Introduction

The Internet of Things (IoT) represents a network of interconnected computing devices equipped with sensors, actuators, and communication interfaces, enabling autonomous data acquisition, processing, and transmission in heterogeneous technology ecosystems [1]. Forecasts indicate that by 2029, there will be approximately 36.5 billion connected IoT devices [2], underscoring the growing influence of this technology in various sectors, including smart homes and business operations [3]. In this regard, IoT offers numerous advantages to businesses, transforming their operations and competitive strategies, thereby improving operational efficiency by automating routine tasks and minimizing the need for manual intervention [4].

Despite these advantages, the adoption of IoT brings with it several challenges [1], such as security issues [5] and challenges related to interoperability and standards [6]. Finally, another important challenge lies in enterprises' ability to accurately assess IoT's technological maturity and the extent of its integration into their organizational frameworks [7].

In this regard, accurately assessing IoT technology maturity within organizations is important because it facilitates informed decision-making regarding resource allocation [8] and provides a clear picture of the organization's current situation and the steps needed to move forward concerning IoT [9]. It also provides a competitive advantage by optimizing these technologies, increasing productivity, enabling real-time data analysis, and improving customer satisfaction [10]. Finally, assessing IoT technology maturity helps to identify potential risks associated with its implementation and integration issues with existing processes [11]. This knowledge indirectly contributes to more effective strategic planning, greater competitive advantage, and business growth.

Now, in the Argentine Republic, and especially in the Buenos Aires Metropolitan Area (AMBA), industrial companies play a fundamental role in the country's economy because they are vital for economic growth and employment generation; in addition, they drive the country's technological and social development [12]. Regarding IoT adoption in Argentine and Latin American companies, it is hampered by several challenges, including inadequate organizational readiness for technology implementation [13], limited empirical evidence on the adoption of this technology in the Latin American context [14], and insufficient government support for its adoption [15], all of which constitute significant obstacles for these types of organizations.

Consequently, several mechanisms have been proposed to measure IoT maturity, mainly through maturity models and frameworks [1]. However, these developments are not standardized for this specific purpose, require contextual adaptation, and frequently fail to adequately address human and organizational aspects [1, 16]. Therefore, accurately implementing tools to assess IoT technological maturity in organizational contexts is important and represents a significant advance in the field [9]. In response to this need, ATLANTIS [17], a multidimensional maturity model for IoT designed to assess technological maturity across diverse organizational perspectives holistically, has been developed. Therefore, the main objective of this research is to assess IoT technological maturity across several industrial organizations in the AMBA in Argentina using the ATLANTIS tool, thereby providing empirical evidence for the domain.

2 Materials and Methods

This research was developed as a non-experimental quantitative study, employing a non-probabilistic convenience sampling that included 37 industrial companies in the AMBA during June and July 2024. The research was methodologically based on the study by Mon and Del Giorgio in [18]. The methodological structure was based on the ATLANTIS multidimensional maturity model [17], specifically designed to assess the adoption and implementation of IoT technologies in industrial organizations, and on a structured questionnaire using a Likert scale. Data analysis involved the application of descriptive and inferential statistical techniques implemented through specialized software. PAST software [19] was used for advanced statistical analysis. Through this methodological approach, we sought to determine the level of IoT technological maturity in organizations and to identify patterns and relationships among the evaluated dimensions, providing a view of the current state of IoT adoption in the AMBA industrial sector.

2.1 Description of the ATLANTIS Maturity Model

ATLANTIS is a multidimensional maturity model specifically designed to assess the adoption and implementation of IoT technologies in industrial Small and Medium Enterprises (SMEs) [17]. This proposal addresses a knowledge gap identified in the domain, i.e., the lack of a comprehensive and specific tool for this type of organization that considers the global nature of IoT, especially in industrial environments [1]. Unlike existing maturity models focusing mainly on specific technological aspects or isolated case studies, ATLANTIS also incorporates organizational and human dimensions based on an accepted taxonomy [20], providing a more comprehensive, holistic, and detailed assessment of IoT in organizations. This multidimensional approach aligns with the growing consensus among experts that successful IoT adoption depends not only on technical capabilities but also on organizational readiness and workforce adaptation [16].

In this regard, ATLANTIS (Fig. 1) considers three fundamental dimensions organizational, technological, and human, each of which is further divided into seven principal components, namely:

- **Device management**: assesses the processes and practices involved in deploying, configuring, managing, and maintaining IoT devices within the organization.
- **Connectivity management**: assesses the organization's capabilities related to data collection, including protocols, standards, data volume management, and downtime considerations.
- **Cloud/edge management**: assesses how organizations process and manage data generated by IoT devices, including data analytics, cloud computing, and Artificial Intelligence (AI) integration.
- **Business integration management**: assesses the integration of IoT into business processes, systems, and strategies, including use cases, data integration, and technology interoperability.
- **Security**: Assesses security challenges and risks associated with the implementation and operation of IoT systems, including security controls, policies, and procedures.

- **Compliance**: assesses the organization's adherence to relevant regulations and ethical considerations when implementing IoT solutions, specifying governance processes, policies, and structures.
- **Contextualization**: assesses the organization's readiness and understanding of the various environmental and operational contexts for implementing IoT solutions, including adaptation to specific requirements, constraints, and challenges.

Finally, each component is further subdivided into specific metrics, classified into four maturity levels: static, reactive, proactive, and innovative. This granular structure enables a detailed assessment of an organization's strengths and weaknesses in IoT adoption within its organizational framework.

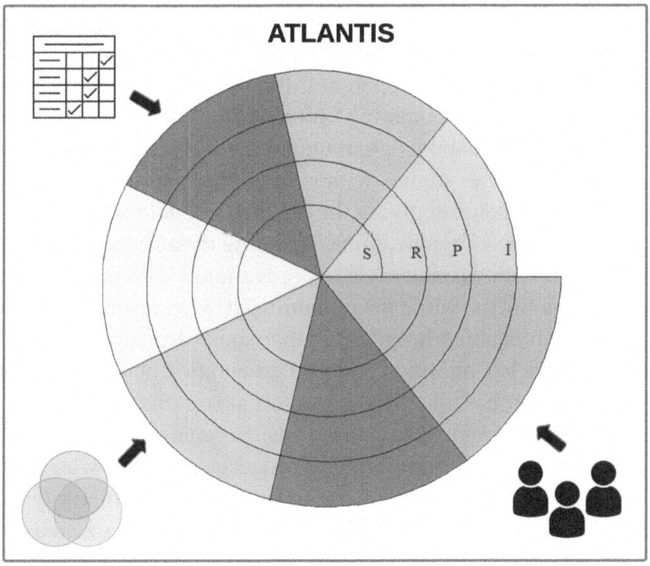

Fig. 1. Proposed ATLANTIS multidimensional maturity model.*Source:* [17].

2.2 Context of the Study Area

Argentina's industrial sector is an important part of the national economy and exhibits a wide range of activities and regional variations. The country has a population of approximately 45 million, of whom a significant portion resides in urban areas. The AMBA alone accounts for almost a third of the population, making it a central hub for industrial activity. Quantitatively, the industrial sector contributes approximately 20% to Argentina's Gross Domestic Product (GDP), with key industries including automobile manufacturing, food processing, textile production, and chemical synthesis [21]. The country has a well-established manufacturing base, and despite economic challenges such as inflation and currency volatility, the sector remains resilient, driven by both domestic demand and exports [22].

The AMBA manufacturing sector faces several challenges, such as economic instability, limited access to finance, and the need for infrastructure upgrades. The adoption of IoT technology in Argentina is on the rise, driven by the need for efficiency and innovation in various industries, particularly in smart manufacturing, predictive maintenance, and supply chain optimization [23]. IoT research and development is also strengthened through collaborations among universities, postgraduate academic programs, research institutions, and private companies. The above factors and strategic economic initiatives position Argentina, particularly the AMBA, as a promising player in the South American IoT domain, with challenges still to be overcome [24].

2.3 Data Collection and Analysis from Organizations in AMBA

For the data collection process for organizations in the AMBA, a non-probabilistic sample was used in June and July 2024, comprising 37 companies. The non-probabilistic nature of the sample was due to the apparent difficulties in identifying all organizations in the country [17]. In addition, obtaining opinions from workers with specific characteristics, such as IoT domain knowledge, required a non-random convenience sampling of participants, as seen in other studies with similar characteristics [18].

In this sense, all participants applying the maturity model had at least 1 year of work experience in their respective organizations, spanning diverse industrial, technological, and educational sectors with varying scales of operation. Of this sample, approximately 60% were employees of SMEs, while the remaining 40% were employees of larger companies. This distribution enabled broader comparisons of results, accurately assessing technological maturity in IoT adoption and implementation across different operational scales and levels of resource availability within organizations.

Data were collected through a structured questionnaire (ATLANTIS implementation) targeting employees of the aforementioned organizations who performed daily IoT-related functions. The participants were introduced to the maturity model and the instrument through digital means, where the maturity of the organizations they belonged to was assessed using a Likert scale.

The data collection process was carried out in three major stages. The first stage consisted of the introduction of ATLANTIS and its specific items. The second stage was the self-assessment, in which each company member evaluated their organization using ATLANTIS as a frame of reference, providing first-hand data on the implementation and use of IoT across various business contexts. Finally, in the third stage, the experts' responses were compiled and analyzed to determine each organization's overall level of IoT adoption maturity, using the weighting system detailed in the next section.

2.4 ATLANTIS Weighting System

This section introduces a weighted scoring system to assess the maturity of IoT adoption in organizations, based on the ATLANTIS maturity model, which has been validated in prior research [17]. This scalable weighting system facilitates individual assessment of each metric, component, and dimension, culminating in an overall maturity score for each organization. It provides an objective assessment of IoT technology at different levels of granularity, allowing organizations to provide detailed information to improve IoT implementation and address its shortcomings.

The weighting system is objective, as it establishes the relative importance of each metric, component, and dimension to successful adoption and implementation based on expert opinion. In addition, the weighting is simple and easy to understand, emphasizing ease of use for evaluators and participating organizations, resulting in broad applicability.

Each metric is evaluated individually and assigned a score ranging from 1 to 4, depending on the level of maturity demonstrated (Table 1):

Table 1. Proposed levels in the ATLANTIS weighting system. **Source:** Original work by the authors.

Level	Score
Static	1
Reactive	2
Proactive	3
Innovative	4

Now, components representing specific functional areas within the IoT ecosystem (e.g., device management, security) are evaluated using a weighted aggregation of their constituent metrics' scores. These weights are expressed as a percentage of the total possible points in ATLANTIS. The determination of these weights was done through a process of aggregating judgments of experts ($n = 8$) with experience in IoT academia, using a survey as a data collection instrument. The resulting weights are in the next Table (Table 2).

Table 2. Distribution of the weights of each component in the weighting system for ATLANTIS. **Source:** Original work by the authors.

Component	Weight (%)
Device management	20%
Connectivity management	20%
Cloud/edge management	15%
Businesses integration management	20%
Security	15%
Compliance	5%
Contextualization	5%

The score for each component (Ci) is calculated as the sum of its individual metric scores multiplied by the component weight (Wi) (Eq. 1).

$$Ci = Wi^{*}\ \Sigma\ (Component\ metric\ score) \tag{1}$$

For dimensions, the score is the sum of all scores obtained for each metric in that dimension, yielding a dimensionless value. Finally, the organization's overall score (G) is the sum of the seven components' scores, with a maximum possible score of 100 (Eq. 2).

$$G = \Sigma\ \mathrm{Ci} \tag{2}$$

where i = 1 through 7.

3 Results

3.1 Initial Exploration of IoT Maturity

This section presents the general analysis of the results obtained from a sample of 37 AMBA companies using the ATLANTIS maturity model and the previously described weighting system (Fig. 2). In general, large companies (BCs) tend to obtain significantly higher overall scores than small and medium-sized companies. In particular, the maximum score for a large company is 54.98 (BC15) and the minimum is 0.44 (BC4), indicating considerable dispersion in digital maturity levels among large companies. In the case of SMEs, the maximum score is 41.8, and the minimum is 4.8, reflecting a high variability similar to that observed in large companies, but with lower maximum values. The above suggests that BC has a significantly higher overall score than SMEs, indicating that SMEs are more advanced in IoT technology maturity, with the difference statistically significant ($p < 0.05$).

Large companies achieved an overall average maturity score of 24.92 points, while SMEs recorded an average of 12.64 points, showing a difference of approximately 12 points on the evaluation scale. Breaking down the maturity scores by components in the BCs (Fig. 3), it is identified that the highest scores are associated with device management, connectivity management, and enterprise integration. In contrast, the compliance and contextualization components appear to yield lower scores in this type of organization. For SMEs, the components with the highest average scores are connectivity management and enterprise integration, while the compliance and contextualization components have the lowest scores, similar to what is observed in large enterprises. There is a significant gap of approximately 12 points between the two groups. Specifically, BCs scored an average of 3.12 points in the Device Management component, compared to 1.12 for SMEs, suggesting a significantly greater capacity to handle and manage IoT infrastructure among larger organizations. Connectivity Management presents one of the most pronounced gaps, with averages of 5.48 and 2.43 points for large enterprises and SMEs, respectively, indicating substantial disparities in data management capability and communication protocols.

Although the difference persists in the Cloud/Edge Management component, a less pronounced gap is observed, with large enterprises averaging 4.32 points and SMEs 2.75

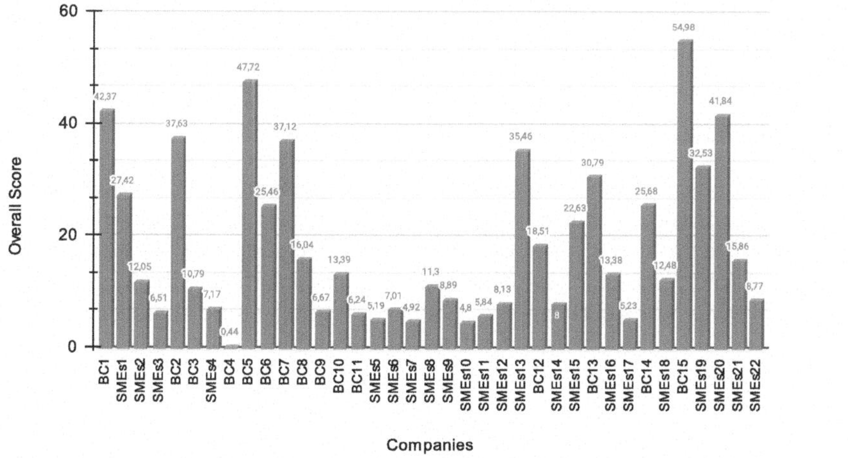

Fig. 2. The overall maturity of AMBA companies is determined using the ATLANTIS maturity model.
Source: Original work by the authors.

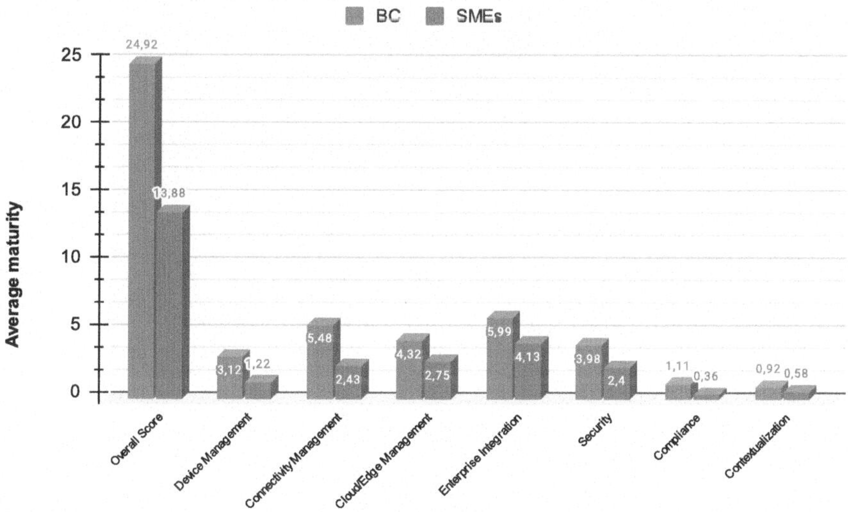

Fig. 3. IoT technological maturity is segmented by components by AMBA organizations.
Source: Original work by the authors

points. As for the Enterprise Integration component, both business groups show strong performance, averaging 5.89 points for large enterprises and 4.13 points for SMEs, suggesting greater maturity in integrating IoT into existing business processes and systems. Finally, the security component reveals a worrying gap, with large enterprises averaging 3.98 points versus 2.40 points for SMEs, which is particularly relevant considering the criticality of security in IoT implementations. Compliance is one of the weakest components for both groups, with averages of only 1.11 points for large enterprises and

0.36 points for SMEs, indicating an urgent need to improve regulatory and governance aspects related to IoT adoption.

3.2 Correlation Between the Variables of Interest

This section presents the statistical correlations (Fig. 4) among the study variables related to IoT technological maturity, measured using the ATLANTIS model as a reference framework. In this regard, prior to applying the correlation tests, the assessment of data normality using statistical tests indicated a non-parametric distribution, which justified the use of Spearman's correlation coefficient (ρ) as a measure of association.

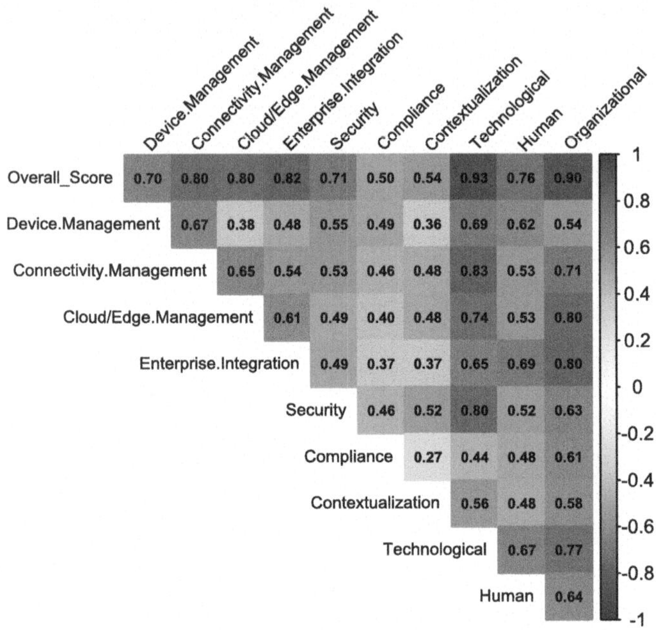

Fig. 4. Statistical correlations between the different variables studied. *Source:* Original work by the authors.

Data analysis indicates significant positive correlations between the overall maturity score and the technological (ρ = 0.92) and organizational (ρ = 0.90) dimensions. In contrast, the correlation between the overall maturity score and the human dimension is moderately high (ρ = 0.75). As for the overall score and its components, higher correlations are observed with connectivity management (ρ = 0.80) and business integration (ρ = 0.82). In contrast, the compliance and contextualization components show the weakest correlations with the overall score. Furthermore, a strong positive correlation was identified between the technological and organizational dimensions (p = 0.76), whereas the human dimension showed moderate correlations with both.

The strong correlation observed between the Technological and Organizational dimensions suggests that IoT technological development may be closely linked to organizational maturity in organizations in the AMBA. Thus, companies with high overall technological maturity tend to have well-developed technological and organizational capabilities. Although the human dimension is important, it shows weaker correlations, which could indicate a development less dependent on the other two dimensions.

Regarding the specific components, device management, connectivity management, and enterprise integration show consistently high correlations with the overall maturity score, suggesting they are critical to a company's overall maturity. This is to be expected, as these components are intrinsically linked in implementing IoT solutions, in which good device management typically requires adequate connectivity and data processing infrastructure. In contrast, the components with lower relative scores, such as compliance and contextualization, present the weakest correlations, identified as potential areas for improvement in organizations, regardless of their scale.

It is important to highlight the strong correlation between business integration and organizational dimension ($\rho = 0.80$), which reinforces the hypothesis that business integration constitutes a significant factor in organizational maturity, as defined in the ATLANTIS model. This emphasizes the importance of acquiring and integrating technology effectively into productive processes. Finally, the moderate correlations of the security component with other components suggest its cross-cutting nature, impacting various maturity dimensions without showing a predominant dependence on a single specific dimension.

Finally, to access the maturity model, you can access the following link (https://freeport.up.railway.app/).

4 Discussion of Results

This study evaluates the IoT technological maturity of different industrial organizations in the AMBA by applying the ATLANTIS maturity model. In this regard, it is important to indicate that, according to the descriptive analysis, it is observed that large companies are more advanced in terms of overall maturity compared to SMEs, reflected in higher scores in several relevant dimensions of the ATLANTIS model, which is in line with other similar studies [25]. In particular, large companies demonstrate statistically significant superiority in the device and connectivity management component, suggesting that they have better infrastructures and processes to handle the technical aspects of IoT. In contrast, no differences were found in the cloud/edge management, enterprise integration, security, and compliance components, indicating that, in these areas, SMEs and large enterprises have comparable capabilities [9], which is what differs from previous results [13], which suggested that Latin American enterprises struggle primarily with IoT organizational integration. Therefore, SMEs could optimize their device and connectivity management capabilities to achieve technological maturity levels comparable to those of large enterprises, while always considering their economic constraints. The above results can serve as a basis for developing specific strategies and public policies to improve IoT technological maturity in different types of enterprises [16].

As for the correlations, the strong relationship between the overall score and the technological components indicates that technological capabilities are a determining factor in achieving high maturity in IoT adoption in ATLANTIS [26]. Thus, companies that invest in infrastructure, data management, and connectivity are more likely to achieve higher overall maturity. Also, the strong correlation between the organizational dimension and the overall score underscores that organizational structure, processes, and culture are relevant factors for successful IoT adoption; technology alone does not guarantee maturity, as a supportive organizational environment is necessary, as indicated in [8]. This finding suggests that a successful journey towards Industry 4.0 requires more than investment in enabling technologies like IoT; it also necessitates parallel advancements in organizational structures, processes, and culture to leverage the potential of interconnected systems fully. In contrast, the moderate correlations observed with the Compliance and Contextualization components could indicate areas where AMBA companies could focus their efforts to strengthen their technological maturity, suggesting a lack of attention to regulatory and ethical issues [26] associated with IoT implementation, as well as a limited understanding of the particular environmental and operational contexts, factors that could differentiate higher levels of maturity [28].

Finally, the results of this research provide concrete empirical evidence for the IoT maturity domain in the specific context of industrial companies in a South American region, offering contextual validation of the ATLANTIS model as a valuable tool for assessing technology maturity. In addition, identifying specific maturity patterns and the correlations between the dimensions offers companies insights, allowing them to assess their strengths and weaknesses and focus their efforts on areas that require more attention [29].

5 Conclusions

This research presents a quantitative assessment of IoT technological maturity in industrial organizations in AMBA - Argentina using the ATLANTIS maturity model, providing valuable empirical evidence and enabling the identification of specific strengths and weaknesses in IoT adoption. The research revealed several significant derivations that contribute to understanding IoT adoption and implementation in industrial environments in Latin America. The main finding is that there is a heterogeneous picture, with a clear distinction in overall maturity between large enterprises and SMEs, with larger organizations demonstrating greater sufficiency, particularly in important components such as device management and connectivity, areas where SMEs have significant gaps, suggesting that the availability of resources plays an important role in achieving higher levels of IoT maturity and, consequently, readiness for broader Industry 4.0 integration. In contrast, overall maturity in the business integration component is a clear strength in both organizations, indicating that they actively incorporate IoT into their core processes.

Along these lines, a strong correlation was found between overall maturity and the technological and organizational dimensions, highlighting the interdependence between technology adoption and the company's structural readiness, suggesting that mere investment in technology does not guarantee maturity unless it is accompanied by adequate organizational adaptation. In contrast, the human dimension showed moderate correlations with other aspects, suggesting that, although important, human factors can develop independently of technical and organizational advances. Next, low correlations between the Security component and overall maturity suggest that organizations may prioritize functionality and integration over security in their IoT implementations, raising the need for policymakers and industry leaders to emphasize security in IoT adoption strategies.

Finally, future work should address this study's limitations by expanding the geographic area beyond the AMBA and including organizations from different sectors. Also, conducting longitudinal studies could provide more information on how IoT maturity evolves and the factors that influence this evolution.

References

1. Pino, A.F.S., Ruiz, P.H., Mon, A., Collazos, C.A.: Mechanisms for measuring technology maturity on the Internet of Things in enterprises: a systematic literature mapping. Internet Things. **25**, 101100 (2024). https://doi.org/10.1016/j.iot.2024.101100
2. Chen, X., et al.: Indoor photovoltaic materials and devices for self-powered Internet of Things applications. Mater Today Energy. **44**, 101621 (2024). https://doi.org/10.1016/j.mtener.2024.101621
3. Kumar, S., Tiwari, P., Zymbler, M.: Internet of Things is a revolutionary approach for future technology enhancement: a review. J. Big Data. **6**, 111 (2019). https://doi.org/10.1186/s40537-019-0268-2
4. Nagy, J., Olah, J., Erdei, E., Mate, D., Popp, J.: The role and impact of Industry 4.0 and the Internet of Things on the business strategy of the value chain-the case of Hungary. Sustainability. **10**, 3491 (2018)
5. Azrour, M., Mabrouki, J., Guezzaz, A., Kanwal, A.: Internet of Things security: challenges and key issues. Secur. Commun. Netw. **2021**, 5533843 (2021). https://doi.org/10.1155/2021/5533843
6. Brous, P., Janssen, M., Herder, P.: The dual effects of the Internet of Things (IoT): a systematic review of the benefits and risks of IoT adoption by organizations. Int. J. Inf. Manag. **51**, 101952 (2020). https://doi.org/10.1016/j.ijinfomgt.2019.05.008
7. Kulkarni, P.M., Gokhale, P., Dandannavar, P.S.: Internet of Things (IoT) adoption: challenges among Small and Medium Scale Enterprises (SMEs). In: Haldorai, A., Ramu, A., Mohanram, S., Zgheib, R. (eds) 4th EAI International Conference on Big Data Innovation for Sustainable Cognitive Computing, pp. 125–134. EAI/Springer Innovations in Communication and Computing (2023). https://doi.org/10.1007/978-3-031-07654-1_9
8. Benotmane, M., Elhari, K., Kabbaj, A.: A review & analysis of current IoT maturity & readiness models and novel proposal. Sci. Afr. **21**, e01748 (2023). https://doi.org/10.1016/j.sciaf.2023.e01748
9. Solis Pino, A.F., Ruiz, P.H., Mon, A., Collazos, C.A., Moreira, F.: Analysis of enterprise Internet of Things maturity models: a review. Appl. Sci. **14**, 9859 (2024). https://doi.org/10.3390/app14219859
10. Ahmetoglu, S., Cob, Z.C., Ali, N.: A systematic review of Internet of Things adoption in organizations: taxonomy, benefits, challenges and critical factors. Appl. Sci. Switz. **12**, 4117 (2022). https://doi.org/10.3390/app12094117
11. Jæger, B., Halse, L.L.: The IoT technological maturity assessment scorecard: a case study of Norwegian manufacturing companies. In: Lödding, H., Riedel, R., Thoben, K.-D., von Cieminski, G., Kiritsis, D. (eds) Advances in Production Management Systems. The Path to Intelligent, Collaborative and Sustainable Manufacturing, pp. 143–150. Springer International Publishing, Cham (2017)

12. Ayalu, G., Abbay, A.G., Azadi, H.: The role of micro- and small-scale enterprises in enhancing sustainable community livelihood: Tigray, Ethiopia. Environ. Dev. Sustain. **25**, 7561–7584 (2023). https://doi.org/10.1007/s10668-022-02359-7
13. Parra-Sánchez, D.T., Talero-Sarmiento, L.H., Guerrero, C.D.: Assessment of ICT policies for digital transformation in Colombia: technology readiness for IoT adoption in SMEs in the trading sector. Digit Policy Regul. Gov. **23**, 412–431 (2021). https://doi.org/10.1108/DPRG-09-2020-0120
14. Grandon, E.E., Aravena Ibarra, A., Araya Guzmán, S., Ramírez-Correa, P.E., Alfaro-Pérez, J.: Internet of Things: factors that influence its adoption among Chilean SMEs [Internet de las Cosas: Factores que Influyen su adopción en Pymes chilenas]. In: Iberian Conference on Information Systems and Technologies, CISTI, pp. 1–6 (2018)
15. Mishrif, A., Khan, A.: Technology adoption as survival strategy for small and medium enterprises during COVID-19. J. Innov. Entrep. **12**, 53 (2023). https://doi.org/10.1186/s13731-023-00317-9
16. Pino, A.S., Ruiz, P., Mon, A., Collazos, C.: A bibliometric analysis of the landscape of measuring technology maturity in the enterprise Internet of Things. Int. J. Electr. Comput. Eng. IJECE. **14**, 4697–4713 (2024) https://doi.org/10.11591/ijece.v14i4.pp4697-4713
17. Pino, A.F.S., Ruiz, P.H., Mon, A., Collazos, C.A.: ATLANTIS: a multidimensional maturity model for evaluating the adoption of the Internet of Things in industrial SMEs. Internet Things. **29**, 101457 (2024). https://doi.org/10.1016/j.iot.2024.101457
18. Mon, A., Giorgio, H.R.D.: Analysis of Industry 4.0 products in small and medium enterprises. Procedia Comput. Sci. **200**, 914–923 (2022). https://doi.org/10.1016/j.procs.2022.01.289
19. Solis, A.F., DA, R.l., Campo Ceballos, D.A., Gaviria López, C.A.: Correlación del contenido de clorofila foliar de la especie Coffea arabica con índices espectrales en imágenes. Biotecnol. En. El Sect. Agropecu. Agroindustrial. **19**, 51–68 (2021) https://doi.org/10.18684/bsaa.v19.n2.2021.1536
20. Hatton, M.: A new taxonomy for IoT reveals new roles and opportunities. Transforma Insights (2023)
21. Bravo, V.: Argentine energy policy during the period 2014–2018. In: Oil and Natural Gas Economy in Argentina: The case of Fracking, pp. 79–248. Springer International Publishing, Cham (2021)
22. Ha, J., Kose, M.A., Ohnsorge, F.: Inflation in Emerging and Developing Economies: Evolution, Drivers, and Policies. World Bank Publications, Washington (2019)
23. Becerra, M., Marino, S., Mastrini, G.: Mapping digital media: Argentina. Buenos Aires (2012)
24. Sánchez, M.A., Ramoscelli, G.: Value creation from the internet of things: exploratory study in Buenos Aires province. Rev Cient. Vis. Futuro. **22**, 170–187 (2018)
25. Zamani, S.Z.: Small and Medium Enterprises (SMEs) facing an evolving technological era: a systematic literature review on the adoption of technologies in SMEs. Eur. J. Innov. Manag. **25**, 735–757 (2022). https://doi.org/10.1108/EJIM-07-2021-0360
26. Lezama-Nicolás, R., Rodríguez-Salvador, M., Río-Belver, R., Bildosola, I.: A bibliometric method for assessing technological maturity: the case of additive manufacturing. Scientometrics. **117**, 1425–1452 (2018). https://doi.org/10.1007/s11192-018-2941-1
27. Bouchikhi, M.E., Weerts, S., Clavien, C.: The Internet of Things deployed for occupational health and safety purposes: a qualitative study of opportunities and ethical issues. PLoS One. **19**, e0315671 (2024). https://doi.org/10.1371/journal.pone.0315671

28. United Nations Educational, Scientific and Cultural Organization (UNESCO), World Commission on the Ethics of Scientific Knowledge and Technology (COMEST): The ethical implications of the Internet of Things (IoT): report adopted in September 2021. UNESCO Publishing, Paris (2023)
29. Pino, A.F.S., Pizarro, D.S.M., Ruiz, P.H., Agredo-Delgado, V., Collazos, C.A., Moreira, F.: Implementing TinyML in Internet of Things devices: a systematic literature review. J. Ind. Inf. Integr. **50**, 101065 (2026). https://doi.org/10.1016/j.jii.2026.101065

Identification of SME Users in Industry 4.0

Alicia Mon(✉), Horacio René Del Giorgio, Silvana Padovano, and María Laura Pepe

Universidad Nacional de La Matanza, San Justo, Buenos Aires, Argentina
{amon,hdelgiorgio,spadovano,mpepe}@unlam.edu.ar

Abstract. The Industry 4.0 paradigm means a revolution in production processes. Companies' adoption of technologies depends on how they assimilate and incorporate new technologies into current processes with the users who operate them in the real-life context of use. This paper presents a study about the state of technology adoption in Small and Medium-sized Enterprises (SMEs) in Latin America, analyzing the ICT products implemented in each of the company's functional areas that interact with the people who operate them and identifying the knowledge and capabilities of actual users for each functional area. For this purpose, the InTIC's® index was used and allowed the measure of a total of 106 companies in different countries and production contexts, from 2020 to 2024. The analysis reveals that 64% of the companies studied have basic technologies, and that user skills vary depending on the functional area in which they operate the technologies in the execution of daily production tasks.

Keywords: ICT Index · Industry 4.0 · Digital Transformation · SMEs · User Profile

1 Introduction

The digital transformation in industrial production has drastically changed production methods in recent years, in terms of internal company processes, value chains, energy use, as well as the necessary skills and knowledge of workers in the different branches of production, generating a transformation in the integration of production areas through digitalization and the creation of new communication channels [1, 2]. This new paradigm influences the strategies and operations of companies, as well as the way in which organizations and consumers interact and exchange value, also allowing the efficient adoption of personalized production and innovation in business models [3–5]. Thus, rapid adaptation of companies to these new technologies is crucial to maintain competitiveness and make the most of the opportunities offered by their implementation in the transformation of products, services, operations and even business models [6]. The success of their adoption will depend on the way in which such technologies are assimilated and incorporated into current traditional production systems.

The ICT products adopted by companies that allow the execution of tasks in different areas require attention to the characteristics of the users, as a basis for advancing in the

H. Luna-García et al. (Eds.): HCI-COLLAB 2025, CCIS 2850, pp. 162–175, 2027.
https://doi.org/10.1007/978-3-032-31223-5_12

analysis of their interaction and in the design of technological products focused on specific ways of operation [7].

Industry 4.0 requires workers to become users of new technologies, performing multiple tasks to adapt to the needs of the industry, while also requiring technological knowledge of a wide range of technological platforms and software applications, imposing production rates previously unknown.

Likewise, training workers in each of the functional areas of a company requires training in specific technical activities combined with broad digital training that considers them as users of the technologies implemented for their daily work and the execution of tasks.

From this perspective, user satisfaction is of moderate importance, given that these are workers who must be trained to solve tasks performed with available technologies, and it is not a matter of choice. Furthermore, knowledge retention is achieved through frequent use.

Knowing users involves identifying their prior knowledge level, how often they use the required technology, what their objectives are, and estimating the impact of their mistakes, considering fatigue, stress, and burnout, as well as the context of use. This will allow users to level their skill and standardize tasks and needs [8].

To identify the specific features of this type of user, a study was conducted to assess the current state of development of Information and Communications Technologies (ICTs) in the manufacturing industry in Latin America, specifically in Argentina, Brazil, Colombia, and Mexico.

This article shows the partial results of a research in which the InTIC's® Index [9] was applied, along with a set of induction, survey and measurement instruments that allowed for the evaluation of the level of adoption of Software, Hardware and Infrastructure products by functional areas, and the main characteristics of the users according to the products and tasks they perform in the different areas.

2 Material and Methods

2.1 Companies' Evaluation Methodology

The evaluation model applied focused on the InTIC's ® index [9], which is structured from the detection of technological products in the Industries and their intersection with their functional areas.

The model evaluates the identified typologies of ICTs implemented in different functional areas within industries, where these technologies fulfill specific functions in the areas where they are implemented. These generic functional areas that the index differentiates are organized into 3 axes, production, logistics and sales for each company depending on the branch of activity it develops and 4 transversal areas that interact with the different functions of the axes. This structure of the index is based on Michael Porter's Value Chain Model [10].

According to the index applied, the Functional Areas identified for industrial manufacturing companies fulfill the basic functions described below:

- *Logistics*: it is an area in which the tasks of entry and exit of materials for production are carried out, as well as the distribution and delivery of what is produced.

- *Production*: it constitutes the area where the production process itself is developed, from the entry of raw materials to the end of the process where the merchandise is ready for distribution. Daily Operations activities can be divided into different production lines within the same organization. In the manufacturing industry, the production function is the core of a company.
- *Sales*: is an area that includes the Sales functions of self-manufactured products as well as Marketing and Commercialization tasks.
- *Management*: constitutes the area in which the decision-making functions are developed, based on the strategic vision of the organization that includes overall management, as well as investment decisions in Infrastructure and Human Resources.
- *Accounting and Finance*: in this area, the economic, financial and accounting operating activities of an organization that determine the operational capacity of the production function are developed.
- *Engineering*: this area includes the design and development activities of products and processes in the different production lines. These functions constitute the axis and support of the Production area and the technological decisions on the operation of the entire company.
- *Purchases*: it is an area that includes the functions of acquiring supplies, raw materials, equipment for all self-manufactured products, as well as the implementation of production processes.

The technological products analyzed by the index are differentiated into 3 ICT components: Software, Hardware and Infrastructure. These 3 components group the different products according to the specificities of each type of technology [11] and are valued, among other options, according to their degree of development in terms of the time they exist as tools used in the market, whether the type of support they provide offers sensitive information to companies, what is the complexity of the problem they solve, whether their use impacts an improvement in processes or on the control of processes, whether it improves the efficiency in the use of resources, whether it improves productivity and whether it reduces operating costs.

This rating may be "1" for a basic contribution for products that have been on the market for a long time, "5" for an average contribution for those products that have been on the market for a while but are still available, and "10" for an advanced contribution for those innovative technology products or those that emerge as new products on the market to be implemented in industries [12].

Once these technological products have been identified and their intersection with each of the areas described, the index allows for the calculation of a score by levels of technological development, with the sum of the weighting of each of the ICT products in a particular industry, which are implemented in each Functional Area, as shown in the following formula (1):

$$Index = \sum Contrib\ (1) + \sum Contrib\ (5) + \sum Contrib\ (10) \tag{1}$$

The sum of the contributions of the scores of all the products allows to determine 3 levels of technological development:

- Basic Level (range between 0 and 120): For companies that have implemented older technology products, each of which adds 1 point.

- Medium Level (range between 121 and 715): For companies that have implemented mid-level technology products, each of which adds 5 points.
- Advanced Level (range between 716 and 1375): For companies that have implemented advanced technology products, each of which adds 10 points.

Not all products included in the Advanced level are cutting-edge, but they are essential for the integration and operation of the others. Therefore, it is possible to extract the subset of Industry 4.0-specific products from this set.

The index's different functional areas allow for the identification of technological products implemented and working in a particular company's areas, as well as the several users operating in those areas with clearly differentiated capabilities and roles.

The ICT products identified by the index are 74 in the different functional areas, within which, those corresponding to the Basic Level are 20, those of the Medium Level are 30 and those of the Advanced Level are 24. As said before, not all the products included in this last Advanced level are of the latest generation, but they are essential for the integration and operation of the others. Therefore, the set of products of the Advanced level defined by the index includes the technological products that make up the industry 4.0 [12].

The first application study of the index was conducted in the municipality of La Matanza, Buenos Aires, Argentina, during the 2019–2021 period. The analysis of the results shows that, of the 45 industries surveyed, 62.50% were at the basic level, 35.00% at the intermediate level, and only 2.50% at the advanced level [11].

Subsequently, in 2023, the index was applied in a collaborative research project between groups from different Latin American countries, and a survey was carried out in a set of 5 companies in Brazil, in the city of São Paulo, 7 in Colombia, in the Cauca region and 15 in Mexico, in the city of Puebla. The results of the application of the index to that set of companies, added to the 45 previously surveyed in Argentina with the same index, allowed to analyze that 64% of the surveyed companies were at a Basic Level, 30.5% at a Medium Level and 5.5% were located at the Advanced Level of technological development [13].

Finally, during 2023/2024 the Index was applied in 34 metalworking companies in Olavarría, Buenos Aires, yielding a result of 24% of companies located at the Basic Level and 76% of companies located at the Medium Level [14].

Based on the index and the set of studies conducted, a total of 106 companies were surveyed using the methods described, using non-statistical random samples, in different regions of Latin America. This allowed for a study of the level of technological development of the companies and a focus on the analysis of users identified from the technological products implemented in each functional area of a company.

2.2 User Analysis Methodology

From observation, focus groups, and user interviews, it was possible to identify the tasks they perform and the work processes to understand the frequencies and sequences of tasks, roles, and the work environment, to specify requirements [8, 15]. In addition, it is possible to go deeper into the interests, motivations, and expectations of users in relation to future development. With information about users, it is possible to define user profiles based on common attributes (information needs, experience, knowledge, access conditions) [15].

In this study, a user analysis was conducted using the ICT index matrix, which separates a company's activities by functional area, identifying the technological products that enable the performance of productive activities. This separation by functional area allows for an analysis of the tasks performed by employees as they are the users of the technologies implemented for that function.

To this end, the products implemented in each area of the 106 companies surveyed were identified, and the level of technological development of each was analyzed in the context of the Latin American SMEs studied.

Based on this analysis of the implemented ICT products, a subset of 10 companies was examined to perform a task analysis in the different functional areas.

To understand the users and their requirements, different information gathering techniques were used in combination [15].

Depending on the different user analysis techniques available, a combination of these is used according to the variables involved in each case, as shown in Table 1.

Table 1. User analysis techniques by variables - Source: Own elaboration

Techniques	Demographics	Skills	Accessibility	Competences	Tasks
Questionnaires	x	x	x		
Interviews	x		x		x
Focus Groups	x				x
User Tests		x	x		x
Non-Participant Observation				X	x

To analyze Industry 4.0 users, the following techniques were applied: questionnaires for demographic variables, non-participant observation for task analysis, and a structured ICT index questionnaire to identify ICT products in use.

3 Analysis of Results

The surveys conducted in the 106 companies made it possible to identify the ICT products implemented in each of the areas where they interact with the people who operate them. The main features of the companies surveyed reveal comparable data that highlight common generic aspects.

The results on the size of the companies surveyed can be seen through Fig. 1, the predominance of micro-enterprises with less than 15 employees (51%) and small companies with a range of 16 to 60 employees (25%), medium-sized companies represent 15%, while large companies represent 9%.

Regarding the technological development level of the 106 companies surveyed, as shown in Fig. 2, the results show that the vast majority have a Basic to Medium level of

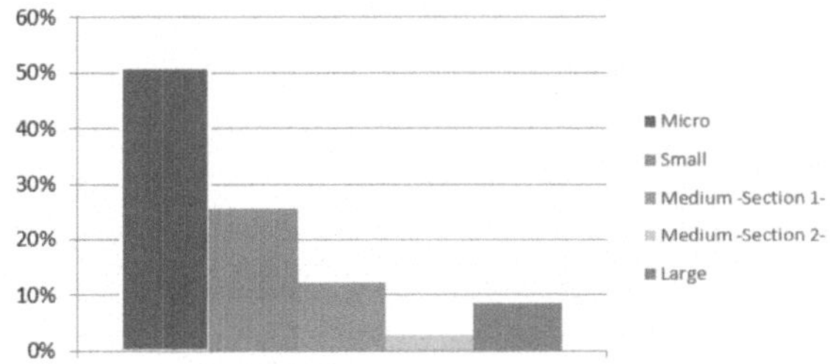

Fig. 1. Distribution according to Size (Total – 106 Industries)*Source:* Own elaboration

development. A closer look at the component data reveals that they are distributed almost equally across the different company sizes; this means that a Microenterprise does not necessarily have a Basic level of development and a Large Enterprise an Advanced level, as might have been expected prior to this analysis.

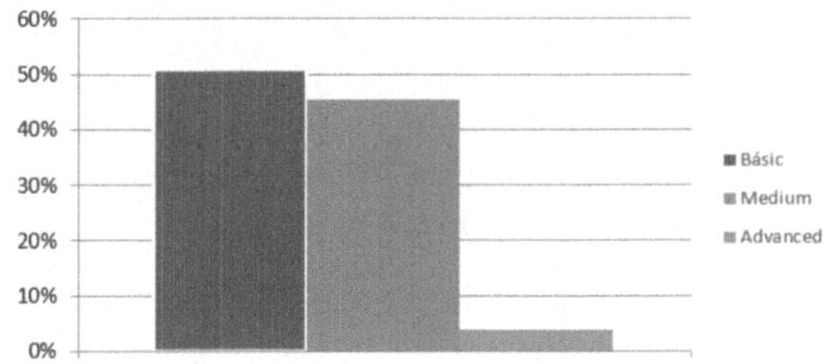

Fig. 2. Distribution according to Score (Total – 106 Industries)*Source:* Own elaboration

Once the overall level of ICT products available in the surveyed companies has been introduced, the technological products are then analyzed disaggregated by functional area, according to their level, as determined by the index. The results obtained in each of the functional areas considered in the study are shown below, given that product users vary significantly in each area.

Logistics Area: The implemented ICTs allow users to perform warehouse management tasks, fleet management, order generation and transportation of items, as well as communication with suppliers, tracking materials and deliveries, and inventory management. An analysis of the technologies applied in the companies surveyed for the Logistics area shows that 53% correspond to Basic technologies, 35% to Medium technologies, and only 12% correspond to Advanced technologies (linked to I4.0), as shown in Fig. 3:

The Advanced Level products that companies have implemented in this functional area and that are operated by users are: Business Intelligence (Cubes, Data Warehouse); IP Telephone Switchboards; Control (PDM); Shared Disks; Computer-Aided Manufacturing (CAM); Big Data Tools; 3D Printers; Computer-Aided Engineering (CAE); Artificial Intelligence – Machine Learning; Advertising Software; Plotters; Programming and Planning (MRP); Augmented Reality; Virtual Reality; Networks for the Internet of Things (IoT); Robots; Sensors; Automation Control Systems; Embedded Systems;

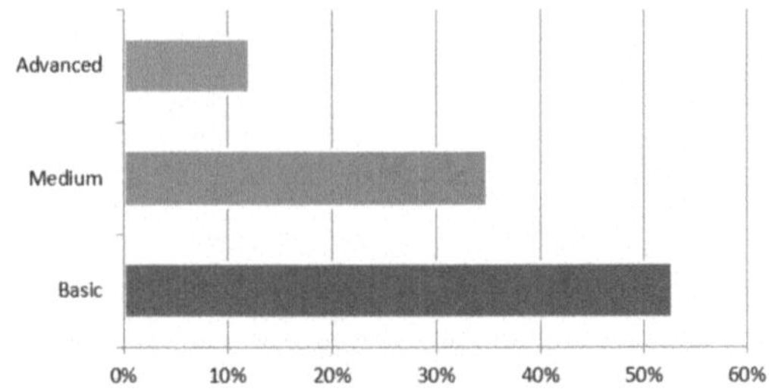

Fig. 3. Distribution according to Score in Logistics*Source:* Own elaboration

SCADA Systems; Energy Control Software; Control Panel/Balanced Score Card and Video Conferencing.

Production Area: The ICT products implemented in companies allow users to carry out the transformation of raw materials into finished products to be sold for consumption or as input for other products in a value chain. ICT products in this area enable the automation of operations, the replacement of human tasks with robots, as well as production control and planning, the reduction of material losses, and quality control on production lines. An analysis of the technologies applied in the surveyed companies for the Production area shows that 46% are Basic technologies, 34% are Medium technologies, and 20% are Advanced technologies, as shown in Fig. 4.

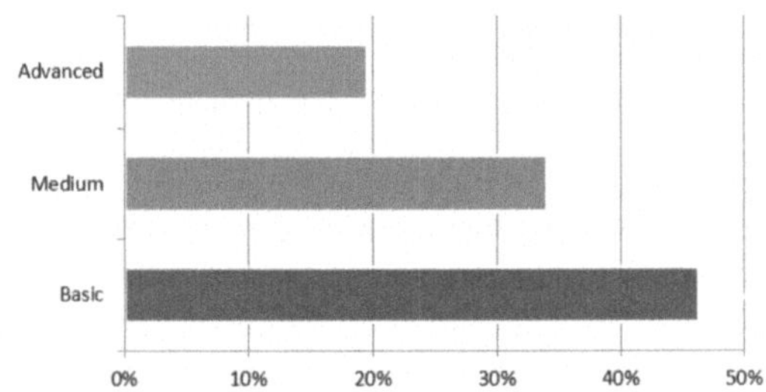

Fig. 4. Distribution according to Score in Production*Source:* Own elaboration

The Advanced Level products that companies have implemented in this functional area and that are operated by users are: Business Intelligence (Cubes, Data Warehouse); IP Telephone Switchboards; Control (PDM); Shared Disks; Computer-Aided Manufacturing (CAM); Big Data Tools; 3D Printers; Computer-Aided Engineering (CAE); Artificial Intelligence – Machine Learning; Advertising Software; Plotters; Programming and Planning (MRP); Augmented Reality; Virtual Reality; Networks for the Internet of Things (IoT); Robots; Sensors; Automation Control Systems; Embedded Systems; SCADA Systems; Energy Control Software; Control Panel/Balanced Score Card and Video Conferencing.

Sales Area: The ICTs adopted in companies allow users to perform sales tasks through different distribution channels in the value chain, including sales through e-commerce and digital marketing, as well as the management of information on market prices, customer relations, and commercial trends. When analyzing the technologies applied in companies in the Sales area, 53% are Basic technologies, 34% are Medium technologies, and 13% are Advanced technologies, as shown in Fig. 5.

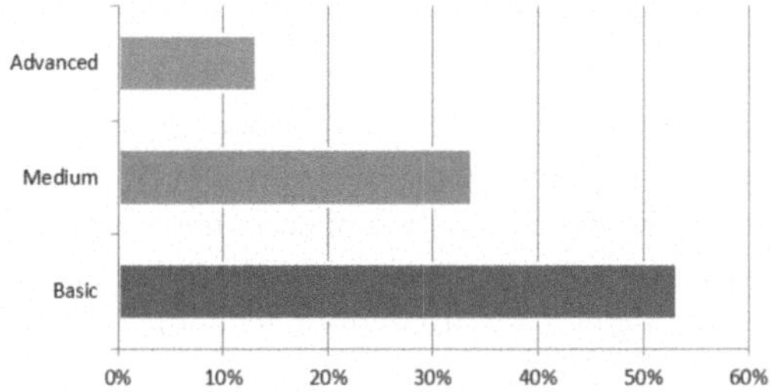

Fig. 5. Distribution according to Score in Sales*Source:* Own elaboration

The Advanced Level products that companies have implemented in this functional area and that are operated by users are: Business Intelligence (Cubes, Data Warehouse); IP Telephone Switchboards; Control (PDM); Shared Disks; Computer-Aided Manufacturing (CAM); Big Data Tools; 3D Printers; Computer-Aided Engineering (CAE); Artificial Intelligence – Machine Learning; Advertising Software; Plotters; Programming and Planning (MRP); Augmented Reality; Virtual Reality; Networks for the Internet of Things (IoT); Robots; Sensors; Automation Control Systems; Embedded Systems; Energy Control Software; Control Panel/Balanced Score Card and Video Conferencing.

Management Area: Business models and decision-making constitute the core functions of this area. The ICT products adopted by companies allow users to manage data sets and the information necessary for decision-making, business planning, and the management of other areas of the organizational structure. When analyzing the technologies applied in the companies surveyed for the Management area, 55% correspond to Basic technologies, 32% to Medium technologies, and 13% to Advanced technologies, as shown in Fig. 6.

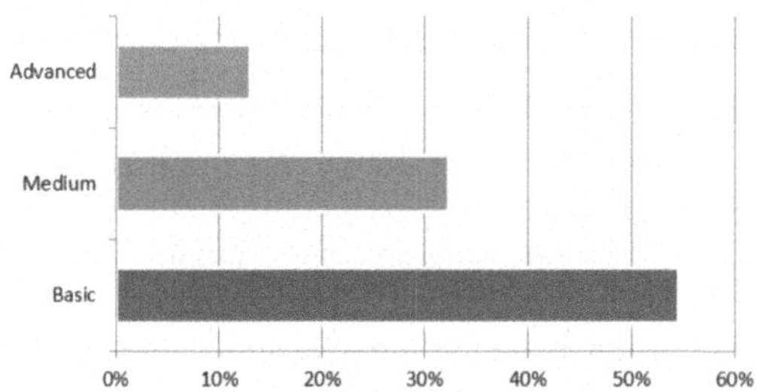

Fig. 6. Distribution according to Score in Management*Source:* Own elaboration

The Advanced Level products that companies have implemented in this functional area and that are operated by users for decision-making are: Business Intelligence

(Cubes, Data Warehouse); IP Telephone Switchboards; Control (PDM); Shared Disks; Computer-Aided Manufacturing (CAM); Big Data Tools; 3D Printers; Computer-Aided Engineering (CAE); Artificial Intelligence – Machine Learning; Advertising Software; Plotters; Programming and Planning (MRP); Augmented Reality; Virtual Reality; Networks for the Internet of Things (IoT); Robots; Sensors; Automation Control Systems; Embedded Systems; Energy Control Software; Control Panel/Balanced Score Card and Video Conferencing.

Accounting and Finance Area: The ICTs adopted in companies allow users to perform accounting tasks related to the purchase of supplies, sales of products, cost analysis, as well as financial management and automation of certain accounting records. When analyzing the technologies applied in companies in the Accounting and Finance area, 54% correspond to Basic technologies, 34% to Medium technologies, and 12% to Advanced technologies, as shown in Fig. 7.

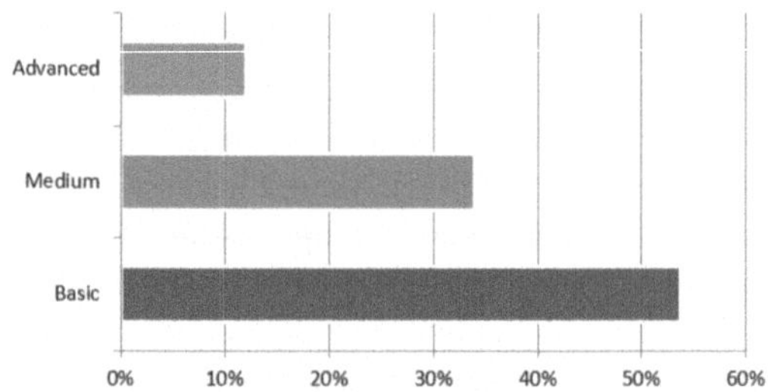

Fig. 7. Distribution according to Score in Accounting and Finance*Source:* Own elaboration

The Advanced Level products that companies have implemented in this functional area and that are operated by users are: Business Intelligence (Cubes, Data Warehouse); IP Telephone Switchboards; Control (PDM); Shared Disks; Computer-Aided Manufacturing (CAM); Big Data Tools; 3D Printers; Computer-Aided Engineering (CAE); Artificial Intelligence – Machine Learning; For Advertising; Programming and Planning (MRP); Augmented Reality; Virtual Reality; Networks for the Internet of Things (IoT); Robots; Sensors; Automation Control Systems; Embedded Systems; SCADA Systems; Energy Control Software; Control Panel/Balanced Score Card and Video Conferencing.

Engineering Area: The ICT products implemented in companies allow users to perform activities such as production process design, traceability, fault detection, new product design, rapid prototyping, and raw material control. An analysis of the technologies applied by companies in the Engineering area shows that 48% are Basic technologies, 35% are Medium technologies, and 17% are Advanced technologies, as shown in Fig. 8.

The Advanced Level products that companies have implemented in this functional area and that are operated by users are: Business Intelligence (Cubes, Data Warehouse); IP Telephone Switchboards; Control (PDM); Shared Disks; Computer-Aided Manufacturing (CAM); Big Data Tools; 3D Printers; Computer-Aided Engineering (CAE); Artificial Intelligence – Machine Learning; Advertising Software; Plotters; Programming and Planning (MRP); Augmented Reality; Virtual Reality; Networks for the Internet

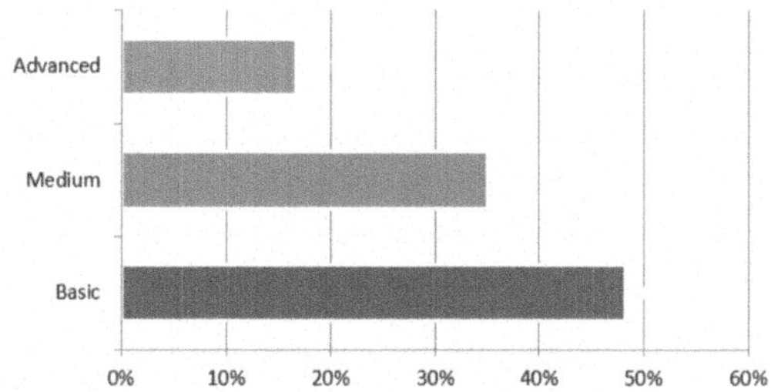

Fig. 8. Distribution according to Score in Engineering*Source:* Own elaboration

of Things (IoT); Robots; Sensors; Automation Control Systems; Embedded Systems; SCADA Systems; Energy Control Software; Control Panel/Balanced Score Card and Video Conferencing.

Purchases Area: The ICTs adopted in companies allow users who operate them to perform purchasing tasks through different channels in the value chain, as well as manage information on market prices and supplier relationships. When analyzing the technologies applied in companies in the Purchasing area, 58% correspond to Basic technologies, 31% to Medium technologies, and 11% to Advanced technologies, as shown in Fig. 9.

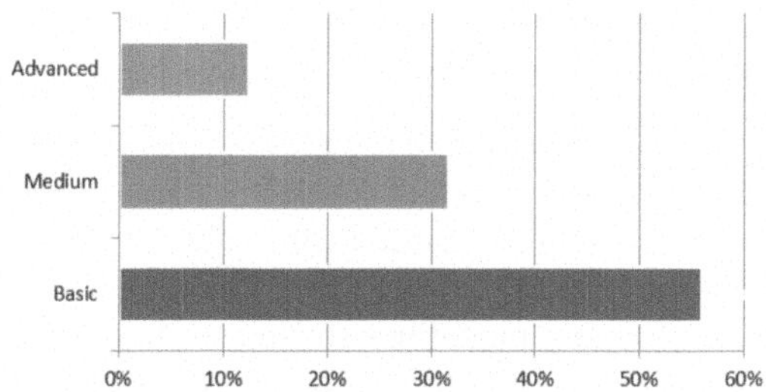

Fig. 9. Distribution according to Score in Purchases*Source:* Own elaboration

The Advanced Level products that companies have implemented in this functional area and that are operated by users are: Business Intelligence (Cubes, Data Warehouse); IP Telephone Switchboards; Control (PDM); Shared Disks; Computer-Aided Manufacturing (CAM); Big Data Tools; 3D Printers; Computer-Aided Engineering (CAE); Artificial Intelligence – Machine Learning; Advertising Software; Plotters; Programming and Planning (MRP); Augmented Reality; Virtual Reality; Networks for the Internet of Things (IoT); Robots; Sensors; Automation Control Systems; Embedded Systems; SCADA Systems; Energy Control Software; Control Panel/Balanced Score Card and Video Conferencing.

As can be seen, the Engineering and Production areas centralize the Advanced Level products. The scope of distribution is highly specialized, making users' skills and prior work experience relevant.

3.1 Analysis of results: Characterization of users by Functional Area

Demographic variables
People differ in the way they learn, think, and solve problems. This is related to their age, gender, physical and cognitive abilities, education, cultural or ethnic background, training, motivation, goals, and personality, and impacts usability [8]. Since the dissemination area is highly specialized, and because the users have recognized profiles and determinable knowledge [15], the following demographic variables were defined for analysis:

Age: People who work in an industry correspond to the economically active group (15 to 64 years old) [16] and, unless there are interns with a medium level of education, they should also be of legal age (18 years old). In the case of managerial levels, the average age in Argentina is 35 years old or older [17] where greater variability is detected is at the operational level, where there are positions that require less or no work experience or previous training. At this point, age determines the historical generation to which each person belongs, with Generation Z (born in the late 20th and early 21st centuries) known as the first "digital natives", which is distinguished from the previous ones by its exclusive characteristics, such as skills in adaptation and use of technology, rejection of traditional ways of working, among others [18].

Gender: The gender variable is irrelevant because these are technologies that require the performance of technical or professional tasks, aimed at a specialized audience in each functional area. It is the specific productive activities in each functional area, and not gender, that are linked to functionality or user experience.

Educational Level: The adoption of technologies for the performance of work functions is impacted by the existence of digital capabilities and skills, which is associated with the training of people [19]. In this variable, the educational level of workers determines the training basis for adapting to the use of technologies in the performance of their tasks. Likewise, the training modalities (technical, humanistic, natural sciences, amongst others) impact the capacities and skills for their adaptation to the context of use. The functional area of Engineering has been identified as the one that requires the highest educational level, while the areas of Production and Logistics have the lowest training requirements.

Work Experience: This variable affects knowledge of the tasks to be performed or the use of technology specific to the functional area of performance. It is a variable that allows determining users' prior knowledge, frequency of use, and the skill categories into which users can be grouped (basic, medium, advanced). It has been identified that the Production area requires the most experience in performing specific tasks in each production unit. The different functional areas require generic experience to varying degrees.

User Skills: Users' interface skills and application proficiency are identified through user testing and observation of users using the software. This can be used to classify users as having basic, medium, and advanced skills. Different functional areas require users with different skill levels to perform their tasks.

Basic Skills: This refers to those using the system for the first time, but there are two situations: they may have little knowledge of the task or interface concepts, or they may have good knowledge of the task but little knowledge of the interface concepts.

Medium Skills: These are expert but intermittent users of a variety of systems, given that they are familiar with the task and several interface concepts, but have some questions or require assistance in using certain more specific or less common functions.

Advanced Skills: These are for users who are fully familiar with task and interface concepts and seek to complete their work quickly, thus demanding response speed and accuracy from the system or application.

The results of the study allow us to identify each of these variables for users in the different functional areas according to a categorization that allows us to evaluate the level of importance for each case, as shown in Table 2.

Table 2. Demographic variables - Source: Own elaboration

Demography	Management	Accounting and Finance	Engineering	Purchases	Logistics	Production	Sales
Age	SR						
Gender	NR	NR	NR	NR	NR	NR	NR
Educational Level	HR	MR	HR	SR	SR	PR	SR
Work Experience	HR	MR	HR	MR	SR	SR	SR
Skills	Medium	Advanced	Advanced	Medium	Basic	Basic	Medium

The evaluation assigns a categorization that assumes the following values:
HR = Highly relevant
MR = Medium relevant
SR = Slightly relevant
NR = Not relevant

This contributes to understanding users' goals and needs and complements knowledge of the tasks they perform and the context of use, to define requirements.

4 Conclusions

The study introduced in this article was conducted using a survey using the ICT index for 106 industrial companies in Latin America from 2020 to 2024. A methodology designed to evaluate the technological capabilities of industrial SMEs and identify their users by functional area and type of task they perform was applied, allowing for a detailed study of some of the demographic variables that distinguish them.

The results show a vision of the integration of Industry 4.0 technologies in SMEs, as well as their users and the ways of existing interaction with the specific technologies with which they operate.

The survey conducted in these 106 companies reveals a predominance of basic and mid-range (medium) solutions in most cases. While a progressive incorporation of advanced Industry 4.0 tools is observed, their implementation is still limited, regardless of company size. This finding contrasts with the idea that larger companies achieve greater levels of technological maturity, suggesting that ICT adoption depends on multiple factors.

Furthermore, the study of user demographics, differentiated by functional area, has allowed us to identify some significant traits, with work experience and skills being the most distinctive variables to analyze when designing technological products for these industries.

These results provide a diagnosis of the current state of digital transformation in industrial SMEs and the importance of focusing the development and implementation of technologies on the users who operate them, given that productivity levels and the success of the transformation will depend on them, considering their specific needs.

References

1. Saavedra Sueldo, C., Perez Colo, I., De Paula, M., Villar, S.A., Acosta, G.G.: ROS-based architecture for fast digital twin development of smart manufacturing robotized systems. Ann. Oper. Res. **322**(1), 75–99 (2022). https://doi.org/10.1007/s10479-022-04759-4
2. Osorio-Gallego, C., Londoño-Metaute, J., López-Zapata, E.: Analysis of factors that influence the ICT adoption by SMEs in Colombia. Intang. Cap. **12**(2), 666–732 (2016)
3. Ávila-Guerrero, F.M., Bernal Díaz, I.V., Monroy Gómez, D.A.: Transformación digital empresarial: revisión de producciones investigativas 2017 – 2021. Rev. Venez. Gerenc. **28**(101), 282–296 (2023). https://doi.org/10.52080/rvgluz.28.101.18
4. Rico-Bautista, D., et al.: Key technology adoption indicators for smart universities: a preliminary proposal. In: Nagar, A.K., Jat, D.S., Marín-Raventós, G., Mishra, D.K. (eds.) Intelligent Sustainable Systems. Lecture Notes in Networks and Systems, vol. 333. Springer, Singapore (2022). https://doi.org/10.1007/978-981-16-6309-3_61
5. Aires, M.D.O., Moraes Rosa, A.C., Mattei Gyori, C.A., Gaby Reis, C.R., Buttignon, K.: Indústria 4.0: a manufatura aditiva como ferramenta de inovação e otimização. Brazilian. J. Bus. **1**(4), 1821–1833 (2019)
6. Trujillo Valdiviezo, G., Rodríguez Alegre, L., Mejía Ayala, D., López Padilla, R.: Transformación digital en América Latina: una revisión sistemática. Rev. Venez. Gerenc. **27**(100), 1519–1536 (2022). https://doi.org/10.52080/rvgluz.27.100.15
7. Collazos, C., Ortega, M., Granollers, A., Rusu, C., Gutierrez, F.L.: Human-computer interaction in Ibero-America: academic, research, and professional issues. IT Prof. **18**, 8–11 (2016). https://doi.org/10.1109/MITP.2016.38
8. Shneiderman, B., Plaisant, C., Cohen, A., Jacobs, S., Elmqvist, N., Diakopoulos, M.: Designing the User Interface: Strategies for Effective Human-Computer. Pearson, Boston (2016)
9. Del Giorgio, H., Mon, A.: Las TICs en las Industrias. Universidad Nacional de La Matanza. Buenos Aires, Argentina (2019). https://indicetics.unlam.edu.ar/es-ar/pdf/libros/Las_TICs_en_las_Industrias.pdf

10. Porter, M.: Competitive Advantage: Creating and Sustaining Superior Performance. The Free Press, Nueva York (1985)
11. Mon, A., Del Giorgio, H.: Analysis of Industry 4.0 products in small and medium enterprises. In: International Conference on Industry 4.0 and Smart Manufacturing (ISM-2021) (2021)
12. Mon, A., Del Giorgio, H.: Technological transformation model for SMEs. In: International Conference on Industry 4.0 and Smart Manufacturing (ISM-2022) (2022)
13. Mon, A., et al.: Industria 4.0 en el contexto latinoamericano: Tendencias y Retos hacia una mejor interacción del Ser Humano con la Tecnología. In: Proceedings of IX Iberoamerican Conference on Human Computer Interaction, pp. 93–97. Universidad Nacional de La Matanza. Buenos Aires, Argentina (2023)
14. Roark, G., De Paula, M., Sueldo, C., Perez Colo, I., Acosta, G.: Transformación Digital en PyMEs Metalmecánicas de Olavarría. Desafíos y Oportunidades. Universidad Nacional del Centro de la Provincia de Buenos Aires – Olavarría – Facultad de Ingeniería (2024). isbn:978-950-658-620-1
15. Gil, E.P., de Lera Tatjer, E., Monjo Palau, A.: Usuarios y sistemas interactivos. FUOC, Barcelona (2009)
16. Argentina.gob.ar: Argentina, nuestro país: Grupos etarios de la población. https://www.argentina.gob.ar/pais/poblacion/proyecciones (2022)
17. Escuela de Negocios, Universidad Torcuato Di Tella: Los perfiles de los gerentes de Argentina y la región: Di Tella en los medios. https://www.utdt.edu/ver_nota_prensa.php?id_nota_prensa=5335&id_item_menu=6 (2011)
18. Maioli, E., Marina, F.: Nuevas generaciones y empleo. Características psico-sociales de las generaciones Z y su inserción en las estructuras organizacionales asociadas al empleo (CABA, 2016). J. Cienc. Soc. Fac. Cienc. Soc. Univ. Palermo. **8**, 88–98 (2016)
19. Comisión Económica para América Latina y el Caribe (CEPAL): Tecnologías digitales para un nuevo futuro. LC/TS, Santiago (2021)

Impact of Keyboard, Joystick, and Skateboard Platform on Usability and User Experience in Digital Games

Ana Grasielle Dionísio Corrêa(✉), Bruno da Silva Rodrigues, Leandro Natale Pupo, and Rogério de Oliveira

Mackenzie Presbiterian University, Rua da Consolação, 930, São Paulo, Brazil
{ana.correa,bruno.rodrigues,leandro.natale,
rogerio.oliveira}@mackenzie.br

Abstract. This study investigates the impact of different interaction devices—keyboard, joystick, and electronic skateboard—on usability and player experience in a snowboarding game developed for PC. The research examines the influence of the device on the player's experience, the impact of performance on the experience, and possible gender differences in relation to device preference and gaming experience. 49 university students, aged between 18 and 59, participated in the study. Participants tested each interaction device for 3 min, with the order of device usage alternated. After each test session, participants responded to the Game Experience Questionnaire (GEQ) to evaluate aspects such as Positive Experience, Negative Experience, Tiredness, and Return to Reality. Performance was measured in terms of score and number of lives lost. The results indicated that device choice significantly influenced negative experience and return to reality (Q1). Player performance had a direct impact on the experience, with better performance leading to a more positive experience (Q2). No significant gender differences were found in device preference or gaming experience, including perception of challenge or overall experience (Q3, Q4).

Keywords: Human-Computer Interaction · Game Experience · Usability

1 Introduction

In recent years, the gaming industry has significantly expanded the variety of interaction devices available to players beyond traditional keyboards and joysticks [1–3]. Innovations such as balance platforms, gesture controls, and virtual reality devices have broadened interaction possibilities [2–6], introducing new challenges for game designers [7]. With these changes, there is a need to adapt game mechanics to these devices without compromising usability and user experience (UX), ensuring that players remain immersed and satisfied [8, 9].

The concepts of usability and user experience, although related, are distinct and essential for interaction design [7]. Usability refers to the efficiency, ease of use, and learnability of players when interacting with devices, addressing aspects such as the

H. Luna-García et al. (Eds.): HCI-COLLAB 2025, CCIS 2850, pp. 176–189, 2027.
https://doi.org/10.1007/978-3-032-31223-5_13

intuitiveness and accuracy of controls. On the other hand, user experience encompasses broader subjective perceptions, including emotions, engagement, immersion, and satisfaction during interaction with the game. Research suggests that non-conventional interaction devices, despite initial adaptation challenges, such as in the case of motion controllers, can significantly enhance both usability and the overall player experience, providing deeper immersion and more active engagement [3–7].

This study aims to investigate how three interaction devices—keyboard, joystick, and electronic skateboard—influence usability and player experience in a PC-developed snowboarding game. Four research questions were addressed: (Q1) Does the interaction device influence the player's experience? (Q2) Does player performance affect the gaming experience? (Q3) Is there a difference between genders regarding preference for the interaction device or perception of challenge? and (Q4) Does gender influence the player's experience?

The results of this study provided insights into the design of interaction devices in PC games, particularly in enhancing player satisfaction and engagement. By investigating how player performance and preferences regarding input devices affect their experiences, the study aims to contribute to the development of strategies that improve usability and provide a more immersive gaming experience. Additionally, the findings will serve as a foundation for future research in the field of human-computer interaction, offering guidelines for creating interfaces that optimize both performance and player enjoyment.

2 Background

Gaming experience is widely influenced by a variety of factors, including the interaction device used, player performance, and individual aspects such as gender and interaction preferences [3, 10]. The choice of input devices has been an area of growing interest, with studies showing that different devices can directly impact player immersion, control, and satisfaction [3, 8]. Research highlights that devices offering greater control and physical feedback, such as motion controllers, provide a more engaging gaming experience [3, 7]. Similarly, studies suggest that the ability to customize input devices according to player preferences can enhance both performance and engagement during gameplay [2, 7].

The influence of performance on the gaming experience has also been well documented. Previous studies suggestions that success in the tasks proposed during the game are associated with a greater sense of pleasure and satisfaction [11, 12]. In contrast, lower performance and frequent failures may lead to frustration and negatively affect the overall player experience [9, 13].

Regarding gender, research indicates that although differences in gaming behavior and preferences may exist, these differences tend to diminish as players gain experience [14, 15]. In this context, device preference and perceived difficulty are more strongly associated with familiarity and skill level than with gender itself [15, 16]. Furthermore, the gaming experience, particularly in terms of immersion, motivation, and satisfaction, appears to be only marginally influenced by gender, with other factors such as gameplay context and player experience playing a more significant role [10–17].

Based on these findings, this study investigates the relationship between input devices, player performance, and gaming experience, focusing on how these variables influence player satisfaction, engagement, and perception of immersion. Additionally, the study examines whether gender directly affects device preference and the quality of the gaming experience, contributing to the field of Human–Computer Interaction and providing insights for the design of more effective and inclusive game interfaces.

2.1 Game Experience Questionnaire - GEQ

The Game Experience Questionnaire (GEQ) is a widely used questionnaire for measuring players' experiences while engaging with a digital game. It assesses various aspects of the player experience, providing a comprehensive view of how the game is perceived in emotional, cognitive, and physical terms. The GEQ is divided into three main versions [18]:

1. Core Game Experience Questionnaire (Core GEQ): This section is used to assess the player's core experience while playing, capturing aspects such as immersion, flow (state of concentration and engagement), competence, tension/stress, challenges, and positive and negative affect.
2. Social Presence Module (Social Presence GEQ): Used to measure the social experience of the game, especially in multiplayer contexts. It evaluates aspects such as empathy, competitive behavior, and the sense of co-presence.
3. Post-Game Module (Post-Game GEQ): Administered immediately after the player finishes the session, it assesses residual sensations from the gaming experience, such as tiredness, satisfaction, or whether the player is still thinking about the game.

2.2 Post-Game Module (Post-Game GEQ)

The Post-Game GEQ, used in this study, consists of 17 Likert-scale questions, where players indicate their level of agreement with statements (e.g., from 1 to 5, where "1" means "strongly disagree" and "5" means "strongly agree"). It includes statements that capture the player's emotional and physical state after the game, such as *"I feel tired," "I still feel excited," "I am satisfied with my performance,"* and *"I am in pain"* (to assess physical discomfort). These questions help us understand how the game impacted the player's well-being after the activity, including effects such as exhaustion, satisfaction, or continued interest in the game. The 17 items are distributed across four components of the post-game experience, as presented in Table 1.

Table 1. Distribution of Post-Game Experience Components [18].

Experience Level	Items
Positive Experience	1, 5, 7, 8, 12, 16
Negative Experience	2, 4, 6, 11, 14, 15
Tiredness	10, 13
Return to Reality	3, 9, 17

The interpretation of the results involves calculating the average scores for the four components based on players' responses to the corresponding items. A high average score for Positive Experience indicates a favorable perception of the gaming session, whereas a high score for Negative Experience points to unfavorable aspects, such as regret or frustration. A high average for Tiredness suggests that the player was physically or mentally exhausted, while a high score for Return to Reality indicates difficulties in readjusting to a normal state after the session. Thus, each component helps identify specific aspects of the post-game experience that can be adjusted to improve player satisfaction and well-being.

2.3 Related Works

In [12], a study was conducted to compare four input devices (keyboard, mouse, joystick, and gamepad) to analyze the degrees of freedom (forward/backward; right/left; up/down; rotation along the x, y, and z axes) in the task of moving a character within a 3D game. The objective for the player was to control the character and navigate through a maze in the shortest possible time. The study involved 34 participants of both genders, aged between 18 and 58 years. Each participant had three attempts, with the two worst attempts being discarded. Data were collected on the time to complete the maze task, distance traveled, and the number of collisions. After the attempts, players answered a questionnaire to assess more subjective measures, such as ease of use, tiredness, accuracy, speed, and preference. The authors concluded that the mouse interface reduced both completion time and distance traveled compared to the other techniques. On the other hand, the gamepad interface increased the number of collisions with the environment.

In [2], a study was conducted to analyze the relationship between the type of game input and the degrees of freedom in a 3D interface. Degrees of freedom (DOF) refer to movements and rotations along the x, y, and z axes. The input devices used in the study included a mouse, a mouse adapted for 3D interfaces, free-motion devices, and isometric desktop devices. To measure the usability of DOFs, the study analyzed aspects such as speed, accuracy, ease of learning, fatigue, coordination (only for controls with more than one DOF), and persistence/acquisition of the device (ease of acquiring the device and whether it remains in position when released). The researchers concluded that no single device fully meets all usability aspects in a 3D application.

A study conducted by [9] suggests that video game control devices for older adults should be adapted to compensate for their motor, sensory, and cognitive limitations. The study involved 24 older adults (12 women, 12 men, with an average age of 69 years) and eight children (average age of 8 years). The experimental setup included two Kinect motion sensors, three computers, three projectors, three video cameras, two audio devices, the video games *Angry Birds* and *Happy Sky*, an Xbox 360 console, a Nintendo Wii, and a touchscreen.

3 Materials and Methods

3.1 The Snowboard Game

The snowboarding game takes place at a winter sports resort, featuring a snowboard slope whose obstacles are represented by tree trunks (see Fig. 1). The game was developed by the authors and runs on the Windows platform (desktop or laptop). It can be controlled using different interaction devices, including a keyboard, joystick (buttons), and an electronic skateboard. The objective is to avoid obstacles that appear randomly at the edges of the track, earning points for each successful dodge. In this game, the player starts with three lives and loses one life upon colliding with an obstacle. If the player loses all three lives, the game ends. In addition to the graphics and game mechanics, a data module was developed for the snowboarding game to collect and store performance data, including score, the time of each collision, and total playtime for each player.

Fig. 1. The snowboarding screens and interaction.*Source:* authors.

The electronic skateboard platform, it connects to the computer via a USB cable, allowing the player to apply pressure on the platform by leaning to shift their center of gravity. This movement controls the base of the platform, enabling the player to move the character within the game.

3.2 Materials and Equipment

The test setup included a chair for participants to sit on and a table for the computer with a keyboard and mouse. The computer used was a Dell laptop with a 15.6″ screen, 2.3 GHz Intel Core i7 processor, 16 GB 1600 MHz DDR memory, and an NVIDIA

GeForce GT 650M 1024 MB graphics card. For the electronic skateboard configuration, the laptop was placed on a table and connected to the electronic skateboard positioned on the floor.

3.3 Study Participants

The participants were randomly admitted to the experiment on a voluntary basis without any monetary compensation. The final sample consisted of 49 university students from different courses. Participants were recruited through convenience sampling via an email invitation sent to student mailing lists at the university. The inclusion criteria required participants of both genders, aged between 18 and 59 years. Exclusion criteria included individuals with diagnosed motor and/or cognitive impairments, a history of epileptic seizures, or reported balance issues.

3.4 Metrics and Data Collection Instruments

The following data were collected:

- Demographic Data: Collected through an online questionnaire to analyze participant profiles, including age, gender, sports habits, and gaming experience.
- Post-Game Experience: Measured using the Game Experience Questionnaire (Post-Game GEQ), administered immediately after gameplay to assess Immersion, Flow, Competence, Positive and Negative Affect, Tension, and Challenge. Responses were recorded using a Likert scale ranging from 0 ("not at all/none") to 4 ("extremely") [18].
- Game Performance: Recorded through the data module, exported as a.csv file with the following specifications: date; time; participantName; score; livesLost.

3.5 Procedures

The experiments were conducted in the Interactive Technologies Research Laboratory at the university, in a room with sufficient space for testing, climate control, and controlled lighting. Initially, participants were invited to read and sign the Informed Consent Form (approved by the Research Ethics Committee, CAAE: 65971322.3.0000.0084) and clarify any doubts. Next, they received a brief explanation about the experiment, its relevance, and the procedures to be followed. At this stage, participants completed a demographic questionnaire to collect information about their personal data and prior gaming experience.

Before starting the test session, participants were introduced to the game, including its objective, rules, and mechanics. At this stage, they were allowed to interact freely and test all three interaction devices (keyboard, joystick, and electronic skateboard) one at a time, without moderator intervention, for approximately 3 min.

After familiarizing themselves with the game and interaction devices, the intervention sessions began. Each participant individually played using all three interaction devices, for 3 min each, with a 1-min break between sessions. The order of device usage was alternated to prevent learning bias.

After each session with an interaction device, the participant answered the Game Experience Questionnaire (GEQ). At the end of the experiment, they were asked to indicate their preferred interaction device. Additionally, performance data were collected, including score and the number of lives lost while using each device.

The total duration of the experiment, from reading and signing the Informed Consent Form (ICF), completing the pre-test questionnaire, free experimentation with the game, interaction sessions with the devices, and filling out the usability questionnaires (GEQ and post-test), was approximately 20 min on average.

3.6 Data Analyse

Four research questions were investigated in this study:

1. Q1. Does the interaction device influence the player's experience?
2. Q2. Does player performance affect the gaming experience?
3. Q3. Is there a difference between genders regarding preference for the interaction device or perception of challenge?
4. Q4. Does gender influence the player's experience?

Depending on the data involved in each research question, an appropriate statistical method was applied for analysis. One-way ANOVA was used for Q1 and Q4. Pearson correlation and the Chi-Square test were applied to analyze Q2 and Q3.

4 Results and Discussions

A total of 49 university participants took part in the study, including 10 female and 39 male participants, with ages ranging from 18 to 49 years (see Table 2).

Table 2. Details of the participants' profiles. Source: authors.

Gender	Age	Participants
Female	$18 < \text{age} <= 21$	7
	$21 < \text{age} <= 30$	2
	$\text{age} <= 30$	1
Male	$18 < \text{age} <= 21$	24
	$21 < \text{age} <= 30$	13
	$\text{age} <= 30$	2
Total	Average = 22	49

Figure 2 shows the frequency of digital game use by men and women, both on computers and mobile devices. It can be observed that men use games more frequently, standing out in the "regularly" and "every day" categories on both platforms. Women, on the other hand, show a more moderate usage pattern, with a greater concentration in

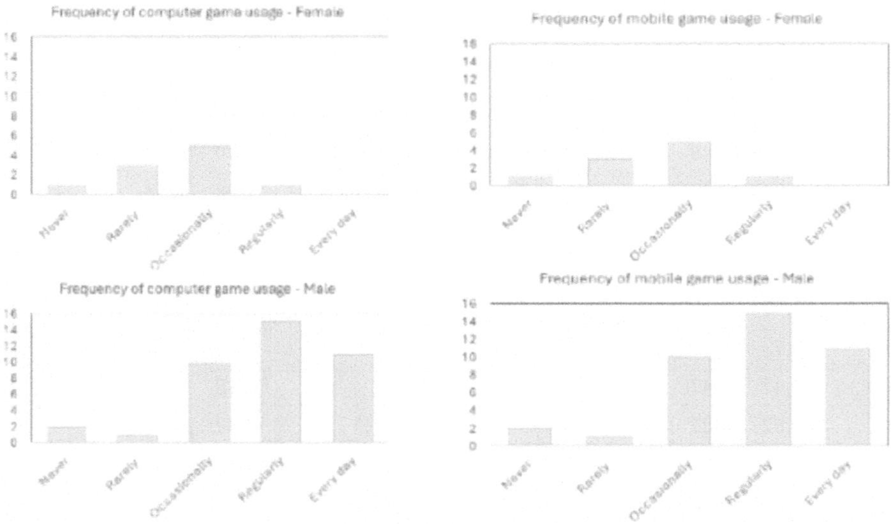

Fig. 2. Frequency of computer and mobile devices.*Source:* authors.

the "rarely" and "occasionally" categories, especially in computer games, although use on mobile devices is slightly more frequent compared to computers.

The analysis of the impact of interaction devices on player experience began with a detailed statistical evaluation of the post-game module components of the GEQ, which covers four main dimensions: positive experience, negative experience, tiredness, and return to reality. For each research question, mean scores and standard deviations were calculated, allowing for a deeper understanding of response variations. Table 3 presents the consolidated results, displaying the mean and standard deviation for each of the four analyzed dimensions across the tested devices.

Table 4 presents the evaluation of player experiences, assessed based on the post-game component. When analyzing positive experience (questions 1, 5, 7, 8, 12, 16), it was found that all three devices achieved high scores, with a slight increase for the skateboard platform (Fig. 3a). Despite this positive experience, the skateboard device also had the highest score in negative experience (questions 2, 4, 6, 11, 14, 15 – Fig. 3b), a score that may be related to player performance during the activity. According to the score obtained in question 11 of the GEQ (*"I felt that I could have performed better"*), players expected to achieve better performance when using the skateboard.

Studies such as those by [4, 7] support this observation, indicating that non-conventional interaction devices, including motion-based controllers and alternative input systems, can provide a more immersive gaming experience. However, these devices may also introduce a steeper learning curve, which can lead to initial difficulties and frustration, particularly for inexperienced users [19]. Despite these challenges, such interaction techniques, including platforms like electronic skateboards, have the potential to enhance player engagement and immersion by promoting more active and embodied forms of interaction [12].

Table 3. Mean GEQ Scores by Question. Source: authors.

Question	Joystick		Keyboard		Skate	
	Mean	Standard Deviation	Mean	Standard Deviation	Mean	Standard Deviation
Q1	2,98	1,48	3,02	1,52	3,49	1,29
Q2	1,04	0,29	1,04	0,29	1,08	0,34
Q3	1,37	0,81	1,39	0,89	1,69	1,1
Q4	1,04	0,2	1,02	0,14	1,22	0,62
Q5	3,47	1,37	3,2	1,35	3,31	1,39
Q6	1,73	0,97	1,55	0,87	1,2	0,61
Q7	2,47	1,47	2,22	1,36	3,18	1,45
Q8	3,82	1,22	3,82	1,13	4,37	0,7
Q9	1,14	0,65	1,08	0,34	1,31	0,71
Q10	1,16	0,66	1,04	0,2	1,22	0,59
Q11	1,78	1,25	1,59	1,27	3,98	1,22
Q12	2,9	1,5	2,69	1,37	2,98	1,31
Q13	1,08	0,45	1,06	0,24	1,12	0,33
Q14	1,45	0,94	1,41	0,98	1,16	0,51
Q15	1,1	0,42	1,12	0,44	1,61	1,08
Q16	3,39	1,4	3,2	1,49	3,24	1,39
Q17	2,35	1,45	2,39	1,44	3,2	1,27

When evaluating the fatigue sensation of players, most participants rated it as mild for all three tested devices (Fig. 4a). Regarding the player's difficulty in disconnecting from the gaming experience (return to reality), it was found that the use of the skateboard platform achieved the highest score among the three interaction devices (Fig. 4b). This difficulty may be related to the higher degree of immersion provided by non-conventional interaction devices. Studies such as [4, 5] suggest that interfaces involving broad body movements and intense physical interaction increase the sense of presence in the virtual environment, making the transition back to reality more challenging [20].

4.1 Influence of Devices on Player Experience (Q1)

To evaluate Q1, a one-way ANOVA test was applied with a significance level of $\alpha = 0.05$. The analysis indicates that the device influenced only negative experience and return to reality.

4.2 Player Performance and its Impact on Experience (Q2)

In evaluating Q2, Pearson correlation was performed with a significance level of $\alpha = 0.05$, where the correlation between the GEQ components and the score obtained by the

Table 4. Post-Game Component Results by Interaction Device. Source: authors.

Post-Game Component	Device	Mean	Standard Deviation
Positive Experience	Skate	3,428571	0,977762
Positive Experience	Joystick	3,170068	1,227808
Positive Experience	Keyboard	3,027211	1,163362
Negative Experience	Skate	1,710884	0,456151
Negative Experience	Joystick	1,357143	0,396746
Negative Experience	Keyboard	1,289116	0,349893
Tiredness	Skate	1,173469	0,427578
Tiredness	Joystick	1,122449	0,462451
Tiredness	Keyboard	1,051020	0,210280
Return to Reality	Skate	2,068027	0,693821
Return to Reality	Joystick	1,619048	0,739119
Return to Reality	Keyboard	1,619048	0,700529

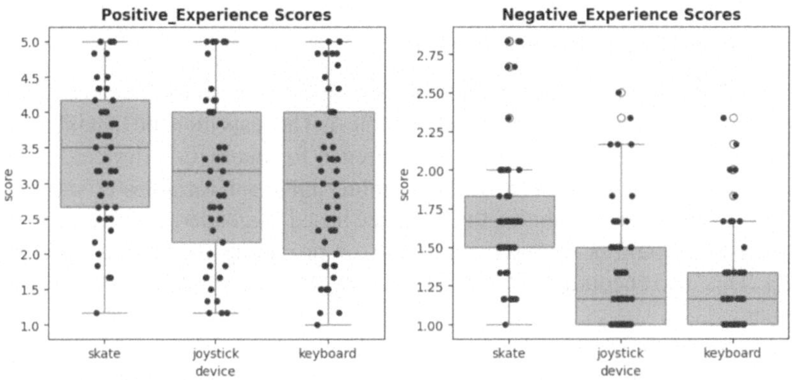

Fig. 3. Scores and distribution obtained through the GEQ questionnaire: (a) evaluating positive experience; (b) evaluating negative experience.
Source: authors.

player during the activity was analyzed. The corresponding statistics and p-values are presented in Table 3.

The correlation analysis suggests that player performance directly influenced their experiences. The performance of players using the skateboard platform resulted in a more positive experience, which is consistent with the higher scores achieved with this device. These findings are supported by previous studies [11, 12], which indicate that player performance is closely related to motivation, satisfaction, and overall enjoyment. When players perform well, as observed with the skateboard platform, their satisfaction and immersion tend to increase. Conversely, poor performance, as observed with the

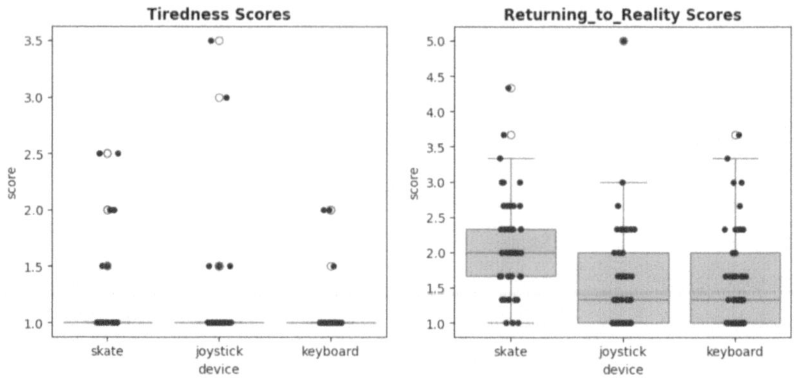

Fig. 4. Scores and distribution obtained through the GEQ questionnaire: (a) evaluating fatigue; (b) evaluating return to reality.
Source: authors.

joystick and keyboard, may lead to frustration and negative impact on the overall gaming experience, reinforcing the importance of designing interaction devices that support player performance.

4.3 Gender and Device Preference (Q3)

The χ^2 (chi-square) test was employed, with a significance level of $\alpha = 0.05$. The results obtained from this analysis are presented in Table 4. The tests indicate that there were no significant gender differences related to preference for interaction devices, suggesting that game and device design can focus on more universal variables of usability and satisfaction, rather than segmenting the audience based on gender. Therefore, device and interface design should be inclusive and focus on providing accessibility, independent of gender. This also encourages a more holistic view of the player experience, avoiding stereotypes.

In the case of the keyboard and joystick, both are widely used in the context of digital games, especially among younger players, who often have prior experience with these devices. On the other hand, the electronic skateboard, being a less conventional interface, may require more adaptation, but at the same time, it may be more intuitive for players accustomed to physical experiences or motion-sensor-based games.

In contrast, older players may have a distinct usage profile: while some may have prior experience with joysticks due to earlier generations of consoles, others may find it more challenging to adapt to non-conventional interfaces, such as the electronic skateboard.

Thus, it is plausible to assume that the gaming experience could differ in a sample composed of older players, either due to resistance to new interfaces, the time needed for adaptation, or possible differences in expectations compared to traditional controls. Future studies could explore this age variable more in-depth, investigating how age impacts the learning curve, acceptance, and immersion in games that use differentiated interaction devices.

Previous studies also suggest that gender does not play a significant role in the choice or preference for interaction devices in games. For example, the research by [14,

15] indicated that, despite some initial differences in exposure to technologies between genders, preferences for devices and the perception of usability tend to converge as gaming experience increases. Additionally, the study by [16] found that gender was not a determining factor in the choice of input devices or in the perception of difficulty in games, reinforcing that usability and experience are more influenced by individual characteristics, such as skills and gaming experience, than by gender.

4.4 Contributions to Satisfaction and Engagement

The results of this study suggest that the choice and optimization of input devices are crucial for providing a more satisfying gaming experience. Games that allow a variety of control devices can attract a broader audience, increase engagement, and reduce player frustration. Additionally, by monitoring the impact of the interaction device on the player's experience, designers can adjust gameplay to improve performance and, consequently, user satisfaction.

Some studies have shown that the choice of interaction devices can significantly influence player satisfaction and engagement. For example, the study by [3] demonstrated that different input devices impact player performance and interaction efficiency, which can affect the overall gaming experience. Additionally, research by [7, 8] indicates that devices that better match player capabilities and provide more intuitive control can improve both performance and perceived usability. These factors, in turn, contribute to increased engagement and satisfaction during gameplay [12].

5 Conclusions

The results presented in this study provide insights into interaction design in PC games, highlighting the effects of input devices on the user experience. These findings can guide the creation of strategies to improve player satisfaction and engagement across different platforms.

Recent studies indicate that non-conventional interaction devices, although they introduce additional challenges, can enhance player engagement. For example, the study by [4] explores how gesture-based interactions using the Leap Motion controller, despite presenting usability challenges, can increase user involvement due to their immersive nature.

Additionally, research on physical interactive systems, such as exergames, suggests that devices requiring greater bodily engagement may demand more effort and adaptation but can also provide a more engaging and immersive gaming experience [5]. These findings, together with studies on interaction design [1], suggest that, despite the challenges associated with non-conventional input devices, such technologies can enhance player experience by increasing engagement and immersion.

This study emphasizes the importance of continuous monitoring of gameplay and user preferences regarding input devices, providing clear guidelines for future research in the field of Human-Computer Interaction. Further studies may explore emerging technologies, such as virtual and augmented reality, to better understand how physical interaction influences usability and immersion.

Future work could also investigate how factors such as session duration and player skill level affect the experience with different devices. Combining performance metrics with subjective evaluations may provide deeper insights into how interaction design impacts player experience. These findings can support both hardware developers and software designers in creating more accessible, intuitive, and engaging gaming experiences.

References

1. Brown, M., Kehoe, A., Kirakowski, J., Pitt, I.: Beyond the gamepad: HCI and game controller design and evaluation. In: Bernhaupt, R. (ed.) Game User Experience Evaluation, Human–Computer Interaction Series, pp. 123–145. Springer, Cham (2015)
2. Zhai, S.: User performance in relation to 3D input device design. ACM SIGGR. Comput. Graph. **32**(4), 50–54 (1998)
3. Lapointe, J.-F., Savard, P., Vinson, N.G.: A comparative study of four input devices for desktop virtual walkthroughs. Comput. Hum. Behav. **27**(6), 2186–2191 (2011)
4. Pirker, J., Pojer, M., Holzinger, A., Gütl, C.: Gesture-based interactions in video games with the Leap Motion controller. In: HCI International 2017, LNCS, pp. 620–633. Springer, Cham (2017)
5. Ferreira, D.R.M., Lima, T.F.M., Assis, G.A., Ruivo, E.L.P., Rodrigues, B.S., Corrêa, A.G.D.: Design of exergames controlled by wearable devices for sensorimotor skills: a framework proposal. In: SeGAH 2022, pp. 1–8 (2022)
6. Barram, Z., Bertozzi, C., Doballapur, V.: Weight controlled electric skateboard (2019)
7. Machado, L., Bernardes, J.L.: A practical evaluation of the influence of input devices on playability. In: HCI International 2016, LNCS, pp. 385–395. Springer, Cham (2016)
8. Rupp, M.A., Oppold, P., McConnell, D.S.: Comparing the performance, workload, and usability of a gamepad and joystick in a complex task. Proc. Hum. Factors Ergon. Soc. Annu. Meet. **57**(1), 1775–1779 (2013)
9. Palacio, R.R., et al.: Usability perception of different video game devices in elderly users. Univ. Access Inf. Soc. **16**, 103–113 (2017)
10. Johnson, D., Nacke, L.E., Wyeth, P.: All about that base: differing player experiences in video game genres and the unique case of MOBA games. In: CHI 2015, pp. 2265–2274 (2015)
11. Christoph, K., Tilo, H.: Effectance, self-efficacy, and the motivation to play video games. In: Playing Video Games, pp. 153–168. Routledge (2012)
12. Fang, X., Chan, S., Brzezinski, J., Nair, C.: Development of an instrument to measure enjoyment of computer game play. Int. J. Hum.-Comput. Interact. **26**(9), 868–886 (2010)
13. Yu, R.W.L., Chan, A.H.S.: Meta-analysis of the effects of game types and devices on older adults-video game interaction: implications for video game training on cognition. Appl. Ergon. **96**, 103477 (2021)
14. Bonanno, P., Kommers, P.A.: Gender differences and styles in the use of digital games. Educ. Psychol. **25**(1), 13–41 (2005)
15. Lucas, K., Sherry, J.L.: Sex differences in video game play: a communication-based explanation. Commun. Res. **31**(5), 499–523 (2004)
16. Shaer, O., Westendorf, L., Knouf, N.A., Pederson, C.: Understanding gaming perceptions and experiences in a women's college community. In: CHI 2017, pp. 1544–1557 (2017)
17. De Grove, F., Cauberghe, V., Van Looy, J.: Development and validation of an instrument for measuring individual motives for playing digital games. Media Psychol. **19**(1), 101–125 (2016)

18. IJsselsteijn, W.A., De Kort, Y.A., Poels, K.: The game experience questionnaire. Technische Universiteit Eindhoven, Eindhoven (2013)
19. Cairns, P.: Engagement in digital games. In: Why Engagement Matters, pp. 81–104. Springer, Cham (2016)
20. Weibel, D., Wissmath, B., Habegger, S., Steiner, Y., Groner, R.: Playing online games against computer-vs.-human-controlled opponents: effects on presence, flow, and enjoyment. Comput. Hum. Behav. **24**(5), 2274–2291 (2008)

Implementation of a Pervasive Video Game with Mobile Sensing Features

Claudio Rubio[1(✉)] and Felipe Besoain[2]

[1] Faculty of Engineering, University of Talca, Curicó, Chile
claudiorubio23@gmail.com
[2] Department of Interactive Visualization and Virtual Reality, Faculty of Engineering, University of Talca, Talca, Chile
fbesoain@utalca.cl

Abstract. This study presents Kaboom, a pervasive game for mobiles devices designed to promote physical activity by integrating real-world movement into its core gameplay mechanics. The objective of the research is to explore how geolocation and step counting sensors can be used to create a responsive and engaging user experience that supports health promotion. Using a using a three-layered architecture, the system collects contextual data via mobile sensors, processes it locally, and stores it in the cloud. A technical feasibility study was conducted on five different smartphones with varying hardware specifications to evaluate sensor calibration consistency, data transmission reliability, and user experience performance. The results showed accurate step counting and route tracking across different android devices, confirming the system's robustness and compatibility. The study also identified challenges such as battery consumption and the need for improved data protection through encryption. Future work will address these issues while incorporating additional sensors and conducting usability tests in real-world conditions.

Keywords: Mobile devices · Mobile Sensing · Videogames · Sensors · Health Promotion

1 Introduction

Physical inactivity is a leading risk factor for non-communicable diseases (NCDs)—chronic medical conditions that are not transmitted from person to person, such as cardiovascular diseases, diabetes, cancer, and chronic respiratory illnesses—and for premature mortality worldwide [1, 2]. According to the World Health Organization (WHO), regular physical activity significantly reduces the risk of several conditions: cancer (8%–28%), cardiovascular diseases such as heart disease and stroke (19%), diabetes (17%), and mental health disorders including depression and dementia (28%–32%) [2]. Between 2020 and 2030, approximately 500 million new NCD cases are expected, with annual treatment costs reaching around $27 billion. Moreover, 4 to 5 million deaths per year could be prevented through more active lifestyles [3].

H. Luna-García et al. (Eds.): HCI-COLLAB 2025, CCIS 2850, pp. 190–201, 2027.
https://doi.org/10.1007/978-3-032-31223-5_14

Multiple strategies have been employed to promote healthy nutrition and physical activity, including social media campaigns [4], multimedia content and prevention initiatives [5], online forums [6], exergames [7], virtual reality platforms [8], and mobile applications [9–11], between others. Among these, video games have emerged as particularly effective tools for delivering educational content through interactive experiences. Beyond education, video games have become influential mediums for political, ethical, and cultural discourse, reshaping how we teach, learn, and engage [12]. One of their main strengths lies in their capacity to create immersive environments that encourage user participation and overcome psychological barriers to behavior change [13]. By placing the player in an active role within a narrative, these experiences promote emotional engagement and increase motivation, making users more likely to adopt and maintain healthy behaviors.

Pervasive technologies such as mobile devices, alongside other virtual strategies, have proven effective in promoting healthy behaviors in diverse areas, including STI prevention [10, 14–16], smoke cessation [10, 14–16] sleep disorders [10, 14–16] and adherence to COVID-19 preventive practices [10, 14–16]. Their ubiquitous presence in daily life allows these devices to influence user habits and routines. Several studies emphasize their potential to collect contextual data, enabling the recognition and interpretation of environmental conditions [17–19]. Through built-in sensors such as GPS, gyroscopes, and step counters, mobile sensing techniques facilitate the intelligent acquisition of real-world data. This capability positions them as key components in the development of applications aimed at encouraging physical activity. Beyond data collection, mobile sensing also enables the design of more responsive interventions by capturing real-time contextual information and adjusting content based on continuous, context-aware inputs.

Contextual information is generally collected through two main approaches: passive and active data collection. In the passive approach, data are gathered indirectly or without requiring user interaction and are not essential for progressing through the experience. For instance, health monitoring applications can track steps, sleep quality, or ambient noise via smartphone sensors in the background. While passive sensing is effective for real-time context recognition, it does not fully take advantage of its potential to enhance immersion or interactivity. This format is appropriate when user attention is minimal; however, when progression depends on the user's environment, a more active and responsive approach becomes necessary.

In contrast, active data collection involves direct user interaction, where contextual inputs play a key role in progressing through the experience. A well-known example is Pokémon Go, a location-based game in which players must physically move through real environments to complete objectives, improving user engagement by linking virtual outcomes to real-world behaviors. When gameplay mechanics respond to physical activity, players become not only cognitively but also physically immersed in the experience. This fusion of movement and narrative promote deeper motivation and supports the development of more sustainable health interventions, in which contextual data not only shapes how progress the narrative but also plays a central role in maintain user motivation.

Given the growing potential of pervasive technologies in behavior change interventions, it is essential to develop strategies that actively recognize environmental factors and embed them into pervasive smartphone games designed to promote physical activity. This study presents a pervasive game for mobile devices specifically developed to incorporate contextual data—such as location and movement—into its core gameplay mechanics. However, embedding environmental information into game design poses several technical challenges, including the real-time capture, processing, and storage of user context. Mobile sensing plays a vital role in addressing these challenges by enabling the continuous collection and interpretation of environmental inputs. These inputs can then be directly translated into gameplay dynamics, allowing for interactive experiences that respond to the user's surroundings and actively motivate physical movement.

The remainder of this paper is structured as follows: the Methodology section describes the system architecture and presents two use cases that illustrate user interaction with the game. The Technical Feasibility Test and Results section introduces the prototype and reports on system performance across multiple devices, including analysis of data collected from step counting and geolocation sensors. Finally, the Conclusion and Future Work section summarizes the study's main contributions and proposes directions for enhancing both the technical implementation and the narrative design of the application.

2 Methodology

This research employs the Design and Creation methodology [20], a structured five-step approach to developing systems and artifacts. These steps include: (1) identifying a problem or opportunity through awareness and observation; (2) suggest a solution that response to necessities; (3) developing modular artifacts con build a prototype; (4) evaluate generate artifacts; and (5) reporting findings and drawing conclusions. Steps 1, 2, and 3 are detailed in this section, while Steps 4 and 5 are addressed in Sects. 3 and 4 of this paper, respectively. This methodology provides a structured approach to designing architectures that support the collection of contextual data in mobile video game environments.

2.1 Problem Awareness and Suggestion

As established in the literature, the prevalence of diseases linked to physical inactivity continues to rise due to increasingly sedentary lifestyles, presenting serious risks to public health. In this context, mobile video games have emerged as promising tools for encouraging healthier behaviors. Designing effective interventions requires an understanding of the user's physical context. To address this, we conceptualized a mobile game that integrates physical activity directly into its core gameplay mechanics using embedded smartphone sensors.

The game take advantage of geolocation and step counting components to create an experience that motivates users to move. By utilizing ubiquitous smartphone sensors, the game responds dynamically to user movement, merging digital play with physical activity. Players are encouraged to walk or run against the clock, promoting exercise through interactive gameplay. Unlike traditional fitness apps, our game uses environmental inputs not only for background tracking but to directly affect gameplay outcomes, establishing a real-time feedback loop between the user's physical actions and virtual progress.

To illustrate how the system operates, we present two general use cases (see Tables 1 and 2 respectively): (1) capturing and storing telemetric data through mobile device sensors; and (2) integrating sensors into gameplay mechanics. These use cases provide an overview of the core processes and interactions between users and the system's architecture.

Table 1. Capturing and storing telemetric data through mobile device sensors. *Source: Authors' own work.*

Use Case:	Capture and store telemetric data in a database.
Actor:	User and System.
Purpose:	Collect sensor data from mobile devices in real time.
Summary:	This use case begins when the player launches the application. The software presents a narrative introducing the game context, gameplay, and system-user interaction. Once the player presses the button to start the experience, they transition to a new scene. In this scene, a countdown timer continuously decreases, and the user can increase the timer value through physical activity. The sensor data is collected locally and later sent to the database for processing. This case concludes when the player runs out of time on the scene's countdown.
Preconditions:	(1) The application must be installed on the user's mobile device. (2) There must be a cloud database capable of collecting data for further processing.

Table 2. Integration of sensors into gameplay mechanics. *Source: Authors' own work.*

Use Case:	Integrate sensor data into gameplay mechanics.
Actor:	User and System.
Purpose:	Incorporate telemetric data into game mechanics.
Summary:	This use case begins when the mobile app requests user permissions to access the device's motion sensors. Once the user grants access, the system starts capturing sensor data: (i) Location and (ii) Step Count. These values are then used to modify the countdown timer in the main scene. This case concludes when the user closes the application or when they run out of time on the countdown.
Preconditions:	(1) The app must request user permissions to collect sensor data from the device.

2.2 Development

Based on the use cases described above, we developed *Kaboom*, a pervasive mobile game designed to promote physical activity by integrating contextual elements derived from geolocation and step count sensors. The game was developed using Unity 3D, version 2021.3.10f1, and programmed in C# [21]. Unity was chosen for its compatibility with the Android platform, its support for sensor integration, and its scalability for iterative development. The design of the gameplay experience was guided by the following key principles:

- Integrate sensor data directly into core gameplay mechanics.
- Provide real-time user feedback, including time extensions and distance traveled.
- Store collected data in a structured format suitable for later analysis.
- Validate the technical feasibility of real time sensing under varied usage conditions

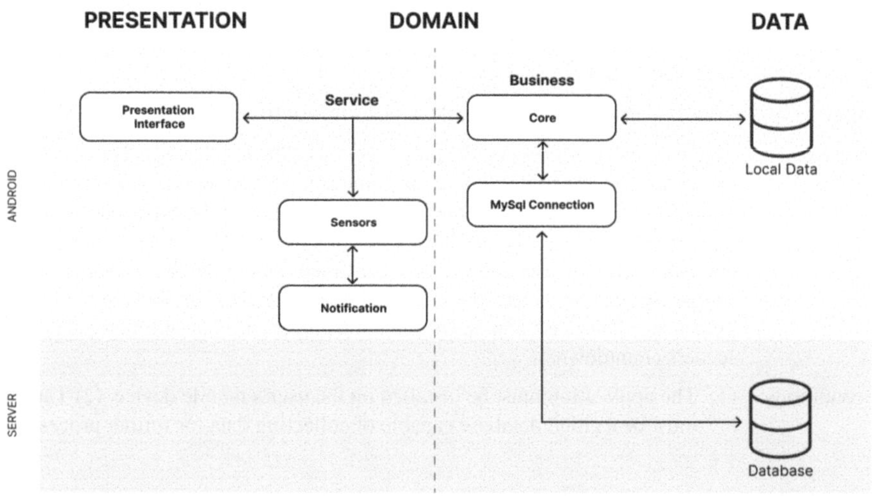

Fig. 1. Solution architecture, a layered diagram representing the client (Android Devices) - Server (Backend) and its components. The architecture was adapted from [22] and incorporates sensors and notifications as functional components.
Source: Authors' own work based on [22]

The development of *Kaboom* focuses on two central components: the solution architecture and the gameplay narrative and mechanics. The architecture defines how data flows through the system and supports future scalability, while the narrative structure focus in player engagement through a coherent and motivating gameplay loop.

Solution Architecture

The solution architecture was designed to support the collection, processing, and storage of telemetric data from mobile sensors. The game revolves around a bomb-and-timer mechanic, where players earn additional time by physically moving, making sensor input a core component of gameplay. The system is organized using a three-layered architecture—Presentation, Domain, and Data—as illustrated in Fig. 1. This structure was chosen to ensure a clear separation of concerns, improving modularity, maintainability, and scalability. The Presentation layer manages the user interface and in-game feedback; the Domain layer handles game logic and sensor interpretation; and the Data layer manages storage operations and asynchronous communication with external services. MySQL was selected as the database solution due to its stability, widespread support, and ability to efficiently handle structured sensor data from multiple clients.

During development, Unity's built-in sensor framework was used to detect movement, with data first cached locally and then transmitted to the cloud. A structured database architecture supported efficient storage and retrieval, enabling both in-game feedback and post-session analysis. To validate the system's robustness, particular emphasis was placed on testing how sensor data integration impacted gameplay in real time across different devices. Performance testing focused on sensor responsiveness, data synchronization, and transmission stability, allowing the team to refine the system and minimize delays or loss. Additionally, feedback mechanisms provided players with real-time updates on time remaining and distance traveled, reinforcing engagement. These iterative evaluations confirmed the system's ability to deliver a consistent and responsive user experience under varying hardware and connectivity conditions.

Narrative and Mechanics

Fig. 2. (a) The main scene, where a central bomb will explode when the timer reaches zero; time is increased through the user's physical activity. (b) The Final scene, displaying game statistics, including score, total time, and steps taken since the game started [22].
Source: Authors' own work.

The game begins with a comic-style introduction in which the protagonist arrives home and discovers a suspicious package containing a bomb. Upon realizing that the bomb's timer increases with physical movement, the character understands that staying active is essential to prevent the explosion. This narrative continues on the main game screen

(Fig. 2a), where players face a bomb and a countdown timer that can only be extended through physical activity. The objective is to keep moving to gain additional time, thereby prolonging the gameplay session until the timer eventually reaches zero and the bomb explodes, triggering the final scene. This mechanic transforms exercise into a core gameplay element, creating immediate consequences directly linked to real-world physical activity.

In the final scene, the comic-style narrative resumes, showing the consequences of the bomb's explosion. At this point, players receive feedback on their performance during the session, presented through three key metrics: (i) overall score, calculated based on (ii) the extra time earned through movement, and (iii) the total number of steps taken, as shown in Fig. 2b. This design not only motivates continued physical engagement but also provides a clear summary of the player's physical and strategic performance. By relating in-game events to real-world behavior, the experience ends in a way that reinforces feedback loops and supports healthy behaviors.

3 Technical Feasibility Test and Results

A technical feasibility study was carried out to evaluate the system's performance and to identify early-stage performance bottlenecks, cross-device inconsistencies, and potential vulnerabilities. The analysis focused on assessing how the application behaves across devices with varying specifications, including processor type, connectivity, operating system, and internet service provider. Table 3 outlines the technical differences among the five devices used during the experimental phase. This information is critical for planning future user testing outside the laboratory environment and for ensuring stable application performance regardless of hardware characteristics.

3.1 Procedure

The application was tested within the same time interval by the same individual. This approach minimized the influence of user-dependent variables, such as stride length and walking speed, ensuring consistent measurement across devices. To improve reproducibility, all devices were fully charged, and background processes were minimized to avoid external interference. The procedure consisted of four stages:

1. The application was downloaded on all devices.
2. Location and Physical Activity Recognition permissions were granted on each device.
3. A 30-min walk around the university campus was completed.
4. The walk ended at the starting point, and the application was then closed on all devices.

3.2 Technical Feasibility Study

The technical evaluation demonstrated that the application performs reliably across a variety of mobile devices with different hardware configurations. Table 3 presents the specifications of the five devices used during testing, including variations in processor type, RAM capacity, battery performance, and network connectivity. Across all devices, the application maintained stable functionality, confirming its robustness and compatibility with heterogeneous hardware environments. Minor fluctuations in GPS accuracy were observed in some devices, primarily due to signal strength and physical obstructions, which aligns with known limitations of geolocation technologies in urban settings. The following device-based observations summarize these results:

- The application maintained stable functionality across devices with diverse specifications, including MediaTek, Snapdragon, and Exynos processors, as well as varying RAM capacities, demonstrating that software works efficiently across a wide range of hardware.
- Despite variations in the operating system (Android versions 10 to 12), the application present stable performance, suggesting strong compatibility and effective software optimization.
- Differences in battery capacity and charging technologies highlighted the need for future power optimization strategies, particularly for devices with limited battery performance.
- Network variation (4G vs. 5G) had no measurable impact on data transmission or gameplay responsiveness, suggesting that the system does not depend heavily on high-bandwidth connections.
- Given the telemetry-based nature of the collected data, it is essential to incorporate robust security measures. Migrating to a solution like Firebase may offer improved encryption and user data protection.

Table 3. Comparison of mobile device technical specifications. *Source: Authors' own work.*

Specification	Moto G54 4G	Xiaomi Redmi Note 8	Samsung S22 Plus	Samsung Galaxy S20 FE	Xiaomi T11 Pro
Screen	6.5 in., Full HD+	6.3 in., Full HD+	6.6 in., Dynamic AMOLED 2X	6.5 in., Super AMOLED	6.67 in., AMOLED
Resolution	2400 × 1080 pixels	2340 × 1080 pixels	2340 × 1080 pixels	2400 × 1080 pixels	2400 × 1080 pixels
Processor	MediaTek Dimensity 720	Qualcomm Snapdragon 665	Exynos 2200 Snapdragon Gen 1	Exynos 990 Snapdragon 865	Qualcomm Snapdragon 888
RAM	4 GB	3 GB	8 GB	6 GB	8 GB
Storage	64 GB	32 GB	128 GB	128 GB	128 GB
Battery	5000 mAh, 30 W fast charging	4000 mAh, 18 W fast charging	4500 mAh, 45 W fast charging	4500 mAh, 25 W fast charging	5000 mAh, 67 W fast charging
Connectivity	4G, Wi-Fi, Bluetooth 5.1	4G, Wi-Fi, Bluetooth 4.2	5G, Wi-Fi 6, Bluetooth 5.2	4G, Wi-Fi 6, Bluetooth 5.0	5G, Wi-Fi 6, Bluetooth 5.2

(*continued*)

Table 3. (*continued*)

Specification	Moto G54 4G	Xiaomi Redmi Note 8	Samsung S22 Plus	Samsung Galaxy S20 FE	Xiaomi T11 Pro
Operating System	Android 11	Android 10	Android 12	Android 12	Android 11
Internet Provider	Claro	Claro	Entel	Movistar	WOM

Additionally, the analysis of sensor-based outputs—such as step count and user trajectory—confirmed that the application generates accurate and consistent measurements regardless of the device used. Figures 3 and 4 illustrate the congruence of this data across devices, reinforcing the integrity of the application's software layer. The experimental phase also revealed two aspects not considered during the design stage: (1) continuous use of the application significantly impacts battery life, highlighting the need for energy optimization strategies; and (2) the sensitivity of the collected telemetry data necessitates the implementation of robust encryption methods to ensure user privacy.

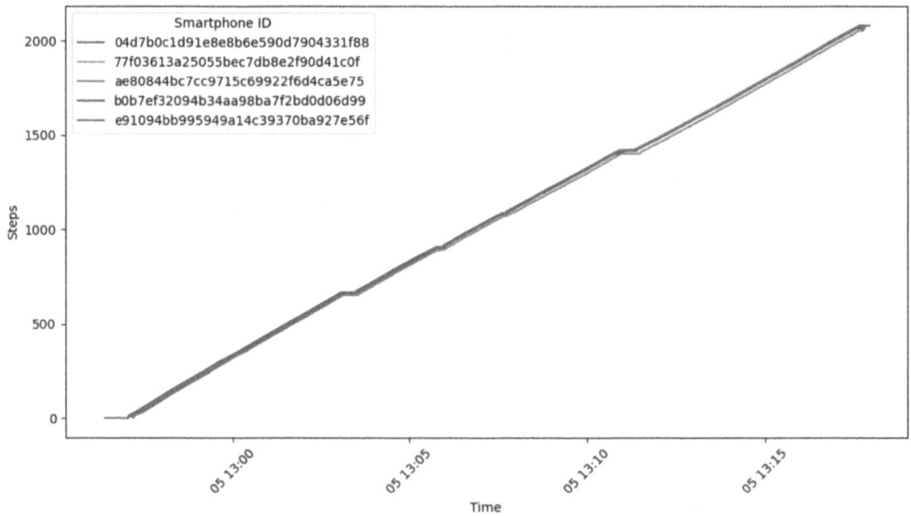

Fig. 3. Step count obtained through different devices within the same period, considering a 30-min interval.
Source: Authors' own work.

In summary, these findings confirm the technical viability of the application and validate Kaboom's architecture for deployment in real-world scenarios beyond controlled laboratory environments. The system demonstrates strong adaptability to diverse hardware configurations and software conditions, making it a promising tool for health-related pervasive gaming interventions. Future iterations should also consider incorporating user experience metrics—such as loading time, UI responsiveness, and memory usage—to complement the technical performance insights and further enhance the system's effectiveness.

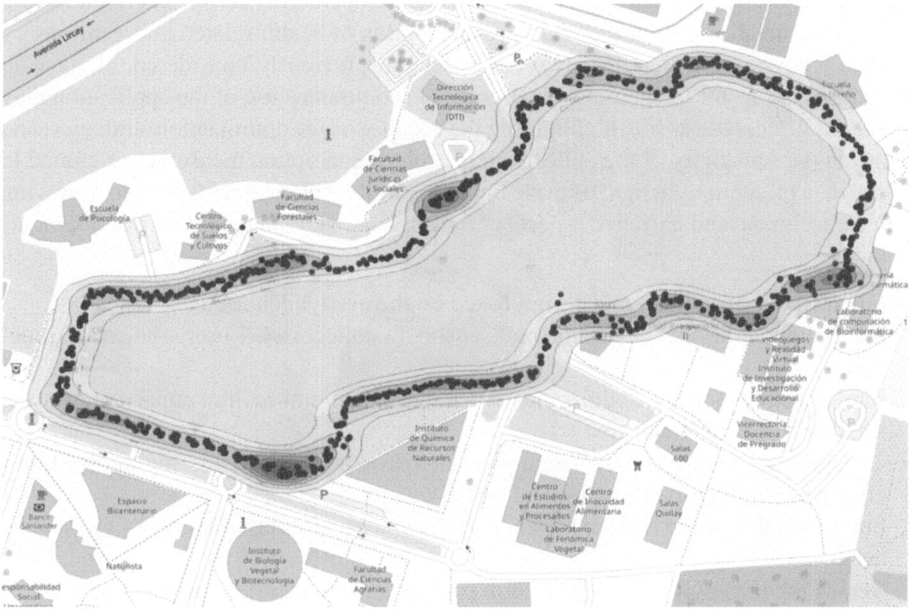

Fig. 4. Heatmap of the trajectory within a 30-min interval. Blue points represent the traveled route, yellow areas indicate mild interaction, while red areas represent zones of higher interaction. *Source:* Authors' own work.

4 Conclusion and Future Work

An application called Kaboom was designed and developed with the goal of promoting physical activity through a video game that integrates contextual components into its core mechanics. This work proposed geolocation and step counting as elements that improve the design of an interactive experience for health promotion. The game's primary mechanic—rewarding physical movement with additional playtime—creates a tangible link between real-world effort and virtual progression.

Our system enables the collection of contextual data through mobile device sensors, which are subsequently stored in the cloud. Each sensor operates as an independent component, allowing for modularity within the system. A key advantage of this implementation is its flexibility: components can be added or removed without requiring complex changes to the system architecture. This modular approach facilitates rapid experimentation with new sensor types, interaction models, or gameplay mechanics, accelerating the process of iterating and improving the system design.

The feasibility study demonstrated that step count data remains consistent across different devices, as shown in Fig. 3. About geolocation, the data indicate that it is possible to accurately track traveled routes and identify high-incidence areas across devices, as illustrated in Fig. 4. Although statistics were gathered from only five devices, the technical diversity among them supports the conclusion that the application can reliably obtain contextual data regardless of hardware specifications. These findings validate the solution's scalability and confirm its interoperability across diverse hardware profiles, a crucial aspect for the widespread adoption of health-related interventions.

The analysis also identified two use cases not previously considered, along with their implications for the gaming experience: (1) continuous use of the application may negatively affect battery life, highlighting the need for usage optimization strategies; and (2) given the sensitivity of the collected data, robust encryption measures are crucial to ensure data protection. In light of these findings, future work should focus on improving both the technical and narrative aspects of the application. Planned future developments include:

- Enhancing the application's design based on the newly identified use cases.
- Integrating additional environmental sensors to collect richer user context information.
- Implementing battery optimization strategies to minimize the impact of sensing activities on mobile devices.
- Conducting usability tests in real-world environments to assess the application's effectiveness in promoting physical activity.
- Improving the narrative design by applying persuasive theories to encourage healthy behaviors.
- Evaluating the application's long-term performance to measure the sustained impact of the experience on daily life.
- Exploring integration opportunities with health monitoring platforms and wearable devices to enrich data collection and cross-validate behavioral outcomes.

Acknowledgments. This research was funded by the National Agency for Research and Development, ANID-Subdirección del Capital Humano/Doctorado Nacional/2023-21232404 and subdirección de proyectos de investigación (FONDECYT) 1241406.

Disclosure of Interests The authors have no competing interests to declare that they are relevant to the content of this article.

References

1. Who, W.H.O.: Enfermedades no transmisibles. World Health Organization: WHO (2023)
2. Who, W.H.O.: Physical activity. World Health Organization: WHO (2019)
3. Santos, A.C., Willumsen, J., Meheus, F., Ilbawi, A., Bull, F.C.: The cost of inaction on physical inactivity to public health-care systems: a population-attributable fraction analysis. Lancet Glob. Health. **11**, e32–e39 (2023)
4. Lohse, B.: Facebook is an effective strategy to recruit low-income women to online nutrition education. J. Nutr. Educ. Behav. **45**, 69–76 (2013)

5. Evans, W.D., Necheles, J., Longjohn, M., Christoffel, K.K.: The 5-4-3-2-1 go! intervention: social marketing strategies for nutrition. J. Nutr. Educ. Behav. **39**, S55–S59 (2007)
6. Cohen, N.L., Carbone, E.T., Beffa-Negrini, P.A.: The design, implementation, and evaluation of online credit nutrition courses: a systematic review. J. Nutr. Educ. Behav. **43**, 76–86 (2011)
7. Castillo, J.F.V., et al.: Design of virtual reality exergames for upper limb stroke rehabilitation following iterative design methods: usability study. JMIR Serious Games. **12**, e48900 (2024)
8. Gao, Z., Lee, J.E., McDonough, D.J., Albers, C.: Virtual reality exercise as a coping strategy for health and wellness promotion in older adults during the COVID-19 pandemic. J. Clin. Med. **9**(6), 1986 (2020)
9. Hingle, M., Nichter, M., Medeiros, M., Grace, S.: Texting for health: the use of participatory methods to develop healthy lifestyle messages for teens. J. Nutr. Educ. Behav. **45**, 12–19 (2013)
10. Besoain, F., Perez-Navarro, A., Aviñó, C.J., Caylà, J.A., Barriga, N.A., de Olalla, P.G.: Prevention of HIV and other sexually transmitted infections by geofencing and contextualized messages with a gamified app, UBESAFE: design and creation study. JMIR Mhealth Uhealth. **8**, e14568 (2020)
11. Besoain, F., Perez-Navarro, A., Ojeda, F., Reyes-Suarez, J.A.: Promoting healthy nutrition behavior using mobile devices and ubiquitous computing. In: Ambient Assisted Living. ICT-based Solutions in Real Life Situations: 7th International Work-Conference, IWAAL 2015, Puerto Varas, Chile, pp. 89–100 (2015)
12. Brown, H.J.: Videogames and Education. Routledge, New York (2014)
13. Molins-Ruano, P., Sevilla, C., Santini, S., Haya, P.A., Rodríguez Marín, P., Gómez-Monivas, S.: Designing videogames to improve students' motivation. Comput. Human Behav. **31**, 571–579 (2014)
14. Finkelstein, J., Cha, E.M.: Using a mobile app to promote smoking cessation in hospitalized patients. JMIR Mhealth Uhealth. **4**, e5149 (2016)
15. Shin, J.C., Kim, J., Grigsby-Toussaint, D.: Mobile phone interventions for sleep disorders and sleep quality: systematic review. JMIR Mhealth Uhealth. **5**, e7244 (2017)
16. Lee, M., You, M.: Effects of COVID-19 emergency alert text messages on practicing preventive behaviors: cross-sectional web-based survey in South Korea. J. Med. Internet Res. **23**, e24165 (2021)
17. Mehl, M.R., Eid, M., Wrzus, C., Harari, G.M., Ebner-Priemer, U.W., Insel, T.R.: Mobile sensing in psychology: methods and applications (2024)
18. van Berkel, N., D'Alfonso, S., Kurnia Susanto, R., Ferreira, D., Kostakos, V.: AWARE-Light: a smartphone tool for experience sampling and digital phenotyping. Pers. Ubiquit. Comput. **27**, 435–445 (2023). https://doi.org/10.1007/s00779-022-01697-7
19. Teng, S., D'Alfonso, S., Kostakos, V.: A tool for capturing smartphone screen text. In: ACM Conferences, pp. 1–24. Association for Computing Machinery, New York, NY, USA (2024). https://doi.org/10.1145/3613904.3642347
20. Oates, B.J., Griffiths, M., McLean, R.: Researching Information Systems and Computing. Sage, London (2022)
21. Unity Technologies: Plataforma de desarrollo en tiempo real de Unity Motor de 3D, 2D, VR y AR. https://unity.com/es (2024)
22. Besoain, F., Gallardo, I.: Think about it: promoting physical activity with a mobile app with a theory-based approach. IEEE Access. **11**, 37021–37030 (2023). https://doi.org/10.1109/ACCESS.2023.3265891

Integrating the Development of Computational Thinking and STEM Competencies in Engineering Education

Pedro del S. Gómez Álvarez(✉) and Julio Ariel Hurtado Alegría

Universidad del Cauca, Popayán, Colombia
{pgomez,ahurtado}@unicauca.edu.co

Abstract. Computational Thinking (CT) and STEM competencies represent essential skills for the next generation of engineers, crucial to driving technological innovation and addressing the complex problems that define the global challenges of the 21st century. The lack of effective strategies for integrating CT and STEM competencies into undergraduate education makes it difficult for students to achieve the CT skills needed to face the challenges of their professional lives. This article presents a model that integrates CT and STEM competencies in the formative activities of engineering (E) students, called CT4E. The model is evaluated through a comparative case study to determine its contribution to the development of CT skills in the context of two introductory engineering courses. The study considered 60 first-semester students of the Engineering Introduction course at the Electronics and Telecommunications Engineering program of the Universidad del Cauca, divided into experimental and control groups. The results obtained from pretest and post-test questionnaires showed a greater increase in key CT skills development, such as abstraction, decomposition, pattern recognition, and algorithmic design, in the group in which the methodology was applied. These promising results support the CT4E model as an effective and replicable tool for strengthening CT and STEM competencies in engineering education (T&E) contexts. Even so, the model requires further refinement cycles, particularly to simplify its application for both teachers and students.

Keywords: Computational Thinking · Engineering Education · STEM Competencies

1 Introduction

Computational Thinking (CT) is a concept whose origin goes back to the work of Seymour Papert at MIT in the 1980s [1] and popularized in recent years through the work of Jeannette M. Wing (2006), defining it as "a way of solving modern engineering problems and designing complex systems that are based on fundamental concepts of computer science", and promoting it as "a fundamental skill used by everyone in the world in the mid-21st century" [2]. This type of thinking represents a universally applicable attitude and skill set. Furthermore, Wing states that "CT is the thinking process involved in formulating a problem and expressing its solution(s) in such a way that an agent - human or machine - can effectively execute it" [2].

H. Luna-García et al. (Eds.): HCI-COLLAB 2025, CCIS 2850, pp. 202–217, 2027.
https://doi.org/10.1007/978-3-032-31223-5_15

In this context, during the last few years, a trend of integrating computer science (hence, CT) into disciplinary education has emerged, especially in the fields of Science, Technology, Engineering, and Mathematics (STEM) [3]. Various research has shown that STEM content and contexts can benefit CT learning. Likewise, incorporating CT in STEM education also enhances students' learning of STEM content [4]. However, the literature on CT is still at an early stage of maturity, especially on how to develop CT in the engineering context [5].

On the other hand, there is evidence that CT is indispensable in modern engineering (T&E); this type of thinking could develop and enhance students' academic competitiveness, problem-solving skills, and system design by exploring and applying computational approaches [6]. However, there have been very few efforts to integrate CT into Technology and Engineering (T&E) education [5].

Kelley and Knowles (2016) define STEM integration in education as "an effort that combines any or all four disciplines of science, technology, engineering, and mathematics in a class, or lesson based on the different connections between different subjects and real-world problems" [7]. CT is indispensable in modern engineering, and it could develop and improve students' academic competitiveness and complex problem-solving skills [8].

Mohtadi et al. (2013) established that students entering engineering (T&E) courses have fewer competencies in STEM subjects, even though they have grown up in an environment with all kinds of computing and electronic devices. Therefore, it is essential to boost research on the integration of CT in Engineering (T&E) [9].

The CT4E model is presented as an extension to the collaborative model for team programming called ChildProgramming [10], to integrate the development of CT and STEM competencies, in formative activities in Engineering (T&E) [11]. This article presents the evaluation of the CT4E model through a comparative case study that aims to identify its effectiveness in the development of CT skills in first-semester engineering students.

The content of the article is organized into several sections covering the theoretical framework, methodology, results, discussion, and conclusions, with recommendations for future research.

2 Theoretical Framework

2.1 Computational Thinking (CT)

The term CT was first introduced by Seymour Papert in the 1980s through his work with the LOGO programming language [1]. In 2006, Jeannette Wing defined it as "the thinking process involved in formulating a problem and its solutions so that they are represented in a way that can be executed by an information processing agent" [2]. Later, refining it in 2017 to emphasize that solutions must be "effectively carried out by an information processor" [12]. Wing argues that CT involves problem-solving, system design, and understanding human behavior based on fundamental concepts of computer science, positioning it as a universally applicable skill set.

Brennan and Resnick (2012) expanded this view by proposing a framework that analyzes CT development through three dimensions: computational concepts, computational practices, and computational perspectives, linked to the visual programming language Scratch [13].

2.2 STEM Education

The acronym STEM was coined by Judith Ramaley in 2001 to integrate science, technology, engineering, and mathematics into learning experiences based on real-world problems [14, 15]. STEM education seeks to develop problem solvers, innovators, and technologically literate students [16]. Kelley and Knowles (2016) define STEM integration as "an effort that combines any or all four disciplines into a class or lesson based on connections between subjects and real-world problems" [7]. This education seeks to provide opportunities for students to be problem solvers, innovators, inventors, confident, logical thinkers, and technologically literate [16]. Key STEM competencies identified in the literature include autonomy, collaboration, use of technology, creativity, critical thinking, and problem-solving through CT and effective information processing [8].

2.3 Technological and Engineering Education (T&E)

According to the ITEEA, T&E education focuses on "how humans modify the world around them to meet their needs or solve practical problems" [17]. It involves designing and developing technological systems, open-ended problem-based activities, and applying technological knowledge to real-world experiences, individually and in teams.

2.4 ChildProgramming

ChildProgramming, developed by Hurtado et al. (2012), is a learning and software construction methodology that integrates playfulness, collaboration, and agility [10]. It operates through three dimensions: cognitive (understanding and appropriating tasks), agile (teamwork guided by agile software development values), and collaborative (knowledge acquisition through peer interaction) [18]. The CT4E model builds upon this framework by extending it to integrate STEM competencies and CT development in engineering education.

3 Related Works

The development of CT in engineering education has been addressed in the academic literature, with multiple approaches and methodological models that seek to strengthen its teaching. The present review of previous works allows for contextualizing the CT4E model in relation to other existing proposals.

3.1 Literature Review

To contextualize the CT4E model, a literature review was conducted following the PRISMA method [19], searching key terms such as "Computational Thinking", "STEM competencies", "Engineering Education", and "Integration" in databases including ACM, ASEE PEER, ERIC, IEEE Xplore, Scopus, SpringerLink, and SpringerOpen. Of the 410 articles reviewed, 21 were selected for their direct relevance; 43% approached CT theoretically, and 57% included experimental results or applied proposals [11]. Following the literature review, the articles were organized into three main categories to facilitate their analysis.

3.2 Computational Thinking and STEM Education

Several studies confirm the value of integrating CT into STEM contexts. Wang et al. (2021) reviewed 55 studies and proposed a problem-based instruction model [3]; Yang et al. (2021) demonstrated positive results using project-based learning in an integrated STEM–CT curriculum [20]. For his part, Sánchez Ludeña (2019) expresses the need to train in technological skills for the current market. Similarly, he states that the sciences should provide methods to understand the natural environment, while technology and engineering provide tools to solve problems, and mathematics strengthens logical thinking [8]. Likewise, Yepes Miranda (2020) presents his study on STEM opportunities in education, describing his approach and strengthening the teaching-learning processes through the systematic review of projects and educational experiences [21]. and Cannady et al. (2025) found, in a study with 600 high school students, that CT skills are consistent predictors of science learning, with block-based programming directly associated with higher CT levels [22]. Finally, Zhou et al. (2024) further showed that scaffolding-based pedagogical approaches significantly enhance CT development in collaborative learning contexts [23].

3.3 Integration of Computational Thinking in Engineering

Wu et al. (2019) identified CT elements in engineering through interviews at Zhejiang University, proposing a digital literacy framework [6]. Likewise, Hacker (2018) developed an instructional model based on informed design for technology and engineering education [5]. For their part, Shoaib and Brophy (2020) established the need for active, constructionist learning environments [24]. while Gross et al. (2014) and Miller et al. (2014) demonstrated through case studies that computational tools and creative exercises optimize CT learning in engineering programs [25, 26]. Atmatzidou and Demetriadis (2014, 2016) confirmed that educational robotics effectively develops CT skills regardless of age or gender [1].

3.4 Assessment of Computational Thinking Skills

Dolgopolovas et al. (2015) showed that only 54.2% of first-year engineering students answered CT tasks correctly, suggesting insufficient school-level preparation [27]. Román-González developed and validated a CT test widely used to measure problem formulation and solution skills [28].

4 CT4E Model: Computational Thinking for Engineering Education in the STEM Context

The CT4E model emerges as an extension of ChildProgramming that integrates STEM competencies and CT skills development in engineering education [11]. It combines concepts, processes, methods, and practices that enable students to tackle complex problems using computational approaches, built upon the cognitive dimension of ChildProgramming and structured around the CT4E Cycle.

4.1 CT4E Conceptual Architecture

The architecture adapts that of ChildProgramming using the situational method engineering approach of Mirbel and Ralyté [29], as defined by Cruz and Rojas [30]. It includes structure, life cycle, actors, dimensions, methodological packages, and activities [11].

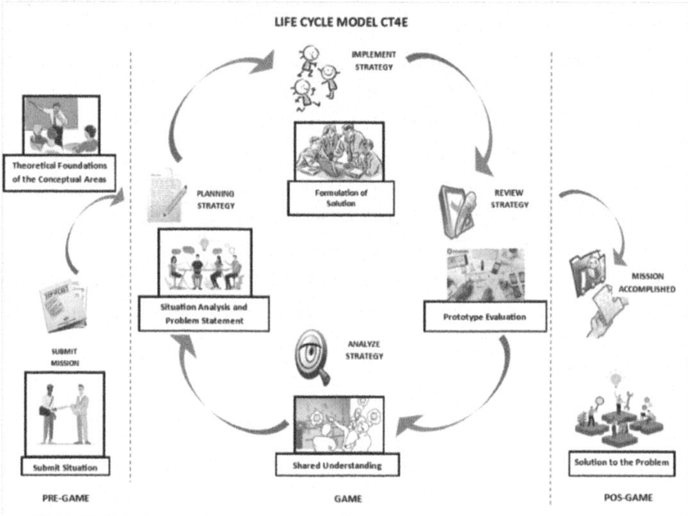

Fig. 1. Life cycle model CT4E. Source: Own research

4.2 CT4E Model Dimensions

The model operates through three interconnected dimensions: the cognitive dimension, which develops CT skills through abstraction, analysis, and logical reasoning in practical activities; the agile dimension, which promotes effective teamwork based on the Agile Manifesto values; and the collaborative dimension, which fosters meaningful learning through peer interaction and cooperative strategies [11].

4.3 CT4E Methodological Packages

CT4E is organized into three packages: Conceptual Areas, covering T&E education concepts, STEM competencies, and CT skills that instructors and students must understand; CT4E Activity Guides, comprising four types of activities that use STEM competencies as tools for CT development in problem-solving; and Recommendations for CT4E Application, a set of session-based guidelines that support teachers in implementing the model [11].

4.4 Definition of CT4E as a process

CT4E follows three iterative phases (see Fig. 1): Pre-Game, where the mission objective is defined, and theoretical foundations are provided; Game, where teams rotate through four stations — plan, apply, revise, and analyze the strategy; and Post-Game, where the evaluated solution is delivered as "mission accomplished" [11].

5 Comparative Case Study

5.1 Study Planning

Objective: to evaluate the contribution of the CT4E model to the development of CT skills in introductory engineering courses with first-semester students of the Electronics and Telecommunications Engineering program at the Universidad del Cauca.

Hypothesis: Implementing the CT4E model in introductory engineering courses favors the development of CT skills in first-semester students.

5.2 Methodology

The study was structured in three phases based on the scientific research cycle of Hurtado (2013), integrating the general guidelines of Bunge and specific guidelines of Shaw [11]:

Exploration phase: Information was collected on STEM, CT, ChildProgramming, and evaluation systems. The literature review used the PRISMA model [19], and the study design followed the guidance of Runeson et al. [31].

Formulation phase: The CT4E model was designed and implemented, integrating STEM competencies into the ChildProgramming methodological framework. Mirbel and Ralyté's [29] situational method engineering approach was followed, addressing requirements capture, selection, and assembly of components.

Evaluation phase: the impact of the model was analyzed through a comparative case study following Runeson et al. [31], measuring its contribution to the development of TC skills in introductory engineering courses.

5.3 Design Comparative Case Study

A comparative case study was designed, consisting of two phases —exploratory and comparative— with first-semester students of Electronics and Telecommunications Engineering and Industrial Automation Engineering, combining qualitative and quantitative data to evaluate the model's effectiveness across different dimensions.

Selection of study participants: The study population consisted of first-semester students of Electronics and Telecommunications Engineering and Industrial Automation Engineering at the Universidad del Cauca, selected based on course availability and willingness to participate.

Context of the research: The study was conducted at the Faculty of Electronic Engineering and Telecommunications (FIET), Universidad del Cauca, Popayán, Colombia, between October 2022 and January 2023, across 10 working sessions of 2 h each.

Variables observed: Quantitative variables included CT skills assessed via pre-test and post-test (abstraction, decomposition, pattern recognition, and algorithm design) and programming quality analyzed with Dr. Scratch (abstraction, modularity, logical thinking). Qualitative variables covered student motivation, active participation, and perceptions of the CT4E model, collected through structured observations and interviews.

Research questions: To evaluate the impact of the CT4E model on the development of CT skills in first-semester students of Electronics and Telecommunications Engineering, a series of research questions were formulated to analyze its contribution to problem-solving, understanding of computational concepts, and student and teacher perceptions of its effectiveness. These questions sought to establish whether the application of the model generated significant improvements in learning within the context of introductory engineering courses and their integration into a STEM environment.

The research questions were as follows:

1. How did the implementation of the CT4E model contribute to the development of CT skills in first-semester Electronics and Telecommunications Engineering students?
2. What impact did the CT4E model have on students' problem-solving skills in the context of an introductory engineering course?
3. How did the application of the CT4E model influence the understanding and use of computational concepts within a STEM environment?
4. Were there significant differences in the development of CT before and after the implementation of the CT4E model?
5. What were the students' and teachers' perceptions of the effectiveness of the CT4E model in their learning process?

These questions allowed obtaining evidence on the effectiveness of the CT4E model in the training of future engineers, validating its application as a strategy in the development of CT.

Instruments and Materials: This section describes the instruments and materials used in the execution of the study, which were selected to ensure a comprehensive evaluation of the results and facilitate the implementation of the activities designed under the CT4E model:

Interviews: a qualitative tool to collect direct information from participants, focusing on their experiences, perceptions, and attitudes towards the study activities.

Pre-test and Post-test: structured questionnaires based on the Marcos Román González test, designed to measure the level of knowledge and skills in TC before and after the intervention.

Observation Protocol: document prepared to record the participation, motivation, and performance of the students during the development of the activities.

Dr. Scratch: the digital tool that allows for automatic evaluation and analysis of the projects developed by students in Scratch, measuring key components such as abstraction, logical thinking, and flow control.

Procedure: The comparative case study was carried out between October 2022 and January 2023 with first-semester students of Electronics and Telecommunications Engineering and Industrial Automation Engineering at the Universidad del Cauca. It was structured in several stages with specific objectives and concrete activities to ensure an effective implementation of the CT4E model. It was carried out in 10 sessions of 2 h, distributed in connected activities (use of Scratch) and disconnected activities. In which the CT4E model was applied, and its impact was evaluated through Scratch activities, Pre-Test and Post-Test tests, and observation of the learning process. The activities developed in each session of the program are detailed below.

5.4 Evolution of the CT4E Model Across the 10 Sessions

To provide detailed insight into the implementation process of the CT4E model, the following Table 1 outlines the evolution of student activities and the methodological focus throughout the 10 working sessions:

Table 1. The evolution of student activities.

Session	Main Activity	CT4E Dimensions	Observations
1	Introduction to the study and pre-test application.	Cognitive	Establishes baseline knowledge; introduces objectives and CT concepts.
2–5	Implementation of programming activities using Scratch.	Cognitive + Agile	Progressive development of computational logic; increased familiarity with abstraction, sequencing, and problem-solving.

(*continued*)

Table 1. (*continued*)

Session	Main Activity	CT4E Dimensions	Observations
6–8	Disconnected activities and collaborative problem-solving in teams.	Collaborative + Cognitive	Emphasis on teamwork, decomposition, and planning; noticeable growth in communication and strategy formulation.
9	Evaluation of final projects using Dr. Scratch.	Cognitive	Projects analyzed for abstraction, modularity, and logical reasoning; quality of code improved significantly.
10	Application of post-test and feedback interviews.	All	Reflections confirm the model's effectiveness; evident growth in CT skills and motivation.

6 Results and Discussion

6.1 Quantitative Results

Quantitative analysis of the impact of the CT4E model on the development of computational thinking (CT) was performed by applying a pre-test and post-test. Four key dimensions were assessed: abstraction, decomposition, pattern recognition, and algorithms.

Comparison of Pre-Test and Post-Test: The results showed a significant increase in student performance after implementation of the model. The following findings stand out:

Abstraction: 12% increase in the ability to identify key structures in computational problems.

Decomposition: 15% increase in the ability to divide problems into manageable subproblems.

Pattern recognition: 10% improvement in the identification of recurring patterns.

Algorithm design: 18% improvement in the ability to structure efficient algorithmic solutions.

These results evidence a significant improvement in the acquisition of TC skills following the application of the CT4E model (see Fig. 2).

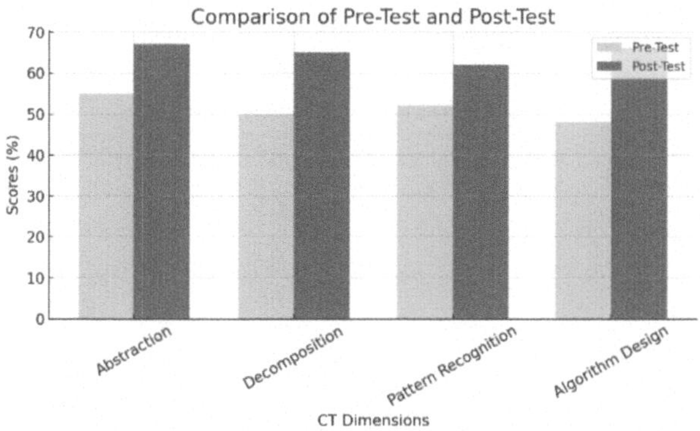

Fig. 2. Pre-Test and Post-Test Comparison - Computational Concepts. Source: Own research

Evaluation with Dr. Scratch: The Dr. Scratch tool was used to analyze the projects programmed by the students in Scratch. An improvement in the indicators of abstraction, modularity, and logical thinking was identified, with an average increase of 20% in the quality of the generated code (see Fig. 3).

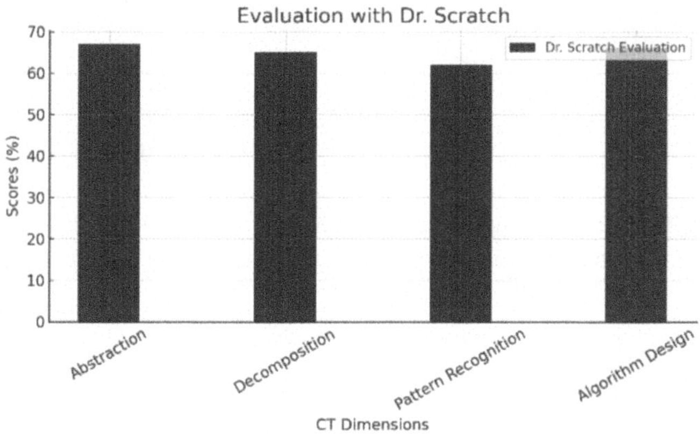

Fig. 3. Results of Dr. Scratch. Source: Own research

Statistical Analysis: Normality tests were applied to verify the distribution of the data, followed by Student's t-tests to evaluate significant differences between the pre-test and post-test. Table 2 below shows the results, which indicate that the observed improvements are statistically significant ($p < 0.05$) (see Fig. 4).

Table 2. Pretest and posttest results.

Dimension	Pre-Test (%)	Pos-Test (%)	Increase
Abstraction	55	67	+12
Decomposition	50	65	+15
Pattern Recognition	52	62	+10
Algorithm Design	48	66	+18

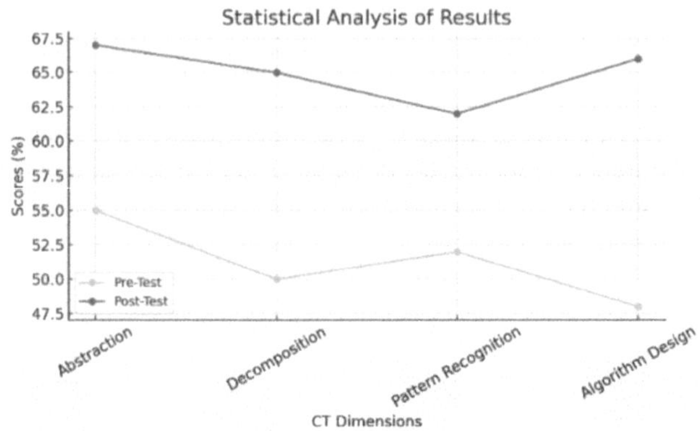

Fig. 4. Statistical Analysis of Results. Source: Own research

Improvement Trend: To visualize the progression in TC skills, a line graph showing the increase in each dimension assessed before and after the implementation of the model is presented.

6.2 Qualitative Results

The qualitative analysis was based on structured observations and interviews with students and teachers. The results reflect a positive perception of the impact of the model on learning.

Classroom Observations:

- Increased student participation and motivation.
- Increased collaborative work and effective communication.
- Improved understanding of computational concepts through hands-on activities (see Fig. 5).

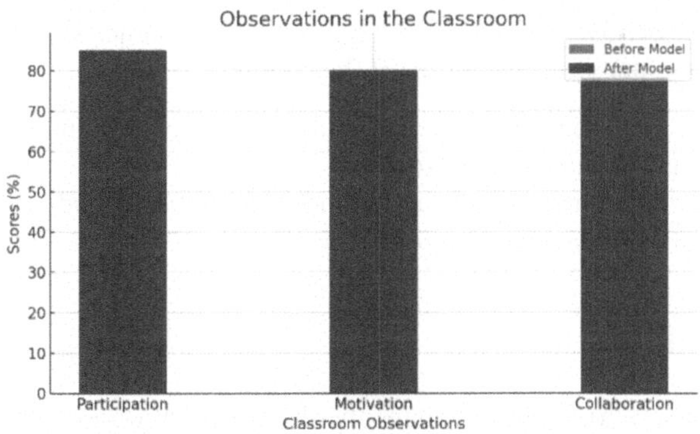

Fig. 5. Classroom Observations. Source: Own research

Student Perception: The interviews revealed that students perceived the CT4E model as a useful and motivating tool for learning programming and computational thinking. The following pie chart shows the distribution of students' perceptions (see Fig. 6):

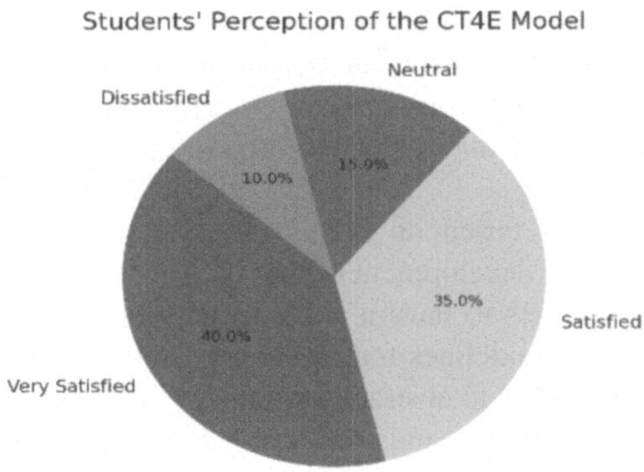

Fig. 6. Students' Perception of the CT4E Model. Source: Own research

6.3 Discussion

Comparison with Previous Studies: The findings obtained are consistent with previous studies on the integration of computational thinking in STEM education settings. Research such as Atmatzidou and Demetriadis (2014) has shown that the combination of practical and theoretical approaches facilitates the development of CT skills.

Educational Implications: The results suggest that the implementation of the CT4E model can be an effective strategy to improve the teaching of TC in introductory engineering courses. In addition, the combination of connected and disconnected activities provides a comprehensive approach that facilitates the understanding of computational concepts.

Limitations of the Study: Sample *Size:* The study was conducted with a small sample of students, limiting the generalizability of the results.

Time of implementation*:* The duration of the study may have influenced the results, as learning CT is a time-consuming process.

External *factors:* Elements such as individual motivation and students' previous experience may have influenced the results.

7 Conclusions

We have obtained a model that integrates the development of computational thinking and STEM concepts in the context of the ChildProgramming methodological approach, with a pilot test that gives us encouraging results.

Through the analysis of the data obtained in the descriptive case study, it is observed that the integration proposed by the CT4E model is feasible, and although integration might not be the only cause of the evaluation results, it does play a very important role in them.

The CT4E model contributes satisfactorily to the management of concepts and application of knowledge in situations of the real context, both in a connected and disconnected way, which promotes motivation in the solution of problems posed in different spaces.

The CT4E integration model is an academic contribution to the Faculty of Electronic Engineering and Telecommunications since it can be used to strengthen the introductory engineering course.

The academic activities based on this integration model are one of the main contributions focused on the development of the TC.

The model allows teachers to have a guide to develop activities within their subjects, which gives students guidelines for problem-solving. These activities encourage students to develop their ability to abstract and identify a problem, prioritize its importance, determine possible solutions, and prototype the most appropriate solution through collaborative work.

8 Future Work

Given the positive impact of the CT4E model, the following lines of future research are proposed:

Expansion of the CT4E model: Evaluate its implementation at different educational levels and in other higher education institutions.

Development of assessment tools: Design more advanced metrics to measure the acquisition of CT skills.

Validation in broader contexts: Apply the model in different regions and with larger samples to evaluate its effectiveness in different educational contexts.

Adaptation for secondary education: Implement CT4E in schools, particularly in grades 10 and 11, to strengthen TC training before university entrance.

Integration with more STEM competencies: Extend its use to other areas of knowledge to strengthen the teaching of scientific and technological disciplines.

Acknowledgments. The authors express their deep gratitude to the Software Engineering Research and Development Group - IDIS of the Faculty of Electronic Engineering and Telecommunications of the Universidad del Cauca, for their support in the realization of this study. Likewise, special recognition is extended to the teachers who facilitated the development of the research in their subjects and provided academic and methodological guidance.

We also thank the first-semester students of Electronics and Telecommunications Engineering and Industrial Automation Engineering, whose participation and commitment made the implementation and evaluation of the CT4E model.

Disclosure of Interests The authors of the article declare that they have no conflict of interest in the work presented.

References

1. Atmatzidou, S., Demetriadis, S.: How to support students' computational thinking skills in educational robotics activities. https://doi.org/10.1016/j.robot.2015.10.008 (2014)
2. Wing, J.: Computational thinking. Commun. ACM. **49**, 33–35 (2006). https://doi.org/10.1145/1118178.1118215
3. Wang, C., Shen, J., Chao, J.: Integrating computational thinking in stem education: a literature review. Int. J. Sci. Math. Educ. **20**, 1949–1972 (2021). https://doi.org/10.1007/s10763-021-10227-5
4. Sengupta, P., et al.: Integrating computational thinking with K-12 science education using agent-based computation: a theoretical framework. Educ. Inf. Technol. **18**, 351–380 (2013). https://doi.org/10.1007/s10639-012-9240-x
5. Hacker, M.: Integrating computational thinking into technology and engineering education. Technol. Eng. Teach. **77**(4), 8–14 (2018)
6. Wu, J., Wang, Y., Kong, H., Zhu, L.: How to cultivate computational thinking-enabled engineers: a case study on the robotics class of Zhejiang University. In: Proceedings of the 2019 ASEE Annual Conference & Exposition. https://doi.org/10.18260/1-2-32901 (2019)
7. Kelley, T.R., Knowles, J.G.: A conceptual framework for integrated STEM education. Int. J. STEM Educ. **3**, 1–11 (2016). https://doi.org/10.1186/s40594-016-0046-z
8. Ludeña, E.S.: La educación STEAM y la cultura "maker". Rev. Padres Maest. J. Parents Teach. **379**, 45–51 (2019). https://doi.org/10.14422/pym.i379.y2019.008
9. Mohtadi, C., Kim, M., Schlosser, J.: Why integrate computational thinking into a 21st century engineering curriculum? In: Proceedings of the IEEE Global Engineering Education Conference (EDUCON). https://doi.org/10.1109/educon.2014.6826132 (2013)
10. Hurtado, J., Alberto, C.C., Tatiana, C.S., Eduardo, R.O.: Child Programming: Una estrategia de aprendizaje y construcción de software basada en la lúdica, la colaboración y la agilidad. (2012)
11. Gómez A., P., Gómez N., Á.: Integrando el desarrollo del pensamiento computacional y los conceptos T&E STEM en el enfoque metodológico de ChildProgramming. Repositorio Universidad del Cauca. http://repositorio.unicauca.edu.co:8080/xmlui/handle/123456789/6279 (2023). Accessed 20 Jun 2023
12. Wing, J.: Computational thinking's influence on research and education for all. Ital. J. Educ. Technol. **25**(2), 7–14 (2017)

13. Brennan, K., Resnick, M.: New frameworks for studying and assessing the development of computational thinking. In: Proceedings of the 2012 Annual Meeting of the American Educational Research Association, Vancouver, Canada, p. 25. (2012)
14. National Science Foundation (NSF): NSF 93–143 guide to programs in the division of research, evaluation and dissemination with specific guidelines for individual programs. (1993)
15. Donahoe, D.: The definition of STEM? Today's Engineer, IEEE-USA. (2013)
16. Morrison, J.S.: Attributes of STEM education: the students, the academy, the classroom. TIES STEM Education Monograph Series. (2006)
17. Dugger, W., Satchwell, R.: ITEEA – Technology for All Americans: a rationale and structure for the study of technology (Rationale and Structure), [online]. https://www.iteea.org/42618.aspx (2022). Accessed 1 May 2022
18. Tenorio Melenje María, M., Trujillo, M.A., Hurtado Alegría, J.A., Collazos, C.: Debugging block-based programs. In: Agredo-Delgado, V., Ruiz, P.H. (eds.) Human-Computer Interaction. Communications in Computer and Information Science, pp. 98–112. Springer International Publishing, Cham (2019). https://doi.org/10.1007/978-3-030-05270-6_8
19. Page, M.J., et al.: Declaración PRISMA 2020: una guía actualizada para la publicación de revisiones sistemáticas. Rev. Esp. Cardiol. **74**(9), 790–799 (2021). https://doi.org/10.1016/j.recesp.2021.06.016
20. Yang, D., Baek, Y., Ching, Y.-H., Swanson, S., Chittoori, B., Wang, S.: Infusing computational thinking in an integrated stem curriculum: user reactions and lessons learned. Eur. J. STEM Educ. **6**(1), 1–12 (2021). https://doi.org/10.20897/ejsteme/9560
21. Yepes Miranda, D.D.: STEM y sus oportunidades en el ámbito educativo. [online]. https://repositorio.unicordoba.edu.co/handle/ucordoba/2774 (2022). Accessed 2 Nov 2022
22. Cannady, M.A., Collins, M.A., Hurt, T., Montgomery, R., Greenwald, E., Dorph, R.: Computational thinking for science positions youth to be better science learners. Educ. Sci. **15**(1), 1–15 (2025). https://doi.org/10.3390/educsci15010105
23. Zhou, R., et al.: Effect of different flow design approaches on undergraduates' computational thinking during pair programming. J. Educ. Comput. Res. **62**(7), 1865–1895 (2024). https://doi.org/10.1177/07356331241268474
24. Shoaib, H., Brophy, S.P.: A literature-based perspective towards learning and pedagogy of computational thinking. In: Presented at the 2020 ASEE Virtual Annual Conference Content Access. https://doi.org/10.18260/1-2-34011 (2020)
25. Gross, S., Kim, M., Schlosser, J., Lluch, D., Mohtadi, C., Schneider, D.: Fostering computational thinking in engineering education: challenges, examples, and best practices. In: Presented at the IEEE Global Engineering Education Conference (EDUCON), pp. 450–459. (2014). doi:https://doi.org/10.1109/EDUCON.2014.6826132
26. Miller, L.D., Soh, L.-K., Chiriacescu, V., Ingraham, E., Shell, D., Hazley, M.P.: Integrating computational and creative thinking to improve learning and performance in CS1. In: Proceedings of the SIGCSE Technical Symposium on Computer Science Education. https://doi.org/10.1145/2538862.2538940 (2014)
27. Dolgopolovas, V., Jevsikova, T., Savulionienė, L., Dagiene, V.: On evaluation of computational thinking of software engineering novice students. https://doi.org/10.13140/RG.2.1.2855.9206 (2015)
28. Román-González, M., Pérez-González, J.-C., Jiménez-Fernández, C.: Test de pensamiento computacional: diseño y psicometría general [Computational Thinking Test: design & general psychometry]. https://doi.org/10.13140/RG.2.1.3056.5521 (2015)
29. Mirbel, I., Ralyte, J.: Situational method engineering: combining assembly-based and roadmap-driven approaches. Requir. Eng. **11**, 58–78 (2006). https://doi.org/10.1007/s00766-005-0019-0

30. Cruz, S.T., Rojas, O.E., Alegría, J.: Un modelo para la enseñanza de la programación de software en niños a través de estrategias colaborativas. Universidad del Cauca. (2013)
31. Runeson, P., Wohlin, C., Hst, M., Ohlsson, M.C., Regnell, B., Wessln, A.: Experimentation in Software Engineering. Springer Publishing Company, Incorporated, Berlin (2012)

Model for the Integration of Automated Tools in the Usability Evaluation of e-Commerce Platforms

Alejandra Yicel Vagas Muñoz[1(✉)], Adriana Marcela Nieto Muñoz[1], and César Alberto Collazos[2]

[1] Corporación Universitaria Comfacauca – Unicomfacauca, Cl. 4 N. 8-30, Popayán, Cauca 190001, Colombia
yvargas@unicomfacauca.edu.co
[2] Universidad del Cauca, Calle 5 No 4 – 70, Popayán, Cauca 190001, Colombia
ccollazo@unicauca.edu.co

Abstract. Usability evaluation on e-commerce platforms, based exclusively on manual heuristic analysis, has critical limitations in terms of subjectivity, time consumption, and lack of scalability that hinder sales optimization. To address these challenges, this study proposes a hybrid model that integrates heuristic evaluations with automated tools, aiming to increase efficiency and objectivity by combining precise metrics with the contextual insight of expert evaluators. Methodologically, a comparative framework was established by applying 16 heuristics and analyzing tools such as Lighthouse, WAVE, and Hotjar to assign improvement scores based on their technical detection capabilities. The results demonstrate that automation significantly optimizes the identification of performance, accessibility, and interaction issues, reducing human bias, although it is acknowledged that design consistency and user perception still require manual interpretation to ensure complete accuracy. This research constitutes a fundamental contribution by establishing the theoretical foundations for scalable hybrid approaches, offering a preliminary proposal with high potential to transform usability evaluation in competitive digital environments, thereby improving the end-user experience.

Keywords: Usability evaluation · Heuristic analysis · Automated tools · E-commerce · Human-computer Interaction

1 Introduction

Evaluating usability on e-commerce platforms is a critical aspect of improving the user experience and increasing the conversion rate. Traditionally, these evaluations have been based on the application of heuristics and the intervention of experts. However, the integration of automated tools can provide a more efficient approach, reducing times and providing quantifiable metrics that facilitate decision-making in interface design. The results obtained in previous studies will serve as a basis for comparing the impact of automation on usability evaluation [1–3].

H. Luna-García et al. (Eds.): HCI-COLLAB 2025, CCIS 2850, pp. 218–235, 2027.
https://doi.org/10.1007/978-3-032-31223-5_16

Table 1. Description of the PICOC method applied to the research. (Source: Own elaboration)

Element	Description
P (Population)	Studies that addressed web platforms were focused, with emphasis on those oriented to e-commerce, given that this type of systems present particular challenges in terms of user experience, navigation, conversion and satisfaction.
I (Intervention)	Research that included the application of automated tools for usability evaluation, such as automatic validators, plugins, interface analysis systems or applied artificial intelligence, was considered.
C (Comparison)	We looked at whether studies compared automated assessments with manual approaches, such as the application of usability heuristics by experts.
O (Outcome)	We searched for studies that reported findings related to the detection of usability problems, the efficiency of the evaluation process, the reduction of time and effort, or the improvement in the user experience.
C (Context)	Research developed in academic, industrial or mixed environments was included, in order to cover different levels of application and practical validation.

1.1 Background Previous Work

The previous work underpins the model by developing sixteen specific heuristics that incorporate seventy-four questions designed to accurately quantify the state of e-commerce platforms. Evaluated by international experts, the study identified critical shortcomings in personalization, navigation, and accessibility, highlighting the imperative need to adapt the criteria to specific user demands in order to obtain superior technical assessments. These findings establish the quantitative baseline necessary for the new automated proposal, enabling a direct comparison between manual and digital approaches that ensures the absolute reproducibility of future results [4].

2 Related Studies on Automated Assessments

To carry out the review of studies related to automated usability evaluations, the PICOC (Population, Intervention, Comparison, Outcome, Context). This framework provides a clear structure for formulating research questions and establishing consistent search, selection, and analysis criteria, which is essential to ensure the validity and relevance of the included studies [5] (Table 2).

2.1 Ramos Mendoza, N. G., & Alarcón Guevara, I. V. (2023). Evaluation of the Quality in use of e-Commerce Platforms

In 2019, with 24 million internet users in Peru and an alarming lack of metrics tools, this study developed an instrument based on the ISO/IEC 25000 standard to audit open-source systems. The methodology evaluates critical attributes such as operability, intelligibility, and learnability, and was applied with scientific rigor to companies with active transactional operations. The empirical results demonstrate that WixCommerce significantly outperforms Weebly, receiving a score of 6.75 versus 4.0 in satisfaction and technical quality following evaluation. This finding validates the imperative need to standardize platform selection through international regulatory frameworks that ensure digital excellence [6, 7].

Table 2. Inclusion and exclusion criteria applied to research. (Source: Own elaboration)

Category	Specific criteria	Justification
Inclusion	Publications between 2013 and 2025	It ensures topicality in relation to automated technologies and recent practices.
	Language: English or Spanish	It facilitates detailed analysis and ensures accurate understanding of the results.
	Practical application of automated tools	Empirical evidence of the use of technology to evaluate usability is sought.
	Analysis of results related to usability (problems, improvements, etc.)	It allows the real impact of the automated intervention to be assessed.
Exclusion	Conceptual works without practical application	They do not provide empirical evidence on the effectiveness of automated tools.
	Studies focused solely on accessibility with no explicit link to usability	The central focus is usability; Works where this is not the main objective are excluded.
	Non-peer-reviewed articles	Priority is given to the quality and academic validation of the included studies.

2.2 Mata, F. J., & Hernández-Ruiz, I. (2019). Usability Evaluation for an e-Commerce Site: Development of a Methodology and its Application to the crg ourmetcoffee.com site

The objective of this study was to propose a reliable methodology for auditing usability in e-commerce ecosystems using the System Usability Scale, whose psychometric robustness was validated through an exhaustive technical analysis of the crgourmetcof fee.com website. The collected data confirms that the platform exceeds acceptability thresholds with an outstanding rating, demonstrating a logical information architecture and flawless transactional flows that mitigate the end-user's cognitive load. In conclusion, the implementation of the SUS emerges as the dominant paradigm for quantifying the customer experience, allowing for the identification of areas for improvement with absolute precision and ensuring that this proposed methodology is infallible [3].

2.3 Paz, F., Villanueva, A., & Pow Sang, J. A. (2015). Usability Evaluation in Web Applications

This study implemented an evaluation process based on Nielsen's heuristics to diagnose academic software products, transforming an initial quality rating of 7% into an optimized interaction architecture. By systematically identifying flaws in navigation and content clarity, the methodology proved highly effective in resolving critical user experience issues following the implementation of the suggested improvements. The results confirm that integrating these evaluations into early stages of development is essential to ensuring a superior final product, validating the technical superiority of this diagnostic approach in modern web applications [8].

2.4 Orienteed. (2023). Test Automation in e-Commerce: Quality and Efficiency

This study highlights the importance of test automation in e-commerce, using tools and scripts to perform usability and performance evaluations with greater efficiency than manual methods. This methodology increases the speed and accuracy of processes by eliminating human error, ensuring consistent results across various operating environments, and enabling the early detection of critical failures. By reducing operating costs and strengthening product robustness, automated systems have established themselves as fundamental pillars of technical quality, making it imperative for companies to adopt them to ensure their competitive relevance [9].

2.5 Sierra González, J. C. (2016). Usability Evaluation Methodology for Web Information Systems

The objective of this study was to propose a structured methodology for evaluating the usability of web systems, emphasizing the need for automation given the complexity and volume of tests required to ensure satisfactory user experiences. This methodological proposal, which spans from planning to the implementation of changes, proved effective in detecting interface flaws, concluding that the integration of automated tools significantly optimizes the time and resources invested without compromising analytical rigor. Finally, in agile development environments, this framework facilitates continuous executions that allow for the constant optimization of the platform without causing critical delays in product delivery [10].

2.6 Valid AI. Best Automated UX Testing Tools for e-Commerce in 2023

The aim of this article was to analyze the top automated testing tools to evaluate user experience (UX) on e-commerce platforms in 2023, highlighting their advantages and applications. The article details several automation tools that are popular in the e-commerce sector, such as tools for usability testing, A/B testing, user behavior analysis, and load simulation. These tools enable development teams to improve the user experience by offering fast and effective testing that identifies issues in the design and functionality of platforms. Proper use of these tools can lead to a better understanding of users' needs, which in turn results in a more user friendly and engaging platform. Businesses should invest in these tools to optimize their performance and better satisfy their customers [11].

3 Discussion on Existing Models and Input on the Model of the Proposed

Usability evaluation in e-commerce has historically relied on SUS scales and international standards, although current automated tools such as Valido AI continue to provide fragmented views of the system. My proposed model revolutionizes this field by integrating automated tools with specific heuristics, overcoming the limitations of isolated approaches through quantifiable reports of high technical precision. Finally, the incorporation of an expert validation phase contextualizes the automated data, consolidating a superior hybrid approach that optimizes operational efficiency and drastically reduces subjectivity in digital audits [3, 4, 6, 11].

4 Proposal for an Automated Assessment Model

A model for the integration of automated tools in the usability evaluation is proposed based on the following 6 phases [12] (Fig. 1):

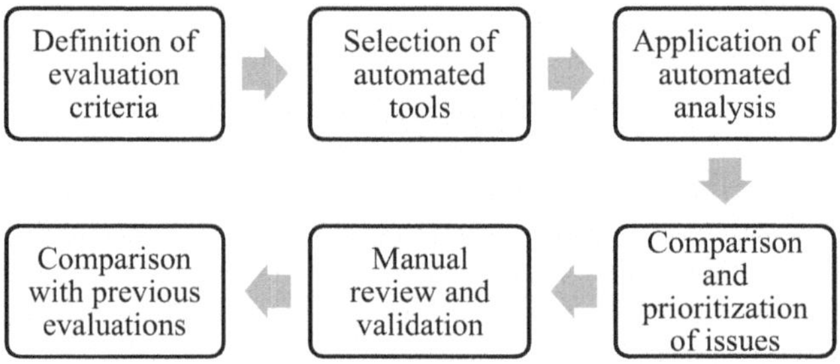

Fig. 1. Phases of the automated assessment model. (Source: Own elaboration)

Table 1 describes each of the phases of the automated assessment model.

This proposed six-phase hybrid model stems from a comprehensive systematic review that integrates manual and automated usability evaluation to ensure complete methodological traceability between expert findings and the technical results obtained. Based on scientific patterns and Gartner reviews, the framework establishes that automation drastically optimizes efficiency in critical areas such as accessibility and performance, although it is unable to replace human perception in subjective dimensions such as visual consistency. Although the theoretical foundation is undeniable, the model awaits validation through pilot testing on real platforms to confirm its absolute technical infallibility [13, 14] (Table 3).

Table 3. Description of the phases of the automated assessment model. (Source: Own elaboration)

Phase No.	Phase	Description
1	Definition of Evaluation Criteria	Selection of specific heuristics for e-commerce platforms.
2	Automated Tool Selection	Identification of appropriate tools for evaluation.
3	Application of Automated Analysis	Use of tools to generate detailed reports on the aspects evaluated.
4	Problem Comparison and Prioritization	Analysis of the findings obtained and determination of critical areas for improvement.
5	Manual Review and Validation	Incorporation of a layer of validation by experts to contextualize the automated results.
6	Comparison with Previous Evaluations	The results obtained through automation will be compared with those of previous studies to assess the impact of the new approach.

5 Towards a More Accurate Assessment of Usability in e-Commerce

E-commerce platforms have evolved significantly, incorporating more sophisticated interfaces and personalized experiences for users. However, ensuring good usability remains a key challenge, as it directly impacts sales conversion, customer retention, and overall user satisfaction [16–19].

5.1 Limitations of the Manual Usability Evaluation

Subjectivity in evaluation. Different evaluators may interpret problems differently, generating variability in the results.

High time and effort. Manually evaluating a complex platform can require hours of analysis, making it costly and difficult to scale.

Difficulty detecting technical problems. Some flaws in performance, loading, and accessibility are not easily identifiable without specialized tools.

Lack of quantifiable data. Many times, manual evaluation is based on qualitative observations without exact metrics on the impact of the problems found.

5.2 Automatic Tools to Evaluate Usability

Currently, there are several tools designed to detect usability problems in digital interfaces, allowing a more objective evaluation.

Lighthouse (Google). Evaluate a website's performance, accessibility, and best practices. Detects loading issues, DOM structure, and response times. Offer optimization suggestions with quantifiable metrics [20].

WAVE (Web Accessibility Evaluation Tool). It analyzes the accessibility of web interfaces, checking for contrasts, alt tags, and semantic structure. Identifies problems that may affect users with visual or cognitive impairments [21].

Hotjar. Track user interaction through heatmaps and session recordings. It allows you to detect browsing patterns and problems in the user experience [22].

5.3 Tool Selection: Comparative Analysis

The choice of Lighthouse, WAVE and Hotjar in the design of the proposed hybrid model, a comparative analysis was carried out with other relevant tools in the field of automated usability evaluation. The objective of this analysis was to identify those options that, in addition to offering useful functionalities, were viable in academic or professional contexts with limited resources and compatible with a heuristic approach.

[20–23]

Table 4. Comparative analysis for the choice of tools. (Source: Own elaboration)

Tool	Type of assessment	Key functionalities	Related Heuristics
Lighthouse	Automated (technical)	Performance metrics, accessibility, SEO, best practices, PWAs	Load time, responsive design, technical errors
WAVE	Automated (visual accessibility)	Accessibility Assessment: Contrast, Structure, Navigation, Labels	Accessibility, readability, clear navigation
Hotjar	User behavior	Heatmaps, session recordings, surveys, and conversion funnels	Visual clarity, intuitive navigation, feedback
Axe	Automated (accessibility)	Advanced WCAG validation, integration with CI/CD pipelines	Accessibility (advanced), structural errors
Siteimprove	Integral (commercial)	SEO analysis, performance, accessibility, detailed regulatory reporting	Multiple technical heuristics (payment required)
CrazyEgg	User behavior	Heat maps, scroll maps, segment analysis	Visual clarity, interaction, user experience

The selected tools offer a wide coverage of the critical areas in web usability: technical performance (Lighthouse), structural accessibility (WAVE) and real user behavior (Hotjar). While alternatives like Axe and Siteimprove stand out for their accuracy or enterprise focus, their implementation may be less accessible or cost-limited, making them less suitable for the proposed approach [24, 25] (Table 5).

Table 5. Comparative analysis for the choice of tools. (Source: Own elaboration)

Tool	Free or Freemium	Ease of use	Browser Integration	Requires advanced technical knowledge	Suitable for educational or research contexts
Lighthouse	Yes (100%)	Loud	Yes (Chrome)	No	Yes
WAVE	Yes (100%)	Loud	Yes (extension)	No	Yes
Hotjar	Partial (basic version)	Medium-High	No	No	Yes
Axe	Yes (limited)	Stocking	Yes	Yes	Partial (requires technical profile)
Siteimprove	No	Loud	No	No	No
CrazyEgg	Partial	Stocking	No	No	Partial (very limited free version)

The selection of free and accessible tools such as Lighthouse, WAVE, and Hotjar ensures a scalable model with a low learning curve, in contrast to corporate or complex solutions like Site improve and Axe. Although WAVE focuses on accessibility, its integration is justified because, according to ISO 9241-171, this dimension is a critical component of usability that directly impacts user effectiveness and satisfaction. Therefore, evaluating accessibility barriers using these tools allows us to identify navigation or readability issues that compromise the overall experience, providing indispensable diagnostic value for optimizing any digital platform [20, 21, 23].

6 Comparison Between Manual Assessment and Automation

To measure the impact of these tools on the heuristic evaluation of e-commerce platforms, a comparative table has been developed based on four key elements.

Evaluation heuristics. Set of 16 principles applied in the evaluation of e-commerce platforms.

Manual scoring. Results obtained from the evaluation carried out by experts without automated tools.

Expected improvement (%). Estimate of the percentage of improvement based on the ability of automatic tools to detect and correct problems.

Projected score. Calculation resulting from applying the expected improvement to manual scoring, reflecting the potential impact of automation.

6.1 Obtaining the Manual Score

The manual scores used in this study come from the article, where a heuristic evaluation applied by six experts was performed [4] (Table 6).

Table 6. Scores assigned to each heuristic after manual evaluation. (Source: [4])

N°	Heuristics	Average of all evaluators	Maximum possible	Difference	Difference in percentage value
H14	Defaults	0.44	3.00	2.56	15%
H15	Reduced latency	0.66	2.00	1.34	33%
H16	E-commerce usability	6.57	14.00	7.43	47%
H7	Diagnose errors	1.88	4.00	2.12	47%
H11	Save Status	1.44	3.00	1.56	48%
H6	Flexibility	3.05	6.00	2.95	51%
H13	Autonomy	1.66	3.00	1.34	55%
H12	Control and readability	2.55	4.00	1.46	64%
H8	Error prevention	2.10	3.00	0.90	70%
H10	Help and documentation	3.60	5.00	1.40	72%
H1	System Visibility and Health	3.82	5.00	1.18	76%
H9	Aesthetic design	3.10	4.00	0.90	78%
H3	User Control	2.38	3.00	0.62	79%
H5	Recognition	4.05	5.00	0.96	81%
H4	Consistency and standards	5.27	6.00	0.73	88%
H2	Connection between the system and the real world	3.60	4.00	0.40	90%

For this analysis, the average of the scores awarded by the evaluators was calculated, which allows a baseline to be established before estimating the impact of automation on the usability evaluation (Table 7).

Table 7. Average of the scores awarded by the evaluators. (Source: [4])

N°	Heuristic	Manual Scoring
H1	Visibility	3.82
H2	Real World Match	3.6
H3	User Control	2.38
H4	Consistency	5.27
H5	Recognition	4.05
H6	Flexibility	3.05
H7	Diagnose Errors	1.88
H8	Error Prevention	2.1
H9	Aesthetic Design	3.1
H10	Help	3.6
H11	Save Status	1.44
H12	Control & Readability	2.55
H13	Autonomy	1.66
H14	Defaults	0.44
H15	Reduced Latency	0.66
H16	E-commerce Usability	6.57

6.2 Methodological Process for Estimating the Expected Improvement

To quantify the impact of automation on usability evaluation, a three-stage approach has been followed (Fig. 2):

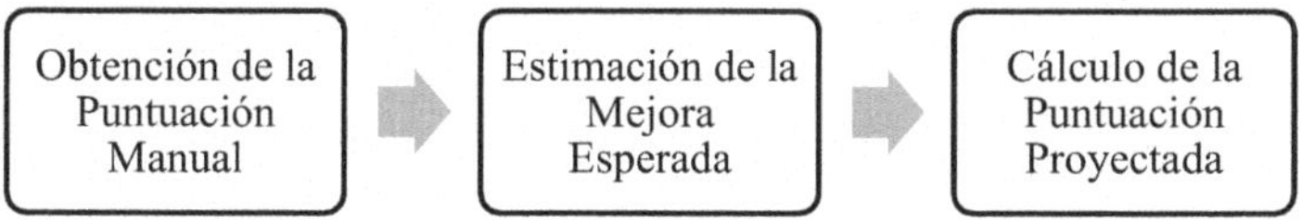

Fig. 2. Phases to quantify the impact of automation on usability evaluation. (Source: [28])

6.2.1 Obtaining the Manual Score

The manual evaluation was done by applying 16 usability heuristics on an e-commerce platform, where each heuristic received a score based on expert perception [4].

Data source. Results of a preliminary heuristic evaluation conducted by experts.

Scoring format. Quantitative scale (low = critical; high = good usability).

Average number of evaluations. Calculation of the average score for each heuristic.

For example. A score of 0.66 for "Reduced Latency" indicates that the loading time is a critical flaw.

6.2.2 Estimate of the Expected Improvement (%)

Estimated Improvement Factors. Table 4 projects the type of automated tool that could be used for the evaluation of each of the usability heuristics and describes the reason for the improvement for each of them [20–22] (Table 8).

Table 8. Description of the type of automated tool and reason for improvement for each heuristic. (Source: Own elaboration)

Heuristic	Tool that helps	Reason for the improvement
H1 Visibility	Lighthouse	Detects visibility issues and system states
H2 Real World Match	Hotjar	Analyze connection with user expectations
H3 User Control	Hotjar	Identify browsing patterns and shortcuts
H4 Consistency	WAVE	Detects inconsistencies in UI standards
H5 Recognition	Lighthouse + WAVE	Assesses visual recognition and structure
H6 Flexibility	Hotjar	Analyze adaptability across different devices
H7 Diagnose Errors	Lighthouse + WAVE	Identify technical and accessibility errors
H8 Error Prevention	WAVE + Lighthouse	Improved form validations and accessibility
H9 Aesthetic Design	Lighthouse + WAVE	Evaluate structure and readability
H10 Help	WAVE	Verify accessibility and visibility of documentation
H11 Save Status	Hotjar	Assesses data persistence and session recovery
H12 Control & Readability	WAVE	Analyze text accessibility and contrast
H13 Autonomy	Hotjar	Detect personalization patterns
H14 Defaults	Lighthouse	Evaluate optimal initial configurations
H15 Reduced Latency	Lighthouse	Identify and optimize charging times

(*continued*)

Table 8. (*continued*)

Heuristic	Tool that helps	Reason for the improvement
H16 E-commerce Usability	Hotjar	Evaluate shopping experience with user data

Factors considered in the improvement estimate. To determine how much each heuristic can improve with automated tools, three key factors were analyzed.

How much does the heuristic depend on subjective vs. objective evaluation? The greater the human (aesthetic) interpretation, the smaller the improvement (5–20%); the greater the objectivity, the greater the impact.

Capabilities of automatic tools. Tools such as Lighthouse, WAVE, and Hotjar have been shown to improve certain aspects by 30–80% in previous studies.

Comparison with previous studies. Use of external references to project the potential for automated improvement in metrics.

Example of an expected improvement assignment. "Reduced Latency" is objective; Lighthouse can measure it accurately and improve load time by up to 80% (Table 9).

Table 9. Expected improvement for all heuristics based on their relationship to automation. (Source: Own elaboration)

N°	Heuristic	Manual Scoring	Expected Improvement (%)
H1	Visibility	3.82	15%
H2	Real World Match	3.6	15%
H3	User Control	2.38	30%
H4	Consistency	5.27	5%
H5	Recognition	4.05	20%
H6	Flexibility	3.05	30%
H7	Diagnose Errors	1.88	45%
H8	Error Prevention	2.1	40%
H9	Aesthetic Design	3.1	20%
H10	Help	3.6	25%
H11	Save Status	1.44	50%
H12	Control & Readability	2.55	25%
H13	Autonomy	1.66	40%
H14	Defaults	0,44	70%
H15	Reduced Latency	0.66	75%
H16	E-commerce Usability	6.57	10%

6.2.3 Calculation of the Projected Score

Once the expected improvement (%), the following formula is applied to calculate the projected score with automatic tools:

$$\textit{Projected score} = \textit{Manual score} \times (1 + \textit{Expected improvement}) \quad (1)$$

It comes from the standard way of calculating a percentage increment in mathematics [28].

Example with an increase of 75%. If a heuristic has a manual score of 0.66 and the expected improvement is 75% (0.75 in decimal), then, for the "Reduced Latency" heuristic.

Manual Score: 0.66

Expected Improvement: 75% (factor 1.75)

$$\textit{Puntuación proyectada} = 0.66 \times (1 + 0.75) = 0.66 \times 1.75 = 1.16 \quad (2)$$

Projected Score: 1.16

If we only multiplied by 0.75, we would get a lower value, which would not correctly reflect the improvement.

7 Comparative Analysis of Manual Evaluation vs. Projection with Automation

The comparison tables present the impact of automation on the heuristic evaluation of e-commerce sites based on four factors: the heuristics evaluated, their initial manual score, the expected percentage improvement using automated tools, and the projected final score following that optimization.

7.1 Interpretation of the Comparison

Manual Scoring. It represents the values obtained in the heuristic evaluation performed by experts without automated tools.

Expected Improvement (%). It corresponds to the estimated percentage of optimization that could be achieved by incorporating automatic tools.

Projected score. It is the result of applying the expected improvement to manual scoring, reflecting the potential of automation in detecting and correcting usability issues (Table 10

Table 10. Projected score by applying the aforementioned form to each of the heuristics (Source: [28])

Heuristic	Manual Scoring	Expected Improvement (%)	Projected Score
Visibility	3.82	15%	4.39
Real World Match	3.6	15%	4.14
User Control	2.38	30%	3.09
Consistency	5.27	5%	5.53
Recognition	4.05	20%	4.86
Flexibility	3.05	30%	3.97
Diagnose Errors	1.88	45%	2.73
Error Prevention	2.1	40%	2.94
Aesthetic Design	3.1	20%	3.72
Help	3.6	25%	4.5
Save Status	1.44	50%	2.16
Control & Readability	2.55	25%	3.19
Autonomy	1.66	40%	2.32
Defaults	0.44	70%	0.75
Reduced Latency	0.66	75%	1.16
E-commerce Usability	6.57	10%	7.23

7.2 Main Findings: Manual vs. Projection with Automation

The comparison table reflects how automated tools can optimize the detection of usability issues on e-commerce platforms. Next, the 16 heuristics are analyzed, grouping them according to the level of projected improvement [4].

Heuristics with High Projected Improvement (40%–75%). These heuristics rely on quantifiable data, so automated tools can optimize their detection significantly (Table 11).

Table 11. Description of problems in manual assessment and how automation tools can improve those problems. (Source: Own elaboration)

Heuristics	Problem in manual evaluation	How automation improves
Reduced Latency (+75%)	Experts may notice delays in loading, but not accurately measure their impact.	Lighthouse analyzes response times and detects performance bottlenecks.

(continued)

Table 11. (*continued*)

Heuristics	Problem in manual evaluation	How automation improves
Defaults (+70%)	The initial system setup can be inconsistent and difficult to evaluate without data from multiple users.	Tools can analyze defaults and assess their impact on usability.
Save Status (+50%)	Assessing whether user data is saved correctly in a session can be tricky.	Hotjar can track interactions and detect if data is lost after a disconnection.
Diagnose Errors (+45%)	Experts can identify errors, but without technical details about their origin.	Lighthouse and WAVE detect technical errors and accessibility automatically.
Autonomy (+40%)	Difficult to assess whether users have enough control over system options.	Hotjar allows you to detect patterns of personalization and accessibility.
Error Prevention (+40%)	Evaluating forms and user flows is subjective and takes time.	WAVE detects errors in forms, and Lighthouse analyzes validations in real time.

Heuristics with Moderate Improvement (20%–35%). These heuristics have some subjectivity, but they can benefit from automation in some ways (Table 12).

Table 12. Description of problems in manual assessment and how automation tools can improve those problems. (Source: Own elaboration)

Heuristics + %Enhancement	Problem in manual evaluation	How automation improves
User Control (+30%)	Assessing how easily users can correct errors is subjective.	Hotjar analyzes interactions and task abandonment in interfaces.
Flexibility (+30%)	Testers may notice a lack of adaptability, but no user behavior data.	Hotjar analyzes how users interact on different devices.
Help (+25%)	Evaluating the effectiveness of online help is subjective.	WAVE detects accessibility issues in the help documentation.
Control & Readability (+25%)	It is based on the evaluators' perception of the clarity of the text.	WAVE evaluates contrast, readability, and visual hierarchy of content.
Aesthetic Design (+20%)	It is subjective and varies according to the evaluator's interpretation.	Tools can detect inconsistent structure, but the design still depends on human judgment.

(*continued*)

Table 12. (*continued*)

Heuristics + %Enhancement	Problem in manual evaluation	How automation improves
Recognition (+20%)	The ease of recognizing elements in the interface varies by user.	Lighthouse can analyze navigation patterns and DOM structure.

Heuristics with Low Projected Improvement (5%–15%). These heuristics rely heavily on human judgment and contextual interpretation, so automation has limited impact (Table 13).

Table 13. Description of problems in manual assessment and how automation tools can improve those problems. (Source: Own elaboration)

Heuristics	Problem in manual evaluation	How automation improves
Visibility (+15%)	Testers can identify whether the system provides sufficient feedback to the user.	Lighthouse can detect hidden or under-visualized elements.
Real World Match (+15%)	Assessing whether the system fits the user's mental model is subjective.	Hotjar can analyze navigation and measure consistency with previous expectations.
Consistency (+5%)	It depends on the evaluator's criteria and cannot be measured with automatic accuracy.	WAVE can detect inconsistencies in structure and labels, but overall consistency still requires human evaluation.
E-commerce Usability (+10%)	It depends on multiple user experience factors.	Hotjar can track buying patterns and Lighthouse can measure performance in payment processes.

8 Implementation and Considerations

The implementation of this study goes beyond theoretical estimation to provide mandatory empirical validation through the strategic selection of representative e-commerce platforms based on their architecture and transactional flow. It is imperative to calibrate metrics that integrate objective data from tools such as Lighthouse with expert heuristic judgment to address the contextual limitations of automation. This hybrid model ensures that aesthetic consistency and subjective perception are not overlooked, establishing a robust evaluation framework that goes beyond simple data collection.

As a future line of work, it is proposed to empirically validate the estimates made in this study, applying automated tools on real platforms and comparing their results with manual evaluations. This will allow adjusting the estimated improvement factors and developing an optimized hybrid model for the evaluation of usability in e-commerce.

9 Conclusions

This study provides a technical analysis of the impact of automation using Lighthouse, WAVE, and Hotjar to optimize heuristic evaluation on transactional platforms. The results demonstrate disruptive potential in terms of accessibility metrics and technical performance, although visual consistency still requires my expert oversight. Consequently, the combination of algorithms and specialized human judgment currently represents the only valid approach.

The proposal establishes estimated improvement factors for each heuristic, making it possible to identify areas where automation optimizes the audit process compared to mandatory manual intervention. However, the model requires empirical validation in real-world environments to mitigate theoretical biases inherent in the current estimates. Future work will refine this hybrid approach, enhancing the scalability and robustness of this new scientific methodology.

References

1. Nielsen, J.: Usability Engineering. Morgan Kaufmann, San Francisco (1993)
2. González, M., Masip, L., Granollers, T., Oliva, M.: Quantitative analysis in a heuristic evaluation experiment. Adv. Eng. Softw. **40**(12), 1271–1278 (2009). https://doi.org/10.1016/j.advengsoft.2009.01.027
3. Mata, F.J., Hernández, I.: Usability evaluation for an electronic commerce site: development of a methodology and its application to the crgourmetcoffee.com site. In: Proceedings of CICEN 2019. (2019). https://doi.org/10.15359/CICEN.1.9
4. Vargas Muñoz, A.Y., Granollers Saltiveri, A., Collazos Ordoñez, C.A.: Analysis and optimization of the usability of e-commerce platforms through evaluation heuristics. (2024)
5. Kitchenham, B.: Guidelines for performing systematic literature reviews in software engineering. EBSE Technical Report EBSE-2007-01. (2007)
6. Ramos Mendoza, B.N.G., Alarcón Guevara, I.V., Leyva Oliver, V.: Evaluation of the quality in use of e-commerce platforms. Thesis, Professional School of Systems Engineering, Faculty of Engineering, Architecture and Urbanism. (2019)
7. ISO/IEC 25000: Systems and software engineering — Systems and software Quality Requirements and Evaluation (SQuaRE). https://www.iso.org/standard/80039.html. Accessed 3 Feb 2025
8. Paz, F., Pow-Sang, J.A.: A systematic mapping review of usability evaluation methods for software development process. Int. J. Softw. Eng. Appl. **10**(1), 165–178 (2016). https://doi.org/10.14257/IJSEIA.2016.10.1.16
9. Orienteed: Test automation in eCommerce: quality and efficiency. https://orienteed.com/es/automatizacion-de-pruebas-en-ecommerce/. Accessed 3 Feb 2025
10. Sierra González, J.C.: Usability evaluation methodology for web-based information systems. (2016)
11. Valido, A.I.: The best automated UX testing tools for ecommerce in. https://www.valido.ai/es/herramientas-pruebas-automatizadas-ux-ecommerce-2023/ (2023). Accessed 3 Feb 2025
12. Zewdu, M.: Automated heuristic evaluation for usability of multiple web interface. https://www.academia.edu/17346353 (2016). Accessed 3 Feb 2025
13. Castro, J.W., Garnica, I., Rojas, L.A.: Automated tools for usability evaluation: a systematic mapping study. In: Lecture Notes in Computer Science, vol. 13315, pp. 28–46. Springer, Cham (2022). https://doi.org/10.1007/978-3-031-05061-9_3

14. Ivory, M.Y., Hearst, M.A.: The state of the art in automating usability evaluation of user interfaces. ACM Computing Surveys. (2001)
15. Kuric, E., Demcak, P., Lang, J.: Systematic literature review of automation and artificial intelligence in usability issue detection. arXiv preprint arXiv:2504.01415. https://arxiv.org/pdf/2504.01415 (2025). Accessed 5 May 2025
16. Masip, L., Granollers, T., Oliva, M.: A heuristic evaluation experiment to validate the new set of usability heuristics. In: Proceedings of the 8th International Conference on Information Technology: New Generations (ITNG 2011), pp. 429–434. IEEE, Las Vegas (2011). https://doi.org/10.1109/ITNG.2011.82
17. Vargas Muñoz, A.Y., Collazos, C.A., Granollers, T.: Evaluation heuristics to improve usability in ecommerce platforms. In: XI Ibero-American Conference on Human-Computer Interaction (JIHCI 2024)
18. Vargas Muñoz, A.Y., Muñoz Sanabria, L.F., Collazos Ordoñez, C.A.: Evaluation heuristics for commercial platforms: systematic mapping study. In: IX Ibero-American Conference on Human-Computer Interaction, pp. 7–24. (2023). https://jihci2023.unlam.edu.ar/es/pdf/LibroActas-JIHCI2023.pdf
19. Heričko, T., Šumak, B., Brdnik, S.: Towards Representative Web Performance Measurements With Google Lighthouse. In: Proceedings of the Conference. Maribor, Slovenia: University of Maribor Press, pp. 39–42. (2021). https://doi.org/10.18690/978-961-286-516-0.9
20. WAVE: Web accessibility evaluation tools. https://wave.webaim.org/. Accessed 3 Feb 2025
21. Hotjar: How to do a usability test evaluation in 5 steps. https://www.hotjar.com/es/test-de-usabilidad/evaluacion/. Accessed 3 Feb 2025
22. Google: Lighthouse | Chrome for developers. https://developer.chrome.com/docs/lighthouse. Accessed 5 May 2025
23. Deque: Accessibility testing tools & software: axe. https://www.deque.com/axe/. Accessed 5 May 2025
24. Siteimprove: Content experiences that capture attention. https://www.siteimprove.com/. Accessed 5 May 2026
25. ISO: ISO 9241-171:2008 – Ergonomics of human-system interaction — Part 171: Guidance on software accessibility. https://www.iso.org/standard/39080.html. Accessed 5 May 2025
26. Harper, S., Yesilada, Y.: Web accessibility and guidelines. In: Web Accessibility, pp. 61–78. Springer, London (2008). https://doi.org/10.1007/978-1-84800-050-6_6
27. Solé, M.O., Granollers, T., Ardévol, M.: Analysis of the viability of solutions for the automation of heuristic evaluation
28. Nextscenario: Percent growth formula. https://nextscenario.com/es/formula-del-porcentaje-de-crecimiento-un-analisis-detallado/. Accessed 3 Feb 2025

Review of Heuristics and Usability and UX Scales for Speech-Based Technologies

Lady K. Gomez[1(✉)], Huizilopoztli Luna-García[1], and César Alberto Collazos[2]

[1] Universidad Autónoma de Zacatecas, Zacatecas 98160, México
{ladykatherine,hlugar}@uaz.edu.mx
[2] Universidad del Cauca, Cauca 76001, Colombia
ccollazo@unicauca.edu.co

Abstract. Technological advancements have led to the widespread adoption of voice interaction technologies in smart speakers, Internet of Things (IoT) devices, mobile applications, and other intelligent systems. Despite their growing presence, several usability challenges persist, hindering their effective integration into users' daily lives. Issues related to natural language understanding, system feedback, error handling, privacy, and user trust negatively affect user experience. Furthermore, the lack of specific heuristics, validated measurement scales, and standardized guidelines limit both the evaluation and systematic development of these technologies, making consistent assessment difficult across different contexts of use. This systematic literature review aims to identify the main knowledge gaps and consolidate recent research on heuristics and usability evaluation methods for voice interaction technologies. Based on an analysis of studies published in recent years, it offers a comprehensive overview of existing approaches, limitations, and trends. The findings contribute to improving the design and evaluation of these systems, while also guiding future research and supporting the development of more user-centered voice interaction solutions.

Keywords: Voice Interaction Technologies · Usability · User experience design · Scales and Heuristic

1 Introduction

Over the past few years, there has been significant technological advancement, which has made it possible to adopt voice interfaces in commercial devices through smart speakers and IoT devices, as well as conversational interaction in mobile devices and others. Although these technologies have advanced significant in development and research, still face usability issues, which causes a problem of adoption by users [1, 2]. These problems can be by the lack of heuristics, usability measurement scales or clear and validated guidelines for the development of these technologies [2], in addition, the lack of consensus on the design of these has represented a barrier to development [3].

The articles [4, 5] define usability as the ability of a system to be used by users to achieve the objectives of creation in an effective, efficient, and satisfactory way. This is

H. Luna-García et al. (Eds.): HCI-COLLAB 2025, CCIS 2850, pp. 236–252, 2027.
https://doi.org/10.1007/978-3-032-31223-5_17

one of the fundamental parts of the success that voice interaction technologies will have. However, a dispersion in literature exists that makes it difficult to integrate the findings, therefore, the difficulty in identifying areas that require improvement. This systematic review aims to address these knowledge gaps by providing a broad view on usability and user experience assessment heuristics or articles that give a broader perspective within voice interaction technologies within the last few years.

This work is organized as follows: in Sect. 2, the research methods and tools used to conduct systematic review are detailed. Section 3 presents the key findings obtained from the studies reviewed. Section 4 introduces a classification framework for categorizing research. Finally, in Sect. 5, he presents potential future work.

2 Research Methodology

For this systematic review, the items established within the Preferred Reporting Items for Systematic Review and Meta-Analyses (PRISMA) [6] were followed, which allows for the appropriate selection of papers, from the database search, the eligibility criteria to the selection process (Fig. 1).

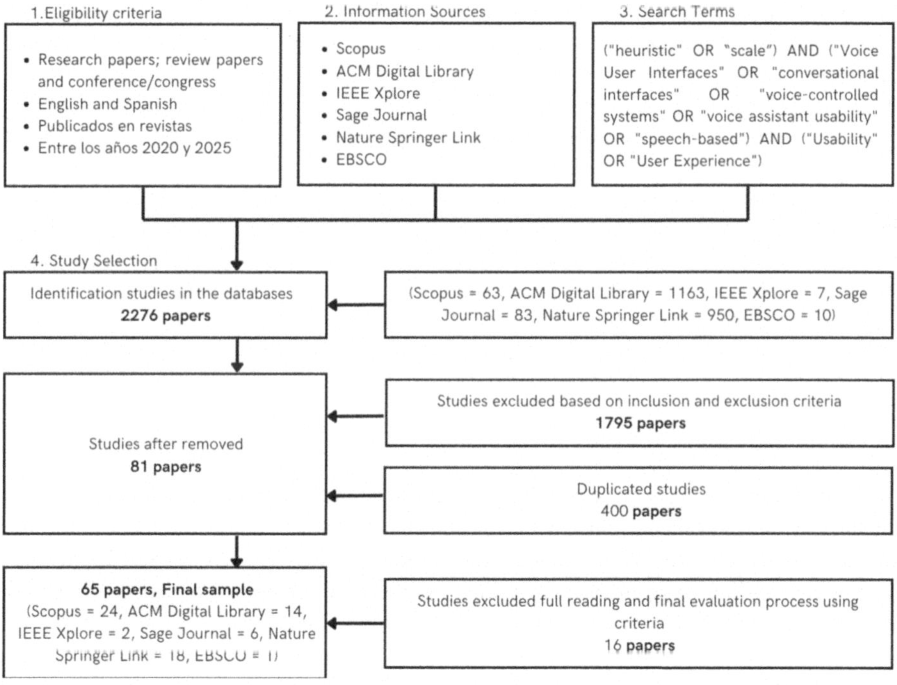

Fig. 1. Flow diagram of systematic review selection process of Preferred Reporting Items for Systematic Review and Meta-Analyses (PRISMA). Source: Author's own work.

2.1 Eligibility Criteria

The research considered for inclusion was published research papers; Review papers and conference/congress papers, between the years 2020 and 2025, written in English or Spanish. Articles not focused on the validation, evaluation of speech-based technologies through heuristics and/or scales or the creation of these, as well as books, brochures and theses are excluded; or articles in languages other than those already mentioned.

2.2 Information Sources

Six databases were considered within the review. ACM Digital Library and IEEE Xplore are selected as the most relevant in computing and technology, Scopus for its predominance and its selection and interdisciplinarity criteria, and the databases Sage Journal, Nature Springer Link and EBSCO for their scientific relevance.

2.3 Search Terms

To appropriately select the research articles, three main terms were selected: "Evaluation", "Voices User Interfaces" and "Usability"; From these terms, related terms are selected for the construction of the search string, which is built based on the steps given by [7]. Selected documents must contain the keywords in the title, abstract, or keywords (Table 1).

Table 1. General Database Query. Source: Author's own work.

Query
("heuristic" OR "scale") AND ("Voice User Interfaces" OR "conversational interfaces" OR "voice-controlled systems" OR "voice assistant usability" OR "speech-based") AND ("Usability" OR "User Experience")

2.4 Study Selection

This selection process made it possible to choose the research articles that are aligned with the objectives of the systematic review, for this purpose the relevant documents were analyzed, evaluated, and identified. This selection study was carried out in different steps, the first is the identification of the studies, for this a search was carried out based on the keywords within the online databases. The second step was to examine the list to include only the articles that meet the criteria of period, type of document, language, from these, the duplicate articles are eliminated. Finally, a complete review of each of the studies was conducted and it was guaranteed that it was related to the objectives of the systematic review.

2.5 Data Collection Process and Synthesis

The search of the articles focused on research and review articles according to the search terms, 2276 studies were identified, divided as follows: Scopus = 63, ACM Digital Library = 1163, IEEE Xplore = 7, Sage Journal = 83, Nature Springer Link = 950, EBSCO = 10. Eligibility criteria were applied through the inclusion criteria for publications in 2020 until February 22, 2025, exclusion through the review of titles, abstracts and keywords that did not include "heuristics", "scale", "usability", "VUI" and "Voice User Interfaces", for which 1402 articles were eliminated, and 400 duplicate papers were identified. The remaining articles were thoroughly examined for selection for final selection. The final dataset included sixty-five articles.

The analysis of the collected data, which is a bibliometric analysis performed to identify the main countries, authors, institutions and sources within the study area, was consolidated using Excel for a detailed analysis. This detailed analysis took into account basic publication data (authors, title, year, accessibility, database, URL, type of article, keywords, number of citations, views, countries related to the publication and institutions), and information about the articles corresponding to the content.

The information collected in Microsoft Excel was analyzed for subsequent data processing, R was used for the visualization of trends and research patterns. The classification of the articles was conducted into various categories according to the objectives of the articles and their contribution to the state of the art, the classification was refined in an iterative way so that all the articles could be classified. In addition, all future research regarding usability heuristics or usability or user experience scales for Voice User Interface is mentioned.

3 Bibliometric Analysis

3.1 Trend in Annual Scientific Publications

For this systematic review, a range of 5 years was considered for the search for articles to consider the most recent articles and research in the area. The evolution of publications from 2020 to 2025 is visible in Fig. 2. In it, you can see the growing number of publications in Heuristics and scales within speech-based technologies. It is denoted that in 2024 there is the largest number of articles published on this topic with eighteen publications, followed by 2023 with thirteen papers published, therefore, it is expected that in the coming years research in this area will intensify.

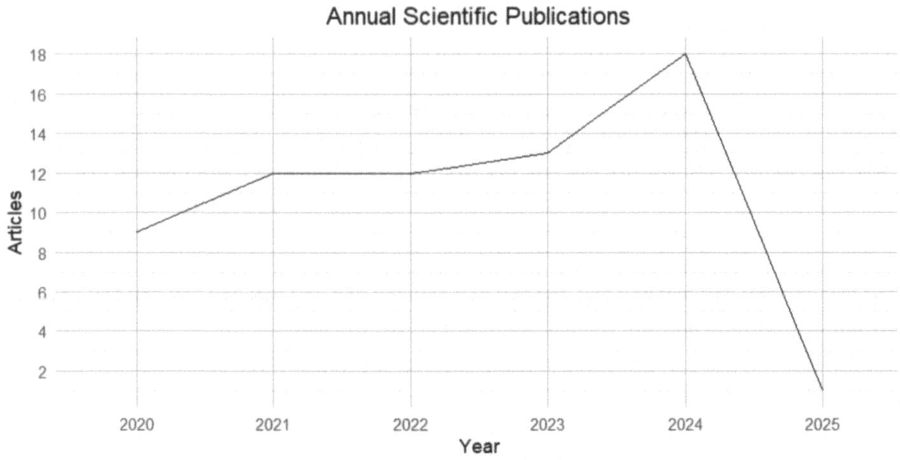

Fig. 2. Annual Scientific Publications. Source: Author's own work.

3.2 Most Influential Authors

The analysis considered factors such as the number of publications, citations and the impact they have through the parameters h_Index that measures productivity and impact, g_Index which measures the total accumulated impact and m_Index that allows adjusting the h-Index by age, likewise, all the authors who participated in the articles were considered. Andreas M. Klein is the author with the most impact and the highest number of publications with six articles and sixty-eight citations, who together with Christine Murad and Cosmin Munteanu have had four publications with thirty-four citations each. Table 2 shows other authors who have also had major influence.

Table 2. Most Influential Authors. Source: Author's own work.

Author	Number of Publications	Total Citations	h_Index	g_Index	m_Index	Start Pub. (2020–2025)
Andreas M. Klein	6	68	4	6	0.8	2020
Christine Murad	4	34	3	4	0.75	2021
Cosmin Munteanu	4	34	3	4	0.75	2021
Martin Schrepp	4	62	3	4	0.6	2020
Maria Rauschenberger	4	27	2	4	0.4	2020
Jorg Thomaschewski	3	61	3	3	0.6	2020

(continued)

Table 2. (*continued*)

Author	Number of Publications	Total Citations	h_Index	g_Index	m_Index	Start Pub. (2020–2025)
Andreas Hinderks	3	45	2	3	0.4	2020
Gustavo López	3	4	2	2	0.66667	2022
Ignacio Díaz-Oreiro	3	4	2	2	0.66667	2022
Luis A. Guerrero	3	4	2	2	0.66667	2022

3.3 Most Influential Countries

Figure 3 shows the countries that have conducted the most research in the last 5 years, Germany has made about eighteen publications, leading together with the United States and Spain with 13 and 7 publications, respectively. China has generated six publications, while Canada, Italy, and Thailand 4 each. On the other hand, the articles published by Costa Rica and Greece were three, and finally India with two research articles finishes the top ten countries with the highest contributions.

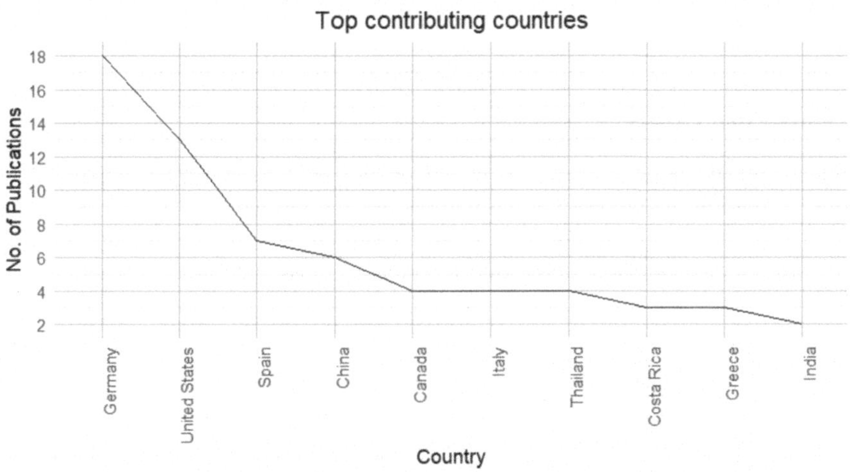

Fig. 3. Top contributing countries. Source: Author's own work.

3.4 Top Contributing Institutions

The institutions that from 2020 to 2025 have made the most contributions to this field of research are led by the University of Applied Sciences Emden/Leer in Germany with 6, followed by the University of Seville with 5 contributions, the company SAP SE and the University of Toronto with 4 publications. Other institutions with a high contribution are shown in Table 3.

Table 3. Top Contributing Institutions. Source: Author's own work.

Institutions	Number
University of Applied Sciences Emden/Leer	6
University of Seville	5
SAP SE	4
University of Toronto	4
IBM Research	3
King Mongkut's University of Technology Thonburi	3
University of Costa Rica	3
University of Waterloo	3
Otto von Guericke University Magdeburg	2
Pädagogische Hochschule Freiburg	2

3.5 Most-Cited Papers

The most relevant articles are those presented in Table 4, where the paper [8] with sixty-eight citations is the one that has had the most relevance.

Table 4. Contributions of the Most-Cited Papers. *Source: Author's own work.*

Paper	Contribution	Total Citations
[8]	This study presents eleven heuristics for evaluating the usability of conversational agents, based on the adaptation of Nielsen's heuristics with chatbots and voice assistants. These were validated through evaluations of diverse types of agents, considering content, interaction design, and privacy. It is important to emphasize the need for a comprehensive approach in the design of these systems.	68
[9]	This article identifies gaps in current practices, proposes two high-level frameworks for guiding future research in measuring voice UX, and evaluates strengths and weaknesses within the identified studies, outlining a path toward accurate measurement of user experience in these types of systems.	36

(*continued*)

Table 4. *(continued)*

Paper	Contribution	Total Citations
[10]	The research article presents the UEQ+ framework, which aims to design UX questionnaires with specific adaptations. Within this framework, three new scales are proposed to measure key aspects in the context of UX. This article also analyzes how the scales can be integrated with the UEQ+ and the need for tools for evaluation.	24
[11]	This document establishes a set of guidelines for conversational user interfaces (CUI) to assist designers in creating more effective and user-friendly interfaces. It also focuses on developing criteria for usability evaluation in interfaces, enabling testing and improvement of future versions. This article adopts a heuristic and linguistic approach, addressing natural language challenges while providing a comprehensive and detailed evaluation.	21
[12]	This article presents three users experience measurement scales for voice assistants, which can be integrated with the UEQ+ framework. The research highlights the importance of considering both task-related and non-task-related aspects in UX evaluation. Additionally, it introduces a modular questionnaire concept for assessing voice interfaces, enabling more precise and tailored measurements for these systems.	20

4 Classification Papers

For this classification, the articles were divided into technologies and design criteria in order to identify the research trends presented within the selected articles. See Table 5.

Table 5. Classification of papers based on design principles. Source: Author's own work.

Technologies	Scale		Heuristic	Design Guide
	UX	Usability		
VPA	8	9	1	3
VUI	9	5	4	7
CUI	3	2	1	2
Conversational Agent	2	6	2	1

From Table 5, it is possible to observe the growing research in technologies such as VPA and VUI. Based on this information and subtopics related to the articles, a categorization of the 65 related articles was carried out. The selected categories can be seen in Table 6.

Table 6. Categories. Source: Author's own work.

Categories	Descriptions
Development and Validation of Measurement Tools for User Experience (UX) in Voice Interfaces	This category identifies articles focused on UX measurement tools, including validation studies. Among them, [13] validates UX scales using the UEQ+ framework for voice assistants such as Alexa, Siri, and Google Assistant. Similarly, [14] evaluates UX measurement tools for voice interfaces like Alexa through surveys and questionnaires. Among the articles dedicated to the creation of measurement tools, [12] focuses on developing and validating new UX measurement scales for VPAs in voice assistants using the UEQ+ framework. Meanwhile, [15] is centered on the creation and validation of a questionnaire designed to assess UX in chatbots, analyzing conversation quality, personality, and user acceptance in university environments. The development of user experience quality for voice interactions is addressed by [10], which focuses on creating three new scales to measure UX quality in voice interactions within the UEQ+ framework, considering aspects such as behavior, response quality, and comprehensibility.
Design and Guidelines for Voice User Interfaces (VUI)	The key studies within this category highlight the need for unified tools and standards. The identified studies focus on the collection and synthesis of VUI design guidelines [16, 17], while others concentrate on usability evaluation scales, utilizing SUS for voice interface assessment [18]. Additionally, studies explore usability evaluation through both adapted and newly developed heuristics for conversational agents and voice assistants [8, 19, 20]. Various articles focus on innovative approaches to enhance VUI usability, such as the use of complementary sounds in interactions [21] and the reduction of cognitive load through natural language to optimize performance [22]. Other studies examine the adoption and perception of VUIs, including emotional expressiveness in chatbots using human and non-human metaphors [23, 24]. Furthermore, the importance of user-centered design is emphasized, integrating VUI design principles [25].

(continued)

Table 6. (*continued*)

Categories	Descriptions
Testing and Usability Evaluation of Voice Assistants (VPA)	These articles focus on VPAs, analyzing the efficiency of SUS and the ISO 9241-11 framework for voice-based personal assistants while evaluating current methods and proposing new evaluation metrics [26–28]. Others concentrate on innovation in VUI evaluation, such as VITAs, a framework based on virtual assistant models that introduces assessment methods for dialogue systems [29, 30]. Another area explored within this category is the impact of latency on user satisfaction and the use of paraphrasing to optimize VPAs [31, 32]. Additionally, the usability of Google Home among non-native English speakers is examined, highlighting the challenges in interacting with VPAs [3].
Cultural and Demographic Factors	Among the cultural factors, the study [33] explores the cultural adaptation of the questionnaires in voice assistants. It is identified that they are not suitable for the evaluation of new contexts, therefore, it is suggested to measure the operational quality and vitality of the assistants. In addition, it emphasizes the creation of updated tools due to technological advances and cultural factors. PMQ is also validated in German and Japanese versions, this validation confirms the flexibility of this culture-independent tool. This article highlights the importance of taking cultural differences into account when designing voice interfaces [34]. Articles focused on demographic factors, [35] focus their study spatially on older adults, revealing the difficulty in the daily use of voice assistants due to the barriers that arise. Emphasis is placed on participatory design and accessibility to improve adoption among this group.
Accessibility and Usability in People with Disabilities	This category deals with user experience and usability in user interfaces for the visually impaired through the study of VoiceOver and Seeing AI tools [36]. As well as people with speech disabilities, where the article [37] focuses on the creation of conversational AI and voice interfaces to improve accessibility on the web. We also found studies focused on motor disability in mixed reality (HoloLens) environments via voice input for noisy environments [38].

(*continued*)

Table 6. (*continued*)

Categories	Descriptions
Specific Contexts	One of the contexts identified for evaluation is voice control systems in vehicles. In [39], it was found that the preference for these systems is focused on tasks requiring high concentration. This study provides valuable insights into preferences, design, and improvements of VCS. Within [40], user frustration while using voice interfaces during driving was investigated, highlighting the feasibility of using voice interfaces to improve UX and regulate emotions in such contexts. Finally, the study [41] focuses on assisting Computer Science students through voice user interfaces, evaluating the prototype using the UEQ. This article offers insights into recent technologies in academic environments.
Health and Wellbeing	Studies related to health and well-being have developed research in the field of mental health through the use of voice assistants for therapeutic support using feedback signals (backchanneling), which promotes emotional disclosure and improves UX [42] In this same branch, a study has been carried out that examines UX through a conversational agent, for self-assessment of their own mental health at home after being diagnosed with affective disorder [43]. The article [44] also creates eleven heuristics to evaluate usability in conversational agents, focusing on reliable content and adoption of daily health routines. In the line of healthy routines in [45], "Workout Pal" is presented, which is a voice interface designed for older adults to support physical activities, in this study design guidelines are specified to improve interaction with older adults.
Video Games and Entertainment	Two articles were found focusing on the category of video games and entertainment. The first, [46], introduces SUStory, a method for evaluating the usability of chatbots for children. This method is based on games and narratives, allowing for the assessment of conversational interfaces in an entertaining context. The second article presents the game "Escape the Echo," which uses voice commands to control game events. By comparing standard voice commands with a text-based approach, it improves accuracy and reduces errors [47].

(*continued*)

Table 6. (*continued*)

Categories	Descriptions
Modal Interaction Preferences and User Behavior	These articles give a perspective from the users, where linguistic characteristics, thematic progression, and predictions are examined, influencing preferences in user responses [48]. And user behavior can also be visualized between traditional and intelligent voice interfaces, providing insights into the convenience and pleasure perceived by users to improve UX and encourage user adoption [49].

5 Future Research

Table 6 shows the future work and challenges to be addressed (Table 7).

Table 7. Future Research. Source: Author's own work.

Challenges
- Development of new evaluation tools and scales for UX in voice systems, to be used across different commercial platforms. Evaluate scales like SUS in various voice contexts. - Conduct more comprehensive research to assess UX using UEQ+ and other evaluation tools for voice assistants across different demographic groups. - Investigate the evolution of voice assistants over time, considering their long-term effects and changes according to user expectations. - Conduct detailed research to establish clear guidelines for accessibility and inclusion, addressing cultural diversity and language. - Consider multimodal interfaces, gesture-based interactions, and contextual recognition filters in various applications. - Adapt GUI interface heuristics to the voice interface (VUI) context and evaluate the tools and resources to support design, also involving industrial designers in this adaptation. - Attention is required to provide privacy guidelines for future development, with further research on security in VPAs. - Consider latency and response delays, investigate their impact in vehicles, stress situations, and explore mitigation strategies. - Investigate the adaptation of voice assistant design to various user profiles, including educational level, age, gender, technological familiarity, prior interaction with voice assistants, and ease of adoption. Additionally, explore the need for speech-based technology customization. - Research accessibility for people with various disabilities, enhance voice recognition accuracy, and tailor interfaces to user needs. - Greater evaluation of voice assistants in the healthcare and automotive sectors to improve UX and usability. From this, improve voice assistants by considering automation and drivers' preferences in traffic. - Investigate complex social interactions and users' emotional responses in contexts related to wellness and health. - Study voice interfaces in games and entertainment applications for evaluating command vocabulary and contextual recognition.

6 Discussion

In this study, the PRISMA methodology was applied, which allowed the identification of the articles according to the objectives of the research, while a replicable, scientific and transparent process is carried out, with which it is possible to identify the articles according to the search criteria, in addition, a categorization of future studies and works was carried out.

This systematic review focused on articles from the past 5 years, allowing for an understanding of how research has advanced in recent years regarding heuristics, guidelines, and evaluation scales for usability and UX in various speech-based technologies. This provides a broader view of the progress made in the field. A total of sixty-five studies were identified that meet the objectives of the article, selected based on the search and selection criteria. From the list of studies, information was summarized through bibliometric statistical analysis to present significant data on user experience and usability in speech-based technologies (VUI, speech-based, CUI, etc.). Information such as publication years, leading countries, authors, and institutions were extracted to identify the major contributors in each category. This reveals the growing body of research in this area in recent years. Additionally, countries like Germany, the United States, and Spain have been at the forefront of research on the topic, with institutions such as the University of Applied Sciences Emden/Leer in Germany and the University of Seville in Spain making notable contributions in this field.

To categorize the articles, different groups were identified through the analysis of objectives. To identify the various research trends through content analysis, a classification framework of nine categories was proposed. These categories are Development and Validation of Measurement Tools for User Experience (UX) in Voice Interfaces, Design and Guidelines for Voice User Interfaces (VUI), Testing and Evaluation of the Usability of Voice Assistants (VPA), Cultural and Demographic Factors, Accessibility and Usability for People with Disabilities, Specific Contexts, Health and Well-being, Video Games and Entertainment, Interaction Modal Preferences, and User Behavior. These categories allow for the classification of articles while extracting important information such as guidelines, heuristics, and new scales for UX and usability evaluation. Additionally, they provide insights into the most researched application scenarios today (video games, education, automotive industry, health). The most studied technologies were voice assistants (VPA) and voice interfaces (VUI), as shown in Table 5. Although there are studies on Conversational User Interfaces (CUI) and conversational agents, these topics have not been as extensively researched in the articles found regarding design criteria. Furthermore, it is possible to observe that among design criteria, heuristics and design guidelines have received the least research attention. The categorization performed is significant as it helps identify critical points such as accessibility, user preferences, and cultural and demographic factors that impact users.

Finally, future challenges and work reveal the need for more research on accessibility, indicating the need for personalization and user-centered design to provide greater adaptability to different demographics such as age, education level, gender, familiarity with technology, and technology adoption, for all speech-based technologies. In addition, to focus future work on emotional responses and complex social interactions, among others.

7 Conclusions

For this study, a systematic literature review was conducted using PRISMA. Different sectors (health, automotive, education, and entertainment) were identified, along with some cultural and demographic factors that involve user experience, usability, and speech-based technologies. Various findings were made, highlighting the need to develop standardized tools to measure UX and usability in voice-controlled technologies, as well as challenges related to privacy and security, culture, language, and user-centered design, with a significant emphasis on personalization and adaptation to users. Additionally, the potential of VUI, CUI, and SUI in contexts such as health, wellbeing, and driving was notably highlighted.

Similarly, as a future agenda, the creation of evaluation metrics, studying the evolution of voice assistants, and improving accessibility are proposed. Therefore, this systematic review generates a theoretical framework for the development of speech-based technologies focused on effectiveness, efficiency, and user satisfaction.

Acknowledgments. To the LITUX group at the Autonomous University of Zacatecas and the IDIS group at the University of Cauca.

References

1. Clark, L. et al.: What makes a good conversation? Challenges in designing truly conversational agents. In: Conference on Human Factors in Computing Systems – Proceedings, vol. 12. (2019). https://doi.org/10.1145/3290605.3300705
2. Murad, C., Munteanu, C.: 'I don't know what you're talking about, Halexa': the case for voice user interface guidelines. In: ACM International Conference Proceeding Series. (2019). https://doi.org/10.1145/3342775.3342795
3. Murad, C., Munteanu, C., Cowan, B.R., Clark, L.: Finding a new voice: transitioning designers from GUI to VUI design. In: ACM International Conference Proceeding Series. (2021). https://doi.org/10.1145/3469595.3469617
4. Fulfagar, L., Gupta, A., Mathur, A., Shrivastava, A.: Development and evaluation of usability heuristics for voice user interfaces. In: Smart Innovation, Systems and Technologies, vol.221, pp. 375–385. (2021). https://doi.org/10.1007/978-981-16-0041-8_32
5. Simor, F.W., Brum, M.R., Schmidt, J.D.E., Rieder, R., De Marchi, A.C.B.: Usability evaluation methods for gesture-based games: a systematic review. JMIR Ser. Games. **4**(2), e17 (2016). https://doi.org/10.2196/games.5860
6. Liberati, A., et al.: The PRISMA statement for reporting systematic reviews and meta-analyses of studies that evaluate healthcare interventions: explanation and elaboration. BMJ. **339**, b2700 (2009). https://doi.org/10.1136/BMJ.B2700
7. Kitchenham, B.: Procedures for performing systematic reviews. (2004)
8. Langevin, R., Microsoft, R.L., Rulai, T.A., Cowan, B., Hirsch, T., Hsieh, G.: Heuristic evaluation of conversational agents. In: CHI Conference on Human Factors in Computing Systems (CHI '21). (2021)
9. Seaborn, K., Urakami, J.: Measuring voice UX quantitatively: a rapid review. In: Conference on Human Factors in Computing Systems – Proceedings. (2021). https://doi.org/10.1145/3411763.3451712

10. Klein, A.M., Hinderks, A., Schrepp, M., Thomaschewski, J.: Construction of UEQ+ scales for voice quality: measuring user experience quality of voice interaction. In: ACM International Conference Proceeding Series, pp. 1–5. (2020). https://doi.org/10.1145/3404983.3410003
11. Sugisaki, K., Bleiker, A.: Usability guidelines and evaluation criteria for conversational user interfaces: a heuristic and linguistic approach. In: ACM International Conference Proceeding Series, pp.309–319. (2020). https://doi.org/10.1145/3404983.3405505
12. Klein, A.M., Hinderks, A., Schrepp, M., Thomaschewski, J.: Measuring user experience quality of voice assistants: voice communication scales for the UEQ+ framework. In: Iberian Conference on Information Systems and Technologies (CISTI), vol. 2020-June. (2020). https://doi.org/10.23919/CISTI49556.2020.9140966
13. Klein, A.M., Kollmorgen, J., Hinderks, A., Schrepp, M., Rauschenberger, M., Escalona, M.-J.: Validation of the UEQ+ scales for voice quality. Comput. Stand. Interfaces. **93**, 103971 (2025). https://doi.org/10.1016/J.CSI.2024.103971
14. Brüggemeier, B., Breiter, M., Kurz, M., Schiwy, J.: User experience of Alexa when controlling music: comparison of face and construct validity of four questionnaires. In: ACM International Conference Proceeding Series. (2020). https://doi.org/10.1145/3405755.3406122
15. Essop, L., Singh, A., Wing, J.: Developing a comprehensive evaluation questionnaire for university FAQ administration chatbots. In: 2023 Conference on Information Communications Technology and Society (ICTAS 2023) – Proceedings. (2023). https://doi.org/10.1109/ICTAS56421.2023.10082753
16. Murad, C., Candello, H., Munteanu, C.: What's the talk on VUI guidelines? A meta-analysis of guidelines for voice user interface design. In: Proceedings of the 5th International Conference on Conversational User Interfaces (CUI 2023). (2023). https://doi.org/10.1145/3571884.3597129
17. Murad, C., Munteanu, C.: 'Voice-first interfaces in a GUI-first design world': barriers and opportunities to supporting VUI designers on-the-job. In: ACM International Conference Proceeding Series. (2022). https://doi.org/10.1145/3543829.3543842
18. Deshmukh, A.M., Chalmeta, R.: Validation of system usability scale as a usability metric to evaluate voice user interfaces. PeerJ Comput. Sci. **10**(1, 17) (2024). https://doi.org/10.7717/peerj-cs.1918
19. Nowacki, C., Gordeeva, A., Lizé, A.-H.: Improving the usability of voice user interfaces: a new set of ergonomic criteria. In: Lecture Notes in Computer Science (including subseries Lecture Notes in Artificial Intelligence and Lecture Notes in Bioinformatics), vol. 12201 LNCS, pp. 117–133. (2020). https://doi.org/10.1007/978-3-030-49760-6_8
20. Heuer, M. et al.: Rethinking interaction with conversational agents: how to create a positive user experience utilizing dialog patterns. In: Lecture Notes in Computer Science (including subseries Lecture Notes in Artificial Intelligence and Lecture Notes in Bioinformatics), vol. 14033, LNCS, pp. 283–301. (2023). https://doi.org/10.1007/978-3-031-35708-4_22
21. Esau-Held, M., Marsh, A., Krauß, V., Stevens, G.: 'Foggy sounds like nothing' — enriching the experience of voice assistants with sonic overlays. Pers. Ubiquit. Comput. **27**(5), 1927–1947 (2023). https://doi.org/10.1007/S00779-023-01722-3/TABLES/5
22. Do, H.J., et al.: Grounding with structure: exploring design variations of grounded human-AI collaboration in a natural language interface. Proc. ACM Hum. Comput. Interact. **8**(CSCW2), 1–29 (2024). https://doi.org/10.1145/3686902/SUPPL_FILE/V8CSCW363AUX.MOV.ZIP
23. Desai, S., Dubiel, M., Leiva, L.A.: Examining humanness as a metaphor to design voice user interfaces. In: Proceedings of the 6th Conference on ACM Conversational User Interfaces (CUI 2024). (2024). https://doi.org/10.1145/3640794.3665535/SUPPL_FILE/AUDIOFILES-CUI
24. Zhu, Q. et al.: Effects of emotional expressive-ness on voice chatbot interactions. p. 11. https://doi.org/10.1145/3543829.3543840

25. Klein, A.M., Kölln, K., Deutschländer, J., Rauschenberger, M.: Design and evaluation of voice user interfaces: what should one consider? In: Lecture Notes in Computer Science (including subseries Lecture Notes in Artificial Intelligence and Lecture Notes in Bioinformatics), vol. 14052, LNCS, pp. 167–190. (2023). https://doi.org/10.1007/978-3-031-35921-7_12
26. Zwakman, D.S., Pal, D., Triyason, T., Vanijja, V.: Usability of voice-based intelligent personal assistants. In: International Conference on ICT Convergence, vol. 2020-October, pp. 652–657. (2020). https://doi.org/10.1109/ICTC49870.2020.9289550
27. Pyae, A.: A usability evaluation of the Google Home with non-native English speakers using the system usability scale. Int. J. Netw. Virtual Organ. **26**(3), 172–194 (2022). https://doi.org/10.1504/IJNVO.2022.122849
28. Dutsinma, F.L.I., Pal, D., Funilkul, S., Chan, J.H.: A systematic review of voice assistant usability: an ISO 9241-11 approach. SN Comput. Sci. **3**(4), 1–23 (2022). https://doi.org/10.1007/S42979-022-01172-3/TABLES/6
29. Li, S., Bu, L., Bai, G., Guo, Z., Chen, K., Wei, H.: VITAS: guided model-based VUI testing of VPA apps. In: ACM International Conference Proceeding Series, pp.1–12. (2022). https://doi.org/10.1145/3551349.3556957
30. Liesenfeld, A., Dingemanse, M.: Interactive probes: towards action-level evaluation for dialogue systems. Discour. Commun. **18**(6), 954–964 (2024). https://doi.org/10.1177/17504813241267071
31. Sogemeier, D., Forster, Y., Naujoks, F., Krems, J.F., Keinath, A.: The importance of timing—an expert evaluation on latencies for voice assistants. In: Proceedings of the Human Factors and Ergonomics Society Annual Meeting. (2024). https://doi.org/10.1177/10711813241260290/SUPPL_FILE/SJ-XLSX-1-PRO-10.1177_10711813241260290.XLSX
32. Guglielmi, E., Rosa, G., Scalabrino, S., Bavota, G., Oliveto, R.: Help them understand: testing and improving voice user interfaces. ACM Trans. Softw. Eng. Methodol. **33**(6) (2024). https://doi.org/10.1145/3654438
33. Koniakowsky, I., Loew, A., Forster, Y., Naujoks, F., Keinath, A.: Context and culture affect the psychometrics of questionnaires evaluating speech-based assistants. In: Adjunct Proceedings - 13th International ACM Conference on Automotive User Interfaces and Interactive Vehicular Applications, AutomotiveUI 2021, pp. 115–118. (2021). https://doi.org/10.1145/3473682.3480276
34. Seaborn, K., Gessinger, I, Yoshida, S., Cowan, B.R., Doyle, P.R.: Cross-cultural validation of partner models for voice user interfaces. In: Proceedings of the 6th Conference on ACM Conversational User Interfaces, CUI 2024. (2024). https://doi.org/10.1145/3640794.3665537/SUPPL_FILE/CUI24-4-SM.PDF
35. Islam, M.U., Chaudhry, B.M.: Learnability assessment of speech-based intelligent personal assistants by older adults. In: Lecture Notes in Computer Science (including subseries Lecture Notes in Artificial Intelligence and Lecture Notes in Bioinformatics), vol. 14042, LNCS, pp. 321–347. (2023). https://doi.org/10.1007/978-3-031-34866-2_24
36. Kim, H.N.: Usability assessment of voice-enabled technologies for users with visual disabilities. In: Proceedings of the Human Factors and Ergonomics Society Annual Meeting, pp. 1–6 (2024). https://doi.org/10.1177/10711813241260395
37. Pucci, E., Piro, L., Possaghi, I., Mulfari, D., Matera, M.: Co-designing the integration of voice-based conversational AI and web augmentation to amplify web inclusivity. Sci. Rep. **14**(1), 1–16 (2024). https://doi.org/10.1038/S41598-024-66725-3/TABLES/5
38. Derby, J.L., Rickel, E.A., Harris, K.J., Lovell, J.A., Chaparro, B.S.: 'We Didn't Catch That!' Using Voice Text Input on a Mixed Reality Headset in Noisy Environments. Proc. Hum. Factors Ergon. Soc. Annu. Meet. **64**(1), 2102–2106 (2021). https://doi.org/10.1177/1071181320641509

39. Huang, C., Yan, S., Xie, W., He, D.: When do users prefer voice control systems in vehicles? a survey of Chinese drivers. Transp. Res. Rec. (2024). https://doi.org/10.1177/03611981241240771
40. Krüger, S., Bosch, E., Ihme, K., Oehl, M.: In-vehicle frustration mitigation via voice-user interfaces – a simulator study. Commun. Comput. Inf. Sci. **1421**, 241–248 (2021). https://doi.org/10.1007/978-3-030-78645-8_30
41. Seeroo, O., Bekaroo, G.: Enhancing student support via the application of a voice user interface system. In: Proceedings of the ACM International Conference Proceeding Series, pp. 1–6. (2021). https://doi.org/10.1145/3487923.3487936
42. Cho, E., Motalebi, N., Sundar, S.S., Abdullah, S.: Alexa as an active listener: how backchanneling can elicit self-disclosure and promote user experience. Proc. ACM Hum. Comput. Interact. **6**(CSCW2), 1–25 (2022). https://doi.org/10.1145/3555164
43. Maharjan, R., Doherty, K., Rohani, D.A., Bækgaard, P., Bardram, J.E.: Experiences of a speech-enabled conversational agent for the self-report of well-being among people living with affective disorders: an in-the-wild study. ACM Trans. Interact. Intell. Syst. **12**(2), 1–25 (2022). https://doi.org/10.1145/3484508/ASSET/1DD513B9-A890-4FB9-810F-EC463C78D50E/ASSETS/GRAPHIC/TIIS-2021-JAN-025-F04.JPG
44. J. Y. Shin and J. Huh-Yoo, Designing everyday conversational agents for managing health and wellness: a study of alexa skills reviews. in PervasiveHealth: Pervasive Computing Technologies for Healthcare, pp. 50–61. (2020). https://doi.org/10.1145/3421937.3422024
45. Desai, S., Hu, X., Lundy, M., Chin, J: Using experience-based participatory approach to design interactive voice user interfaces for delivering physical activity programs with older adults. In: ACM International Conference Proceeding Series, pp. 180–190. (2023). https://doi.org/10.1145/3623809.3623827
46. Chen, S., Markopoulos, P., Hu,.J.: SUStory: usability evaluation of conversational interfaces for children with a narrative on a game board. In: Proceedings of the 6th Conference on ACM Conversational User Interfaces (CUI 2024), pp. 1–10. (2024). https://doi.org/10.1145/3640794.3665565
47. Zargham, N., Fetni, M.L., Spillner, L, Muender, T., Malaka, R.: 'I know what you mean': context-aware recognition to enhance speech-based games. In: Proceedings of the CHI Conference on Human Factors in Computing Systems, pp. 1–10. (2024). https://doi.org/10.1145/3613904.3642426/SUPPL_FILE/PN7883-SUPPLEMENTAL-MATERIAL-1.PDF
48. Sargsyan, L., Choi, S., Kim, S.H.: Investigating user preferences for conversation design of voice assistant systems using linguistic features. Proc. Hum. Factors Ergon. Soc. Annu. Meet. **67**(1), 91–96 (2023). https://doi.org/10.1177/21695067231192609
49. Cheng, S.: Understanding users' voluntary switching behavior for user interfaces of intelligent personal assistant devices. Inf. Syst. Front. **2024**, 1–24 (2024). https://doi.org/10.1007/S10796-023-10459-6

Between the Tangible and the Intangible: Mu + Art 2024 as a Model for Digital Preservations of Art with a Cultural Value

Anyela Patricia Villamizar Carrillo(✉), Campo Elías Flórez-Pabón, and José Jacinto Gelves Ordóñez

Facultad de Artes y Humanidades, Universidad de Pamplona, Pamplona 543050, Colombia
{anyela.villamizar,ceflorez,jojagel}@unipamplona.edu.co

Abstract. This study analyses the preservation of traditional art in digital environments from the Mu + Art 2024 exhibition at the University of Pamplona. The research, with a qualitative approach, was based on structured interviews with four participants and was articulated around six key categories: fundamental aspects, evaluation of the event, user experience, digital referents, documentation and preservation, as well as accessibility and cultural value. The results indicate that effective digital preservation requires a balance between applying advanced digital technologies and protecting the authenticity and essence of traditional art. The discussion highlights the importance of maintaining artistic integrity during the digitization process, suggesting that the combination of technological innovation and care for authenticity is essential for the preservation of the cultural value of art in its migration to digital platforms. In conclusion, the research emphasizes that the preservation of traditional art in digital environments requires strategies that integrate technology and authenticity to ensure the preservation of its cultural identity

Keywords: Digital Accessibility · Digital Art · Artistic Digitization · Digital Gallery · Cultural Heritage · Digital Preservation · Artistic Education · Cultural Value

1 Introduction

Higher education is an ideal space for the construction of knowledge, and the University of Pamplona, Colombia, hosts Musci plus Art (Mu + Art), a yearly event that searches to offer spaces between traditional art and digital technologies, aiming to preserve traditional art, thus proposing challenges for educational and cultural exhibition processes. Since the COVID 19 pandemic, the latest versions of the event make a transition from works done in traditional art to digital formats.

This qualitative research focuses on techniques and implementations of visualization technologies, considering cultural and educational considerations for the preservation of art. The analysis was classified into six categories to answer the following research question: how can the preservation of traditional art be nurtured from educational processes

H. Luna-García et al. (Eds.): HCI-COLLAB 2025, CCIS 2850, pp. 253–270, 2027.
https://doi.org/10.1007/978-3-032-31223-5_18

through its circulation in digital art exhibitions? Alternating technological innovation with the preservation of artistic culture.

In the same sense, the event allows the generation of spaces of diffusion and knowledge, which nuance the idea of the cultural value that the works of traditional art have in their sense of identity, strengthening the tradition of the border region where this event is held. This transforms new technologies into ideal spaces to expand art, knowledge of art, knowledge of the artist and the networking that artistic creation entails.

2 Origins of Mu + Art

Since 2017, the Degree in Artistic Education of the University of Pamplona has created an academic space to show artistic management [(performing arts: theatre, circus and dance), music, visual arts (painting, sculpture, architecture and photography), literary arts (poetry and narrative), audiovisual arts (film and video) and electronic arts (digital arts, interactive installations and use of electronic technology)] to the public in the region, in different techniques acquired by undergraduate students. It is worth clarifying that the event does not handle all the different arts that have been mentioned, but focuses originally on the performing arts, some areas of visual and musical arts, besides evidencing the learning of essential skills for the integral formation of the artist. This resulting activity is called Mu + Art, which emerges from the classroom as a teacher's initiative to create a space for exhibition that celebrates artistic and cultural diversity, and is implemented as a significant universe for the development and promotion of art. It is characterized as a converging point between creators and spectators, where the different artistic manifestations dialogue with the social and cultural environment of the region. The exhibition transcends the academic sphere, resulting in a catalyst of experiences that connect art with the community, fostering artistic awareness and strengthening links between the educational institution and society [3, 12, 26].

With the aforementioned, Mu + Art becomes the opportunity for the undergraduate students to display the result of their work in the classroom prior to the curatorial process, to exhibit in a gallery in the region.

Once the works of students and external artists which meet the requirements for the event from the perspective of traditional art are selected, the installation of the respective exhibition rooms is done, as well as the inauguration of the artistic event where the exhibits of music, theater, painting, sculpture, dance, among others, are shown.

In 2020, the event faces the COVID-19 pandemic, a problem that allowed us to conceive this activity from a virtual space. The use of emerging technologies for the exhibition of art shown in galleries allows the implementation of new strategies that involve digital art. This brought up a fundamental challenge in the digitization of traditional art to digital art [11, 15]. The development of a digital gallery that leads to a specialized website, in order to expose the most outstanding works of the curatorship, was considered [17]. This process not only allowed the virtual exhibition of the works, but also opened new possibilities to improve the exhibition experience, networking, knowledge of art, knowledge of the artist, among others, facing the event to the different problems that are found in virtuality, such as improving navigability and the way in which exhibition processes can be carried out to Internet users, the use of emerging technologies such as Virtual Reality (VR), Augmented Reality (AR) and Mixed Reality (MR) - [10, 14, 37, 43, 49]. This implies that the main problem of this research focuses on the following question: how can the preservation of traditional art be nurtured from educational processes through its circulation in digital art exhibitions?

This question encompasses two essential aspects: first, the effective documentation that traditional artistic processes must possess and the review of the different techniques of art visualization in digital environments [47], finding spaces for the appreciation of the artist's creative process, which promotes the appreciation of cultural heritage, cultural richness, cultural assets, cultural legacy and cultural heritage in the region [6, 39].

It is important to give veracity in the development of artistic processes, as well as in the processes of the transfer of the work from real spaces to virtual spaces, without putting the originality of the work of art into question [8]. In this same sense, this digital transformation from traditional artworks to the processes of digitalization of traditional art and the conception of digital art is not limited to reproductive processes in technical format, such as photography, scanning, or modeling, if not that it should be sought that the virtual or digital spaces generate 'another' experience that can be immersive as the VR, RA, RM that, resignify the narrative of artistic creation, and cover other aspects beyond visual reproduction, not as the arrival point of the digitization of traditional art, but as it becomes open to emerging technologies. It should be clarified that this process includes the documentation and preservation of essential aspects such as the techniques used in its creation, the cultural processes and the historical contexts that gave life to each piece [20]. This ensures that art does not lose its heuristic sense, since the digital platform must ensure several aspects, including accessibility, as well as the preservation of the historical value of the work of art.

As for the event of Mu + Art in its latest versions, it has managed to cure the exhibitions, migrate the information of the artists and face the challenge of adapting the works to an incipient digital gallery that depends on the context. Although these digital platforms are transformed into an innovative complement, they must maintain the authenticity of the artistic experience by adapting works to virtual formats, which involves solving issues related to the preservation of textures, material nature and original techniques in the digital environment and the experience of the observer [30] as mentioned above.

3 Frame of Reference

3.1 Origins of Mu + Art

After the VIII version of the Mu + Art "Knowledge, experiences and reflections in artistic education" in the year 2024, the event is consolidated as the most important academic space in the region, where art is the leitmotif where each of the creators present the human side of regional artists in this exhibition; this speaks of the teaching-learning process that has been happening over the years in this formative event.

The first version, in 2017, was born from the teachers' interest to show the artistic products made in the classroom by students at the Julio Pérez Ferrero public library of Cucuta; in 2018, the Mu + Art took a leap towards the community. Quinta Teresa in the city of Cucuta became the new setting for the exhibition entitled "Between the

Arts: Learning to Teach". For 2019, the third version set another milestone, moving classrooms to reality, demonstrating that art is also handled and lived in community.

The year 2020 brought unexpected challenges. The pandemic transformed the world and Mu + Art as well. The fourth version was adapted to the virtual format with the theme "Contexts", giving life to a digital platform that attracted more than 2,400 visitors. During lockdown, art became a window to hope and a means that broke physical boundaries. The return to face-to-face encounter took place in 2021 with the theme "Resilience: The Art of Living". This fifth version took the exhibition to the Unicentro shopping mall in the city of Cucuta and to the Casa Águeda Gallardo de Villamizar Museum in the city of Pamplona. Art came out to people, telling stories of overcoming and hope.

In 2022, the sixth edition, entitled "Resilience and Hope", motivated undergraduate students and the national, regional and border (Colombo-Venezuelan) community to a continuous reflection of reality through art. In general, various disciplines were integrated into the event such as art, education and psychology, to create works that reflected the reconstruction after the health crisis experienced with COVID-19. However, the event also presents a maturity and advance in the way viewers approach art through the digital medium. The process of digitizing traditional art on the Web becomes latent and, as a result, the impact of regional artists at national and international level is extended through the diffusion that occurs with social networks on the Internet.

In 2023, Mu + Art focused on the roots and movements of its territory. The seventh edition, called "Art, Territory and Border", allowed students to address issues such as migration, identity and cultural diversity in the face of a globalized world that includes multicultural heritage. Each work was transformed into a narrative about the place they inhabit and the stories that are intertwined in their borders, which offers each one its corresponding cultural richness. The artist portrays what happens in every moment, what appears in everyday life. The day-to-day is the best way to be inspired and to create resistance against what happens in the territory and on the Colombian-Venezuelan border. Thus, art is the catalyst of these experiences, which are filtered beyond the regional through what is digitalized in the event. This is how art in the region overflows and socializes with the "others", with those who do not want to close their eyes to what happens in the territory of Norte de Santander.

In 2024, the eighth edition celebrated the return of the academic event to Quinta Teresa, with the theme "Knowledge, Experiences and Reflections in Artistic Education". This event consolidated Mu + Art as a cultural and academic referent in the North and South region of Santander, highlighting the importance of artistic education as an engine of social transformation in both departments, thus projecting the need for the event to be transformed into a national and international congress where art in Colombia and the Andean region is shown.

The university and the northeastern community, especially the inhabitants of the city of Cucuta, have created a collection of fundamental life lessons through Mu + Art, that are transformed into experiences that bring the community and the Bachelor of Arts program together, in related issues to art and culture, at a regional and national level, where physical spaces are created to foster culture, art and creation in various settings and cities. This indicates that art is the common language that brings citizens, students and teachers in the undergraduate program together, creating a cultural event that educate artists, educators and the wider community.

In addition, it is a new source of peace in the region, as it creates a place to talk about identity and hope under the banner of cultural value through the arts, impacting different audiences.

4 Theoretical Framework

4.1 Digital Art Preservation

Preservation of art through digital media is relatively a new field that is being explored by researchers in the area of digital art, but it is fascinating as it brings disciplines such as preservation, technology, cultural heritage and data management together. According to Rothenberg [1, 23, 26, 34, 42], the goal is not only to save files, but to ensure that they remain accessible and useful in the future, and that the issue of obsolescence moves into the background. According to Granger, the theory of preservation based on emulation, proposes the recreation of past technological environments, in order to allow the access to digital works that would otherwise become obsolete, is the appropriate way at this moment to ensure non-obsolescence, since this approach not only seeks to protect art, but also to incorporate advances in digital security, to ensure its long-term integrity in the art world [26, 39, 49].

On the other hand, Mu + Art has initiated this process aimed at the digital preservation of the artistic samples presented and is in an incorporation process that respects traditional artistic practices. The first versions of these events done through a Web space have a simple but powerful idea: beginning to digitize the works presented by means of large-scale photography, so that those who cannot go to the face-to-face gallery can taste the virtual space. Nevertheless, the Web space faces the challenges of the digital world [24, 42] in art-related issues, as aspects such as format and display environments become relevant, since if they are not updated in works, they will be obsolete within a matter of years, as Dekker proposes [16]. It is worth mentioning that, when talking about the conservation of digital art, not only preservation is talked about, but also aspects such as the historical, technical and cultural context of the artist and the observer.

4.2 Modern Methods for Artwork Digitization

In recent years, technology has advanced in subjects related to applied sciences, and in the previous year, 2024, the role of Artificial Intelligence (AI) in the different disciplines of knowledge has become massive [4, 5, 9, 41]. These developments affect the cultural heritage that is latent in each society, which allows the processes of digitization of artworks to take on meaning and significance in the face of digitization. For example, the fact of scanning something in 2D generates a different perception from the use of 3D scanners, which propose another worldview of art and of the artist in the viewer's sensitive experience. This implies that, thanks to this technology, sculptures and historical monuments have been digitized, opening new doors for their study and appreciation [28, 29, 46].

However, 3D scanners are not the only advances that should be previewed, but issues such as virtual reality (VR) and augmented reality (AR) must also be analyzed, which will change and alter the way art is perceived and interacted with. World-class museums like the Louvre and the British Museum already offer immersive virtual tours, where visitors can explore artworks from the comfort of their own homes. In addition, artificial intelligence (AI) is being used to restore and analyze artworks, uncovering details that the human eye could not perceive [37]. It is as if technology was giving us a magnifying glass to see art with a clarity that has never been imagined [21].

In the specific case of Mu + Art, these practices are not there yet, but continuous improvement processes are already working on the way how processes such as VR and AR can be included in the artistic event [30], improving the approach of digitizing art samples presented by artists from the region.

4.3 Migration of Traditional Art to Digital Media

The transition from traditional art to digital art is not exempt from challenges [24]. One of the greatest obstacles is the unplanned or unintentional technological obsolescence. Imagine creating a digital work today, only to find that in a few years the format in which it was saved is no longer supported. This requires careful planning and constant investment in technology to prevent the works from falling into oblivion.

On the other hand, a delicate issue is the loss of authenticity and "creativity" in digital works. This is a theme which Drucker takes up when he revisits the ideas of Benjamin [7], arguing that reproduction or technical copying dehumanizes said work of art; in other words, it begins to erase or blur the elements that make it unique, that give value to it in a given time and space. This reality in the face of the digital is magnified, since the work of art is open to the infinite of the reproduction of the technique, without quality loss, generating an art without soul, dead art, lacking the necessary "aura" that human production embodies [19, 32], questioning issues such as the value and authenticity of digital and digitized art compared to traditional works.

Such problematization raises the issue of intellectual property, which exposes how there is a facility with which digital works can be copied and distributed on the internet without the artist's consent, leading to legal and ethical conflicts [29]. To address this problem, technologies such as Non-Fungible Tokens (NFT) have emerged, which allow artists to verify the authenticity and ownership of their digital creations. This is an innovative solution, but also a reminder that the world of digital art continues to evolve and face new challenges, and that Mu + Art must be at the forefront of this reality, in order to respond to the reality of the world we live in [14, 18].

On the other hand, Mu + Art has initiated this process aimed at the digital conservation of the shown artistic samples and is in a process of incorporation that respects traditional artistic practices. Thus, the first versions of these events are beginning to be imbued to the digital world, through a Web space which has a simple but powerful idea: to begin to digitize the works by means of large-scale photography, so those who cannot go to the face-to-face gallery can taste the virtual space. However, the Web space faces the challenges of the digital world [2, 42] in art-related issues, since aspects such as format and display environments become important, given that if they are not updated in works, they will be obsolete within a matter of years, as Dekker proposes [16]. It should be clarified that, when talking about the preservation of digital art, not only the preservation is addressed, but this also involves taking aspects such as the historical, technical and cultural context into account.

5 Methodology from the Research Perspective

5.1 Approach and Design

The proposed research used a qualitative methodology, allowing a preservation of the thoughts and perceptions of the respondents. Similarly, the research has a cross-sectional design and a descriptive approach, that allows the exploration of opinions and experiences about the preservation of traditional art in its digital migration.

5.2 Participants

Key informants were intentionally selected and classified into three groups:

1. Two external experts: Knowledgeable about navigability processes and interested in art.
2. An art teacher: From a public university, also considered expert in the subject.
3. A citizen of the region: Who actively participates in artistic activities.

In regards to the exclusive use of interviews as an exclusive means to carry out research, this is justified in the sense that there is greater depth in data collection, meaning that detailed information from the respondents' perspective is provided, which is crucial when evaluating an event like the Mu + Art, since the hermeneutic and semiotic sense that is given to the digital, but also to the work, can be deepened. In the same order, there is greater flexibility and adaptability in the proposal to create the interview, which makes it easier to explore emerging themes and improve the context and narrative around the artistic experiences of research participants.

This does not imply that there are no limitations in the research because, although an archive of the event was referred to make an archival observation when presenting the works of the previous versions of the Mu + Art, this was more an obstacle than a methodological advantage in the development of the research, because it did not offer the necessary quality, as the information available on this repository was limited. This generates lack of depth in what is to be observed and a biased view of what has been achieved with the current version of the event that was analyzed.

5.3 Data Collection Techniques

A structured interview of 12 questions was used, validated by expert judgement. Interviews were conducted online (TEAMS) and lasted 30 to 40 min. Informed consent was obtained from all participants.

5.4 Categories for Analysis

The interviews were analyzed in six categories:

1. Fundamental aspects: Perceptions and thoughts.
2. Mu + Art Evaluation: Design and content.
3. User experience: Loading speed and navigability.
4. Digital galleries: Referents in design and functionality.
5. Documentation and preservation: Techniques and processes.
6. Access and cultural value: Tools and strategies.

5.5 Data Analysis

It was carried out through content analysis, with the double-expert gaze validation to ensure axial classification and location of information in the aforementioned categories.

5.6 Research Problem

The problem focuses on how to preserve traditional art during its migration to the digital format, specifically in the effective documentation of artistic processes and visualization techniques in digital galleries, in the context of Mu + Art.

5.7 Main Objective

To explore effective strategies for the documentation of artistic processes and the implementation of visualization techniques in digital galleries, allowing the preservation of traditional art.

6 Analysis and Results

From the content analysis that classified the information from the interview, significant findings were identified in six key categories for the development and improvement of the Mu + Art digital gallery, where it is clarified that, in order for the scope of research to have implications on the subject of universal order, and for these results to be applicable to other events and digital spaces in a transversal way, they must be adapted to the specific situations of each research. Thus, the categories analyzed were:

First category: fundamental aspects (perceptions and thoughts):

Regarding the question "what is a digital gallery?" Three units of analysis were found: virtual exhibition space; technological platform for diffusion; and subjective digital experience.

With respect to "what is meant by digital art?" Three units of analysis were found: Digital transformation process; digital tools; and mediated artistic experience.

For the study of the digital gallery and digital art in this research, trends from a functional and technological vision are found, expressed by three participants and with a critical thinking that leads to think about the importance of the usage of technical aspects in the area expressed by another participant.

There is a similarity among the respondents on the functionality, exhibition and diffusion of digital galleries, in which interpretations can be made about their authenticity, value, navigability and access in digital media, where functionality and legitimacy are evaluated as important factors of the works, making the idea of preservation of digital art an aspect that is glimpsed in the idea of digital art [26, 43] (Table 1).

Table 1. Comparative table on fundamental aspects of art

Participant	Definition of digital gallery	Definition of digital art	Perspective on traditional art
1	Online space for versatile multimedia exhibitions	Form of expression that uses digital technology and computational tools.	Physical expression, more "rustic", through traditional means.
2	Virtual space for the exhibition and diffusion of digital and digitized works.	Visual expression through the use of software/hardware as an essential part of the creative process.	Emphasizes the transformation from physical to digital.
3	Virtual environment focused on the exhibition and diffusion of digital artworks.	Any form of visual expression that uses software/hardware as an essential part of the visual expression.	Physical form of expression with traditional techniques.
4	Storage of artificial copies of feelings.	Incomplete experience of subjectivation and ephemeral statement.	Emphasizes on the authenticity and the direct emotional experience.

Second category: Mu + Art evaluation

On the other hand, for the question "what aspects of Mu+Art's design and content do you consider most effective?" Four (4) units of analysis were found: content structuring; navigation experience; design elements; and interactive functionalities.

Some responses are categorized, such as: "thematic organization with topics that facilitate exploration", "diversity of artistic manifestations", "classification in art, science and environment". Respondents: E1, E2 and E3. In the same sense, the question "what elements of the interface were less intuitive?" Three units of analysis were found: structural problems; accessibility limitations; and lack of interactivity. There, we found answers such as: "unclear navigation", "works listed without apparent order", "unattractive topic structure", "lack of hierarchical organization". Respondents: E1, E3 and E4.

The respondents suggest that the Mu + Art digital gallery has favorable aspects in its initial browsing process, and its processes of organizational structure accessibility, and interaction tools should be worked on. The initial content presentation is highlighted as a strength, but they identify that information must be systematically reorganized and a more robust accessibility system such as mobile navigation must be handled. In the same way, the interviewees mentioned variables such as: Content Organization, Navigability, Visual Design, Accessibility, Multimedia Content, Speed and Performance, Interactive Aspects, and Information Structure, which represent that the event is migrating from traditional art format to digital media [7, 18, 29].

Third category: User experience

Now on the topic of: "how would you rate loading speed and ease of navigation between sections?", three (3) units of analysis were found: technical performance; navigability between sections; and accessibility to content. Some answers found are as follows: "*the navigation structure is not coherent*", "*it is not accessible at the exact point*", "*internal links inefficient*", "*need for clearer menus*". Respondents: E1, E2, E3 and E4.

Another point is: "what aspects of content organization would improve your experience?", where three units of analysis were found: structural organization; search tools; and interactive elements. Some of the answers are: "*better structure and hierarchy*", "*organize works by techniques and authors*", "*implement preview*", "*a specific or better hierarchical structure*". Respondents: E1, E2, E3 and E4.

The study indicates that technical performance holds a significant position, in which it is a positive process, but the navigation experience should be worked on, since respondents indicate that a clearer structure must be implemented, as well as more efficient search tools, ways to contact artists, among others. In the same way, aspects such as loading speed, navigability between sections, content organization and suggestions for improvement proposed below: "*A more robust information architecture is suggested to be developed, with emphasis on the hierarchical organization of content and the implementation of advanced search tools to improve user experience*". This implies that, once again, the Mu + Art already recreates a first experience of transition from traditional art to digital media [29].

Fourth category: Digital galleries

Particularly, the topic of: "what digital art galleries do you consider to be benchmarks in terms of design and functionality?", three units of analysis were found: main references; outstanding characteristics; and differential elements. Responses are identified as: "*3D virtual tour*", "*high resolution*", "*interactive tools*", "*immersive experiences*", "*detailed visualization*". Respondents: E1, E2, E3 and E4.

Gathering information on: "what specific features of these galleries would you like to see implemented in Mu+Art?", three units of analysis were found: technical tools; integration elements; and educational aspects, with answers such as: "*partnerships with other universities*", "*interdisciplinary platform*", "*institutional connections*", "*networks of artistic collaboration*". Respondents: E2 and E3.

Google Arts & Culture, MOMA, Tata Gallery, Louvre Museum are taken as international referents, emphasizing advanced technical characteristics and immersive experiences of each of them, which would allow a process of improvement comparatively. In the same way, implementing high quality visualization tools and establishing institutional connections is suggested, as well as improvement in the technical aspects of visualization in the Mu + Art digital gallery.

These galleries had their form of visualization and validation, the immersive experience, the development of interactive tools, and the contextual content they developed as highlights; in the same way, once they told us about these galleries, some implementation suggestions for the Mu + Art were made, such as some tools of visualization techniques, paying a lot of attention to the organization and exploration in the gallery as is proposed, placing an emphasis on the placement and integration of the information [19], as it is a process where attention needs to be on the educational and cultural aspects, and some additional functions such as integrated purchasing, advanced search systems and customized exhibition spaces. Thus, digital galleries work for the preservation of digital art in the developed versions at Mu + Art [43].

Fifth category: Documentation and preservation

On the other hand, about "what are the best practices for effectively documenting artistic processes in the context of the digitization of traditional art?", three units of analysis were found: documentation processes; digital preservation techniques; and information management. Some identified responses are: "*high quality scanning*", "*3D scanning*", "*gigapixel images*", "*backups on secure servers*". Respondents: E1, E2, E3 and E4.

Similarly, on "which visualization techniques can maintain fidelity to traditional techniques?", three (3) units of analysis were found: visualization tools; access strategies; and security measures. Responses are categorized as: "*protection of rights*", "*blockchain*", "*cloud copies*", "*physical servers*", "*accessible databases*". Respondents: E1, E3 and E4.

The study indicates that an integral starting point towards digital preservation can exist, which reviews high quality technical aspects, aiming to maintain the authenticity of the works. A more rigorous preservation is possible, such as high-resolution implementation, 3D processes, backup and storage systems, metadata, and full accessibility and implementation of security processes that allows the preservation of the artistic experience. In this way, from its beginnings, the documentation and preservation at the event emphasizes on the conservation of digital art, by creating the Website, in order to have a collection of what happened at the event [26].

Sixth category: Accessibility and cultural value

In regard to "what features should be implemented to improve accessibility to the virtual gallery?", three (3) units of analysis were found: accessibility tools; content adaptability; and inclusive functionalities. On the other hand, on "how can digital platforms guarantee accessibility and preservation of historical and cultural value?", three (3) units of analysis were found: cultural preservation; educational dissemination; and digital sustainability. Respondents indicate concerns for accessibility, cultural preservation, diffusion and sustainability, as emphasis is placed on the need to implement inclusive tools while maintaining and transmitting the cultural significance of the works, since the four participants talk about the processes of Artistic Process Documentation, Digital Preservation Techniques, Visualization, and Access and Security Strategies, and the importance of developing a platform that integrates universal accessibility functionalities is suggested, with effective strategies for the presentation and diffusion of the cultural value of digital art. This implies that preservation must consider the accessibility and cultural value of the event, in order for the migration from traditional art to digital media to be reproduced in future versions [18].

7 Discussion

7.1 Fundamental Aspects of Digital Galleries

In the discussion about the Fundamental Aspects of Digital Galleries, the technological functionality to show the culture where the digital gallery exposes the artistic experience is manifested. This process aligns with what Paul [30] calls "new media aesthetics", where the technological interface constitutes an integral component of the work. Mu + Art, as an academic project, faces the unique challenge of mediating between tradition and innovation, suggesting that the differential value of these galleries lies in their ability to create "digital contact zones" that facilitate dialogues between local artistic communities and global audiences. This extended perspective places digital galleries as instruments of pedagogical and cultural transformation, that constantly negotiate between the preservation of authenticity and the exploration of new expressive possibilities of the digital medium.

7.2 Evaluation of Mu + Art

The evaluation of Mu + Art in this research found a differentiation in the limitation of the organizational structure, the accessibility and navigability of the Web site process, which is referenced in the findings, regarding to the fundamental principles of user-centric design [30] where visibility and feedback are essential for the digital experience, being the reason why the respondents defined it with deficiencies in the structure of the mentioned themes and the accessibility for users with different abilities, stating that it does not meet these principles found on the Web site. Mu + Art currently lacks contextual navigation indicators that guide the route and available options, suggesting that the improvement of the platform requires not only technological refinements but a fundamental reconsideration on how to translate the sensory experience of art into a digital interaction language consistent with the expectations of various user profiles.

7.3 User Experience

The current context of the analysis of the user experience of the Mu + Art reveals differences between the technical performance referring to the loading speed and the ease of navigation, as well as a great concern for the architecture of the information implemented in the navigation tools [19]. The interviews identified the need to implement search tools and an architecture of the structure; to give efficiency with the principles of Morville [32] the "information architecture" is not merely structural but semantic, creating meanings through the navigation itself, so it is possible to affirm that usability and findability on the website must be improved, as they are aspects found in interviews. It is identified that Mu + Art needs to evolve towards an experience design that does not simply facilitate efficient search, but creates immersive digital narratives, where navigation itself becomes an extension of artistic experience, a fundamental aspect for academic digital galleries that seek to transcend mere representation, to become spaces of interpretation and construction of knowledge.

7.4 Referents in Digital Galleries

Referencing international digital galleries reveal a more complex phenomenon than the simple functional or technical comparison initially identified. What is significant is not the technological sophistication of platforms like Google Arts & Culture or the Louvre, but what Schweibenz [45] conceptualizes as the "deterritorialization of the museum experience" in virtual spaces. While the respondents mentioned desirable technical features, a deeper analysis reveals that these platforms have managed to transcend visual representation to create new ontologies of digital artistic experience. Schweibenz's theory about virtual museums proposes that these spaces are not replicas but distinct cultural entities with their own experiential logics, where virtuality is not a limitation but an expansion of the traditional museum concept. This perspective suggests that Mu + Art should aim not to emulate the superficial characteristics of its referents, but to develop a specific paradigm of digital presentation that responds to its specific educational context and the cultural particularities of the works it hosts, considering that advanced visualization tools are means to facilitate new forms of aesthetic experience and knowledge construction, not ends in themselves.

7.5 Documentation and Preservation

Findings suggest that documentation and preservation at the Mu + Art require techniques to maintain the authenticity and integrity of the works, emphasizing the need to implement high-resolution techniques and robust storage systems as proposed [11] in the process of digital preservation in museums, indicating that it requires not only perfection in digitization processes, but also comprehensive strategies to maintain the cultural integrity and long-term accessibility of digitized works. For Mu + Art, this implies that effective preservation consists not only of implementing advanced technologies, but of developing an interpretative apparatus which documents the relations between the work, its production context and the multiple cultural readings it elicits, creating what might be called "culturally situated digital objects" that keep not only the images alive but the narratives, meanings and contexts that make them culturally relevant.

7.6 Accessibility and Cultural Value

The derived implications of Mu + Art's accessibility and cultural value analysis indicate that accessibility tools and preservation of cultural value are required. The expressed perceptions indicate that inclusive tools and cultural preservation strategies are required, and coincide with accessibility [19, 45] in cultural spaces as agents of social change, where accessibility is not a technical appendix but a foundational principle that determines who can participate in the construction of digital cultural discourse and must be adapted for meaningful experiences that maintain authenticity, process that the respondents identify. Mu + Art must evolve towards a model of transformative accessibility that not only facilitates access to predetermined content, but also invites diverse communities to co-create meanings and narratives around the represented cultural heritage, incorporating traditionally marginalized perspectives and facilitating intercultural dialogues that enrich the collective understanding of regional art, thus turning the digital platform not only into a repository of works but into a dynamic space for collaborative cultural construction.

8 Conclusions and Recommendations

The analysis of the study conducted at Mu + Art indicates that digital preservation and documentation of artistic processes is not only a technical issue, but also a process with cultural recall and artistic authenticity. In this case, experts agree that high-resolution digitization, 3D processes and robust back-up systems are processes that allow works to be preserved in a better way. Emphasis is placed on the fact that, beyond technology, information should receive importance through the implementation of cybersecurity and metadata, which fulfil their role in protecting works from external processes, and thus ensure future access while preserving the historical and cultural value.

The research identified specific shortcomings in the current digital gallery, particularly in navigability, information architecture and accessibility for users with different abilities. The interviews highlighted the importance of developing inclusive tools that eliminate access barriers, and educational strategies that contextualize the works.

In this study, the categories of accessibility and preservation of works as cultural value were found as focal points in the development of digital galleries. The collected information highlights the need to create an inclusive tool that allows art to be exhibited for all populations; also, to find educational diffusion strategies that not only show the works, but also tell stories and contextualize their meaning, which requires innovation in the processes of keeping artistic works in time to keep history. Finally, the goal is clear: to build bridges between art and society, ensuring that their cultural value transcends the barriers of time and space.

8.1 Recommendations

In order to form an Inclusive and Sustainable Digital Future in perspectives of Mu + Art improvement, for the preservation of traditional art measured by technology, specific recommendations include: reorganizing the navigation structure, implementing advanced search systems, adopt visualization techniques comparable to referents such as *Google Arts & Culture*, and develop documentation protocols that preserve both the work and its creative process.

- *For the development of Documentation and Preservation processes in events of this type:*

    - High Resolution and 3D Techniques: Adopt cutting-edge technologies that capture every detail of the works, preserving their essence and authenticity.
    - Backup and Storage Systems: Implement solid infrastructures that ensure the durability of digital works against technological obsolescence.
    - Metadata Management: Meticulously organize and document each work, facilitating future access and study.
    - Security Measures: Protect digital works with advanced protocols that guarantee their integrity and prevent cyber threats.

- *To improve the accessibility and cultural value of Mu + Art:*

  - Inclusive Tools: Design accessible platforms that remove barriers and allow everyone to enjoy art, regardless of their abilities.
  - Educational Outreach: Create programs that not only show the works but also educate about their historical and cultural context.
  - Digital Sustainability: Adopt practices that ensure long-term preservation, balancing innovation and environmental responsibility.
  - Cultural Functionalities: Integrate features that enrich the user experience, such as advanced search systems, customized exhibitions and integrated purchase options, always respecting the cultural value of the works.
  - Appreciation of the artist: unveiling his art, considering his perceptions and interests, supporting him about the knowledge of the technology to be able to use them and navigate the knowledge society with his art.

Finally, this implies understanding that the digitization of art is not only a response to the technological challenges of our time, but an opportunity to re-imagine how we interact with culture. Combining advanced preservation techniques with an inclusive and educational approach ensures that art remains a bridge between the past, present and future. This effort not only preserves works but also democratizes access to knowledge and enriches our understanding of the world. Ultimately, the digital preservation of art is an act of care and respect for our cultural heritage, a legacy that deserves to be protected and shared with future generations.

Acknowledgments. This article is associated to the research project entitled: Teaching of philosophy in the schools of Norte de Santander, downtown, Cucuta and its metropolitan area, code 400-156.012-157 (GA311-BP-2024), from the CONQUIRO research group of the Philosophy program at the Faculty of Arts and Humanities of the University of Pamplona, (Col-Lat.).

References

1. Abarca, J.E.O.: El arte en la era digital: teorizaciones, desafíos y reflexiones. Aitías Rev. Estud. Filos. Cent. Estud. Humanísticos UANL. **5**(10), 1–27 (2025)
2. Acevedo-Rincón, J.P., Flórez-Pabón, C.E.: TelEduc: a virtual learning environment for teaching and learning at the University of Campinas. Brazil. J. Phys. Conf. Ser. **1161**(1), 012023 (2019). https://doi.org/10.1088/1742-6596/1161/1/012023
3. Albar Mansoa, P.J.: Prácticas artísticas para el bienestar colectivo. Diálogos entre arte, salud, educación artística y sociedad. Octaedro. (2025)
4. Albar Mansoa, P.J.: La Inteligencia Artificial de generación de imágenes en arte:¿ Cómo impacta en el futuro del alumnado en Bellas Artes?. (2024)
5. Arroba, F.O.: La inteligencia artificial y la transformación de las expresiones artísticas. Uru: Rev. Comun. Cult. **10**, 65–84 (2024)
6. Cameron, F., Kenderdine, S.: Theorizing Digital Cultural Heritage: A Critical Discourse. MIT Press, Cambridge (2007)
7. Basile, M.V., Garziera, G., Facus, A.L.: Arte y patrimonio universitario: el "Tesoro" de la Escuela de Bellas Artes (FAD-UPC). Avances. **34**, 75–90 (2025)

8. Benjamin, W.: La obra de arte en la época de su reproductibilidad técnica. https: //www.marxists.org (1936)
9. Bentkowska-Kafel, A., Denard, H., Baker, D.: Paradata and Transparency in Virtual Heritage. Ashgate Publishing, Farnham (2012). https://doi.org/10.4324/9781315599366
10. Boy-Guilén, L.E., Sánchez-Palacios, L.G., Cieza-Mostacero, S.E.: Originalidad de obras de arte digital generadas por IA: Una revisión sistemática de la literatura. AiBi Rev. Investig. Adm. Ing. **13**(2), 1–11 (2025). https://doi.org/10.15649/2346030X.4582
11. Cabero-Almenara, J., Gallego, M.R., Llorente-Cejudo, C.: Realidad mixta, virtual y aumentada: tecnologías para el aprendizaje. Texto Livre. **18**, e49561 (2025). https://doi.org/10.1590/1983-3652.2025.49561
12. Cameron, F.: The Future of Digital Data, Heritage and Curation in a More-than Human World. London, Routledge. https://www.taylorfrancis.com/books/mono/10.4324/9781003149606/future-digital-data-heritage-curation-fiona-cameron (2021)
13. Cariati, R.: Cultura de pensamiento: el catalizador de experiencias de aprendizaje. In: El aula vivencial: De la clase recitada a la experiencia de aprendizaje, p. 49. (2025)
14. Castellano Ortiz, E.: Sistemas NFT y certificación de autenticidad: aplicación de nuevas tecnologías a la conservación del arte digital. REIDOCREA. **13**(39), 592–604 (2024). https://doi.org/10.30827/reidocrea.v13i39.31420
15. De la Fuente, M.H., Narros, C.J., Seijo, S.P.: Perspectivas de la realidad virtual y aumentada en el discurso informativo, persuasivo y artístico. In: En Experiencias inmersivas: realidad virtual y realidad aumentada en periodismo, publicidad y artes, pp. 19–36. Tirant Humanidades, Valencia (2024)
16. De la O Cerino, E.R., López Martínez, C.E.: Arte tradicional en la era digital: desafíos y estrategias para la comercialización de tiras bordadas de tabasco. LATAM Rev. Latinoam. Cienc. Soc. Humanid. **5**(3), 539–547 (2024). https://doi.org/10.56712/latam.v5i3.2057
17. Dekker, A.: Collecting and Conserving Net Art: Moving Beyond Conventional Methods. Routledge, London (2018)
18. Din, H., Hecht, P.: The Digital Museum: A Think Guide. American Association of Museums, Washington, D.C. (2007)
19. Dowling, M.: Is non-fungible token pricing driven by cryptocurrencies? Finance Research Letters. doi:https://doi.org/10.1016/j.frl.2021.102097 (2021)
20. Drucker, J.: The virtual codex from page space to e-space. In: Comparative Textual Media: Transforming the Humanities in the Postprint Era, pp. 199–224. University of Minnesota Press, Minneapolis (2013)
21. Eisner, E.W.: The Arts and the Creation of Mind. Yale University Press, New Haven (2002)
22. Elgammal, A., Liu, B., Elhoseiny, M., & Mazzone, M.: CAN: creative adversarial networks, generating "art" by learning about styles and deviating from style norms. https://arxiv.org/abs/1706.07068 (2017)
23. Fernandes, F.O., Prado, G.: Conservación del arte digital: desafíos, oportunidades y estrategias innovadoras. ANIAV - Rev. Investig. Artes Vis. **16**, 89–102 (2025)
24. Flórez-Pabón, C.E., Cabeza-Herrera, O.J., Oses-Gil, A.: Interacción y gamificación: enseñanza de la filosofía en la Universidad de Pamplona. Tril. Cienc. Tecnol. Soc. **15**(29), e2439 (2023). https://doi.org/10.22430/21457778.2439
25. García, C.P.: El crecimiento del Mercado de Arte Digital. Estud. Ciénega. **8**, 139–148 (2024)
26. García Morales, L.: Conservación y restauración de arte digital. Tesis doctoral, Universidad Europea de Madrid (2011)
27. Granger, S.: Emulation as a digital preservation strategy. D-Lib Mag. **6**(10), 1–10 (2000). https://doi.org/10.1045/october2000-granger
28. Greene, M.: Releasing the Imagination: Essays on Education, the Arts, and Social Change. Jossey-Bass, San Francisco (1995)

29. Huerta, R., Rodríguez-López, R.: Educación digital, creaciones artísticas y formación del profesorado. Arte Individuo Soc. **37**(1), 193–207 (2025)
30. Lessig, L.: Free Culture: How Big Media Uses Technology and the Law to Lock Down Culture and Control Creativity. Penguin Press, New York (2004)
31. Ligarretto Feo, R.: Media-Arte Digital: educación artística experimental para la media literacy. Calle 14 Rev. Investig. Campo Arte. **19**(36), 370–389 (2024). https://doi.org/10.14483/21450706.21297
32. Moreno, L.D.R.: Inmaterialidades. Problemas de conservación del arte de los nuevos medios. De Arte: Rev. Hist. Arte. **16**, 227–238 (2017)
33. Morville, P.: Information Architecture for the World Wide Web: Designing for the Web and Beyond. O'Reilly Media, Sebastopol (2015) https://books.google.com.co/books?id=dZaJCgAAQBAJ&printsec=frontcover&hl=es&source=gbs_ge_summary_r&cad=0#v=onepage&q&f=false
34. Norman, D.: The Design of Everyday Things: Revised and Expanded Edition. Basic Books, New York (2016) https://www.academia.edu/40621043/The_Design_of_Everyday_Things_Don_Norman
35. Oliveira Fernandes, F., Prado, G.: Conservación del arte digital: desafíos, oportunidades y estrategias innovadoras. ANIAV - Rev. Investig. Artes Vis. **16**, 89–102 (2025). https://doi.org/10.4995/aniav.2025.23183
36. Paul, C.: Digital Art (World of Art). Thames & Hudson, London (2022) https://www.academia.edu/78928735/Digital_Art_Now
37. Pescarin, S.: Museums and virtual reality. J. Cult. Herit. **15**(3), 1–4 (2014). https://doi.org/10.1016/j.culher.2013.10.008
38. Prieto Andreu, J.M.: Revisión sistemática sobre aprendizaje colaborativo mediante realidad virtual, realidad aumentada y realidad mixta. Teor. Educ. Rev. Interuniv. **37**(1), 151–186 (2025). https://doi.org/10.14201/teri.31921
39. Ramírez, J.F.M., Del Castillo, A.: Itinerarios de la materia: medialidad, circulación y obsolescencia tecnológica en algunas prácticas artísticas desde México. Artnodes: Rev. Arte Cienc. Tecnol. **15**, 61–69 (2015)
40. Ramos, L.M., Tuñón, M.: La economía naranja y el valor del arte en la sociedad contemporánea. Cuad. Coyunt. **3**(1), 23–41 (2025). https://doi.org/10.48204/J.cc.n1.a6781
41. Rodríguez-Ortega, N.: Inteligencia artificial y campo del arte. https://riuma.uma.es/xmlui/bitstream/handle/10630/19525/32.pdf (2020)
42. Rosenthal, D.S.H., Robertson, T., Lipkis, T., Reich, V., Morabito, S.: Requirements for digital preservation systems: a bottom-up approach. Int. J. Digit. Curat. **1**(2), 1–11 (2005). https://doi.org/10.2218/ijdc.v1i2.5
43. Rothenberg, J.: Ensuring the longevity of digital documents. Sci. Am. **272**(1), 42–47 (1999). https://doi.org/10.1038/scientificamerican0195-42
44. Rubio-Tamayo, J.L., González, H.E.: La realidad virtual y extendida como medios para la convergencia del arte, la ciencia y la tecnología: potencial expresivo y representación del medio inmersivo-interactivo. J. Sound Silence Image Technol. **8**, 127–149 (2025)
45. Sandell, R.: Museums Moralities and Human Rights. Routledge, London (2016) https://www.researchgate.net/publication/318585210_Museums_Moralities_and_Human_Rights
46. Schweibenz, W.: The virtual museum: an overview of its origins, concepts, and terminology. Mus. Rev. **4**(1), 1–29 (2019) https://www.researchgate.net/profile/Werner-Schweibenz/publication/335241270_The_virtual_museum_an_overview_of_its_origins_concepts_and_terminology/links/5d5ac020a6fdcc55e8192ede/The-virtual-museum-an-overview-of-its-origins-concepts-and-terminology.pdf
47. Sinthanayothin, C., Wongwean, N., Bholsithi, W.: Interactive virtual 3d gallery using motion detection of mobile device. In: International Conference on Mobile IT Convergence, pp. 120–125. IEEE, Piscataway (2011)

48. Srinivasan, R., et al.: Digital museums and diverse cultural knowledge: moving past the traditional catalog. Inf. Soc. **25**(4), 265–278 (2009). https://doi.org/10.1080/01972240903028714
49. Valera, S.C., Valdés, P.F., Viñas, S.M.: NFT y arte digital: nuevas posibilidades para el consumo, la difusión y preservación de obras de arte contemporáneo. Artnodes: Rev. Arte Cienc. Tecnol. **28**, 2 (2021)
50. Velásquez Saavedra, M.E.: Realidad mixta y su relación con los museos: remodelando la interacción con los Adolescentes. Publ. Investig. **18**(2), 1–15 (2024). https://doi.org/10.22490/25394088.8913

Towards a Collaborative Framework for the Implementation of Digital Transformation Processes in Higher Education Institutions: A Comparative Analysis

Alex A. Torres[1(✉)], César Alberto Collazos[2], and Alicia Mon[3]

[1] Corporación Universitaria Comfacauca-Unicomfacauca, Popayán, Colombia
atorres@unicomfacauca.edu.co
[2] Universidad del Cauca, Popayán, Colombia
ccollazo@unicauca.edu.co
[3] National University of La Matanza, Buenos Aires, Argentina

Abstract. This study presents a systematic literature review to analyze existing digital transformation models for Higher Education Institutions (HEIs) and proposes a collaborative framework to support the implementation of digital transformation processes across their core missions. Using the PRISMA methodology, an initial set of 95 articles was identified, of which 15 were selected for in-depth analysis. The findings reveal four main categories of models: digital maturity, data governance, digital collaboration, and technology adoption. Among the 15 studies analyzed, digital maturity models were the most prevalent (six studies), while only five specifically addressed the Latin American context, where resource constraints and institutional resistance continue to hinder digital transformation initiatives. The review also highlights the absence of standardized assessment criteria for measuring digital maturity and the limited research on collaborative approaches to digital transformation in higher education. To address these gaps, this study proposes a collaborative framework that integrates digital maturity assessment, data governance strategies, and interinstitutional cooperation to support sustainable implementation. The framework emphasizes capacity building, the establishment of strategic partnerships, and the development of governance policies. This research contributes to the academic discussion by consolidating the most effective elements of existing models and providing a structured approach tailored to Higher Education Institutions in Latin America and other emerging economies. Future research should empirically validate the proposed framework and develop standardized digital maturity metrics.

Keywords: Digital transformation · digital maturity models · collaborative framework · data governance · technology adoption · Latin America

H. Luna-García et al. (Eds.): HCI-COLLAB 2025, CCIS 2850, pp. 271–287, 2027.
https://doi.org/10.1007/978-3-032-31223-5_19

1 Introduction

1.1 Background

Digital transformation (DT) has become a strategic priority for Higher Education Institutions (HEIs) in the second decade of the twenty-first century (Benavides et al., 2023). This evolutionary process uses digital capabilities and technologies to modernize business models, operational processes, and user experiences that generate value (Rodríguez-Abitia & Bribiesca-Correa, 2021), emerging as a key element to strengthen teaching, research, social projection, and university management.

The adoption of emerging technologies such as online learning, artificial intelligence, and data analytics has enabled universities to adapt to the demands of the knowledge society (UNESCO, 2022; OECD, 2021; Weller, 2020). However, digital transformation has not been homogeneous and faces significant barriers, particularly in Latin America, where digital divides, low technological investment, and resistance to organizational change persist (World Bank, 2023).

According to Miranda et al. (2021), Colombia faces a considerable lag in technological infrastructure, especially in regional institutions such as Unicomfacauca, which underscores the need for digital transformation strategies adapted to the local context.

Various models have been proposed to guide this process in universities. Among them, digital maturity models stand out (Venkatesh et al., 2021; Westerman et al., 2019), data governance (Alenezi, 2021; Janssen et al., 2020), technological adoption (García-Peñalvo, 2022; Selwyn, 2020) and inter-institutional collaboration (OECD, 2021; Ramírez-Montoya et al., 2022).

These models directly inform the design of the framework proposed in this study: for example, the technology adoption approach of Venkatesh et al. (2021) nurtures the technological dimension of the framework, while the data governance model of Janssen et al. (2020) guides the digital information management component.

However, there is still no consolidated collaborative framework that facilitates the effective implementation of digital transformation in HEIs with different levels of technological maturity. This situation evidences the need to carry out a systematic review of the literature and a comparative analysis of existing models, to determine their applicability in specific contexts such as that of Unicomfacauca, a higher education institution located in Popayán, Cauca, Colombia.

1.2 Importance of the Study

Despite the growing academic and governmental interest in university digital transformation, gaps persist in the literature, among which the following stand out:

- Lack of standardization in digital transformation models for HEIs (OECD, 2021; UNESCO, 2022; Westerman et al., 2019).
- Scarcity of empirical evaluations on digital maturity in Latin American universities (World Bank, 2023; Miranda et al., 2021).
- Limited evidence on internal and inter-institutional collaboration in the implementation of digital transformation processes (Alenezi, 2021; Janssen et al., 2020).

- Poor adaptability of existing models to contexts with specific technological and organizational constraints (García-Peñalvo, 2022; Selwyn, 2020).

This systematic review seeks to close these gaps through a comparative analysis of digital transformation models in HEIs, establishing the basis for the design of a collaborative framework adapted to the realities of Unicomfacauca and other institutions in Latin America.

1.3 Research Problem

Although digital transformation is recognized as a critical factor for the modernization of universities, a collaborative framework that allows its structured and sustainable implementation has not yet been developed. The research problem is formulated as follows:

How to implement a collaborative digital transformation framework to improve mission processes in a higher education institution?

This problem arises from the lack of standardized criteria to measure digital maturity, the lack of internal and external collaboration between HEIs, and the need to adapt global models to the particular realities of Latin America.

1.4 Objective of the Review

The overall objective of this systematic review is to:

Define a collaborative framework for the implementation of digital transformation processes in Higher Education Institutions, contributing to the continuous improvement of mission processes.

Specific objectives:

- To analyze the state of knowledge about digital transformation models in higher education.
- To compare the methodological approaches used in the TD models and to evaluate their applicability in Unicomfacauca.
- To identify the digital maturity criteria in the reviewed studies and their relevance for the measurement of TD in HEIs.
- To determine gaps in the literature and propose a collaborative framework for Latin America.

1.5 Research Questions

To answer the problem posed, the following research questions have been formulated. Main Question: How to implement a collaborative digital transformation framework to improve mission processes in a higher education institution? The Secondary Questions are described in Table 1.

This paper provides an overview of the research papers published in this field through a systematic literature review (RSL) of digital transformation models or frameworks in HEIs. The sections of the document are structured as follows: The Introduction section presents the current RSL related to digital transformation models or frameworks for

Table 1. Research Questions

No	Question
P1	What are the digital transformation frameworks or models defined for higher education institutions or universities?
Q2	What level of collaboration do TD models in higher education present?
Q3	What are the most widely used criteria to measure digital maturity in universities?
Q4	What are the main gaps in the literature on digital transformation in Latin American universities?
Q5	How can a digital transformation model be adapted to Unicomfacauca?

HEIs, defining the importance of the study, the research problem, the objectives and the research questions. In the Methodological section, the authors present the protocol followed, the process of extracting the relevant data and describe the results of the process. The Discussion section provides a discussion to answer research questions. Finally, the Conclusions and Recommendations section describes the inferences.

2 Methodology of the Systematic Review

This research is based on the PRISMA protocol (Preferred Reporting Items for Systematic Reviews and Meta-Analyses) proposed by Moher et al. (2009), which allows for the identification, selection, evaluation, and rigorous synthesis of scientific evidence related to digital transformation in higher education institutions.

The methodological process was carried out in four main phases:

1. Identification: Search for articles in scientific databases.
2. Screening: Removal of duplicates and preliminary review of titles and abstracts.
3. Eligibility: Evaluation of quality and relevance through complete reading.
4. Inclusion: Final selection of articles for detailed analysis.

After completing all phases of the process, 15 studies were selected for final analysis.

2.1 Data Sources

The bibliographic search was carried out in the Scopus database, selected for its relevance and coverage in high-quality scientific publications, especially on issues of digital transformation in higher education (Mar et al., n.d.). Mendeley software was also used to manage references, remove duplicates, and encode information, and Microsoft Excel was used to organize the extracted data.

2.2 Search Strategy

The search strategy was meticulously designed to ensure comprehensiveness and relevance, adapting to the research questions and guidelines of the PICO framework. Table 2 describes the terms used in this research for the construction of the search string. The search was carried out in the Scopus database, considering the studies carried out between 2019 and 2024.

Table 2. Search Terms

Main Term	Related Terms
Digital Transformation	Digital Transformation, Digital Transformation, Digital Transformation Models, Digital Transformation Framework, Digitalization, digitization
Higher Education Institutions	Universities, universities, Education, education
Search string used	
(("Digital Transformation") OR ("Digital Transformation") OR ("Digitalization") OR ("Digitization") OR ("Digital Transformation Model") OR ("Digital Transformation Models") OR ("Digital Transformation Framework") OR ("Higher Education Institutions") OR ("Higher Education Institutions" OR ("Universities") OR ("Universities") OR ("Education") OR ("Education")	

2.3 Study Selection

Studies were selected according to the criteria described below.

Inclusion and Exclusion Criteria

The authors (Budgen & Brereton, 2006) They clarified that research identified through electronic and manual searches can be unequivocally excluded based on the title and abstract, which requires obtaining a full copy. In addition, redundant references were systematically removed using Mendeley software. Inclusion and exclusion criteria according to the methodology allowed us to filter out studies that are not relevant around the defined questions. In this case, the following articles are taken as inclusion criteria:

1) Publications in indexed scientific journals and refereed conferences.
2) Studies published between 2019 and 2024.
3) Studies that propose digital transformation models or frameworks applicable to HEIs or universities.
4) Articles in English and Spanish. 5) Studies that include digital maturity measurement and inter-institutional collaboration.

The following items are excluded criteria:

1) Studies that do not propose a structured model of digital transformation.
2) Publications without peer review (blogs, opinion articles).
3) Documents with a focus on other sectors (companies, health, etc.).
4) Duplicate studies or without access to the full text.

Item Selection Process

The selection process was carried out in four phases, following the PRISMA model:

1) Identification: 95 studies were found after applying the search strategy in the Scopus database.
2) Screening: 0 duplicate studies were eliminated.
3) Eligibility: We reviewed titles and abstracts, excluding 24 studies that did not meet the criteria.
4) Inclusion: Finally, 15 articles were selected for detailed analysis.

Figure 1 describes a summary of the PRISMA protocol.

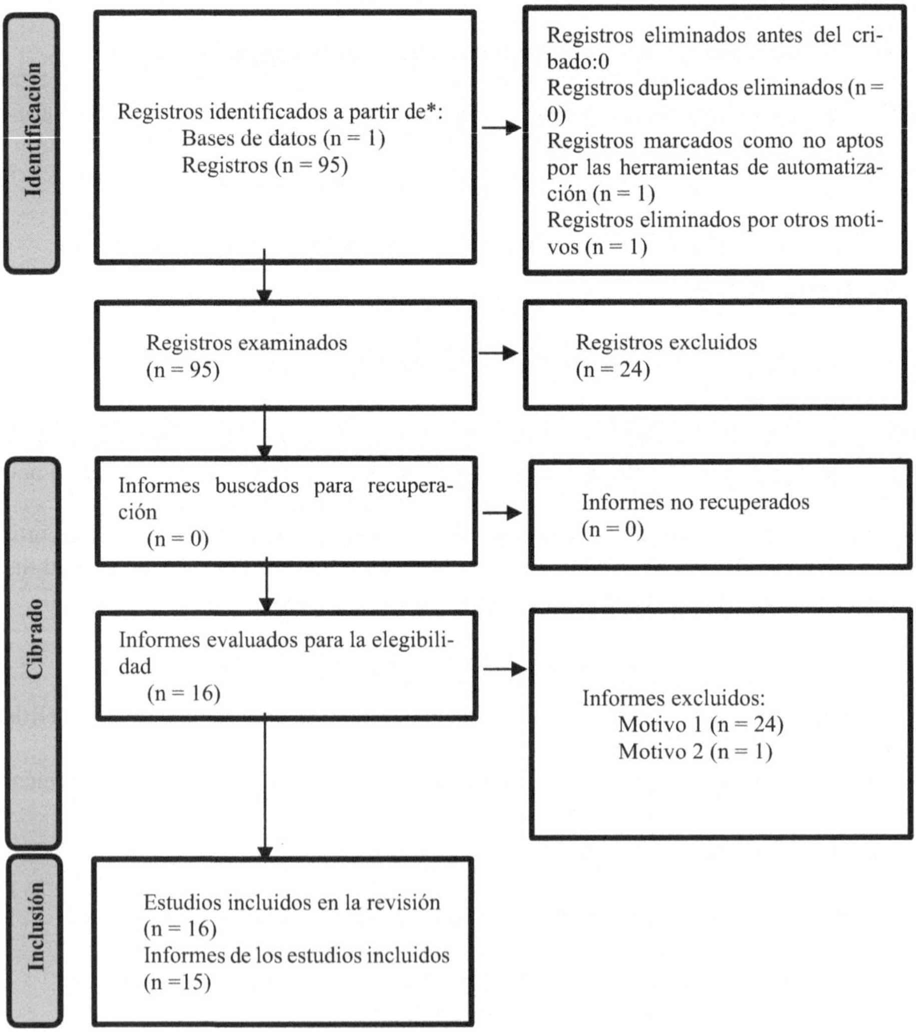

Fig. 1. PRISMA Protocol Application

2.4 Assessment of Study Quality

To measure the quality of the selected studies and determine the relevant ones, a questionnaire was developed structured in five key questions, with a scoring system of three values ($-1, 0$ and $+1$). Table 3 shows the questions to be considered in order to evaluate the studies and the score assigned according to the possible answers.

Table 3. Quality Assessment Criteria

Questions	Evaluation scale
The study proposes a framework, route or set of elements described in detail to carry out digital transformation processes in HEIs or universities The study presents results of the implementation of a digital transformation model or framework in HEIs or universities The study presents collaborative work initiatives to support digital transformation processes in universities The research presents the construction of a digital transformation model and/or collaborative work in organizations Do you describe the benefits and challenges that come with adopting digital transformation processes in organizations?	Measurement scale: Yes = 1.0 Partially = 0.5 No = 0.0 Measurement Strategy: Maximum rating: 7.0 Minimum rating: 2.0 Minimum acceptance score: 2.5

Table 4. Characteristics of the studies analysed

Features	Categories	No. of Studies
Geographic Region	Latin America	5
	North America	3
	Europe	4
	Asia	2
	Global	1
Research Method	Qualitative	6
	Quantitative	5
	Mixed	4
Scope of Application	Public universities	6
	Private universities	4
	Individual Case Studies	3
	General models applicable to multiple universities	2

2.5 Data Extraction and Analysis

Design of Data Extraction Forms. The computer software used for data management and analysis of the information contained in the articles included Mendeley and Microsoft Excel. Mendeley was used to monitor the articles obtained by querying the database, effectively eliminating redundant references and classifying the information within each article, making distinctions by applying different colors according to the designated category. In contrast, to document and organize the data generated from the downstream protocol, Microsoft Excel was used. The workbook was structured with several tabs, meticulously recording each distinct phase. Full information can be accessed in the supplementary materials.

Data Extraction Procedures. The methodology used for data collection was systematically structured in three distinct phases. Analysis of the information: The dissection and categorization of the data were performed using an inductive analytical approach. The textual segments that provided answers to the research questions were distinctively marked using varied color coding, facilitated by Mendeley software. This methodological approach allowed for deeper engagement with the text and facilitated a meticulous process of examination and categorization. In phase 2, Information classification: the coding of the labels with the intention of attributing representative meaning to the highlighted data was established simultaneously during the information analysis phase. And finally phase 3, Information extraction: each segment of the text that was emphasized during the information analysis phase was systematically classified according to the codes outlined during the classification phase. To effectively manage the resulting information, a spreadsheet application was employed. Which can be accessed through the following link: https://surl.li/tpdrqn.

2.6 Information Synthesis

As a synthesis method, the information from selected studies was extracted and structured by adapting the bibliographic files proposed by Hoyos Botero (Botero, 2000): Identification (title, authors, year of publication, keywords), type of study, objective of the study, type of model/framework, dimensions of the model, components of the model, method/approach, scope of application, level of collaboration, measurement of maturity, main findings, gaps/gaps in the literature, main conclusions, relevance for the development of the collaborative framework, applicability in Colombia (Unicomfacauca).

3 Results

This segment is organized according to the research and mapping queries synthesized from the evaluation of the articles, after the process of analyzing the information outlined in the review protocol. In addition, the data obtained from the review protocol is aggregated into the spreadsheet: https://surl.li/tpdrqn.

3.1 Included and Excluded Studies

After applying the selection process based on the PRISMA methodology, a total of 95 relevant studies were identified for the analysis of digital transformation models in higher education institutions. Of these, 80 articles were excluded for not meeting the inclusion criteria, resulting in a final sample of 15 studies that make up the basis of analysis.

3.2 General Characterization of the Studies Analyzed

The selected studies cover various geographical regions, research methodologies and fields of application. The following table summarizes its characteristics:

This characterization reflects that the focus on digital maturity models responds to the priority of systematically assessing the state of digitalization in universities, especially in regions in the process of technological consolidation such as Latin America.

3.3 Main Models/frameworks of Digital Transformation in Universities

The models identified in the literature can be grouped into four main categories, as shown in Table 5:

Table 5. Main models of digital transformation in universities

Identified Models	Description	No. Studies	Studies
Digital Maturity Models	They evaluate the level of institutional digitalization based on key dimensions such as infrastructure, digital skills, and technological adoption	6	Rodríguez et al. (2021), Martínez et al. (2021), Giand et al. (2021), Timokhova et al. (2022), Langseth et al. (2023), Castro et al. (2023)
Data Governance Models	They focus on the management and administration of digital information within universities, ensuring security and efficiency in academic and administrative processes	3	Abdulfattah et al. (2020), García et al. (2021), Taher et al. (2023)
Digital Collaboration Models	They promote the integration of multiple actors within the university ecosystem (administrators, teachers, students, and external entities) to facilitate digital transformation	4	Alenezi et al. (2021), Castillo et al. (2021), Quaicoe et al. (2023), Ramírez-Montoya et al. (2022)

(continued)

Table 5. (*continued*)

Identified Models	Description	No. Studies	Studies
Technology Adoption Models	They analyze the implementation of emerging technologies and their impact on educational and administrative processes	2	Aditya et al. (2023), Nurhas et al. (2022)

The preponderance of digital maturity models reflects the need for universities to systematically measure their digital progress to guide strategic decisions.

3.4 Patterns and Trends

Based on the analysis of the selected studies, the following trends are identified:

- Predominance of digital maturity models (40% of the studies), evidencing that measuring the level of transformation is an institutional priority.
- Greater frequency of qualitative approaches, suggesting that digital transformation is still studied more as an exploratory phenomenon than a quantifiable one.
- There is little presence of data governance models, possibly due to siloed academic structures, where each agency manages its information in isolation.
- Emerging digital collaboration models, fundamental in universities with limited resources, although still poorly integrated into formal strategies.

3.5 Comparative Analysis of Digital Transformation Models

- Digital transformation models in higher education institutions present significant differences in terms of their approach, level of collaboration and applicability.
- Digital Maturity Models have been the most widely used due to their ability to assess the degree of digitalisation in universities. However, their effectiveness depends largely on the adoption of standardized metrics and their alignment with institutional objectives. These models usually have a medium-high level of collaboration, since they require the involvement of multiple internal actors, such as teachers, administrators and students.
- Data Governance Models focus on the efficient management of digital information, but their applicability in higher education is limited compared to more regulated sectors, such as corporate or government. These models have a medium level of collaboration, since they involve technical areas of the universities, but not necessarily the academic community as a whole.
- Digital Collaboration Models have proven to be effective in the integration of key actors within the university ecosystem. Unlike digital maturity models, they emphasize cooperation between different institutions, including partnerships with the private sector and government agencies. Its main limitation is the lack of mechanisms for measuring digital maturity, which makes it difficult to systematically assess it. However, they have a high level of collaboration, making it easy to implement in resource-constrained environments.

- Finally, the Technology Adoption Models focus on the incorporation of new digital tools in teaching and academic administration. Although its application is broad, its approach is based on technological implementation without necessarily considering a structured framework for digital transformation. These models tend to have a low-medium level of collaboration, since they are often driven by administrative decisions without a process of active participation of the entire university community. Table 6 consolidates the comparative analysis of Digital Transformation Models.

Table 6. Comparative Analysis TD Models

Model/Frame	Level of Collaboration	Maturity Measurement	Methods Used	Applicability in HEIs
Maturity Digital	Medium - High	Yes	Qualitative/Quantitative	High
Governance Data	Medium	Yes	Qualitative	Moderate
Collaboration Digital	High	No	Mixed	High
Adoption Technology	Low - Medium	No	Quantitative	Moderate

3.6 Gaps and Challenges Identified in the Literature

Gaps. The systematic review has identified several gaps in the literature on digital transformation in higher education institutions. Among them, the lack of comprehensive models that combine elements of digital maturity and inter-institutional collaboration stands out. Many models focus on only one dimension, leaving aside a holistic approach that considers both the technological infrastructure and the participation of different actors within the institution.

Another important gap in the literature is the scant research on the impact of data governance in universities. Although there are data management models applied to other sectors, their adaptation to the educational field remains a challenge. The lack of standards for data management in academic institutions limits evidence-based decision-making and the efficiency of administrative processes.

In addition, the need to develop standardized metrics to evaluate digital transformation in universities is observed. Currently, models use heterogeneous indicators, making it difficult to compare between institutions and measure progress over time.

- Lack of comprehensive models that combine digital maturity and inter-institutional collaboration.
- Little research on the impact of data governance in universities.
- Need to develop standardized metrics for the evaluation of digital transformation in HEIs.

Challenges. The challenges in the implementation of digital transformation in higher education vary from technological aspects to organizational barriers. A key challenge is the effective implementation of models in universities with limited resources. Many institutions face difficulties in adopting digital models due to budget constraints, which impede investments in infrastructure and training.

Another challenge is the training of teachers and administrators in digital skills. The adoption of new technologies requires educational actors to develop skills that allow them to use them effectively. Without continuous training strategies, digital transformation may be limited in its actual impact.

Finally, the integration of collaborative models with sustainable institutional policies represents a significant challenge. The lack of alignment between digital strategies and institutional planning can generate isolated efforts that fail to consolidate over time. It is necessary to establish regulatory and governance frameworks that allow the continuity and expansion of digital initiatives in higher education.

- Effective implementation of models in universities with limited resources.
- Training of teachers and administrators in digital skills.
- Integration of collaborative models with sustainable institutional policies.

4 Discussion

4.1 Critical Analysis of the Identified Models

Digital transformation models in higher education institutions present diverse approaches ranging from digital maturity assessment to data governance and inter-institutional collaboration. From the comparative analysis carried out, significant differences were identified in terms of approach, applicability and effectiveness of each model.

Digital Maturity Models stand out for their ability to provide a clear measurement of the state of digitalization of universities. However, its limitation lies in the need for standardized metrics and their dependence on internal structural factors. In contrast, Data Governance Models have proven to be fundamental for the efficient management of digital resources, although their approach is more technical and less pedagogical.

Digital Collaboration Models have emerged as a key strategy to enhance digital transformation, allowing cooperation between different actors in the university ecosystem. However, its success depends to a large extent on the existence of clear strategic alliances and institutional policies. Finally, Technology Adoption Models have been widely implemented, but in many cases they lack an organizational structure that guarantees their sustainability over time.

4.2 Evaluation of the Applicability of the Models in Latin American Universities

The application of the revised models in Latin American universities faces multiple challenges. Institutions in the region often have limitations in technological infrastructure, investment in digitalization, and teacher training in digital skills. While Digital Maturity

Models can be useful for establishing initial diagnoses, their effective implementation requires significant resources.

Data Governance Models, on the other hand, have not yet been widely applied in Latin American universities, which represents an opportunity for future research and practical applications. In contrast, Digital Collaboration Models have shown greater viability in the region, especially through inter-university consortia and international cooperation programs.

4.3 Reflection on the Adaptation of These Models in Unicomfacauca

In the context of Unicomfacauca, the adoption of a digital transformation model must consider the institutional reality, including its technological and organizational capacity. A hybrid approach that combines elements of digital maturity, digital collaboration, and data governance could be an effective strategy to ensure sustainable implementation.

The university could benefit from adopting digital maturity metrics to assess its progress, while also strengthening inter-institutional collaboration with other universities and government bodies. Data management must play a crucial role in this process, ensuring that information is used strategically for academic and administrative decision-making.

4.4 Implications for Future Research

Proposal of a Collaborative Framework for Digital Transformation for HEIs Based on Analyzed Models. To structure the collaborative framework, the authors propose to identify key dimensions and fundamental components based on the models analyzed. These dimensions will allow a structured and sustainable implementation of digital transformation in higher education institutions.

Dimensions of the Collaborative Framework:

1. Strategic Dimension:

   - Development of institutional plans for digital transformation.
   - Definition of key performance indicators (KPIs).
   - Creation of policies for the adoption of technology and digitalization of processes.

2. Technological Dimension:

   - Implementation of robust digital infrastructure (cloud computing, Big Data, AI).
   - Use of online learning platforms and digital tools.
   - Evaluation of interoperability of technological systems.

3. Organizational Dimension:

   - Promotion of digital culture within the university.
   - Training and continuous training in digital skills.
   - Creation of multidisciplinary teams to lead digital transformation.

4. Data Governance Dimension:

- Establishment of regulations for data management.
- Implementation of information security and privacy strategies.
- Use of data analytics for institutional decision-making.

5. Collaboration and Networking Dimension:

- Promotion of internal collaboration within the university between different dependencies, faculties and research centres.
- Creation of participation mechanisms for key actors within the institution (administrators, teachers, students and directors).
- Creation of strategic alliances with other universities, governments and the private sector.
- Promotion of networks for the exchange of knowledge and experiences in digitalisation.
- Development of co-financing initiatives for digital transformation.

Key Components of the Framework:

- Diagnosis and Measurement of Digital Maturity: Tools and methodologies to evaluate the current level of digitalization of the institution.
- Implementation and Monitoring Strategies: Operational planning with clear phases and evaluation mechanisms.
- Training and Awareness: Training programs for teachers, administrators and students.
- Monitoring and Continuous Improvement Systems: Periodic evaluations to adjust strategies and ensure the sustainability of the process.
- Digital Governance Regulations and Policies: Guidelines that regulate the use, protection and exploitation of technology in higher education.

This collaborative framework allows for an effective integration of technology, data governance and institutional cooperation, ensuring that digital transformation in universities is a continuous, structured process that can be adapted to different contexts.

Based on the analysis carried out, a collaborative framework is proposed that integrates the most effective elements of the revised models. This framework is based on the following principles:

- Digital Maturity Assessment: Implement a diagnostic system to measure the level of institutional digitalization.
- Data Governance: Develop strategies for the management and protection of digital information.
- Inter-institutional collaboration: Promote strategic alliances with other universities, companies and public bodies.
- Continuous Training: Train teachers and administrators in the use of digital technologies to ensure effective adoption.

- Financing Strategies: Identify sources of financing for the sustainability of digital transformation processes.

4.5 Validity Risks

The analysis of digital transformation models must consider certain limitations that may affect their applicability and effectiveness. Among the main risks identified are:

- Bias in study selection: Most of the studies reviewed come from specific contexts, which may limit the generalizability of findings.
- Difficulty in implementation: Some models require high levels of investment and advanced technical capabilities.
- Lack of continuity: Without a clear institutional policy, digital transformation initiatives may not be sustainable over time.

These risks must be considered when applying any model in universities with limited resources or complex organizational structures.

5 Conclusions and Recommendations

5.1 Main Findings

This systematic review reveals that digital maturity models dominate the landscape of digital transformation in higher education. However, there is a marked scarcity of studies focused on Latin America, showing that global models tend to overlook regional nuances such as budget constraints, technological gaps, and cultural differences in university governance.

The findings also highlight the absence of standardized criteria for measuring digital maturity and the limited research on collaborative approaches inside and outside universities. These gaps underscore the need for transformation frameworks adapted to local realities, emphasizing both internal collaboration between agencies and inter-institutional cooperation.

The review consolidates the contribution of a collaborative framework, integrating digital maturity, data governance and strategic collaboration as essential elements for a sustainable digital transformation.

5.2 Contributions of This Review to the Academic Community

Practical Implications for Universities Seeking to Implement Digital Transformation

Based on the findings, higher education institutions – especially in Latin America – are recommended to consider:

- Realistic Initial Diagnosis: Adapt the digital maturity measurement tools to the budgetary limits and technological infrastructure capacities of institutions such as Unicomfacauca.

- Strategic Training: Design digital training programs prioritizing basic and strategic competencies in teachers and administrative staff, adjusted to the available resources.
- Contextualized Data Governance: Establish data management policies that balance efficiency and simplicity, considering institutional capabilities in information security.
- Local Collaboration and Networks: Promote regional inter-university alliances and educational consortia to share technological resources, experiences and digital transformation strategies.

5.3 Limitations of the Systematic Review of the Literature

This review has important limitations:

- North Atlantic bias: Most studies come from Europe and North America, underscoring the need to build tailored frameworks for Latin America and other emerging economies.
- Heterogeneity of Measurement Criteria: The diversity of metrics used makes rigorous comparison between models difficult.
- Poor Empirical Validation: Many revised models lack evaluations in real contexts, limiting their practical applicability.
- Single Source of Information: The review was based exclusively on Scopus studies, leaving room to expand future searches to databases such as Web of Science, IEEE Xplore or SciELO for a more complete picture.

5.4 Recommendations for Future Research

Future Research Lines

- Development of Regionally Adapted Models: Design digital transformation frameworks that respond to the socioeconomic and cultural needs of Latin America.
- Empirical Validation of the Proposed Framework: Implement pilots in Latin American universities to adjust and refine the suggested collaborative framework.
- Standardized Measurement of Digital Maturity: Create assessment instruments that are internationally comparable but locally adaptable.
- Integration of Emerging Technologies: To study the impact of Big Data, Artificial Intelligence and Blockchain on the mission processes of Latin American universities.

Acknowledgements. The authors express their deep gratitude to the Ministry of Science, Technology and Innovation of Colombia (MinCiencias) for the financial support granted through Call No. 933 of 2023, which has been fundamental for the development of this research within the framework of the doctoral training program. This support has allowed the realization of this study, contributing to the advancement of knowledge in Digital Transformation and its application in the strengthening of mission processes in higher education.

Declaration of Interests. The authors declare that there are no financial, commercial, personal, or academic conflicts of interest that may have influenced the results or interpretation of the data presented in this study.

References

Academic Sources and Scientific Articles

1. Abdulfattah, A.: Towards an integrated model of data governance. J. Digital Educ. **12**(3), 45–67 (2020)
2. Aditya, R.: Digital transformation in early childhood education. Educ. Technol. Rev. **18**(2), 112–129 (2023)
3. Alenezi, M.: Deep dive into digital transformation in higher education. High. Educ. Stud. **14**(1), 32–50 (2021)
4. Castro, J.: Digital transformation in higher education institutions: implementation model. Int. J. Educ. Innovation **25**(4), 67–85 (2023)
5. García, M.: Avoiding the dark side of digital transformation in teaching. Digital Learn. J. **15**(2), 78–93 (2021)
6. Langseth, K.: The role of support units in digital transformation. Eur. J. Higher Educ. **20**(3), 145–163 (2023)
7. Martínez, R.: A roadmap for digital transformation (radical solutions for digital transformation in universities). Educ. Res. J. **27**(1), 88–105 (2021)
8. Marks, S.: Digital transformation in higher education: challenges and opportunities. J. Higher Educ. Policy **19**(4), 98–117 (2020)
9. Nurhas, A.: Understanding the challenges of rapid digital transformation. Digital Policy Strategy Rev. **10**(3), 50–68 (2022)
10. Quaicoe, L.: School-based digital innovation challenges and way forward conversations about digital transformation. Educ. Technol. Soc. **22**(1), 200–219 (2023)

Institutional Reports and Reference Documents

11. World Bank. Digital Transformation in Higher Education in Latin America and the Caribbean (2023)
12. OECD. Digital Education Policies and Transformation in Higher Education. OECD Publishing (2021)
13. UNESCO. Guidelines for Digital Transformation in Universities (2022)

Methodological References

14. Moher, D., Liberati, A., Tetzlaff, J., Altman, D.G., The PRISMA group.: Preferred reporting items for systematic reviews and meta-analyses: the PRISMA statement. PLoS Med **6**(7), e1000097 (2009). https://doi.org/10.1371/journal.pmed.1000097

Towards a Mental Model-Driven Approach for User Interface Development: Evolving DataForm

William J. Giraldo O.(✉) and Cristian D. Palechor S.

Universidad del Quindío, Armenia, Colombia
wjgiraldo@uniquindio.edu.co, cdpalechors@uqvirtual.edu.co

Abstract. User interface development often faces usability challenges due to discrepancies between developers' conceptual models and users' mental models. This paper introduces an enhanced model-driven approach centered on DataForm, a formal language designed to capture, structure, and operationalize users' mental models in UI design. We extend DataForm to support visual customization, rendering flexibility, and real-time propagation through a modular architecture that separates business logic from interface representation. Integrated into the Task and Data Model-Based User Interface Development (TD-MBUID) framework, DataForm enables model-driven prototyping and dynamic updates. Its abstract syntax is formalized to allow hierarchical structuring of data and interface elements, while propagation mechanisms ensure synchronization between the back-end and the front-end. A case study in a virtual learning environment demonstrates the approach's potential to enhance interface adaptability, streamline UI evolution, and improve alignment between system behavior and user cognition. While preliminary results are promising, they are based on a structured implementation scenario. Further experimental validation with end users is necessary to empirically assess the extent to which DataForm supports cognitive alignment and usability improvements across diverse interaction contexts.

Keywords: Human-Computer Interaction · Mental Models · Model-Based User Interface Development · DataForm · UI Rendering · UI Propagation · User-Centered Design

1 Introduction

When individuals interact with information systems, they develop a subjective internal representation of the system and their role within it [1]. However, these systems are often designed from the developer's perspective, creating a discrepancy between the system's conceptualization and the user's perception [2]. This misalignment can make adaptation difficult and negatively impact productivity. Studies have demonstrated that aligning the user's mental model with the system's structure improves interaction efficiency and overall performance [3]. To address this challenge, various tools have been developed to model user cognition, such as DataForm, which represents mental models in user

H. Luna-García et al. (Eds.): HCI-COLLAB 2025, CCIS 2850, pp. 288–303, 2027.
https://doi.org/10.1007/978-3-032-31223-5_20

interfaces. However, DataForm has limitations in visual representation, as it does not incorporate aesthetic properties such as typography, colors, or borders. The study of mental models in Human-Computer Interaction (HCI) has gained increasing relevance, particularly in the design of model-based interfaces. The capture, representation, and rendering of these models are essential to ensure alignment with the system's structure. From a User-Centered Design (UCD) perspective, the goal is to preserve user subjectivity while minimizing the influence of developers.

TD-MBUID (Task and Data Model-Based User Interface Development) has been established as a conceptual framework within UCD to capture mental models through DataForm. Its implementation in interface design enables the structuring of a development workflow that reduces biases and ensures alignment with the user's mental model.

This research explores various conceptual definitions of mental models to provide a clear and consistent understanding of the term. Subsequently, it examines how the capture, propagation, and rendering of mental models can be integrated to enhance interaction and usability in interactive systems.

2 Mental Models

The concept of mental models is widely used across various disciplines, including psychology, education, engineering, and Human-Computer Interaction (HCI), among others. However, its interpretation is not uniform and varies significantly depending on the theoretical framework in which it is applied. A common challenge arises when there is no shared understanding of what constitutes a mental model: two individuals may discuss the concept without successfully conveying their comprehension, as if they were speaking different languages, frameworks, or reference models [4]. This ambiguity complicates the precise identification of its components and, consequently, the understanding of mental models.

2.1 Mental Model from a General Perspective

The notion of mental models, originally proposed by Kenneth Craik [5], represents a small-scale cognitive simulation of how the world functions, enabling individuals to anticipate events, reason, and generate explanations. Mental models serve as internal cognitive representations that allow individuals to interpret their environment, make decisions, and solve problems. Their definition varies across disciplines, including psychology, education, engineering, and Human-Computer Interaction (HCI) [6]. These dynamic structures are shaped by prior experiences and evolve through learning [7]. Additionally, mental models can be understood as reasoning mechanisms in working memory or as sets of beliefs that guide decision-making and user interaction with their environment. They function as filters for processing new information and structuring knowledge [8]. In system interaction, mental models play a crucial role in usability, as interfaces must align with user perception to optimize the user experience [9]. From a functional perspective, mental models are essential for manipulating cognitive artifacts, enabling users to construct solutions based on pre-existing mental structures [1]. These representations are flexible and adaptive, reconfiguring as new knowledge is acquired [10]. Their study is fundamental to enhancing human-technology interaction, ensuring that interactive system design reflects the way users conceptualize and operate within the digital world.

2.2 Mental Models in HCI

In Human-Computer Interaction (HCI), a mental model represents the subjective perception that users construct regarding how a system functions, based on their beliefs, prior experiences, and acquired knowledge [11]. Through these models, users interpret the interface, predict its behavior, and make decisions during interaction [12]. A design that aligns with mental models improves efficiency and reduces cognitive load [13].

However, mental models are dynamic and vary across users, making it essential to design coherent and predictable interfaces [14]. In software engineering, these models also influence system development, as they reflect the assumptions and values of developers regarding software design and usage [2]. Ensuring alignment between the mental models of the development team and those of users is crucial to guaranteeing product quality and usability. A well-defined mental model facilitates communication, coordination, and the effective implementation of development methodologies, preventing discrepancies that could negatively impact user satisfaction [15, 16].

2.3 Mental Models in MBUID

Model-Based User Interface Development (MBUID) utilizes declarative models to structure and generate user interfaces, reducing complexity through abstraction and automation of interactive components [17]. In this approach, mental models play a crucial role, as the representation of interaction must align with the user's perception of the system. MBUID organizes the interface into data, task, domain, and user models, ensuring that they reflect the user's expectations and prior knowledge [18]. Additionally, it incorporates a context model to adapt interaction based on dynamic factors such as environment, device, and temporal constraints [19]. Within this framework, the mental model is expressed through these declarative models, representing the user's internal understanding of the system, shaped by their experience and prior assumptions [20]. Thus, MBUID translates user needs into concrete structures and behaviors, ensuring that interfaces remain aligned with user expectations and cognitive processes.

2.4 Mental Models in TD-MBUID

TD-MBUID proposes a methodology that integrates data and task modeling for interface development. The incorporation of the mental model concept in TD-MBUID enables the design of interfaces aligned with how users perceive and organize information. By focusing on the structured representation of data and tasks, this methodology minimizes interpretation biases, ensuring that the interface accurately reflects the user's knowledge of the system.

TD-MBUID is grounded in principles of perception, establishing that the human brain does not process data or tasks directly; rather, perception begins when sensory stimuli are received from the environment (Fig. 1). Following structuralist principles—such as the Gestalt laws of visual perception, the brain identifies forms, groups entities, and constructs meaning from perceived objects (data).

Within this framework, TD-MBUID introduces DataForm, an independent model designed specifically to represent the user's interpretation emerging from interaction with stimuli. This model complements other components within MBUID, which capture different aspects of the user's mental model, including task structures and domain-specific data.

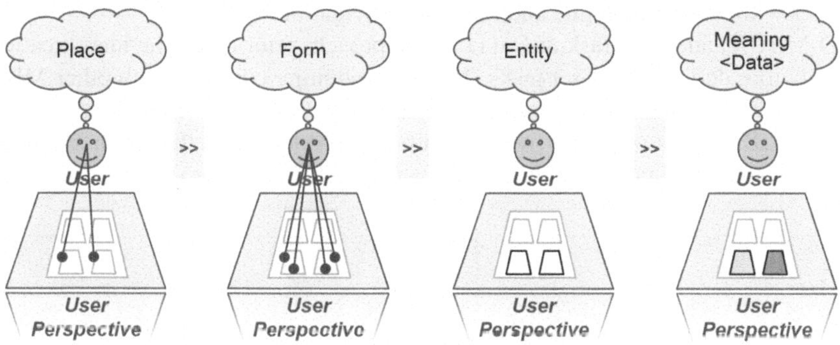

Fig. 1. Perceptual Process.Source: Own elaboration.

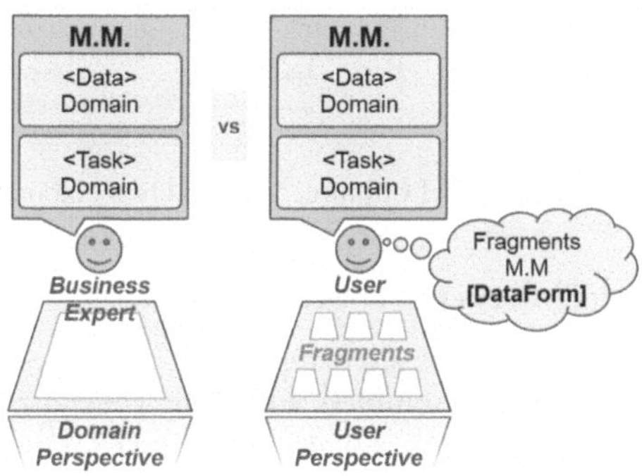

Fig. 2. Divergence Between Business Expert and User Mental Models. Source: Own elaboration.

TD-MBUID asserts that, while users possess a prior mental model regarding business domain data and tasks, user interfaces should not directly represent these elements, as they originate from the mental models of experts or developers. Instead, interfaces should be designed based on the specific needs of each user type, allowing them to interact with data in a focused manner, aligned with their individual workflows and contextual scenarios.

Business data and task models are defined by domain experts and structured through entities that are primarily understood by experts and developers. These representations provide a holistic view of the business, but users only interact with selected fragments (Fig. 2), rather than the complete dataset, during their engagement with the system. Consequently, interface design must prioritize presenting data in an accessible and contextually relevant manner, ensuring that users can efficiently execute their tasks within the system.

User interface (UI) information undergoes fragmentation due to device constraints and rendering space limitations. This partitioning structures the interaction design by distributing navigation and dialogue. Low partitioning results in large interfaces with extensive dialogue and minimal navigation, whereas high partitioning leads to smaller interfaces with limited dialogue and increased navigation.

TD-MBUID adopts a Task & Data (TD) approach, prioritizing the identification of UI data before defining the user tasks. This methodology contrasts with other MBUID approaches, which first model tasks and then design the UI. Crucially, user interfaces in TD-MBUID do not originate from domain data models but rather from a structured mental model capture process conducted in a controlled laboratory setting (Fig. 3).

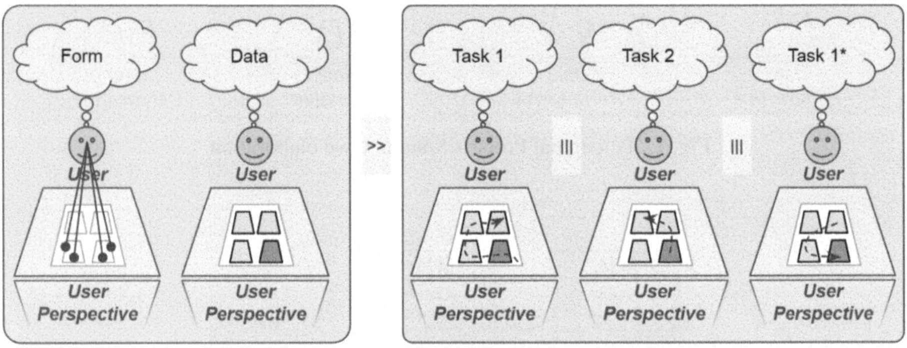

Fig. 3. Mental Model Capture. Source: Own elaboration.

Mental Model Capture Process in TD-MBUID (Fig. 4):

1. User Identification: Key user types are categorized.
2. Laboratory Setup: A team is assembled with four specialized roles: (a) Business domain data & tasks, (b) Form & UI design, (c) DataForm modeling, (d) User management
3. Capturing the Mental Model of Data: Conducted in three phases: (a) Data identification, (b) Establishing relationships between data elements, (c) Data representation analysis (examining sketches, layout, adjacency, and semantics).
4. Paper-Based Form Structuring: Forms are drafted without buttons or technology, ensuring that they support the entire transaction flow to capture the full interaction model before UI partitioning.
5. Capturing the Mental Model of Tasks: (a) Scenario-based task presentation, (b) Cognitive walkthrough with paper-based forms, where users demonstrate how they would perform tasks, (c) Task model identification.
6. Partitioning Forms: Forms are segmented according to rendering constraints, and steps 3, 4, and 5 are repeated.

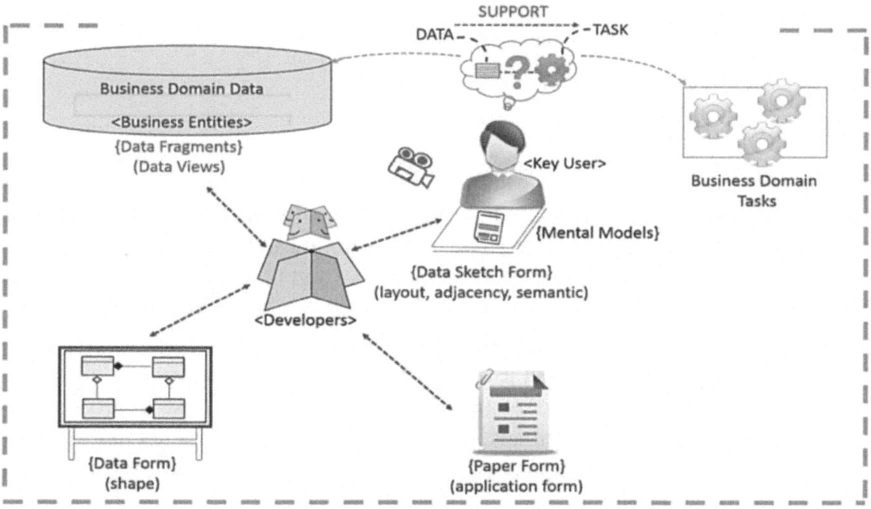

Fig. 4. DataForm Management. Source: Own elaboration.

7. DataForm & Interaction Model Development: Navigation and dialogue structures are refined based on the insights obtained

TD-MBUID is a user-centered development framework that considers the majority of human factor information to be captured at the business modeling level (the physical level) (Fig. 5). At this stage, technology is absent, and only human interactions are considered.

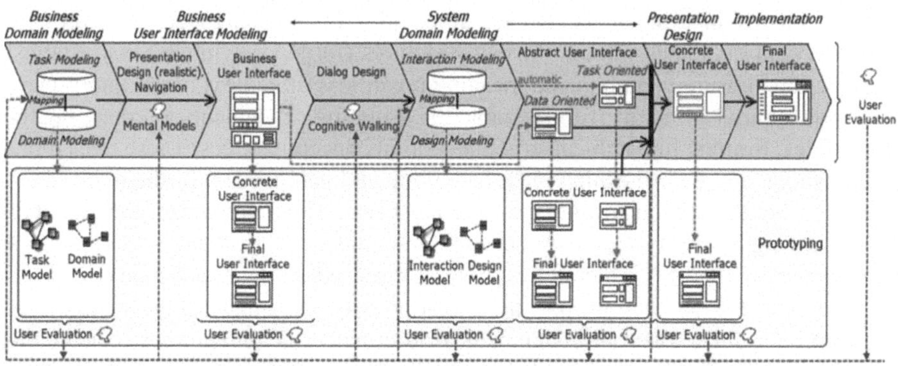

Fig. 5. TD-MBUID Development Framework. Source: Own elaboration.

TD-MBUID proposes the "Business User Interface (BUI)" (paper-based forms), which represents the user's mental model without technology, "without buttons." The user interface results from balancing the BUI with automatically identified user interfaces derived from task models. TD-MBUID introduces prototyping and evaluation cycles involving the user at all stages [21].

2.5 Final Considerations

Mental models function as cognitive simulations of reality, enabling individuals to reason, anticipate, and make decisions. In Human-Computer Interaction (HCI) and software development, their proper application enhances usability and user satisfaction. However, the discrepancy between the user's mental model and that of the developer remains a common challenge in software engineering, which can be addressed through user-centered methodologies and iterative validation. This research conceptualizes the mental model as the internal representation users construct based on interface stimuli, encompassing both its formation and adaptation during interaction. Unlike approaches that infer these models from design artifacts, this study proposes their explicit representation in DataForm—an artifact that captures data, shapes, and visual elements—facilitating analysis and application in interactive interface development.

3 DataForm

The DataForm language arises from the combination of the terms "data" and "form." While data represent objects and the content of the world, form encapsulates meaning, logical structure, and relationships between these objects. This language was developed to capture and represent the structure and meaning of the user's mental model in a way that facilitates its use in the development process while minimizing the influence of subjective biases from other stakeholders.

Humanity has previously created other languages with characteristics similar to DataForm, such as natural languages and mathematics. In these languages, an expression consists of data organized through formal structures (forms or symbols) that establish hierarchies and ensure unambiguous meaning regardless of context or the interpreter's role. These symbols or signs (form) enable the grouping of elements to create higher-order entities, forming hierarchical structures, often conceptual trees. These trees represent the whole, and their meaning must be unique and independent of the interpreter's perspective. For this reason, symbols or signs must ensure an ordered interpretation, typically following a priority-based structure. For example, in a mathematical expression such as: $a = b + 3(c + d)$, a hierarchy of operator precedence is established (Fig. 6). In this expression, the "="operator has the lowest priority, meaning that the values on its right must be evaluated before assignment. Additionally, the parentheses indicate that the operation "$c + d$" is computed before multiplication by 3. The sequence of evaluation can be decomposed into the following groups:

[g1: a], [g2: b + 3(c + d)], [g3: b], [g4: 3(c + d)], [g5: 3], [g6: c + d], [g7: c], [g8: d].

Anyone familiar with this language understands that group 6 is executed first and can also determine its interpretation. Thus, by correctly using DataForm, all stakeholders interpret each mental model in the same way. Given this example, one can conclude that this mathematical expression follows a DataForm structure, meaning it consists of

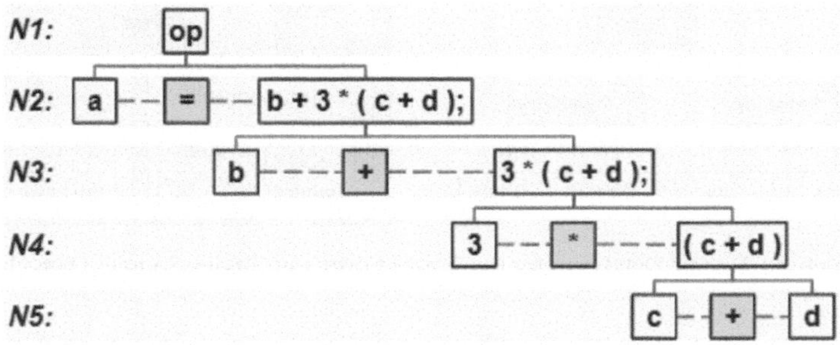

Fig. 6. Structural Tree of DataForm for the Expression a = b + 3(c + d).
Source: Own elaboration.

explicit data (e.g., a, b, 3, c, d), emergent data (higher-order concepts such as group 2, group 4, and group 6), and forms such as =, +,, and parentheses (, +,)

Upon close examination, this structure closely resembles that of Concurrent Task Trees (CTT), where correct implementation is achieved by grouping elements based on priority [19]. In this sense, CTT can be considered a type of DataForm.

Now, if we consider data elements such as trip, origin, destination, dates, and airport, and incorporate a hierarchical structure of the type "is part of," it becomes possible to construct a mental model of a round-trip journey with its respective flights organized hierarchically (Fig. 7). For example:

trip {outbound {flight 1 {origin {*date, airport,*}, destination {*date, airport,*}},
flight 2 {origin {*date, airport,*}, destination {*date, airport,*}}
},
return {flight 1 {origin {*date, airport,*}, destination {*date, airport,*}},
flight 2 {origin {*date, airport,*}, destination {*date, airport,*}}
},
}

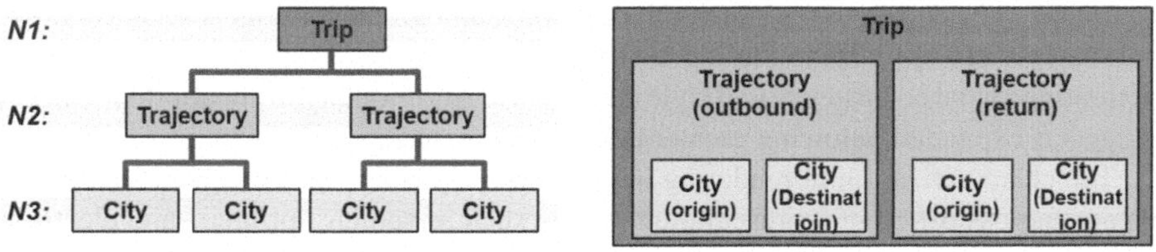

Fig. 7. Structural Tree of DataForm for the Travel Form.Source: Own elaboration.

According to the Royal Spanish Academy (RAE), a group is defined as the totality of elements or objects possessing a common property that distinguishes them from others, such as living beings.

TD-MBUID establishes group formation through containment relationships based on a "whole-part" structure, where the common property is the parent-child relationship. This is expressed as follows: "The outbound origin and the outbound destination are part of the outbound group; they are contained within it."

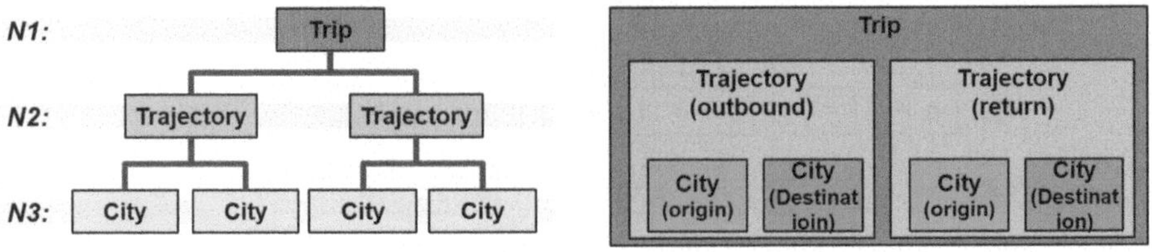

Fig. 8. Structural Tree of DataForm for the Travel Form with Styles.Source: Own elaboration.

This approach stems from the fact that DataForm was initially conceived for the design of paper-based forms and their corresponding user interfaces. However, what happens if similar attributes or characteristics need to be assigned to both the origin and destination cities? In such a case, it would be necessary to support the creation of new trees that structure different types of groups, this time based on formal characteristics such as appearance (Fig. 8).

While the "is part of" relationship is still used, it now shifts from a containment relationship to a sharing relationship. This is expressed as follows: "The outbound origin and the return origin are part of the blue group; they are shared between outbound and return segments, respectively."

To move toward a framework guided by mental models, it is essential to define a more advanced version of the DataForm language—one capable of capturing the information necessary to support the representation, propagation, and rendering of modern user interfaces.

4 Adaptation of the DataForm Language

The adaptation of the DataForm language aims to enhance its ability to represent the user's mental model by improving presentation, rendering, propagation, and information transfer. Advanced CSS properties are introduced for visual customization, including personalized backgrounds, adaptable typography, and graphical effects such as borders and shadows. To optimize rendering, a modular approach based on CSS rules is adopted, facilitating visual consistency and style inheritance. Additionally, compatibility with new widgets is expanded, allowing greater flexibility in interface creation.

The characterization of rendering in DataForm considers the constraints of the visible area across different representation media, such as screens, printers, and electronic devices. Tools such as the viewport and media queries are employed to adapt visualization to different contexts, optimizing user experience and ensuring accessibility across various environments.

Regarding mental model propagation, an interconnection is established between the rendering engine and the data server, ensuring seamless information flow from the database to the user interface. This is achieved through data transformations, synchronization via RESTful APIs or WebSockets, and distribution to visual elements using bindings and events. The separation of data and presentation through ViewPart and ViewModel enables interface updates without altering the underlying data structure.

The characterization of the ViewModel in DataForm defines its essential properties, ensuring efficient data management. It includes support for both simple and nested properties to represent hierarchical structures, serialization and deserialization into formats such as JSON, interoperability with various systems, and support for multiple data types.

The conceptualization of the DataForm model is structured into three key areas: (1) Form Conceptualization, eliminating the distinction between containers and individual elements to enhance flexibility; (2) Style Properties Conceptualization, introducing a modular hierarchy based on CSS to ensure visual consistency and style reuse; and (3) Rendering Conceptualization, defining restrictions at both global and individual levels, allowing each element to manage its rendering space independently. A concept dictionary is introduced to formalize key terms such as attributes, properties, visual traits, and rendering mechanisms.

Finally, the formalization of the DataForm language redefines its syntax to improve extensibility. UML diagrams are employed to model its structure and facilitate property reuse through concepts such as ModelElement and ConfigurableElement. The concrete syntax is analyzed from the perspective of modeling tools, concluding that XML representation within the Eclipse Modeling Framework (EMF) enables structured serialization and model manipulation, though its use as a visual design language remains limited. In conclusion, the formalization of DataForm reinforces its role as a structural modeling tool, providing a robust foundation for its integration into model-based user interface development.

5 Definition of Architectural Mechanisms for DataForm Rendering and Propagation

This study defines the architectural mechanisms necessary for the rendering and propagation of the DataForm language, establishing a structure that enables the effective representation of the user's mental model within the interface. The definition of these mechanisms is divided into three phases: first, the reference architecture is described, identifying the key components and their interactions within the system; second, the static and dynamic structure of the architectural mechanisms is established, detailing how they support the rendering and propagation of DataForm; and third, an in-depth analysis of each component is conducted, identifying its role in the data transformation process.

5.1 Definition of the Mechanisms

The DataForm model requires a processing structure that ensures the correct transmission of data and its transformation into visual elements within the user interface. To achieve this, mechanisms are defined to convert the user's mental model into presentation structures that align with their cognitive expectations. Three fundamental aspects are presented:

Static structure of architectural mechanisms: This section describes the integration of TD-MBUID, an environment developed to facilitate the creation of model-based interfaces, enabling the definition of DataForm's abstract syntax and synchronizing its representation with the system. Within TD-MBUID, the Editor UI allows the generation of DataForm model instances, while VP Sync is responsible for storing and propagating these instances to the back-end.

Architectural uses: This section analyzes the essential operational flows for model propagation. One of the primary processes is the synchronization of the ViewPart from TD-MBUID (Fig. 9), which begins with the definition of the interface in the Editor UI and the subsequent serialization of the model in the database through VP Sync. This process enables the dynamic update of the interface in the front-end without requiring manual code modifications.

Details of rendering and propagation mechanisms: The components responsible for transforming data into interactive visual elements are introduced. ViewPart and ViewModel Sync in the front-end request data from the back-end, interpreting and propagating them within the UI Framework for rendering. Synchronization in the back-end ensures the conversion of the business model into a ViewModel, guaranteeing that the interface accurately reflects the system's structure.

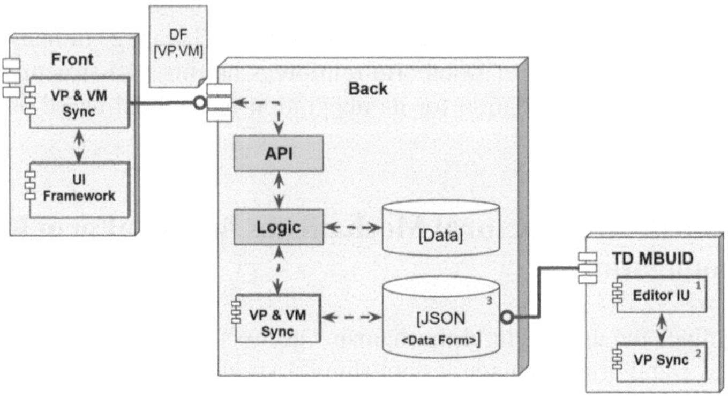

Fig. 9. Proposed Architecture for DataForm Propagation.Source: Own elaboration.

5.2 Proposed Architecture

The proposed architecture consists of three interconnected layers: Front-End, Back-End, and Database. The Front-End encompasses the UI Framework along with the ViewPart and ViewModel Sync, which are responsible for rendering and managing data requests to the Back-End. The clear separation between business logic and presentation enhances maintainability and allows for dynamic interface updates. The Back-End comprises the API, the logic layer, and ViewPartSync, ensuring the transformation of business data into structured visual components ready for rendering. Finally, the Database acts as a central repository, storing both the DataForm structure and its associated interface data, facilitating seamless data retrieval and synchronization within the interactive system.

The DataForm loading process from the front-end is executed through ViewPart Sync, which sends requests to the API to retrieve the stored visual representation from the database. Once the data is processed, the UI Framework converts it into an interactive user interface. Similarly, the ViewModel update process allows real-time data modifications without altering the interface structure, ensuring proper synchronization between the database and the user view.

The architectural mechanisms defined in this work provide a robust infrastructure for DataForm rendering and propagation. Integrating these mechanisms within a modular architecture facilitates the dynamic updating of the interface, enabling the user experience to adapt to different contexts. Moreover, the separation between the business model and the interface model ensures a flexible and scalable implementation, optimizing the transformation of mental models into interactive visual structures.

6 Case Study

The case study examines the integration of the DataForm language within a virtual learning environment developed by the research group, aiming to enhance the rendering and propagation of the user interface.

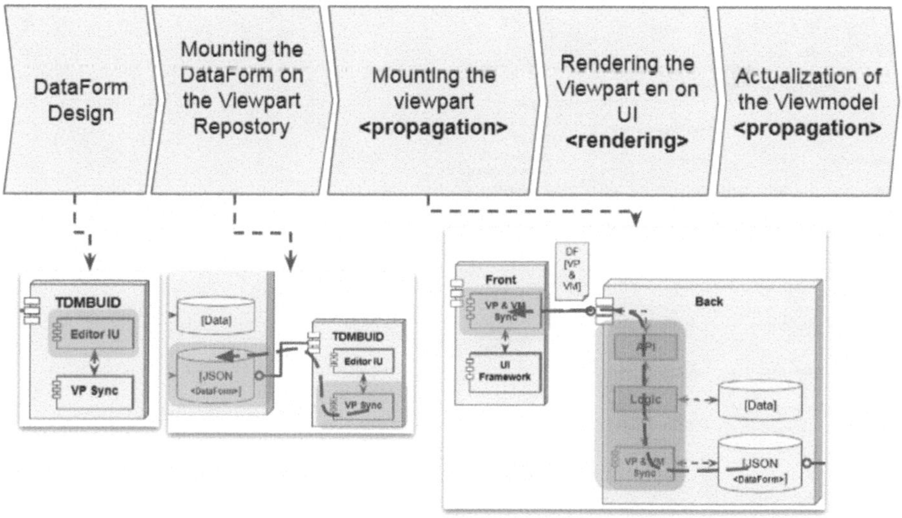

Fig. 10. Flow Diagram for the Case Study.Source: Own elaboration.

The process begins with the **design of the DataForm in TD-MBUID**, where an instance of the model is generated, specifying shape and visualization properties (Fig. 10). The DataForm is then **serialized and synchronized** in **JSON format** within the database, enabling its retrieval and utilization by the backend. This mechanism ensures that data remains accessible to the system while optimizing its representation in the **user interface**.

The **TD-MBUID environment** facilitates **model-driven development** through the **Eclipse Modeling Framework** (EMF), allowing for validation and code generation (Fig. 11). Within this environment, **ViewParts** are designed and later integrated into the **UI Framework engine**, which is responsible for rendering. This engine, based on **Google Apps Script**, separates widgets into **HTML** and **JavaScript libraries**, allowing the UI Manager to dynamically register and render components. The **implementation of DataForm** within this architecture enables v**iew representation through structured models instead of static code**, ensuring **greater flexibility and scalability** within the **virtual learning environment's user interface**.

7 Results

The case study validated the effectiveness of DataForm's rendering and propagation mechanisms through its implementation in TD-MBUID, the UI Framework Engine, and Firebase. It was demonstrated that serialization to JSON enables the independent propagation of forms and data, ensuring a clear separation between the view and the model.

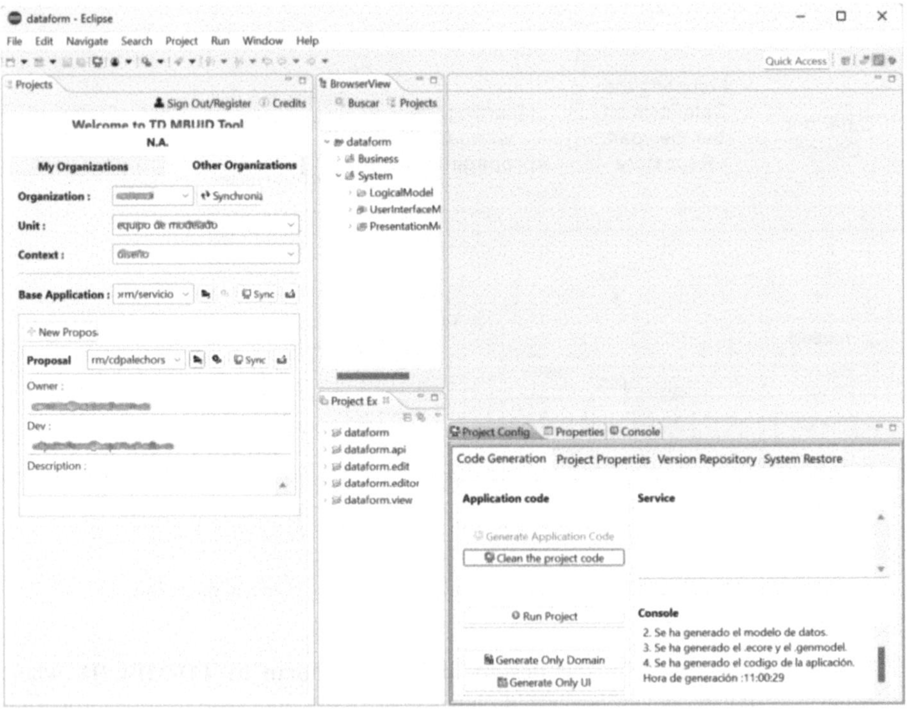

Fig. 11. Environment of TDMBUID on eclipse.Source: Own elaboration.

Furthermore, the study confirmed that DataForm is not dependent on a specific backend. Its integration with Firebase eliminated the need for custom-written endpoints, proving its adaptability to different environments without impacting the user interface logic.

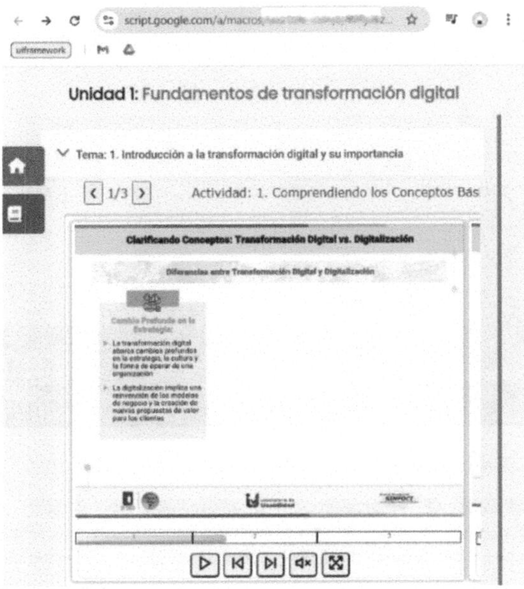

Fig. 12. Course Platform Home Page.Source: Own elaboration.

In the frontend, the implementation replaced a fixed-code structure with a model-based approach, enabling dynamic interface updates at runtime. As a result, any modification to the ViewPart in TD-MBUID is automatically reflected in the educational platform.

Figure 12 presents an interface rendered using the UI Framework's rendering algorithm, where content synchronization is managed through the ViewModel. In contrast, the platform's homepage (Fig. 13) functioned solely as a redirection page and was not generated using the described rendering mechanisms.

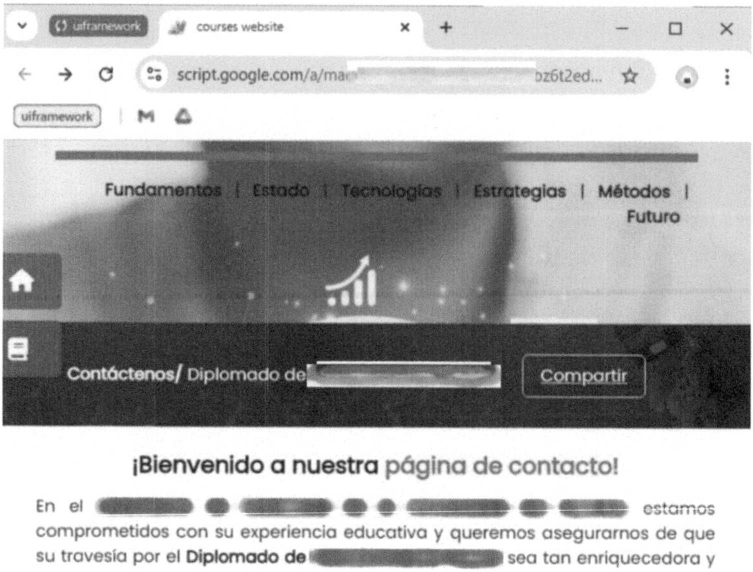

Fig. 13. User Interface from a DataForm Model.Source: Own elaboration.

8 Conclusions

This study established a robust foundation for the evolution of the DataForm language, enhancing its capacity to represent, transform, and propagate user mental models within model-driven interface development. The research identified key structural relationships between user and business expert mental models, resulting in the design of a conceptual framework for their explicit representation. The formalization of DataForm's abstract syntax improved its extensibility, while rendering and propagation mechanisms were defined to support dynamic user interface updates across different platforms. A case study within a virtual learning environment demonstrated the feasibility and adaptability of the proposed architecture in a controlled setting. However, to fully assess the impact of DataForm on user cognition and usability, future work should focus on conducting empirical experiments with end users in diverse contexts. These studies will be essential to validate the cognitive alignment promoted by DataForm and to refine its integration into real-world software development processes.

References

1. Kim, M.K., McCarthy, K.S.: Using graph centrality as a global index to assess students' mental model structure development during summary writing. Educ. Technol. Res. Dev. **69**, 971–1002 (2021). https://doi.org/10.1007/s11423-021-09942-1
2. Sulong, S., Sulaiman, S.: Exploring blind users' experience on website to highlight the importance of user's mental model. In: Abdullah, N., Wan Adnan, W.A., Foth, M. (eds.) User Science and Engineering, pp. 105–113. Springer, Singapore (2018)

3. Xie, B., Zhou, J.: The influence of mental model similarity on user performance: comparing older and younger adults. In: Zhou, J., Salvendy, G. (eds.) Human Aspects of IT for the Aged Population, pp. 569–579. Springer, Cham (2017)
4. Hofstede, G.H., Hofstede, G.: Culture's Consequences: Comparing Values, Behaviors, Institutions and Organizations Across Nations. Sage, Thousand Oaks (2001)
5. IEEE: IEEE Standard Glossary of Software Engineering Terminology. IEEE, New York (1990). https://doi.org/10.1109/IEEESTD.1990.101064
6. Craik, K.J.W.: The nature of Explanation. Cambridge University Press, Cambridge (1967)
7. Denzau, A.T., North, D.C.: Shared mental models: ideologies and institutions. Kyklos. **47**, 3–31 (1994)
8. Jing, W.: Study on the relationship between mental model of designer team and factors in remote collaboration. In: Stephanidis, C. (ed.) HCI International 2016 Posters' Extended Abstracts, pp. 46–51. Springer, Cham (2016)
9. Mohammed, S., Dumville, B.C.: Team mental models in a team knowledge framework: expanding theory and measurement across disciplinary boundaries. J. Organ. Behav. **22**(2), 89–106 (2001). https://doi.org/10.1002/job.86
10. Jones, N.A., Ross, H., Lynam, T., Perez, P., Leitch, A.: Mental models: an interdisciplinary synthesis of theory and methods. Ecol. Soc. **16**, 13 (2011)
11. Gray, S.A., Gray, S., Cox, L.J., Henly-Shepard, S.: Mental modeler: a fuzzy-logic cognitive mapping modeling tool for adaptive environmental management. In: Proc. 46th Hawaii Int. Conf. on System Sciences (HICSS), pp. 965–973 (2013). https://doi.org/10.1109/HICSS.2013.399
12. Markman, A.B.: Knowledge Representation. Psychology Press, New York (2013)
13. Norman, D.A.: The Psychology of Everyday Things. Basic Books, New York (1988)
14. OMG: Meta Object Facility (MOF) Specification 1.4. Object Management Group (2002)
15. Nielsen, J.: Mental Models and User Experience Design. (2010). https://www.nngroup.com/articles/mental-models/
16. Jonassen, D.H.: Operationalizing mental models: strategies for assessing mental models to support meaningful learning and design-supportive learning environments. In: Proc. CSCL, pp. 182–186 (1995). https://doi.org/10.3115/222020.222166
17. Sinreich, D., Gopher, D., Ben-Barak, S., Marmor, Y., Lahat, R.: Mental models as a practical tool in the engineer's toolbox. Int. J. Prod. Res. **43**, 2977–2996 (2005). https://doi.org/10.1080/00207540500057373
18. Canon-Bowers, J.A., Salas, E., Converse, S.: Shared mental models in expert decision making. In: Castellan, N.J. (ed.) Individual and Group Decision Making, pp. 221–246. Lawrence Erlbaum, Hillsdale (1993)
19. Balijepally, V.G., Nerur, S., Mahapatra, R.K.: Effect of task mental models on software developer's performance: an experimental investigation. In: Proc. HICSS, pp. 5442–5451 (2012). https://doi.org/10.1109/HICSS.2012.9
20. Giraldo, W.J.: Marco de desarrollo de sistemas groupware interactivos basado en la integración de procesos y notaciones (2010)
21. Loeffler, D., Hess, A., Maier, A., Hurtienne, J., Schmitt, H.: Developing intuitive user interfaces by integrating users' mental models into requirements engineering. In: Proc. HCI (2013). https://doi.org/10.14236/EWIC/HCI2013.14
22. Luyten, K.: Dynamic user interface generation for mobile and embedded systems with model-based user interface development (2004)
23. Hartson, R., Pyla, P.S.: The UX Book: Process and Guidelines for Ensuring a Quality User Experience. Elsevier, Waltham (2012)
24. Giraldo, W.J., Arias, M.R., Collazos, C.A., Molina, A.I., Ortega, C.M., Redondo, M.A.: Fast functional prototyping of user interfaces based on DataForm models. In: Proc. Computing Colombian Conference (10CCC), pp. 172–179 (2015)

Understanding Accessibility Needs of Blind Authors on CMS-Based Websites

Guillermo Vera-Amaro and José Rafael Rojano-Cáceres(✉)

School of Statistics and Informatics, University of Veracruz, Xalapa, Veracruz, Mexico
{gvera,rrojano}@uv.mx

Abstract. This paper addresses the limited attention given to blind users as content creators in Content Management Systems (CMS), a gap that remains underexplored in web accessibility research. For blind authors, effective interaction with CMS platforms requires more than technical compliance; it demands interfaces designed with semantic clarity, predictable navigation, and meaningful feedback for screen reader users. This study investigates the accessibility barriers blind users face when performing key tasks—such as page creation, menu editing, and image publishing—using CMS platforms. A two-fold evaluation was conducted using automated tools and manual usability testing with three blind and one sighted participant, complemented by expert analysis based on the Barrier Walkthrough method. Results showed that block-based interfaces were particularly challenging, often marked as accessible by automated tools but resulting in critical usability issues during manual evaluation. The use of a text-based editor, the integration of AI-generated image descriptions, and training aligned with screen reader workflows, significantly improved usability and autonomy. These findings underscore the limitations of automated assessments and highlight the importance of user-centered design practices. Enhancing CMS accessibility requires consistent navigation structures, reduced reliance on visual interaction patterns, and the integration of AI tools that support blind content authors throughout the content creation process.

Keywords: Web Accessibility · Usability Study · User Experience · Artificial Intelligence · Blind Users · Content Management System

1 Introduction

Websites are the primary sources of information and services on the internet [1], and according to the Global Digital Report, around 66% of the world's population has internet access [2], highlighting the need for tools that enable website creation without advanced technical skills [3]. Content management systems (CMS) have become important tools for this purpose, powering over 60% of websites globally [4]. These platforms offer user-friendly interfaces, but many still present significant accessibility barriers for blind users [3], despite efforts to align with WCAG standards [5].

Approximately 16% of the global population—around 1.3 billion people—live with disabilities [6], including visually impaired content creators who face challenges using

H. Luna-García et al. (Eds.): HCI-COLLAB 2025, CCIS 2850, pp. 304–320, 2027.
https://doi.org/10.1007/978-3-032-31223-5_21

CMS tools to produce content for both blind and sighted users. In the United States alone, 26% of adults (67 million individuals) have some form of disability [7]. Unfortunately, accessibility is often treated as an afterthought, with some products omitting its implementation altogether [8]. This is partly due to reliance on automated evaluation tools [9], which perform syntactic checks—like verifying alternative text or proper HTML structure—while failing to assess critical semantic aspects such as page hierarchy, element roles, and overall usability. These aspects are essential for effective navigation by screen reader users [8], yet many CMS platforms are not born-accessible [10].

This study evaluates the accessibility of CMS components, focusing on navigation, form interaction, and content management from the perspective of blind authors. Through workshops with blind participants on a dedicated website, we identify usability challenges and assess how effectively a CMS supports accessible content creation. Our main contribution is to document the accessibility needs of blind authors in CMS environments through an empirical approach, emphasizing that key semantic aspects—such as structure, element roles, and functional purposes—are often undetected by automated tools but are critical for a usable and accessible experience.

The remainder of this paper is organized as follows: Sect. 2 and Sect. 3 reviews relevant literature on web accessibility and CMS platforms, Sect. 4 outlines the research methodology, Sect. 5 presents the key findings, followed by a discussion in Sect. 6. Limitations of the study are addressed in Sect. 7, and finally, Sect. 8 summarizes the conclusions and suggests directions for future research.

2 Background

Web accessibility according to the World Wide Web Consortium (W3C) [11], promotes that websites and technologies are usable by people with disabilities. The Web Accessibility Initiative (WAI) [12] plays a key role through standards like the Web Content Accessibility Guidelines (WCAG), while the Authoring Tool Accessibility Guidelines (ATAG) 2.0 [13] promote best practices for making CMS platforms accessible [14].

People with visual impairments require screen readers to access information online. Screen readers agents convert on-screen content into speech [8], relying on semantic HTML and ARIA (Accessible Rich Internet Applications) roles to interpret page structure [15]. Poor semantic markup impairs navigation, creating barriers for visually impaired users. Automated tools can detect basic issues like missing alt text but often fail to evaluate deeper semantic structures, such as proper heading hierarchies [8]. Attempts to improve this include machine learning approaches for identifying ARIA landmarks [16], browser extensions using natural language processing for navigation aids [17], and systems for automatically injecting landmarks [18]. However, consistent with HCI principles on usability and real-world performance [19], true accessibility evaluation requires combining automated assessments with user-based testing [20].

CMS platforms enable content creation without advanced technical skills [21], in that sense WordPress powers 43.6% of all websites globally [4]. This translates to a content management systems market share of 61.7% because 29.4 of websites do not use a CMS solution. Despite their flexibility, many CMS platforms present accessibility challenges, such as inconsistent navigation and poor screen reader support [3]. Addressing these issues requires adherence to the WCAG and user-centered design practices [22], including semantic labeling and keyboard navigability [5]. Artificial intelligence tools, like automated image description generators [23], support accessibility by reducing manual effort and improving multimedia engagement for blind users [24].

Accessibility evaluations often combine qualitative (user-centered) and quantitative (automated) approaches [20]. While inspection methods focus on technical compliance, observation methods capture user experiences and real interaction challenges [25]. Prior studies suggest that integrating both approaches provides more comprehensive insights [1]. This research adopts a combined strategy, aligning with HCI principles of usability and user empowerment [19], by integrating automated evaluations with blind user testing to uncover both technical and experiential barriers.

3 Related Work

We conducted a literature review on accessibility in CMS-based platforms using the search string *("content management systems" OR "wordpress") AND "accessibility"* in the Scopus and Web of Science databases, focusing on barriers encountered by blind users. The search yielded 92 results, among which several relevant studies were identified. Pascual et al. [26], who evaluated Blogger and WordPress, highlighting challenges due to insufficient guidance for accessible design and incomplete adherence to WCAG and ATAG standards, without assessing administrative functions. Similarly, Calvo et al. [27] evaluated Moodle [28], revealing significant barriers for screen reader users in content management workflows.

Regarding content editors, Sanchez-Gordon et al. [22] improved accessibility in TinyMCE and Summernote editors by adding image insertion controls, while López et al. [29] analyzed six CMS platforms, finding that none fully met ATAG guidelines [13]. In a later study, they proposed a methodology to identify and correct accessibility issues [30]. Additionally, Csontos and Heckl et al. [3] explored tools to address issues like missing alt text and poor semantic structure while Acosta et al. [31] defined a method for evaluating the accessibility of online content editors.

CMS-specific solutions include a WordPress plugin by Causarano and Paternò et al. [21], integrated with MAUVE++ for real-time feedback. Zilak et al. [32] also assessed a WordPress prototype using automated evaluations and surveys, though notably without involving screen reader users, limiting real-world insights into usability.

Overall, most studies rely on automated tools for accessibility evaluations, with fewer involving expert reviews and even fewer including blind users. To the best of our knowledge, no previous research has combined automated analysis with usability testing involving blind users as content creators. This study aims to fill that gap, focusing on the barriers they face and providing a foundation for future research.

4 Method

This research employs a modified version of the WCAG Evaluation Methodology (WCAG-EM) [33], similar to the approach proposed by Acosta-Vargas et al. [34] with adaptations aligned to our objectives as illustrated in Fig. 1. It integrates quantitative evaluation using automated tools and qualitative analysis through empirical testing with blind users managing CMS content. Manual evaluation also incorporates expert review via the Barrier Walkthrough (BW) method [35].

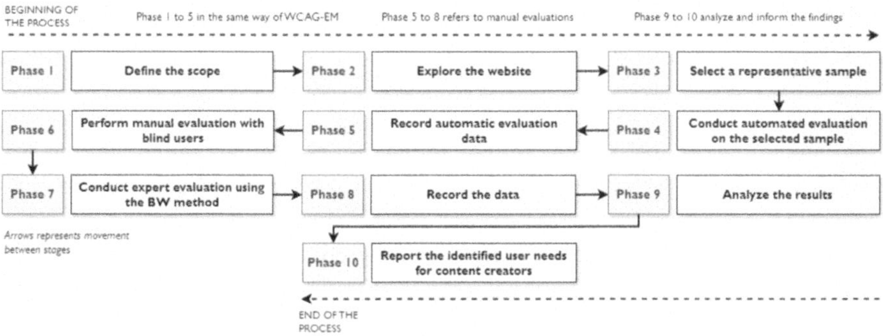

Fig. 1. Proposed research method (adapted from [34]).

4.1 Conduction of the Study

The method was applied to CMS tasks typically challenging for blind authors, such as those listed in Table 1. Each task was first evaluated using an automated tool, followed by empirical testing across three sessions with blind participants. Barriers identified were rated for severity based on impact on task performance following the BW method.

Phase 1: Defining the Scope. This study explores the accessibility needs of blind authors, focusing on four research questions:

- **RQ1**. What is the correlation between automated and manual evaluation?
- **RQ2.** How can AI assist in tasks requiring visual input?
- **RQ3.** How does training impact user performance?
- **RQ4.** What challenges do blind authors face in CMS?

WordPress 6.7.1 was deployed on an Ubuntu 24.04.1 virtual machine with MySQL 8.0.41 and Apache 2.4.58. WordPress was selected for its open-source nature, plugin extensibility [36], and alignment with WCAG 2.2 Level AA standards [5], offering features like semantic HTML and keyboard navigation [37, 38]. Training materials specifically designed for screen reader users were developed and published online across three sessions. All sessions were recorded and qualitatively analyzed based on participant feedback.

Phase 2: Exploring the Website. The CMS interface was analyzed to identify accessibility-relevant functionalities. Built with HTML, CSS, JavaScript, and PHP, it contains dynamic elements that may create barriers for screen readers. Key components include the Toolbar (1) for administrative quick task, the Main Navigation Menu (2) for core feature management, and the Work Area (3) for content creation. Other sections, such as the Page Title (4), Action Notices (5), Filter Area (6), and the Main Content Area

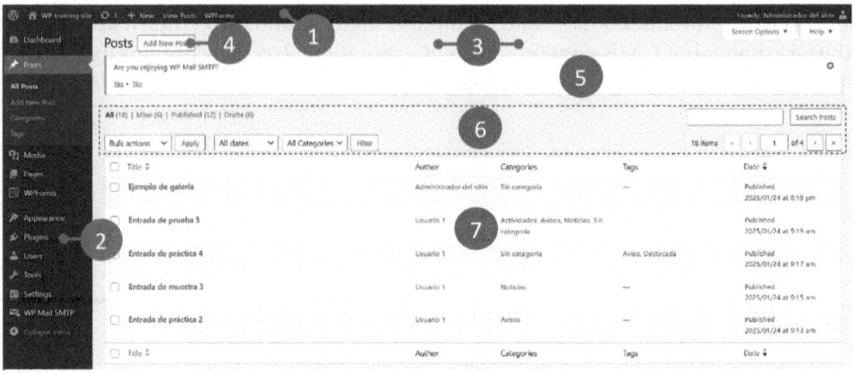

Fig. 2. CMS administration interface highlighting key sections (own elaboration).

(7), are shown in Fig. 2. This exploration highlighted barriers, particularly in complex interaction areas.

Phase 3: Selecting a Representative Sample. Since this study focuses on content creation, public-facing website design was not evaluated. A pilot session with a blind user helped define key tasks that blind content authors need to perform in a CMS, following prior research [36], summarized in Table 1.

Table 1. Identified tasks to perform with automated evaluations (own elaboration).

Id	Task	CMS page	Errors	Alerts	E + A
T01	Login and enter credentials	wp-login	0	1	1
T02	Navigate through menus	wp-admin	3	17	20
T03	Use block-based editor	post-new-block	2	17	19
T04	Use text-based editor	post-new	16	23	39
T05	Create and manage categories	edit-tags	14	23	37
T06	Manage media files	upload	4	18	22
T07	Create image galleries	post-new-gallery	19	24	43
T08	Configure homepage and blog page	options-reading	2	17	19
T09	Adjust general site settings	options-general	2	20	22
T10	Edit main menu	nav-menus	23	25	48
T11	Configure social media widget	widgets	2	17	19
T12	Customize design	customize	125	118	243
T13	Install and activate complements	plugins	14	20	34
T14	Create and manage forms	form-builder	78	49	127

Phase 4: Automatic Evaluation on the Selected Sample. WAVE was selected for automated evaluation due to its effectiveness in identifying accessibility issues and WCAG 2.2 support [39]. The WAVE Chrome extension was used for its ease of deployment and visual reporting [14, 40]. Key CMS pages listed in Table 1 were evaluated.

Phase 5: Record Automatic Evaluation Data. Accessibility scores from the WAVE evaluation were recorded and organized, and the full dataset[1] is publicly available to ensure transparency and reproducibility.

Phase 6: Perform the Manual Evaluation with Blind Users. A manual assessment followed, involving five participants: three blind users experienced with screen readers (NVDA and JAWS), a sighted user for visual support, and an instructor with over ten years of CMS experience. Participant demographics are detailed in Table 2.

Table 2. Participants demographic information (own elaboration).

Id	Gender	Role	Sight Condition	Screen Reader Experience	Screen Reader
P1	M	Author	Blind	18 years	JAWS
P2	M	Author	Partially Blind	15 years	NVDA
P3	F	Author	Partially Blind	16 years	NVDA
P4	M	Author	Sighted	–	None
P5	M	Instructor	Sighted	1 year	NVDA

A pilot test with one blind participant helped refine the evaluation process, including task duration and accessibility setting and ensuring comfort by allowing participants to use personal keyboards. The manual evaluation included: (1) assessing initial user experience without CMS training, (2) evaluating the same sections as in automated assessment, and (3) conducting three 2-h training sessions. The first session provided a verbally described overview by the instructor sharing his screen; the second involved the instructor using NVDA, sharing both the screen and audio; and the third focused on complex areas with challenging navigation flows, again using screen reader technology. All sessions were recorded to collect user feedback on their experiences.

Phase 7: Conduct Expert Evaluation Using the BW Method. Manual evaluation data, gathered from user observation and feedback, were analyzed using an adapted Barrier Walkthrough (BW) method [35]. BW identifies barriers that hinder CMS usability. Observations were converted into quantitative data, following prior studies [1, 32]. Barriers were rated on impact (effect on usability) and persistence (frequency of occurrence). Impact was rated from None (0), Minor (1), Significant (2), to Critical (3), while persistence was based on barrier frequency (See Table 3). The final severity score was determined by combining impact and persistence, following the BW method guidelines. If either impact or persistence was 0, the severity was classified as "None". A "Minor"

[1] All data supporting this study are available at: https://doi.org/10.17632/4f9ptj34nb.2

severity was assigned when impact was 1 and persistence was 1 or 2. A "Significant" severity was given if impact was 2 and persistence was 1 or 2. A "Critical" severity was given if impact was 3 or persistence reached 3 (See Fig. 3). A CMS-specific adaptation of the original barrier list for blind persons was developed, incorporating WCAG accessibility principles [41], which provide the foundation for accessible web content and establish that must be Perceivable, Operable, Understandable, and Robust for effective access and use (See Table 4).

Table 3. Severity rating scale, barrier occurrences and persistence levels (own elaboration).

Impact	Meaning	Barrier occurrences	Persistence
0	None	0 and 1	0
1	Minor	2 and 3	1
2	Significant	4 and 5	2
3	Critical	Greater than 5	3

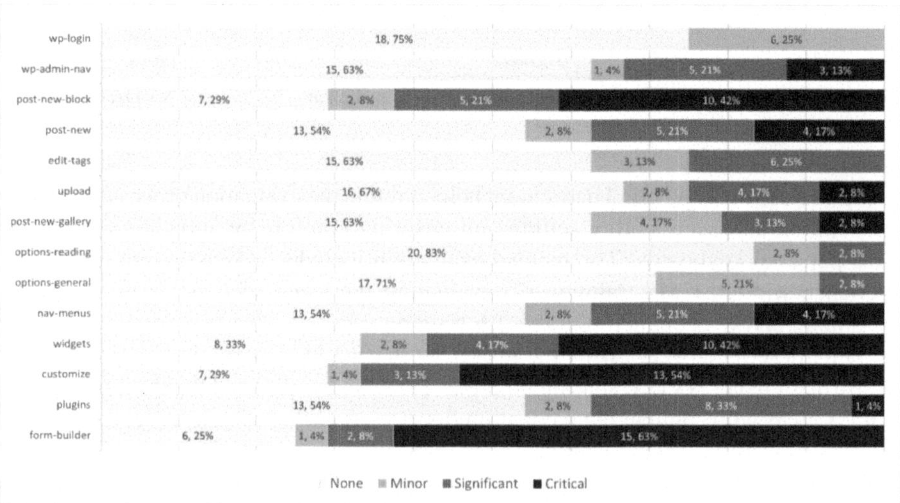

Fig. 3. Summary of severity levels for each evaluated CMS task (own elaboration).

Table 4. Sample of evaluation with the BW method for the T03 task (own elaboration).

Id	Barrier	Principle	Success Criteria	Impact	Persistence	Severity
B01	Rich images lacking equivalent text	Perceivable	1.1.1	1	0	None
B02	Color is necessary	Perceivable	1.4.1, 1.4.3	1	1	Minor
B03	Opaque objects	Perceivable	1.1.1	1	0	None
B04	Functional images lacking text	Perceivable	1.1.1, 1.4.5	1	0	None
B05	Tables with no structural relationships	Perceivable	1.3.1	0	0	None
B06	Tables with no summary	Perceivable	1.3.1, 1.3.2	0	0	None
B07	Forms that are badly linearized	Perceivable	1.3.2	2	0	None
B08	Generic links	Operable	2.4.4, 2.4.9	1	0	None
B09	Ambiguous links	Operable	2.4.4, 2.4.9	1	2	Minor
B10	Dynamic menus in JavaScript or CSS	Operable	2.1.1, 2.1.3, 4.1.2	0	0	None
B11	Mouse events	Operable	2.1.1, 2.1.3	0	0	None
B12	Keyboard traps	Operable	2.1.2	0	0	None
B13	Too many links	Operable	2.4.10	1	1	Minor
B14	Forms with no LABEL tags	Operable	3.3.2, 1.3.1	2	0	None
B15	Non separated links	Operable	2.4.4, 2.4.9	1	0	None
B16	Skip links not implemented	Operable	2.4.1	1	0	None
B17	No keyboard shortcuts	Operable	2.1.1, 2.1.4	1	1	Minor
B18	No page headings	Operable	2.4.6, 1.3.1	1	1	Minor
B19	Page without titles	Operable	2.4.2	1	0	None
B20	Difficulty locating the save button	Operable	2.4.3, 1.3.2	2	0	None
B21	Form with redirect	Understandable	3.2,2, 3.2.5	1	1	Minor
B22	New windows	Understandable	3.2.1, 3.2.5	2	0	None
B23	Language markup	Understandable	3.1.1, 3.1.2	1	0	None
B24	Dynamic changes	Robust	4.1.2, 4.1.3	2	0	None

Phase 8: Record the Data. Barrier Walkthrough evaluation data, including impact, persistence, and severity scores, were systematically recorded. Each task evaluation was documented individually and recorded on tables (see Table 4). The complete dataset is available for reference, and summarized results are shown in Table 5.

Phase 9: Analyze the Results. The lowest-rated area was the block editor, with a Critical severity of 10, followed by Customize Design with a score of 9. The highest-rated task was Login, followed by Set general settings (See Fig. 3). Correlation analysis between automated and manual evaluations was performed (See Fig. 4). These findings, discussed in detail in the Sect. 5.

Phase 10: Report on the Content Creator's User Needs. A major requirement is consistent and predictable navigation structures, as screen reader users rely on navigation semantics. Visual blocks, dynamic menus, inconsistent heading structures, and ambiguous links created confusion and increased cognitive load.

Table 5. Summary of BW severity levels for all manual evaluated tasks (own elaboration).

Id	Task	None	Minor	Significant	Critical
T01	Login and enter credentials	18	6	0	0
T02	Navigate through menus	15	1	5	3
T03	Use block-based editor	7	2	5	10
T04	Use text-based editor	13	2	5	4
T05	Create and manage categories	15	3	6	0
T06	Manage media files	16	2	4	2
T07	Create image galleries	15	4	3	2
T08	Configure homepage and blog page	20	2	2	0
T09	Adjust general site settings	17	5	2	0
T10	Edit main menu	13	2	5	4
T11	Configure social media widget	8	2	4	10
T12	Customize design	7	1	3	13
T13	Install and activate complements	13	2	8	1
T14	Create and manage forms	6	1	2	15

5 Results

This section analyzes the findings in response to each of the research questions.

5.1 RQ1. What is the Correlation Between Automated and Manual Evaluation?

To measure the linear relationship between automated evaluation scores and manual user testing severity, the correlation coefficient (1), was applied using the *CORREL*() función in a spreadsheet software. This coefficient quantifies the strength and direction of the relationship, ranging from −1 to 1. A value of 1 indicates a perfect positive correlation, greater than 0 signifies a positive correlation, zero represents no linear relationship, and −1 denotes a negative correlation [1].

$$r = \frac{\sum(x-\overline{x})(y-\overline{y})}{\sqrt{\sum(x-\overline{x})^2\sum(y-\overline{y})^2}} \tag{1}$$

The correlation analysis revealed varying relationships between the automated evaluation scores and manual severity ratings. As shown in Fig. 4, a moderate negative correlation ($r = -0.58$) with "None" severity suggests that as the number of errors and alerts reported by automated tools increases, the likelihood of having no issues decreases. A weak negative correlation ($r = -0.45$) was found with "Minor" severity, while "Significant" severity showed a very weak negative correlation ($r = -0.14$), indicating little to no relationship. Conversely, "Critical" severity showed a moderate positive correlation ($r = 0.69$), suggesting that higher automated error scores align with an increased presence of critical barriers, though some discrepancies remain.

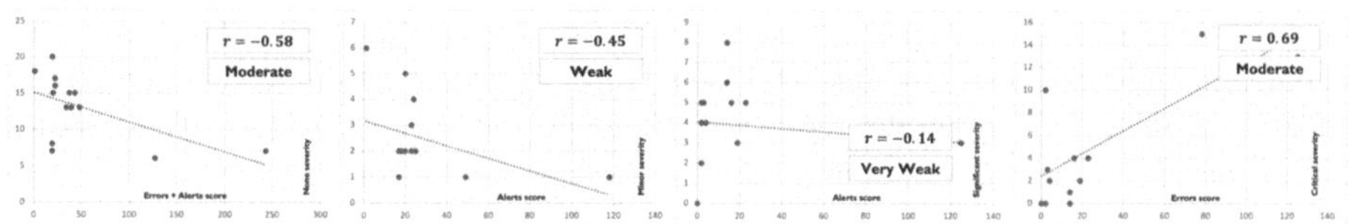

Fig. 4. Scatter plots showing the linear correlation between automated and manual evaluations (own elaboration).

5.2 RQ2. How Can AI Assist in Tasks Requiring Visual Input?

AI-based tools proved valuable in addressing specific accessibility barriers, particularly those related to visual content lacking alternative text. This directly aligns with WCAG 2.2 criterion 1.1.1 (Non-text Content), which although not one of the most frequently violated overall, becomes critically impactful when associated with functional images (Barrier B04), as confirmed by multiple severe cases in our evaluation. During publishing tasks, blind authors often uploaded images without alt text, making them invisible to screen reader users. The integration of AI-powered plugins into WordPress enabled the automatic generation of descriptive alt text, reducing the need for sighted assistance and supporting more independent content creation workflows.

5.3 RQ3. How Does Training Impact User Performance?

Before training, blind participants struggled with interface navigation, especially in block-based layouts, often encountering keyboard traps and relying on inefficient strategies such as excessive tabbing, as reported in [18]. These issues relate to WCAG criteria 2.1.2 (No Keyboard Trap) and 2.4.3 (Focus Order), as well as Nielsen's heuristics on user control and visibility of system status [19]. After targeted instruction, user performance improved significantly. Participants navigated more efficiently, used headings effectively, and completed tasks with greater success. The second session, where the instructor used NVDA alongside participants, was particularly impactful. Hearing synchronized feedback from both the instructor's and their own screen reader helped participants better understand navigation sequences, reducing confusion and enhancing learnability and efficiency.

Training emphasized screen reader commands and semantic navigation strategies, enabling users to better identify form fields (WCAG 1.3.1), operate menus, and publish content while reducing errors—supporting both error prevention and help and documentation heuristics. The use of assistive technology in training created a shared learning environment that eased cognitive load and allowed users to follow instructions more intuitively, confirming that training methods aligned with assistive workflows can significantly improve usability for blind content creators.

5.4 RQ4. What Challenges Do Blind Authors Face in CMS?

Blind content authors encounter substantial usability challenges in CMS environments due to poor semantic structure, lack of consistent feedback, and visual interaction patterns. Automated evaluation revealed a median of 14 errors and 22 alerts per page, while manual testing identified 4 critical, 5 significant, and 2 minor severities. The most critical barriers included too many links (B13) and difficulty locating the save button (B20), reflecting violations of principles related to efficiency and error prevention. These issues disrupt the user's mental model and increase the time and effort required to complete tasks.

From a Human-Computer Interaction (HCI) perspective, poor affordances in block-based editors—relying on drag-and-drop interactions [42]—hinder learnability and lead to "dead ends" where navigation fails. Barriers such as ambiguous links (B09), dynamic menus without ARIA roles (B10), and keyboard traps (B12) correspond to frequent violations of WCAG criteria 2.4.4, 2.1.1, and 4.1.2. These directly impact operability and reduce user control, requiring blind users to rely on inefficient strategies like excessive tabbing. In contrast, criteria such as 1.1.1 (alt text) and 3.1.1/3.1.2 (language identification) showed lower severity, indicating better baseline compliance.

A notable cognitive burden stems from insufficient or inaccessible status messages, tied to criterion 4.1.3 (B24), which limits feedback during content creation. This lack of immediate system response violates HCI heuristics related to visibility of system status. Similarly, excessive or irrelevant link groups (B13) reduce navigational clarity, increasing error likelihood. Although tools powered by AI help generate alt text [43], these must be fully integrated into the CMS to support blind authors effectively and reduce visual dependency. Classic text-based editors like TinyMCE yielded better performance due to their predictable layout and keyboard compatibility, enhancing efficiency and user satisfaction. These findings emphasize the need for CMS platforms to move beyond visual paradigms and adopt inclusive design practices that align with both WCAG compliance and core HCI principles.

6 Discussion

Automated tools like WAVE can identify basic accessibility issues but fall short in assessing real usability and user experience [14]. This was evident in the evaluation of the block-based editor, which was marked as accessible yet proved highly problematic during manual testing. Critical barriers were significantly more frequent than minor or significant ones, especially under the Robust principle—often due to inaccessible dynamic changes and lack of appropriate feedback (WCAG 4.1.3). The Operable principle also showed notable violations related to navigation and keyboard interactions (WCAG 2.1.1, 2.4.4). In contrast, Understandable criteria—such as labels and language identification (WCAG 3.1.1, 3.1.2)—were less frequently violated. As a result, some CMS pages offer moderate accessibility, whereas others present significant challenges (See Fig. 5). Pages with simpler, sequential structures (e.g., login or general settings) aligned better across automated and manual evaluations. However, visual interfaces such as the Customizer and Form Builder consistently scored poorly, indicating that layout complexity and visual-centric design increase cognitive load and hinder usability. These findings highlight the need for learnable interfaces that provide consistent navigation models and reduce ambiguity in user flows—especially for blind users relying on screen readers.

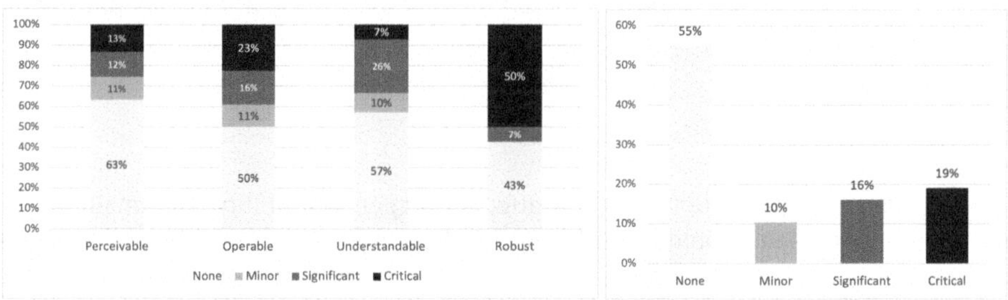

Fig. 5. Distribution of severity levels of identified barriers across accessibility principles (own elaboration).

From a HCI lens, the training modality had a strong impact on user performance. Sessions where the instructor used NVDA improved learnability and task efficiency, reinforcing the importance of synchronized feedback and multimodal instruction. Furthermore, the use of AI-powered tools to generate alt text supported error prevention and user autonomy, enabling blind authors to produce accessible content with less reliance on sighted support. However, these improvements reveal a deeper issue: usability barriers often stem not from user limitations, but from systems that overlook inclusive design principles [44].

CMS development must evolve beyond checklist compliance and embed user-centered design into its development lifecycle. This involves involving disabled users in evaluations, integrating manual testing, and ensuring that design decisions address real-world challenges faced by blind content authors—not only to meet accessibility standards, but to uphold digital inclusion as a fundamental right.

6.1 HCI Design Recommendations for Accessible CMS

From a user-centered design perspective, the findings suggest concrete improvements for CMS developers and theme/plugin designers. First, CMS interfaces should avoid drag-and-drop mechanics that exclude screen reader users and instead prioritize keyboard operability and semantic clarity (WCAG 2.1.1, 1.3.1). Dynamic components, such as expandable menus or modals, must be properly labeled with ARIA roles to ensure clarity and feedback (WCAG 4.1.2, 4.1.3). Navigation structures should be predictable and support heading-based movement (WCAG 2.4.1, 2.4.6), minimizing cognitive load. Additionally, form elements must include visible labels and provide status confirmation messages (WCAG 3.3.2), reducing errors and supporting learnability. Finally, integrating AI-driven tools to assist with tasks such as image description aligns with the autonomy needs of blind users and should be offered as a native option, not just as third-party extensions.

7 Limitations

This study has some limitations that may affect result generalizability. The small sample size of four participants could be considered a constraint; however, it adheres to established protocols recommending a maximum of five visually impaired users to ensure consistent feedback [25, 45]. A pilot test was also conducted with one blind user to refine the procedure. Another limitation involves the BW method, which, while providing valuable insights, depends on expert judgment and can introduce bias. To address this, participant feedback was used to validate findings. Additionally, only one automated tool was used—intentionally—to maintain consistency and evaluate its correlation with manual testing rather than tool comparison. Finally, since the study was conducted remotely, direct observation was limited. This was mitigated by encouraging participants to share their screens during the pilot and describe their navigation processes, helping identify consistent patterns and enhancing result reliability.

8 Conclusions and Future Work

This study examined the accessibility barriers faced by blind content creators when using CMS platforms. Through the combined application of the BW method [35] and the WCAG-EM [33], we identified critical usability issues related to navigation consistency, semantic clarity, and content management workflows. The findings reinforce that blind authors often struggle not because of personal limitations, but due to systemic design choices that prioritize visual interaction. Tailored training, particularly aligned with screen reader workflows, proved transformative, significantly improving users' efficiency and autonomy.

Future work could extend this research by integrating empirical approaches like BW with multiple automated evaluation tools, allowing for a more comprehensive analysis across various user profiles and disabilities. Comparative studies involving other CMS platforms could uncover more accessible solutions or inspire improvements to WordPress, especially regarding block-based interfaces that currently present severe challenges. Expanding user testing to include low vision, motor-impaired, and deaf users would also offer a broader perspective on inclusive CMS design.

Ultimately, addressing the accessibility needs of blind content creators transcends technical enhancements—it aligns with the broader imperative of recognizing accessibility as a fundamental digital right. Ensuring that CMS platforms are operable, perceivable, understandable, and robust is not optional, but essential to fostering equitable participation in digital spaces. Accessible content creation environments empower blind authors to contribute fully and independently to the web, supporting the core principles of universal design and human-centered computing.

Acknowledgments. This work is supported by SECIHTI under scholarship CVU: 1351657.

Disclosure of Interests. The authors have no competing interests to declare that are relevant to the content of this article.

References

1. Acosta-Vargas, P., Antonio Salvador-Ullauri, L., Lujan-Mora, S.: A heuristic method to evaluate web accessibility for users with low vision. IEEE Access. **7** (2019). https://doi.org/10.1109/ACCESS.2019.2939068
2. Kemp, S.: Digital 2024: Global overview report. https://datareportal.com/reports/digital-2024-global-overview-report. Last accessed 29 Jan 2025
3. Csontos, B., Heckl, I.: Improving accessibility of CMS-based websites using automated methods. Univ. Access Inf. Soc. **21**, 491–505 (2022). https://doi.org/10.1007/s10209-020-00784-x
4. W3Techs: Usage statistics and market share of content management systems. (2025). https://w3techs.com/technologies/overview/content_management. Last accessed 26 Jan 2025
5. WordPress Foundation: Accessibility coding standards. https://developer.wordpress.org/coding-standards/wordpress-coding-standards/accessibility/. Last accessed 26 Jan 2025
6. WHO: Global report on health equity for persons with disabilities. https://www.who.int/publications/i/item/9789240063600. Last accessed 10 Jun 2024

7. CDC: Disability and health overview. https://www.cdc.gov/ncbddd/disabilityandhealth/disability.html. Last accessed 03 Dec 2024
8. Bajammal, M., Mesbah, A.: Semantic web accessibility testing via hierarchical visual analysis. Proc. Int. Conf. Softw. Eng. **1610–1621** (2021). https://doi.org/10.1109/ICSE43902.2021.00143
9. Ismailova, R., Inal, Y.: Comparison of online accessibility evaluation tools: an analysis of tool effectiveness. IEEE Access. **10** (2022). https://doi.org/10.1109/ACCESS.2022.3179375
10. Lazar, J.: A framework for born-accessible development of software and digital content. In: Lecture Notes in Computer Science (including subseries Lecture Notes in Artificial Intelligence and Lecture Notes in Bioinformatics), pp. 333–338. Springer, Cham (2023). https://doi.org/10.1007/978-3-031-42293-5_32
11. Henry, S.L.: WCAG 2 overview. https://www.w3.org/WAI/standards-guidelines/wcag/. Last accessed 21 May 2024.
12. W3C WAI: About W3C WAI. https://www.w3.org/WAI/about/. Last accessed 21 Sep 2024
13. Henry, S.L.: Authoring tool accessibility guidelines (ATAG) overview. https://www.w3.org/WAI/standards-guidelines/atag/. Last accessed 30 Jan 2025
14. Acosta-Vargas, P., Acosta, T., Lujan-Mora, S.: Challenges to assess accessibility in higher education websites: A comparative study of Latin america universities. IEEE Access. **6** (2018). https://doi.org/10.1109/ACCESS.2018.2848978
15. Nurthen, J., Cooper, M., Henry, S.L.: WAI-ARIA overview. https://www.w3.org/WAI/standards-guidelines/aria/. Last accessed 21 May 2024
16. Watanabe, W.M., de Lemos, G., Nascimento, R.W.: Accessibility landmarks identification in web applications based on DOM elements classification. Univ. Access Inf. Soc. **23**, 765–777 (2024). https://doi.org/10.1007/s10209-022-00959-8
17. Silva, J.S.R., et al.: In-page navigation aids for screen-reader users with automatic topicalisation and labelling. ACM Trans Access Comput. **17**, 1–45 (2024). https://doi.org/10.1145/3649223
18. Aydin, A.S., Feiz, S., Ashok, V., Ramakrishnan, I.: SaIL: saliency-driven injection of ARIA landmarks. In: Proceedings of the 25th International Conference on Intelligent User Interfaces, pp. 111–115. ACM, New York, NY, USA (2020)
19. Nielsen, J.: 10 Usability heuristics for user interface design. https://www.nngroup.com/articles/ten-usability-heuristics/. Last accessed 02 Nov 2024
20. Luján-Mora, S., Masri, F.: Evaluation of web accessibility: a combined method. In: Information Systems Research and Exploring Social Artifacts: Approaches and Methodologies, pp. 314–331. IGI Global Scientific Publishing (2012)
21. Causarano, G., Paternò, F.: Facilitating development of accessible web applications. In: Human-Centered Software Engineering, pp. 47–62. Springer, Cham (2024). https://doi.org/10.1007/978-3-031-64576-1_3
22. Sanchez-Gordon, S., et al.: Implementation of controls for insertion of accessible images in open online editors based on WCAG guidelines. Case studies: TinyMCE and summernote. In: Advances in Intelligent Systems and Computing, pp. 315–326. Springer, Cham (2019)
23. Tiwary, T., Mahapatra, R.P.: Web accessibility challenges for disabled and generation of alt text for images in websites using artificial intelligence. In: 2022 3rd International Conference on Issues and Challenges in Intelligent Computing Techniques, ICICT (2022)
24. Yadav, A.R., Yadav, S.S., Kamoji, S.: Artificial intelligence enhanced content management systems: integration, considerations, and useful examples. In: Proceedings - 2023 3rd International Conference on Pervasive Computing and Social Networking, ICPCSN, pp. 283–288 (2023)

25. Ferreira, S.B.L., Da Silveira, D.S., Capra, E.P., Ferreira, A.O.: Protocols for evaluation of site accessibility with the participation of blind users. Procedia Comput. Sci. **14**, 47–55 (2012). https://doi.org/10.1016/J.PROCS.2012.10.006
26. Pascual, A., Ribera, M., Granollers, T.: Perception of accessibility errors to raise awareness among Web 2.0 users. In: ACM International Conference Proceeding Series (2012)
27. Calvo, R., Iglesias, A., Moreno, L.: Accessibility barriers for users of screen readers in the Moodle learning content management system. Univ. Access Inf. Soc. **13**, 315–327 (2014). https://doi.org/10.1007/S10209-013-0314-3
28. Dougiamas, M.: The moodle story. https://moodle.com/about/the-moodle-story/. Last accessed 02 Feb 2025
29. López, J.M., Pascual, A., Masip, L., Granollers, T., Cardet, X.: Influence of web content management systems in web content accessibility. In: Human-Computer Interaction, pp. 548–551. Springer, Berlin, Heidelberg (2011)
30. López, J.M., Pascual, A., Menduĩa, C., Granollers, T.: Methodology for identifying and solving accessibility related issues in web content management system environments. In: W4A 2012 - International Cross-Disciplinary Conference on Web Accessibility (2012)
31. Acosta, T., Acosta-Vargas, P., Salvador-Ullauri, L., Luján-Mora, S.: Method for accessibility assessment of online content editors. In: Advances in Intelligent Systems and Computing, pp. 538–551. Springer, Cham (2018)
32. Zilak, M., Keselj, A., Besjedica, T.: Accessible web prototype features from technological point of view. In: 2019 42nd International Convention on Information and Communication Technology, Electronics and Microelectronics (MIPRO), pp. 457–462. IEEE (2019)
33. Henry, S.L., Abou-Zahra, S.: WCAG-EM overview: website accessibility conformance evaluation methodology. https://www.w3.org/WAI/test-evaluate/conformance/wcag-em/. Last accessed 21 May 2024
34. Acosta-Vargas, P., Salvador-Ullauri, L., Pérez-Medina, J.L., Gonzalez, M., Jimenes, K., Rybarczyk, Y.: Improving web accessibility: evaluation and analysis of a telerehabilitation platform for hip arthroplasty patients. Adv. Intell. Syst. Comput. **959**, 508–519 (2020). https://doi.org/10.1007/978-3-030-20040-4_46
35. Brajnik, G.: The barrier wlakthrough method. https://people.uniud.it/node/3465. Last accessed 01 Feb 2025
36. Avila, J., Sostmann, K., Breckwoldt, J., Peters, H.: Evaluation of the free, open source software WordPress as electronic portfolio system in undergraduate medical education. BMC Med. Educ. **16**, 1–10 (2016). https://doi.org/10.1186/S12909-016-0678-1/FIGURES/3
37. WordPress Foundation: WordPress accessibility handbook. https://make.wordpress.org/accessibility/handbook/. Last accessed 26 Jan 2025
38. Serra, G., Fara, P., Casini, D.: Enhancing the availability of web services in the IoT-to-edge-to-cloud compute continuum: a WordPress case study. In: Proceedings - 2023 26th Euromicro Conference on Digital System Design, DSD, pp. 602–609 (2023)
39. WebAIM: About WAVE. https://wave.webaim.org/about. Last accessed 30 Jan 2025
40. Manca, M., Palumbo, V., Paternò, F., Santoro, C.: The transparency of automatic web accessibility evaluation tools: design criteria, state of the art, and user perception. ACM Trans. Access Comput. **16** (2023). https://doi.org/10.1145/3556979
41. Campbell, A., Adams, C., Bradley, R.: Introduction to understanding WCAG 2.2. https://www.w3.org/WAI/WCAG22/Understanding/intro#understanding-the-four-principles-of-accessibility. Last accessed 21 Feb 2025
42. WP Accessibility Team: Accessibility tickets, tasks, and reports. https://make.wordpress.org/accessibility/handbook/get-involved/tickets-tasks-reports/. Last accessed 26 Jan 2025
43. Leotta, M., Mori, F., Ribaudo, M.: Evaluating the effectiveness of automatic image captioning for web accessibility. Univ. Access Inf. Soc. **22**, 1293–1313 (2023). https://doi.org/10.1007/s10209-022-00906-7

44. Chundury, P., Thakkar, U., Reyazuddin, Y., Jordan, J.B., Elmqvist, N., Lazar, J.: Understanding the visualization and analytics needs of blind and low-vision professionals. In: ASSETS 2024 - Proceedings of the 26th International ACM SIGACCESS Conference on Computers and Accessibility (2024)
45. Nielsen, Jakob.: Why you only need to test with 5 users. https://www.nngroup.com/articles/why-you-only-need-to-test-with-5-users/. Last accessed 02 Nov 2024

Virtual Reality and the Metaverse for Developing Self-efficacy Variables in Future English Teachers

Evangelina Garcia-Marquez[1](✉), Juan Manuel Gonzalez-Calleros[2], and Alfredo Garcia-Suarez[2]

[1] Facultad Ciencias de la Electrónica, Benemérita Universidad Autónoma de Puebla, Puebla, México
bve230875@viep.com.mx

[2] Facultad Ciencias de la Computación, Benemérita Universidad Autónoma de Puebla, Puebla, México
{jmgonzalezcalleros,alfredo.garciasuarez}@viep.com.mx

Abstract. Speaking in English has consistently been a challenge for learners, particularly for future teachers regarding oral production. This article examines the relationship between self-efficacy variables and oral communicative competence (OCC) in pre-service English teachers, exploring the potential of immersive virtual environments such as Virtual Reality (VR) and the Metaverse. A literature review identified key factors—perceived English proficiency, language ego, inhibition, language anxiety, and communicative interaction—that influence self-efficacy and OCC. To investigate these relationships, a pilot experiment was conducted with four English-teaching trainees from a teacher training college in Mexico. Participants engaged in discussions using BigScreen, a VR application within the Metaverse, utilizing Meta Quest 2 and Meta Quest 3 headsets. Pre- and post-test questionnaires indicated a direct relationship between self-efficacy and the identified variables, particularly classroom efficacy, instructional efficacy, and efficacy in exemplifying meanings. Statistical analysis was performed using Python, applying linear and multiple correlation techniques to evaluate these relationships.

Keywords: Virtual Reality · Metaverse · Oral Communicative Competence · Self-efficacy · Pre-service English Teachers

1 Introduction

Virtual Reality (VR) and the Metaverse have emerged as innovative tools in English as a Foreign Language (EFL) instruction [1–4]. The teaching and learning of English remain subjects of interest in both research and classroom practice [5–7]. In recent years, Mexico has continued to exhibit a medium to low level in terms of English language proficiency and linguistic skills as a foreign language [8, 9].

Today, digital and technological resources are prevalent in classroom environments [10, 11], as they enable different types of interactions and cognitive constructions with

H. Luna-García et al. (Eds.): HCI-COLLAB 2025, CCIS 2850, pp. 321–336, 2027.
https://doi.org/10.1007/978-3-032-31223-5_22

students and subject matter. The use of technology in the classroom fosters innovation, motivation, and creativity [12–14]. It facilitates continuous natural communication among participants [15, 16], and feedback occurs organically, allowing students to reflect on their own learning process and performance [2, 17].

VR and the metaverse are being considered as potential platforms for developing various linguistic skills, as well as for analyzing the impact of this type of technology on pre-service English teachers [18–20].

It was in 2018 when the use of Virtual and Augmented Reality became a pedagogical option, mainly due to the launch and increased accessibility of technological devices such as Oculus Meta glasses, later rebranded as Meta Quest 2 and 3 [21–23]. The latter are the latest advancements in mixed reality headsets released by Meta. Following these launches, the use of immersive VR has increasingly become an option to support teaching and learning processes across various disciplines, extending beyond entertainment and gaming [3, 24, 25].

This article aims to describe the phases of the pilot study conducted with pre-service teachers specializing in English at a Higher Education Institution in Mexico. The application selected for this quasi-experiment was BigScreen, available on the Meta Horizon platform, which serves as Meta's digital library for downloading or acquiring both immersive and mixed reality applications for Meta Quest 3 headsets.

This work presents a detailed description of the pilot study, whose purpose was to evaluate the relationships and correlations of variables identified in the literature concerning self-efficacy in oral communicative competence in English. To achieve this, a conceptual theoretical framework was developed to contextualize the definitions and meanings retrieved. Additionally, a state-of-the-art review and an analysis of previous studies were conducted, using systematic literature reviews that considered objectives and conclusions.

Furthermore, relevant assessment instruments were identified and evaluated to measure linguistic self-efficacy in English, teaching self-efficacy in the classroom, as well as the results of a post-intervention semi-structured interview designed to capture participants' experiences. The analysis of these questionnaires results was analyzed using Python and Visual Studio Code for data visualization.

In the discussion section, the relationships and correlations identified in the pilot study are compared with findings from the literature, particularly regarding variables such as the perceived ability to use English, the ability to give clear commands in class, and the linguistic ability to express personal ideas and basic concepts in English. Finally, in the conclusion section, we resume main ideas recovered from the pilotage mediated by immersive Virtual Reality (iVR).

2 Theoretical Framework

In this section, we present the main theories related to Oral Communicative Competence (oCC), VR, and the Metaverse, with the aim of conceptualizing the terms used and identifying the variables proposed by these theories concerning.

2.1 Variables Involved in Oral Communicative Competence in English

Oral communicative competence (oCC) in English began to be studied in the mid-20th century when pedagogical and linguistic theorists became increasingly concerned with understanding how language is produced [26]. In this article, we will discuss the Communicative Theory proposed by Dell Hymes (1980), who argued that the ability to communicate extends beyond the application of orthographic, grammatical, and morphosyntactic rules of language. He emphasized that communicative competence is more than just a response to an external stimulus inherent to human beings [27].

Hymes stated that oCC is related to a set of skills, abilities, and both external and internal factors of linguistic, sociolinguistic, and pragmatic nature. In other words, language serves a specific communicative function depending on the speaker's context [26, 27]. This theory bases communicative competence on a series of metalinguistic factors, including: (1) Where and when communication takes place; (2) Who speaks and who listens, (3) What message is conveyed, (4) The purpose of the discourse, (5) The intonation used; (6) The communication channel, (7) The type of discourse perceived and (8) Interaction norms and Discourse genre [26, 27]. These factors highlight that communication is not only about linguistic accuracy but also about the appropriateness and effectiveness of language use in social interactions [28].

Also, in the teaching and learning processes of English as a second language, several factors influence oCC elements such as pronunciation, fluency, accuracy, affective factors, and interaction effects are highly related to how language is produced [28, 29]. One of the major observable obstacles among English learners is the fear of making mistakes, of not being understood, or of sounding foolish and being judged by the listener [30]. Similarly, the ability to determine what to say, when to say it, and how to say it significantly affects how oCC is developed in English. Several individual and contextual factors directly impact oCC in English, including age, exposure to the language, phonetic ability, linguistic identity and ego, and motivation and concern for good pronunciation [26, 27].

OCC in English is one of the core linguistic skills that inherently depend on interaction and purpose. Speaking is not just about producing grammatically structured or well-intonated words but about sharing meanings, agreements, and negotiating understanding [28]. These interaction skills are closely related to the speaker's decision-making, imagination, reactions, and reciprocity in communication [28–30]. These aspects reinforce the idea that oCC in English is not merely about linguistic knowledge and a linguistic level but also about social and pragmatic effectiveness in communication and self-perception performing the language.

2.2 Virtual Reality and Metaverse for Educational English purposes

Virtual Reality is defined as a computer-generated simulation of a virtual world that can involve vision and other senses, allowing the user to feel immersed [1, 2, 4, 6, 7]. VR incorporates realism, interaction, and immersion, the latter being the subjective sensation of being in a specific place [2, 31–33].

Immersive Virtual Reality (iVR) not limited to three-dimensional simulations generated by a computer; instead, it now incorporates devices such as VR headsets, which enable users to experience total immersion in a virtual world [1, 2, 4, 6]. VR involves realism, interaction, and immersion, reinforcing the subjective feeling of presence in a virtual environment [31, 33]. Key variables such as sense of presence and interaction are essential to achieving a fully immersive experience [2, 22, 32].

- **Sense of Presence in iVR.** The sense of presence within an iVR space refers to feeling physically present in a virtual environment, even though the user is fully aware that their physical body is located elsewhere [2, 4]. If the virtual space is well-designed, users can experience a stronger sense of presence in that environment. A higher sense of presence leads to longer engagement within the space; however, achieving this is not an easy task as it requires careful consideration of interactions, activities, and potential physical discomfort the user may experience [1, 32].
- **Physical Space in iVR.** The "physical space" in iVR refers to different aspects of the virtual environment, as these spaces are determined by the objectives, interactions, or activities planned by the designer [2, 4]. There are four key categories: Visual Enhancements, Interaction within the Virtual Environment, Control Enhancements and Monitoring Enhancements.
- **Engagement in iVR.** The term engagement refers to the psychological construct that describes the emotional, cognitive, and behavioral connection an individual establishes with an activity, task, project, or environment [1, 18]. The level of engagement during immersion is closely linked to motivation to complete the task, interaction levels, and various cognitive processes that enable users to connect with the activity or task [19].

On the other hand, the metaverse is understood as a three-dimensional virtual space where users can interact through avatars [2–4]. The term metaverse has evolved from pre-existing concepts that have taken various forms over the past two decades [4]. Among these concepts are the so-called virtual worlds [34]. The key variables related to the metaverse include sense of presence, avatars, personal space, and natural interfaces [4, 5].

3 Preview Works

To determine the gap in the literature, a literature search covering the last 10 and five years up to the present was conducted. This search was based on search strings that incorporated key terms related to emotional factors identified in the foundational references, oral communicative competence in English as a foreign language, the use of experiential technologies, and instructional models in education. The reviewed terms included <<Autoeficacia OR self-efficacy AND future teachers>>, <<Entornos virtuales de aprendizaje AND Virtual Reality AND 3d virtual environment>> and <<modelos tecno-pedagógicos AND modelos integración AND education>>.

Each document review was guided by specific objectives, OB-1. Determining the related factor according to the literature on Oral Communicative Competence (oCC) in English; OB-2. Identifying types of technology-mediated educational interventions that have been implemented; OB-3. Analyzing the contributions and suggestions derived from these interventions; OB-4. Identifying the methodologies used in these studies and

OB-5. Examining the results, conclusions, and discussions from these documents to conduct critical discussions on the selected materials

Although literature exists that addresses the combination of these search concepts, a gap in the literature was identified when these concepts are integrated into the training of English language teachers. From the analysis of the reviewed documents, these literature gaps were identified. Table 1 below presents a synthesis of the literature findings, organized according to the previously mentioned objectives that guided the literature review.

Based on the analysis of previous studies, the variables identified in the literature that impact the oCC are presented [2, 19, 24]. According to the literature, these variables are linked to the speaker's feelings and emotions [14, 16, 17].

- **Self-Esteem.** This variable plays a fundamental role in cognitive processes [17]. Students develop their self-esteem, self-confidence, and awareness of their own level of efficacy through experiences gained from interacting with the world [7]. There is a direct relationship between self-esteem and oCC in English [1].
- **Self-Efficacy**. This variable is identified as a key affective factor that determines both the quantity and quality of oCC in English [16, 26, 27]. Self-efficacy directly influences confidence and oral production performance [14, 16, 17]. If a speaker does not develop confidence in their oCC, they are less likely to use English effectively [17].
- **Willingness to Communicate**. This variable can be understood as a result of the perceived level of self-efficacy [14, 16, 17]. The level of successful experiences a speaker has in their oral communication will determine their willingness to interact in the language [17].
- **Risk-Taking**. This affective variable is directly related to self-esteem and self-efficacy [2, 5, 17]. It refers to the ability to make intelligent guesses, meaning the willingness to take the risk of communicating in a second language and making mistakes [5]. Taking risks in speaking facilitates interactions [7], as it allows the speaker to constantly face uncertainty and the potential for errors, including the possibility of appearing ridiculous [16, 17]

Through the analysis of previous studies, it can be concluded that self-efficacy is one of the affective factors most closely related to oCC. It is evident that self-efficacy is strongly linked to other identified affective variables, making it a key focus for study, as it has been consistently highlighted in previous research as an intervening variable [14, 16, 17]. Perceiving oneself as capable of communicating in English influences how the language is used, the words chosen, and the extent to which it is employed [19]. This makes self-efficacy the variable of interest in the training of future English teachers [1].

4 Methodology

The present article presents a pilot study conducted under a quantitative methodological approach [36]. A quasi-experimental pilot workshop was conducted, and the variables analyzed were self-efficacy in speaking English and self-efficacy in teaching.

Two Likert-scale instruments were applied (1) Self-Efficacy Scale for English Learning [37] and (2) Teachers' Sense of Efficacy Scale, TSES Spanish Long Version [38].

Table 1. Synthesis of the literature findings.

Objective	Key literature notes	References
OB-1	The concept of Self-Efficacy was identified, rooted in Albert Bandura's Self-Efficacy Theory (1997). Variables identify: Self-knowledge, level of effort, and self-monitoring = Self-efficacy beliefs. Linguistic anxiety in a second language (English). Performance experiences (Content and cognitive-pedagogical mastery).	[7, 14, 16, 17]
OB-2	Virtual Learning Environments (VLEs) have been implemented to: develop English learning strategies, motivate language acquisition, foster creativity, analyze reactions and perceptions during virtual visits, study effectiveness in concept acquisition, examine the relationship between device type/immersion and information retention ability, and develop oral skills.	[1]-[3, 4, 33]
OB-3	The use of VLEs fosters collaborative work. There are a growing interest and need for the design and creation of context-specific VLEs. It is noted that technology enhances motivation, self-confidence, and the quality of participants' English. It is necessary to apply a techno-pedagogical model to achieve a functional and comprehensive integration. The lack of methodology makes it difficult for teachers to select appropriate tools for VR. Immersive technology is often implemented, which can lead to either the success or failure of educational technology integration.	[12, 17, 25, 35]
OB-4	ACOT, ARCS, ADDIE, TPACK, and SAMR are interactive design models used in educational immersive technology. Technologies applied were classified as simple HMD, such as Google Cardboard, VR360° videos, Expedition and Unity, GoPro VR Player, Avatar, HMD-VR Box, HMD: Oculus Quest Headsets / Oculus Go Headsets, 3D MAX, and VR HMD using HTC VIVE.	[1, 6, 7, 17]
OB-5	VLEs motivate language acquisition, plus foster creativity, and develop lingual skills in English, especially Speaking skills. New immersive technologies and the use of metaverse emerged as suggested technology and platform for conducting future research.	[1, 7, 22, 24]

Source: Authors own elaboration.

The categories from these questionnaires were analyzed using data informatics linear and multiple correlation techniques by Python, complemented these information semi-structured interviews were conducted with participants to obtain deeper insights into their perceptions and overall experiences for future considerations.

The objective of this pilot study was to determine the relationships and correlations between self-efficacy in the hability in communicating in English language and the self-efficacy related with students' engagement, instructional strategies and abilities learning English language in future English teachers. Additionally, participants' English proficiency levels were assessed according to the Common European Framework of Reference for Languages (CEFR) using the categories of the Preliminary English Test (PET) [39]. This measurement was conducted to determine participants' English proficiency levels and whether they were influenced by immersion in the BigScreen environment. Variables such as willing to communicate, motivation, attention and perception were capture in video for future analysis and discussion.

4.1 Participants

A group of four pre-service English teachers was invited to participate, selected through convenience sampling, as they represent an interest group and are accessible to the researcher. The participants in the pilot study were two women and two men, aged between 20 and 30 years, with little to no experience in the use of VR.

During the first part of the pilot study, the participants signed an informed consent form and completed an initial questionnaire with demographic data.

4.2 Workshop Design

1. The first step in designing the workshop was a meeting of the research team. The pilot study was structured as a four-hour workshop. It was planned that immersion would take place in pairs, as all participants were in the same physical room. Also, the instruments to be tested and validated during this pilot study were determined.

2. Subsequently, the software was selected. The selected software was BigScreen (BS) (see Fig. 1), as it offers a multi-user platform allowing interaction among up to participants in the same virtual room. It also provides features such as customizable environments, invitation options, and interactive tools within the virtual space in its free version.

Fig. 1. Example of the BigScreen home screen used. Source: Authors own elaboration.

3. Within the BS environment, the classroom setting was selected, which simulated being inside a traditional classroom. This choice was made in alignment with the SAM-R model [13], specifically in the substitution and augmentation stages, to enhance the classroom experience. In the same way, a classroom-themed environment was chosen as the interaction space due to its familiarity, allowing participants to experience it within VR, enabling them to interact, explore, and become acquainted with the technology (see Fig. 2). BS also features a screen that allows integration with applications such as YouTube (see Fig. 3) and Netflix, as well as the ability to project content from a computer within the virtual environment.

Fig. 2. Selected screen: Classroom environment in BigScreen Source: Authors own elaboration.

Fig. 3. Classroom environment in BigScreen with YouTube Source: Authors own elaboration.

For access BS, avatars are generated by default based on gender (see Fig. 4). While some customization options are available, such as skin tone, outfits, and accessories, the free version does not allow for extensive modifications.

Another advantage is the mobility within the environment (see Fig. 5), as it allows users the freedom to move around, providing different viewpoints. It also includes sub-menus that enable users to interact within the environment rather than remaining static. These interactions include writing, throwing tomatoes, having popcorn, and drinking soda (see Fig. 6). These tools help beginner participants become familiar with the technology, controls, graphics, and immersion, reducing the risk of cybersickness [41].

Fig. 4. Example avatar in the environment BS Source: Authors own elaboration.

Fig. 5. Mobility inside environment BS Source: Authors own elaboration.

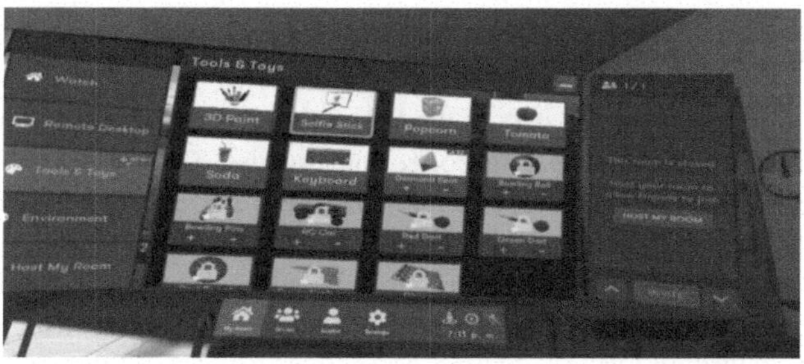

Fig. 6. Tool and toys menu inside BS Source: Authors own elaboration.

4. Pilot planning. Both in-person and virtual meetings were held to determine the logistic of the workshop. Table 2 presents the key phases, components, and considerations that emerged from these meetings.

The qualitative data collected will be analyzed separately at a later stage. In this article, only the quantitative results and data obtained from the previously mentioned instruments will be analyzed.

Table 2. Workshop Structure in the Metaverse (BS): Key Phases and components

Phase	Description
1. Initial Planning	Selection of speech-triggering situations in BS. Topic selection: Artificial Intelligence, aligning with the conference theme. Definition of timing, duration, and required resources. Consideration of recording and material collection.
2. Design and Testing of the Interaction Environment	Evaluation of Meta Quest 2 and 3 for role assignment. Structuring peer interaction to foster trust and engagement. A researcher moderating and posing trigger questions.
3. Workshop Implementation	Phase 1: Introduction and informed consent process. Phase 2: Training in VR headset usage. Phase 3: Immersion session (15–20 min). Phase 4: Reflection, discussion, and completion of exit questionnaires.
4. Data Collection and Analysis	Non-immersed participants documented thoughts in a dashboard in Spanish. Collection of ideas, expectations, and insights.

Source: Authors own elaboration.

4.3 Workshop Implementation

The workshop was conducted as part of the Educational Conference and had a duration of four hours. Fig. 7. shows the data collection process. During the workshop, three additional participants joined; however, their data was not considered, as they did not belong to the target population.

Participants were informed that interactions would be recorded. Additionally, they were advised to immediately notify the support staff in the room if they experienced any discomfort, including nausea, dizziness, vertigo, visual overload, eye strain, or any other symptoms of cybersickness [41] during immersion. This process was repeated for three cycles.

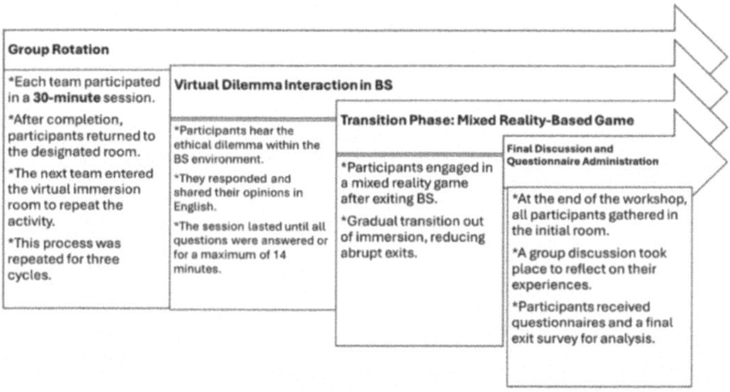

Fig. 7. Data Collection Process Source: Authors own elaboration.

5 Data Analysis

Once the workshop concluded, participants completed two questionnaires. The first was the Self-Efficacy Scale for English Learning [37], which used a Likert scale from 1 to 5, where 1 represented "I am incapable of doing that" and 5 represented "I am very capable of doing that". This questionnaire measured variables such as oral production ability, listening ability, sources of self-efficacy and self-efficacy perception, verbal persuasion or linguistic ego, physiological and emotional states, and general self-efficacy.

The second questionnaire was the Teachers' Sense of Efficacy Scale (TSES) [38], which used a Likert scale from 1 to 9, where 1 corresponded to "Nothing at all" and 9 to "For the most part". The variables analyzed in this instrument included efficacy in student engagement, efficacy in instructional strategies, and efficacy in classroom management. Both instruments were analyzed based on their respective variables. All participants completed the questionnaires using a QR code that directed them to a Forms survey. For the quantitative analysis of these variables and to determine possible relationships or correlations between them, Python 13.3.1 and Visual Studio Code were used.

6 Results

Based on the identified instruments, an average score analysis and response frequency analysis were conducted. A total of four responses from the target population were examined, with the items categorized and analyzed accordingly. The relationship between oCC and listening competence was specifically analyzed, as this variable proved to be significant during the immersion experience.

These data were processed using Visual Studio Code, which utilizes Python 13.3.1 for data processing and statistical analysis, and two heat maps were generated as a colorimetric visualization tool. These heatmaps allowed for interpretations and predictions regarding the relationships observed based on the collected responses.

The variables from both instruments were triangulated to determine their averages and correlations. Fig. 8 presents the average relationships between oral communicative

```
Pilotaje= pd.read_excel('Pilotaje_SOMECE.xlsx')
Pilotaje
```

	Participantes	CA_PROM	CCo_PROM	EEE	EISs	EGA
0	1	4.000000	4.000000	6.750	7.250	6.875
1	2	3.571429	4.000000	7.750	7.500	7.375
2	3	3.428571	3.428571	7.500	6.625	6.875
3	4	3.285714	3.428571	4.875	5.625	5.625

Fig. 8. Analysis of Average Relationships Between Instrument Variables Source: Authors own elaboration.

competence and listening competence, as measured by the linguistic skills scale, along with the self-perception strategy variables related to classroom management.

Once the relationships between the items of the variables were analyzed, their interpretation was carried out. The results indicate a direct relationship between the perception of linguistic skills related to listening competence, which emerged as a receptive variable influencing the participant's oral production. Similarly, a relationship was identified between both competences and classroom management skills in pre-service English teachers.

Based on these average values, a relationship matrix was generated to compare oCC and listening ability against perceived self-efficacy in the classroom. Additionally, the absolute value of all correlations between the variables from the two applied instruments were calculated. Using predictive modeling techniques, Figure 9 presents these relationships. On the orange side, which demonstrated the correlation between perceived self-efficacy in speaking English and perceptions of teaching strategies, student engagement strategies, and classroom management strategies are shown. On the green side, the correlation between these same perceived strategies and listening comprehension ability is displayed.

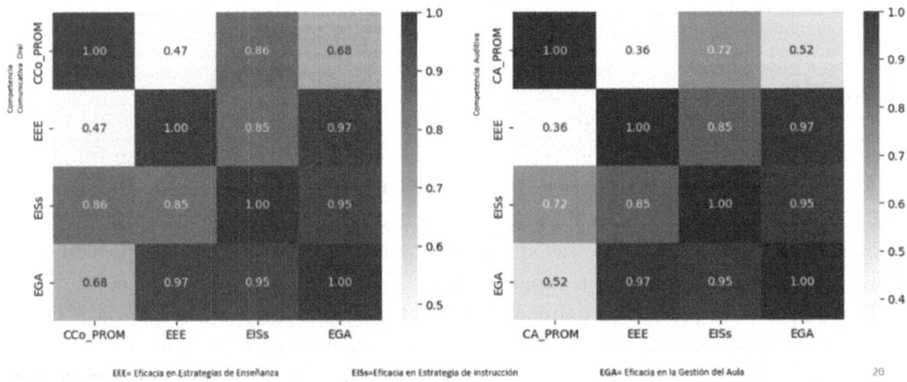

Fig. 9. Predictive modeling Heatmap Source: Authors own elaboration.

These results show us, that the color intensity observed in the heat maps suggests a notably high correlation between oCC and listening competence, particularly when paired with the perceived efficacy to select student engagement strategies. This correlation, point out the interdependent nature of speaking and listening skills within the communicative language framework [26–28]. This heat map's color offers a visual representation of the relations and correlations between oCC and listening competence, guiding pre-service English teachers in making decisions about which strategies are effective for different proficiency levels or learning contexts.

7 Discussion

The article aims to demonstrate the relationship and correlation that can be determined through the use and implementation of the following questionnaires: (1) Self-Efficacy Scale for English Learning [37] and (2) Teachers' Sense of Efficacy Scale [38], along with participants' English proficiency level and their experience within a metaverse environment BS.

The relationship between variables related to Efficacy in Classroom Management shows a stronger correlation with both oCC and listening competence. However, these results cannot be considered conclusive because of the limited number of participants. The findings remain exploratory within the context of pre-service English teachers, aiming to characterize the optimal user profile and provide recommendations.

Self-efficacy is referenced as an affective factor related to oCC [22] and is also linked to how language is used in the classroom, how information is processed, how learning and teaching occur, and the learning strategies employed [2]. The relationship between classroom management and oCC-Listening competence appears as a significant variable. Therefore, it is important to further investigate participants' responses through interviews.

Immersion in Virtual Reality (VR) proves to be an engaging and innovative tool [23]; however, for some participants, it can also be overwhelming. Even individuals with prior experience with screens and video games may find an immersive environment massive. This factor should be considered, as some participants may be reluctant to participate, communicate, or interact within the virtual environment [6, 7, 25].

The implementation of the metaverse as a strategy to develop oCC through immersive experiences can be considered enriching [23, 25]. However, it is essential to identify the optimal user profile for this type of technology. Developing an immersion protocol is necessary. The lack of a replicable immersive strategy limits the use of the metaverse especially Meta Horizon, making it less frequently to be implemented with pre-service English teachers from specific contexts.

8 Conclusions

Immersive virtual environments like virtual reality and the metaverse effectively capture student attention [21–23]. But their implementation must follow a controlled and safe protocol. Not all users are suited for VR, and prior gaming or computer experience does not eliminate the risk of cybersickness [41].

Being in BS within the classroom scenario fosters a sense of belonging, yet participants expect interactive activities. Triangulating self-efficacy scales [37, 38] helps predict correlations between oral and listening skills in English and perceived classroom efficacy. To refine implementation, listening skills should be evaluated using PET Cambridge criteria [39], and qualitative analysis should be expanded. A larger-scale intervention is needed to establish a structured protocol for integrating metaverse-based learning, ensuring accessibility and proper familiarization with VR tools.

References

1. Bahari, A.: Affordances and challenges of teaching language skills by virtual reality: a systematic review (2010–2020). E-Learning Digit. Media. **19**(2), 163–188 (2022). https://doi.org/10.1177/20427530211036583
2. Chen, H.-J.: Gather in the metaverse: learning outcomes, virtual presence, and perceptions of high- and low-achieving pre-service teachers of English as a foreign language. Educ. Inf. Technol. **29**(7), 8549–8577 (2024). https://doi.org/10.1007/s10639-023-12135-3
3. Murala, D.K.: METAEDUCATION: state-of-the-art methodology for empowering feature education. IEEE Access. **12**, 57992–58020 (2024). https://doi.org/10.1109/ACCESS.2024.3391903
4. Slater, M., Barngrover, M., Friedman, D., Lopez-Tarruella, A., Niamut, O.: A metaverse for the good. In: Slater, M., Barngrover, M., et al. (eds.) A Metaverse for the Good: Design, Application and Understanding, p. 215. Frontiers Media SA (2024)
5. Wilks, J.L., Jacka, L.: Second life, first experiences: using virtual worlds in teacher education. Aust. J. Teach. Educ. **38**(4) (2013). https://doi.org/10.14221/ajte.2013v38n4.10
6. Sousa-Ferreira, R., Campanari-Xavier, R.A., Rodrigues-Ancioto, A.S.: La realidad virtual como herramienta para la educación básica y profesional. Rev. Cient. Gen. José María Córdova. **19**(33), 223–241 (2021). https://doi.org/10.21830/19006586.728
7. Yudintseva, A.: Virtual reality affordances for oral communication in English as a second language classroom: a literature review. Comput. Educ. X Real. **2**, 100018 (2023). https://doi.org/10.1016/j.cexr.2023.100018
8. Mexicanos primero.: Sorry. El aprendizaje del inglés en México, p. 2030. Mexicanos Primero, Visión (2015)
9. Cid De León, E.M.: Resultados de exámenes de nivel de inglés en México: revisión sistemática de investigaciones. Alternancia Rev. Educ. Investig. **5**(9), 53–67 (2023). https://doi.org/10.33996/alternancia.v5i9.1103
10. Vicario-Solórzano, M.: Perspectivas y usos de las TICC en la educación. Centro de Estudios Superiores en Educación (2011)
11. Borromeo García, C.A., Fernández Pérez, J.A., Ramírez Martinell, A.: La tecnología en la enseñanza de idiomas: evolución a través de los métodos. (2018)
12. Crompton, H. et al.: Examining technology use within the ADDIE framework to develop professional training. Eur. J. Train. Dev. **48**(3/4), 422–454 (2024). https://doi.org/10.1108/EJTD-12-2022-0137
13. Drugova, E., Zhuravleva, I., Aiusheeva, M., Grits, D.: Toward a model of learning innovation integration: TPACK-SAMR based analysis of the introduction of a digital learning environment in three Russian universities. Educ. Inf. Technol. **26**(4), 4925–4942 (2021). https://doi.org/10.1007/s10639-021-10514-2
14. Luo, Z., Li, H.: Competence, preparation, and relaxation: contributing factors to EFL student teachers' self-efficacy and teaching performance in microteaching training. Heliyon. **10**(4), e26216 (2024). https://doi.org/10.1016/j.heliyon.2024.e26216

15. Harmandaoğlu Baz, E., Balçıkanlı, C., Cephe, P.T.: Introducing an innovative technology integration model: echoes from EFL pre-service teachers. Educ. Inf. Technol. **23**(5), 2179–2200 (2018). https://doi.org/10.1007/s10639-018-9711-9
16. Pozas, M., Letzel, V., Frohn, J.: An empirical study exploring pre-service teachers' profiles and their prospective ICT integration: is it a matter of attitudes, self-efficacy, self-concept or concerns? J. Comput. Educ. **11**(1), 237–257 (2024). https://doi.org/10.1007/s40692-022-00254-8
17. Ma, Y.: The triarchy of L2 learners' emotion, cognition, and language performance: anxiety, self-efficacy, and speaking skill in lights of the emerging theories in SLA. Front. Psychol. **13**, 1002492 (2022). https://doi.org/10.3389/fpsyg.2022.1002492
18. Barrot, J.S.: Using social networks for English teaching and learning. Lang. Teach. **56**(2), 181–196 (2022). https://doi.org/10.1152/ajplegacy.1975.229.6.1641
19. Fedorova, O., Shumskyi, O., Golikova, O., Kutsenko, I., Serdiuk, N., Zahorodna, O.: Microlearning in forming the students' English competencies with VR involvement. Brain. Broad Res. Artif. Intell. Neurosci. **13**(1 Sup1), 388–402 (2022). https://doi.org/10.18662/brain/13.1Sup1/326
20. Boonmoh, A., Kulavichian, I.: Exploring Thai EFL pre-service teachers' technology integration based on SAMR model. Contemp. Educ. Technol. **15**(4), ep457 (2023). https://doi.org/10.30935/cedtech/13567
21. Christoforou, M.: Enhancing the ESP lesson with IMMERSE: a pedagogical example of a metaverse language learning platform. (2019)
22. Godwin-Jones, R.: Emerging spaces for language learning: AI bots, ambient intelligence, and the metaverse. Lang. Learn. **27**(2), 6–27 (2023)
23. AlSaleem, I.A., B.: The Efficiency of metaverse platforms in language learning based on Jordanian young learners' perceptions. Arab World Engl. J. **14**(1), 334–348 (2023). https://doi.org/10.24093/awej/vol14no1.21
24. Peixoto, B., Pinto, R., Melo, M., Cabral, L., Bessa, M.: Immersive virtual reality for foreign language education: a PRISMA systematic review. IEEE Access. **9**, 48952–48962 (2021). https://doi.org/10.1109/ACCESS.2021.3068858
25. Li, M., Yu, Z.: A systematic review on the metaverse-based blended English learning. Front. Psychol. **13**, 1087508 (2023). https://doi.org/10.3389/fpsyg.2022.1087508
26. Brown, H.D.: Principles of Language Learning and Teaching. Pearson Longman (1980)
27. Brown, H.D: Teaching by principles: an interactive approach to language pedagogy. (1994)
28. Bygate, M.: Speaking. Oxford University Press (2003)
29. Brown, G., Yule, G.: Teaching the Spoken Language. Cambridge University (1999)
30. Spitzberg, B.H.: Communication competence as knowledge, skill, and impression. Commun. Educ. **32**(3), 323–329 (1983). https://doi.org/10.1080/03634528309378550
31. Fussell, S. G., et al.: (2019). Usability testing of a virtual reality tutorial. Proceedings of the Human Factors and Ergonomics Society Annual Meeting, 63(1), 2303–2307. doi:https://doi.org/10.1177/1071181319631494
32. Mustafa, B.: Using 3D animation and virtual reality in educations. Technium Soc. Sci. J. **27**, 269–289 (2022). https://doi.org/10.47577/tssj.v27i1.5393
33. Wang, M., Tong, J., Lu, H.: Digital Twin technology of metaverse based on game engine in the campus application scenarios. Acad. J. Eng. Technol. Sci. **7**(2) (2024). https://doi.org/10.25236/AJETS.2024.070223
34. Naim, M.K., Hua, D.T.K.: Metaverse in language learning on communicative competencies-mini review. (2024)
35. Creswell, J.W., Creswell, J.D.: Research design: qualitative. In: Quantitative, and Mixed Methods Approaches, 5th edn. SAGE (2018)
36. Sansores, S.A.: El sentido de autoeficacia en el aprendizaje del inglés de estudiantes de secundaria pública. Universidad de Quintana Roo (2018)

37. Tschannen-Moran, M., Woolfolk-Hoy, A.: Teacher efficacy: capturing and elusive construct. Teach. Teach. Educ. **17**, 783–805 (2021)
38. English, C.: Cambridge English: Preliminary (B1 Preliminary / PET). Cambridge University Press (2016)
39. Stanney, K. et al.: Identifying causes of and solutions for cybersickness in immersive technology: reformulation of a research and development agenda. Int. J. Hum.-Comput. Interact. **36**(19), 1783–1803 (2020). https://doi.org/10.1080/10447318.2020.1828535

What is Happening to Critical Thinking in University Students in the Era of Artificial Intelligence?

Leonardo Saavedra[1,2(✉)], Carlos Alberto Peláez[1], Andrés Solano[1], Rodrigo J. Ocampo G.[1], and David F. Ramirez-Moreno[1]

[1] Universidad Autónoma de Occidente, Cali, Colombia
{lsaavedra,capa,afsolano,rocampo,dramirez}@uao.edu.co
[2] Universitat Politècnica de Catalunya, Barcelona, Spain

Abstract. Innovation is essential in higher education to equip professionals with the skills needed to advance the democratization of artificial intelligence. Building on this premise, we conduct a comparative study examining the impact of education mediated by Generative Artificial Intelligence (GenAI) versus traditional approaches, with critical thinking competence at its core. This article reviews the state of the art on GenAI mediated training processes and their influence on critical thinking. The review was conducted between September and December 2024, yielding 161 initial results. After applying the inclusion and exclusion criteria, 23 documents relevant to the research questions were identified. Our findings suggest that integrating GenAI into teaching, evaluation, and other academic practices is crucial for delivering effective learning experiences that enhance students' critical thinking skills. GenAI can enhance critical thinking through structured frameworks and real-time feedback, but it requires strategic pedagogical integration to avoid technological dependence. The teacher's role is fundamental as a cognitive facilitator, guiding students toward independent reasoning while promoting critical AI literacy.

Keywords: Higher education · generative artificial intelligence · critical thinking

1 Introduction

Artificial Intelligence (AI) is radically transforming how information is accessed and knowledge is produced [1]. AI-based tools now generate text, images, and other content with a level of sophistication that once required expert human intervention [2]. However, the democratization of this technology poses unique challenges for higher education, particularly in cultivating critical thinking (CT) skills among college students [3].

The proliferation of AI-generated content increases the risk of spreading misinformation and bias. Without strong CT skills, students may accept and disseminate information without questioning its veracity or source [4]. CT is crucial for evaluating information quality, accuracy, and reliability, enabling students to distinguish between

H. Luna-García et al. (Eds.): HCI-COLLAB 2025, CCIS 2850, pp. 337–351, 2027.
https://doi.org/10.1007/978-3-032-31223-5_23

content based on solid academic and scientific foundations and material that is inaccurate, misleading, or deceptive [5]. Moreover, Generative Artificial Intelligence (GenAI) can facilitate dishonest academic practices, such as unintentional plagiarism or an overreliance on automated sources [6]. Therefore, developing CT skills reinforces academic integrity and promotes AI tools' ethical, responsible use.

Pedagogically, fostering CT empowers students to become autonomous and adaptive learners, elevating independent study's significance within their educational journey [7]. In an era where knowledge and technology evolve rapidly, the ability to analyze, synthesize, and evaluate information is more valuable than memorizing static content [8]. CT competencies prepare students to tackle complex problems, spur innovation, and actively contribute to advancing their disciplines.

At a societal level, graduates with CT skills are better prepared to engage in informed debates and make decisions that positively impact society [9]. Higher education, therefore, is responsible for cultivating citizens capable of navigating and constructively influencing an increasingly complex world.

Based on the above, this article reviews the state of the art on the impact of CT on GenAI-mediated training processes as part of an institutional project comparing traditional face-to-face educational models. The findings indicate that higher education must evolve by integrating GenAI to create effective learning experiences that bolster CT skills. Addressing CT development is necessary and imperative in today's university education, ensuring students are prepared for an interconnected world dominated by emerging technologies. Failure to do so could widen the global digital divide between populations in highly industrialized and emerging economies and hinder the preparation of future university graduates.

This paper comprises six sections: the introduction, the background, the research methodology, the analysis of results, the discussion, and the references.

2 Background

A universal definition of critical thinking (CT) is lacking. As a complex concept, CT has been described as an attitude, a logical process, purposeful reflection, and a developmental journey. Glaser [10] introduced CT as an attitude coupled with the rational application of skills in problem-solving, while Ennis [11] emphasized its logical, product-oriented nature, such as correctly evaluating statements. Other authors [12–15] view CT as a process of rational, purposeful reflection, and subsequent research [16] has highlighted that CT skills also depend on an individual's predispositions.

This multidimensional concept involves the ability to analyze, evaluate, infer, synthesize, and explain information and autonomously regulate one's thinking [17–20]. Although defining CT for university students remains a debated topic, educators and employers agree that college graduates often lack adequate CT skills. The complexity of CT compounds this challenge; its specific components tend to vary across disciplines, leading to discipline-specific definitions and operationalizations in higher education [21].

Lai [22] proposed that CT definitions should be categorized by the author's field of study, identifying three primary psychological, philosophical, and educational approaches. Psychological definitions focus on cognitive skills, emphasizing the mental activities involved in CT. For example, [23] defines CT as "a metacognitive process that, through reflective and intentional judgment, increases the chances of producing a logical conclusion to an argument or a solution to a problem."

In the educational realm, CT is often equated with higher-order thinking, as outlined in Bloom's taxonomy [24]. In this framework, cognitive skills are classified by complexity, with higher-order thinking encompassing analysis, synthesis, and evaluation.

Experts agree that CT comprises both skills and dispositions. The skills involve analyzing and evaluating arguments and applying methodological, statistical, and causal reasoning. Dispositions refer to the willingness to engage in effortful thinking, being open and fair-minded when evaluating claims, and remaining skeptical of unsubstantiated assertions. Assessing both is crucial, as possessing the skills without the corresponding disposition (or vice versa) may hinder effective critical thinking [25].

Successful KT requires cognitive ability and the interest and willingness to engage in reflective, embodied, and emotional processes [26]. It is insufficient to question; one must be fully committed to the inquiry process. This perspective aligns with UNESCO guidelines [3], emphasizing the importance of inclusive and sustainable AI in enhancing human capabilities. The Application and Strategic Thinking level builds on this foundation by encouraging students to apply knowledge reflectively, consider multiple variables, and anticipate future scenarios, preparing them to collaborate with GenAI to design informed solutions aligned with sustainability goals and long-term vision. Furthermore, the Creativity, Innovation, Lifelong Learning, and Adaptability levels stress the need for flexible minds capable of envisioning possibilities and making visionary connections. Together, these competencies complement analytical skills and foster continuous learning, empowering students to become agents of change in a dynamic global environment. Several pedagogical strategies have been proposed to cultivate CT:

- Problem-Based Learning (PBL): Encourages students to tackle complex problems and promotes the analysis and synthesis of information [18].
- Structured Debates and Discussions Allow students to explore and defend diverse viewpoints, enhancing argumentation and critical evaluation [27].
- Direct Instruction in CT Skills: Involves dedicated sessions on identifying fallacies, analyzing arguments, and evaluating sources [17].
- Reflective Tasks and Self-Assessments: Foster metacognition by helping students identify strengths and areas for improvement in their reasoning [28].
- Use of Technologies and Simulations: Integrates digital tools and generative AI to create dynamic learning environments that offer immediate feedback and simulate real-life scenarios [29].

These strategies can be adapted within curricula to foster critical thinking effectively.

3 Research Methodology

This study employed a systematic literature review, adhering to the guidelines established in [30] and utilizing the PRISMA framework [31]. It examines key findings on the impact and challenges of critical thinking (CT) within GenAI-mediated training processes in higher education.

The methodology was structured around three main components: defining research questions, establishing inclusion and exclusion criteria for the literature, and designing comprehensive search protocols.

3.1 Research Questions

Table 1 presents the research questions that define the scope of this systematic review.

Table 1. Research questions.

Code	Question	Motivation
RQ1	What is the impact of GenAI-mediated learning on critical thinking compared to the effects of traditional educational models in a face-to-face environment?	It is important to investigate whether AI improves students' assessment, autonomy, and reasoning or limits the development of critical thinking. Comparing these approaches will enable the design of educational strategies that enhance AI's ethical and reflective use without compromising the capacity for analysis and informed decision-making.
RQ2	How should higher education processes evolve by including GenAI to enable satisfactory learning experiences that enhance critical thinking in students?	It is essential to redefine pedagogical strategies so that AI does not replace human reasoning but amplifies it. This requires an educational design that balances automation with reflection to ensure students develop intellectual autonomy and critical skills in digital environments.

Source: Authors' own work.

3.2 Information Resources and Search Strategies

Search protocols were established to explore articles and book chapters across various databases that address the research questions outlined in the previous section. These databases were chosen for their relevance to GenAI research and its role in critical thinking within higher education. Table 2 lists the primary search terms used to develop these protocols.

Table 2. Research protocols.

Databases	Sentences
ScienceDirect	"critical thinking" AND "higher education" AND "constructs" AND "artificial intelligence" "artificial intelligence generative" AND "higher education" AND "thinking skills"
Springer	"Artificial Intelligence" AND ("Education" OR "Learning" OR "Teaching") AND "Higher Education" AND "Critical Thinking" "Generative Artificial Intelligence" AND ("Education" OR "University" OR "Pedagogy") AND "thinking skills"
Taylor & Francis	"Education" AND "Artificial Intelligence" AND "Critical Thinking"
IEEE	"generative artificial intelligence" AND "critical thinking" AND "higher education" AND "assessment" AND "learning outcomes" AND "education

Source: Authors' own work.

3.3 Inclusion and Exclusion Criteria

A set of inclusion and exclusion criteria was defined for the selection and classification of the articles chosen for the systematic review study. These criteria can be reviewed in Table 3.

Table 3. Inclusion and exclusion criteria.

Inclusion Criterion	Exclusion Criterion
IC1: Studies focused on GenAI in education	EC1: The document is not available for download
IC2: Studies written between 2020 and 2024	EC2: Published before 2020
IC3: English language	EC3: GenAI in education is not the main focus
IC4: Primary research (books, papers, thesis)	EC4: Not in English
	EC5: Not primary research (report, letter, poster)

Source: Authors' own work.

3.4 Data Recovery

A Microsoft Excel template was used to record the retrieved data, ensuring efficient organization and effective collaboration throughout the review process. After applying the search protocols and inclusion/exclusion criteria, the results were initially sorted by the database consulted. For each article, the following details were recorded: (a) the search protocol used, (b) publication title, (c) authors, (d) year of publication, (e) source (e.g., journal, conference paper), (f) abstract, (g) DOI/ISBN/ISSN, and (h) a brief analysis of the source.

The review was conducted between September and December 2024, yielding 161 initial results. After applying the inclusion and exclusion criteria, 23 documents relevant to the research questions were identified. Table 4 summarizes the outcomes of this methodology.

Table 4. Results Summary.

Database	Search results	Relevant documents
ScienceDirect	99	12
Springer	25	2
IEEE	27	7
Taylor & Francis	10	2
Total	161	23

Source: Authors' own work.

4 Results Analysis

Reference [32] proposed a framework to enhance students' critical thinking (CT) in synthesizing AI-generated information. Grounded in cognitive psychology, education, and interdisciplinary thinking, the framework integrates Bloom's taxonomy, Paul and Elder's metacognitive model [33], and Shanto's ChatGPT-based approach [34]. It identifies CT skills, analysis, interpretation, inference, evaluation, explanation, and self-regulation, organized into five interconnected phases: familiarization, conceptualization, inquiry, evaluation, and synthesis. The study demonstrates that progressing from lower-order to higher-order thinking enhances clarity, depth, integration of perspectives, and coherent argumentation. This framework thus serves as a key reference for evolving higher education processes to incorporate GenAI in ways that foster CT.

In [34], the authors developed and evaluated AI-CRITIQUE (AI-based Critical Reflection and Insightful Thought Unleashed for Education). This conceptual framework leverages ChatGPT to promote CT skills in higher education. Despite calling for further research, the framework offers a promising approach by outlining seven key activities: (1) identifying learning objectives, (2) selecting appropriate GenAI tools, (3) formulating specific questions, (4) generating ideas and perspectives, (5) evaluating and analyzing, (6) synthesizing information, and (7) reflecting on learning. Preliminary evidence indicates that students' cognitive levels shifted from mere recall to more meaningful rationalization, as assessed by the levels of the thinking model [35]. Although this study does not compare traditional educational models, it offers an interesting approach to understanding the impact at the CT level of GenAI-mediated training processes.

Reference [36] conducted a literature review to map both the opportunities and challenges of AI in education. The authors classified AI's functions in student learning into four categories: (1) assigning tasks based on individual competence, (2) facilitating human-machine conversations, (3) analyzing student work for feedback, and (4) enhancing adaptability and interactivity in digital environments. In teaching, AI supports adaptive strategies, augments teachers' capabilities, and aids professional development; in assessment, it provides automatic grading and performance prediction; and in management, it improves platforms, personalizes services, and supports evidence-based decision-making. The review also categorizes student outcomes, motivation, academic performance, 21st-century skills, and non-cognitive aspects. It raises ethical concerns (e.g., plagiarism, privacy, biases) while warning that overreliance on GenAI may undermine core cognitive skills. This review highlights the opportunities and challenges of AI in education and provides recommendations for future research across educational domains and learning outcomes.

In [37], the authors identify challenges for AI in education, such as a lack of personalized learning resources, inadequate data for predictive models, disconnects between AI technologies and teaching practices, and the risk of widening the digital divide. They also note limited teacher knowledge, negative attitudes toward AI, and insufficient research on its socio-emotional impacts. Considering this study, a series of challenges remain to be addressed in the short term.

Collectively, the studies reviewed present two complementary perspectives: one set proposes frameworks aimed at enhancing CT in GenAI-mediated education, while another highlights the risks and challenges associated with its use. These works underscore the importance of interdisciplinary collaboration and teacher training to integrate AI effectively into university evaluation processes [38]. Moreover, findings indicate that while AI can support CT, certain human capacities remain irreplaceable, such as cultural sensitivity, resilience, and socio-emotional learning [39].

Reference [40] emphasizes the positive impact of promoting AI literacy among teachers, advocating for comprehensive AI education in teacher training programs. It argues that mere exposure to GenAI tools is insufficient; educators must develop a creative and ethical mindset to integrate these technologies effectively in classroom activities. AI literacy curricula should extend beyond technical knowledge to include ethical considerations and responsible use, ensuring that teachers remain proficient and ethically grounded as higher education evolves. This study demonstrates the need to develop higher education processes by incorporating GenAI, building on a solid foundation of AI literacy among educators as architects of educational systems.

In [41], the role and implications of ChatGPT and GenAI in higher education are explored. The study stresses that empowering GenAI requires collaborative efforts among stakeholders to address emerging challenges in curriculum, assessment, technology, and governance. By fostering CT, students are encouraged to critically question and analyze AI-generated content, recognize biases, and make informed decisions, ultimately preparing them for a GenAI-driven future. This study highlights the need to evolve higher education processes by incorporating GenAI to enable successful learning experiences that enhance CT.

Darwin et al. [42] investigated the use of AI for achieving language proficiency (English as a foreign language) and its impact on CT. They found that while AI can enhance CT through activities like literature review, data analysis, and experimental design, students also expressed concerns over issues such as limited personalization, echo chambers, reliability, and the handling of nuanced information. Reference [43] applies Critical Discourse Studies to assess AI's broader impact on higher education. It considers issues of intellectual property, social impact, and language use. It stresses the need for critical evaluation to address historical inequalities embedded in training data, promoting equity and inclusion.

In [44], the authors demonstrated that AI could implement five evidence-based teaching strategies, using multiple examples, varied explanations, diagnosing misconceptions, distributed practice, and low-stakes testing, to enhance lesson effectiveness and student learning. AI tools, particularly large language models, can assist in generating instructional materials and providing feedback, thereby augmenting teacher capacity without replacing the essential human elements of teaching. It is clear that as AI continues to develop, researchers and educators will need to consider both the benefits and limitations of using AI for educational purposes and develop guidelines for its ethical and effective use.

Reference [45] stresses the urgency of evaluating AI's potential to bolster ethics, creativity, and CT in higher education while identifying its possible negative impacts. The study highlights that low student participation in digitally supported classes and AI-based grading, which may favor rote reproduction over innovative ideas, underscore the importance of courses that stimulate intellectual and creative engagement supported by active teacher involvement.

In [46], findings indicate that integrating AI tools into human-centered teaching strategies can foster students' ability to evaluate and employ AI effectively and critically. The authors offer recommendations in three areas: (1) teaching strategies (e.g., multimodal AI tools and agile environments), (2) reflective learning (emphasizing collaborative and reflective practices), and (3) ethical and critical engagement (balancing AI and human input with ethical considerations). This study emphasizes the need to integrate comprehensive AI education into the curriculum to ensure that the next generation of students has the knowledge, skills, and ethical framework to leverage AI responsibly and innovatively.

A study [47] examined the effects of explicit training on using GenAI tools in language teaching, revealing substantial impacts on curricula, learning activities, and assessment. However, it also noted the absence of a dedicated competency framework addressing contemporary trends. In conjunction with findings from [48, 49], these studies stress the need to enhance teacher training so educators can integrate GenAI effectively inside and outside the classroom.

Reference [50] highlights that GenAI's influence on learning outcomes, pedagogy, and assessment is critical for workforce advancement. Based on students' perspectives, the study argues for transforming higher education to prepare learners for a GenAI-driven society. It introduces new learning outcomes, such as AI literacy and interdisciplinary creative learning, and recommends future research on workforce competencies, self-assessment measures, and innovative pedagogies. The study also identifies key educational domains (education, teaching, assessment, and administration) and outlines benefits, including increased motivation [51], improved academic performance [52], enhanced collaborative and self-regulated skills [53], and strengthened non-cognitive aspects [54]. These results invite questioning and reflection on the skills that future professionals should foster and suggest a detailed study of the new learning outcomes necessary for higher education, such as AI literacy.

Hashmi and Bal [55] explored transparency and accountability using GenAI, proposing a framework that educates students on responsible AI use. Their roadmap encourages the integration of AI tools into teaching rather than imposing bans, recommending curriculum expansion to include AI skills training alongside ethics and fundamentals. This framework lays the foundation for evolving higher education processes to prepare students for an AI-dominant future. This article lays a foundation for evolving higher education processes by incorporating GenAI to enable successful student learning experiences.

Essien et al. [56] used Bloom's taxonomy (remember, understand, apply, analyze, evaluate, create) to assess CT development via AI text generators. Their study, which examined potential, challenges, and benefits, highlighted key issues such as reliability, ethical concerns, digital literacy, and bias. While ChatGPT supported understanding and application, progress at the highest level and creation remained limited. The findings underscore the importance of teacher guidance in the ethical use of AI and call for further research on diverse competency frameworks.

Moorhouse et al. [57] redesigned tasks and assessments in light of GenAI's capabilities, recommending that assessments foster creativity and CT by incorporating contextual elements, authenticity, and alternative knowledge representations. Similarly, Liu and Pásztor [58] found that while Problem-Based Learning generally promotes CT, further research is needed to evaluate its effectiveness across various educational contexts. Together, these studies support integrating GenAI into higher education to strengthen CT.

Michel-Villarreal et al. [59] examined GenAI's classroom integration through questions posed to ChatGPT regarding its challenges and opportunities. Their findings suggest that ChatGPT can effectively facilitate feedback, tutoring, and debate, reinforcing the need for empirical research into practices that maximize GenAI's benefits while understanding user experiences. Sedlbauer et al. [60] provided evidence that ChatGPT can improve students' CT by enhancing their ability to analyze, detect errors, and engage in discussions. They also noted that GenAI's impact extends to socio-emotional dimensions, which can both support and challenge personal integrity and stability.

Gammoh [61] discussed the challenges of incorporating GenAI tools, such as ChatGPT. Teachers expressed concerns that these technologies might compromise fundamental CT skills and foster dependency, reducing active, autonomous participation. To counter these risks, the study recommends revising assessment strategies to include discussions, presentations, and group projects while maintaining essential human elements like emotional interaction and personalized support. It also calls for robust detection tools and an ethical framework to manage GenAI's integration.

Bond et al. [62] emphasize the importance of collaborative research in AI in higher education, highlighting CT's role in its effective application. Their recommendations include developing adaptive learning systems, integrating interdisciplinary approaches, creating automated assessments with personalized feedback, and implementing intelligent tutoring systems. They argue that educational tasks should transcend memorization, providing spaces for critical analysis. They also call for further research on how these tools affect skills such as informed speculation and evidence-based reasoning.

Ruiz-Rojas et al. [63] evaluated CT development from university students' perspectives using tools like ChatGPT, You.com, and Chat PDF. Their findings suggest that GenAI can enhance CT and collaborative work if students are motivated to question and explore solutions. However, the study also highlights risks such as algorithmic biases, data privacy issues, and ethical concerns, emphasizing the need for training in the critical use of AI and examining its impact on didactics and micro-curricular activities.

Thiga [64] explored GenAI's dual role in CT development, proposing that it should be used as an assistant, not a teacher replacement, to encourage critical analysis of its outputs. She recommends implementing systematic questioning strategies (focusing on veracity, logic, and ethics), designing collaborative learning experiences, and prioritizing assessments that foster informed judgment and self-regulation. Thiga calls for further research on balancing GenAI's ease of use with the preservation of ethical and logical reasoning skills, offering an initial framework for ethically integrating GenAI into higher education.

Finally, AlAfnan [65] presented an educational taxonomy and framework designed to prepare students for the ethical, analytical, and adaptive challenges posed by the information age and GenAI. His model stresses the need for students to critically evaluate AI-generated responses based on truthfulness, integrity, and ethics. Building from foundational Knowledge and Understanding to higher levels of Synthesis and Evaluation, the framework emphasizes discerning source relevance. It incorporates ethical and moral reasoning to promote responsibility, respect, and fairness in decision-making. This comprehensive framework offers a robust response to current challenges, empowering students with the tools they need to lead ethically, critically, and creatively in the age of IA.

These studies provide a comprehensive panorama of how GenAI impacts CT and higher education. They propose frameworks and pedagogical strategies to enhance CT and address the challenges and ethical considerations necessary for integrating GenAI effectively, underscoring the need for ongoing interdisciplinary collaboration, rigorous research, and innovative teacher training programs.

5 Discussion

Based on the state-of-the-art findings for the first research question (RQ1), GenAI-mediated formative processes offer significant advantages for developing critical thinking (CT) skills, albeit with inherent challenges. Frameworks such as AI-CRITIQUE [31, 33] demonstrate that GenAI can enhance advanced CT abilities, analysis, synthesis, and evaluation through structured activities like formulating specific questions, evaluating AI responses, and engaging in metacognitive reflection. While traditional educational models have emphasized inquiry communities, classroom debates, project work, and case analysis, exploring additional opportunities that foster reflective and critical judgment skills is imperative.

Regarding limitations, [58] notes that GenAI can foster dependency if not used strategically, potentially reducing students' cognitive autonomy. Moreover, biases in AI-generated content underscore the importance of critical AI literacy. Traditional models offer direct human interaction that nurtures empathy and interpersonal collaboration, qualities that may be less evident in GenAI-mediated environments. Thus, assessing GenAI's impact on both cognitive and emotional development is essential.

Integrating GenAI into higher education creates opportunities to enhance CT by generating simulated environments and providing real-time feedback [28]. This technology complements traditional pedagogical strategies and promotes deep, reflective learning; however, it must be accompanied by methodologies that balance skill development to prevent overdependence on technology. Empirical studies such as [33, 35] indicate that students using GenAI-based frameworks progress from memory-based thinking to more rational, reflective approaches, outperforming traditional environments. Yet, limitations remain regarding developing originality and creativity [45, 56]. To counter this, tasks should include debates, group projects, and problem-solving exercises encouraging active interaction with GenAI tools [37] and activities promoting abstraction, idea expression, and spontaneous creativity. Additionally, there is a need for CT processes among decision-makers in the implementation and use of GenAI in education.

For the second research question (RQ2), it is essential to reconfigure the teacher's role. Teachers must be trained in using GenAI to ensure ethical, effective integration that promotes creativity and constructive criticism [33, 37]. Moreover, curriculum design should integrate competencies related to the critical use of GenAI, such as bias assessment, ethical reasoning, and transferring knowledge to new contexts [54, 64]. Multiple studies highlight that the teacher's role is strategic in this GenAI era; without sufficient support and guidance, students risk becoming overly dependent on technology, which could undermine their CT abilities. Teachers must be valued as subject matter experts and facilitators of cognitive development, guiding students to develop independent and critical reasoning skills.

Reflective processes should also be promoted in students, encouraging them to question and validate GenAI-generated information, thereby strengthening their intellectual autonomy [40, 62]. Educational plans should incorporate modules on ethics and responsible AI use to address concerns such as algorithmic biases and data privacy [63]. As AI becomes more integrated into decision-making processes, understanding its ethical implications will be critical for future professionals.

In summary, incorporating GenAI into higher education requires a pedagogical approach that places CT at its core by:

- Designing authentic tasks that foster creativity, ethical inquiry, and problem-solving;
- Strengthening AI literacy so that both students and teachers can critically assess the limitations, biases, and potentials of generative tools;
- Create AI assistants that promote the development of students' CT skills rather than simply providing answers to questions and
- Promoting metacognitive reflection to help students identify and question the implicit assumptions in AI-generated content, with critical discourse analysis as a transversal tool [43].

In the short term, it is important to create AI assistants that are as similar as possible to digital tutors who answer students' questions and ask them questions to help them think better. To do so, teachers must configure their assistant's purpose, specify behavioral instructions (for example, a Socratic questioning approach or a Hegelian dialectic approach), and provide the response format, warnings, and restrictions. Teachers should consider user experience (UX) design guidelines for GenAI-based systems and recommendations for their applications [66].

While GenAI tools have significant potential to enhance CT skills compared to traditional educational models, their strategic and responsible implementation is crucial. Addressing challenges such as defining specific CT skills and dispositions, establishing concrete guidelines for CT teaching and assessment, and clearly outlining performance levels for CT in future workplaces remains imperative.

Finally, a critical question that permeates and frames the objectives of this review concerns the disquieting possibility confronting the roles of professors, tutors, and mentors: Might GenAI technologies supplant them in certain formative processes within higher education?

From a strictly logical perspective, some scholars posit that such a replacement is feasible shortly [67]. The development and deployment of AI-based assistants, endowed with the capacities for dialectical or Socratic engagement with users —particularly university students—could, in theory, achieve the expected outcomes associated with CT without necessitating the intervention or accompaniment of a human educator, tutor, or mentor. Scholars argue that AI assistants, through structured dialogues, can foster logic and rationality in students at a level comparable to or even exceeding human instructors, as current language models already support high-quality, rational discourse across diverse topics and disciplines.

However, from a broader and interdisciplinary standpoint—encompassing developmental psychology, cognitive psychology, and neuroscience—other scholars highlight the profound disruptions and deficits that would likely ensue from the complete exclusion of human educators at any stage of the university learning process [68]. According to this view, the consolidation and affirmation of CT necessarily involve interactions with human agents who, in face-to-face engagements, enact the full spectrum of emotional experiences, such as surprise, wonder, and uncertainty.

This review adopts an optimistic stance regarding the concern above [69]. It envisions a future wherein collaborative engagement among human mentors, students, and AI assistants will foster the emergence of *collaborative intelligence*. In such a model, triadic conversations —involving human tutors, students, and non-organic AI agents— will synergistically expand human action, learning, and development possibilities.

References

1. Collie, R.J., Martin, A.J.: Teachers' motivation and engagement to harness generative AI for teaching and learning: the role of contextual, occupational, and background factors. Comput. Educ.: Artif. Intell. **6**, 100224 (2024)
2. The AI community building the future. (n.d.). https://huggingface.co/
3. UNESCO. Critical thinking and generative artificial intelligence. https://www.ibe.unesco.org/en/articles/critical-thinking-and-generative-artificial-intelligence. (2024)
4. Lim, W.M., Gunasekara, A., Pallant, J.L., Pallant, J.I., Pechenkina, E.: Generative AI and the future of education: ragnarök or reformation? A paradoxical perspective from management educators. Int. J. Manag. Educ. **21**(2), 100790 (2023)

5. Song, Y., Roohr, K.C., Kirova, D.: Exploring approaches for developing and evaluating workplace critical thinking skills. Think. Skills Creat. **51**, 101460 (2024)
6. Zhai, X.: ChatGPT user experience: implications for education. SSRN, 4312418 (2022)
7. Cáceres, M., Nussbaum, M., Ortiz, J.: Integrating critical thinking into the classroom: a teacher's perspective. Think. Skills Creat. **37**, 100674 (2020)
8. Van Le, H., Chong, S.L.: The dynamics of critical thinking skills: a phenomenographic exploration from Malaysian and Vietnamese undergraduates. Think. Skills Creat. **51**, 101445 (2024)
9. Geng, X., Zhan, Y., You, H., Zhao, L.: Exploring the characteristics of undergraduates' critical thinking development in peer interaction via epistemic network analysis. Think. Skills Creat. **52**, 101553 (2024)
10. Glaser, E.M.: An experiment in development of critical thinking. Teach. Coll. Rec. **43**(5), 1–18 (1942)
11. Ennis, R.H.: A logical basis for measuring critical thinking skills. Educ. Leadersh. **43**(2), 44–48 (1985)
12. Brookfield, S.D.: Developing Critical Thinkers: Challenging Adults to Explore Alternative Ways of Thinking and Acting. Jossey-Bass (1987)
13. Ennis, R.H.: Critical thinking and subject specificity: clarification and needed research. Educ. Res. **18**(3), 4–10 (1989)
14. Paul, R.: Critical thinking: what every person needs to survive in a changing world. NASSP Bull. **75**(533), 120–122 (1991)
15. Sternberg, R.J.: Thinking styles: keys to understanding student performance. Phi Delta Kappan. **71**(5), 366–371 (1990)
16. Facione, P.: Critical Thinking: A Statement of Expert Consensus for Purposes of Educational Assessment and Instruction (The Delphi Report) (1990)
17. Halpern, D.F.: Teaching critical thinking for transfer across domains. Am. Psychol. **53**(4), 449–455 (1998)
18. Hmelo-Silver, C.E.: Problem-based learning: what and how do students learn? Educ. Psychol. Rev. **16**(3), 235–266 (2004)
19. Lipman, M.: Thinking in Education, 2nd edn. Cambridge University Press (2003)
20. Bouckaert, M.: The assessment of students' creative and critical thinking skills in higher education across OECD countries: a review of policies and related practices. OECD Education Working Papers, 293 (2023)
21. Jacobs, P.M., Ott, B., Sullivan, B., Ulrich, Y., Short, L.: An approach to defining and operationalizing critical thinking. J. Nurs. Educ. **36**(1), 19–22 (1997)
22. Lai, E.R.: Critical thinking: a literature review. Pearson's Res. Rep. **6**(1), 40–41 (2011)
23. Dwyer, C.P., Hogan, M.J., Stewart, I.: An integrated critical thinking framework for the 21st century. Think. Skills Creat. **12**, 43–52 (2014)
24. Anderson, L.W., Krathwohl, D.R.: A Taxonomy for Learning, Teaching, and Assessing: A Revision of Bloom's Taxonomy of Educational Objectives. Addison Wesley Longman (2001)
25. Bensley, D.A., Murtagh, M.P.: Guidelines for a scientific approach to critical thinking assessment. Teach. Psychol. **39**(1), 5–16 (2012)
26. Lindebaum, D., Fleming, P.: ChatGPT undermines human reflexivity, scientific responsibility and responsible management research. Br. J. Manag. **35**(2), 566–575 (2024)
27. Kennedy, R.: In-class debates: fertile ground for active learning and the cultivation of critical thinking and oral communication skills. Int. J. Teach. Learn. High. Educ. **19**(2), 183–190 (2007)
28. Rivas, S.F., Saiz, C., Ossa, C.: Metacognitive strategies and development of critical thinking in higher education. Front. Psychol. **13**, 913219 (2022)
29. Mao, J., Chen, B., Liu, J.C.: Generative artificial intelligence in education and its implications for assessment. TechTrends. **68**, 58–66 (2024)

30. Kitchenham, B., Charters, S.: Guidelines for performing systematic literature reviews in software engineering. Technical Report EBSE-2007-01, School of Computer Science and Mathematics, Keele University, and Department of Computer Science, University of Durham, UK (2007)
31. Page, M.J., McKenzie, J.E., Bossuyt, P.M., Boutron, I., Hoffmann, T.C., Moher, D.: The PRISMA 2020 statement: an updated guideline for reporting systematic reviews. Int. J. Surg. **88**, 105906 (2021)
32. Yusuf, A., Bello, S., Pervin, N., Tukur, A.K.: Implementing a proposed framework for enhancing critical thinking skills in synthesizing AI-generated texts. Think. Skills Creat. **53**, 101619 (2024)
33. Paul, R., Elder, L.: The Miniature Guide to Critical Thinking Concepts and Tools. Rowman & Littlefield (2019)
34. Shanto, S.S., Ahmed, Z., Jony, A.I.: Enriching learning process with generative AI: a proposed framework to cultivate critical thinking in higher education using ChatGPT. Tuijin Jishu J. Propuls. Technol. **45**(1), 3019–3029 (2024)
35. Lee, H., Jeon, J., Lee, H.: Development of framework and rubric for measuring students' level of systems thinking. J. Korean Assoc. Sci. Educ. **38**(3), 355–367 (2018)
36. Zhai, C., Wibowo, S., Li, L.D.: The effects of over-reliance on AI dialogue systems on students' cognitive abilities: a systematic review. Smart Learn. Environ. **11**(1), 28 (2024)
37. Chiu, T.K., Xia, Q., Zhou, X., Chai, C.S., Cheng, M.: Systematic literature review on opportunities, challenges, and future research recommendations of artificial intelligence in education. Comput. Educ. Artif. Intell. **4**, 100118 (2023)
38. Xia, Q., Weng, X., Ouyang, F., Lin, T.J., Chiu, T.K.F.: A scoping review on how generative artificial intelligence transforms assessment in higher education. Int. J. Educ. Technol. High. Educ. **21**(1), 40 (2024)
39. Chan, C.K.Y., Tsi, L.H.Y.: Will generative AI replace teachers in higher education? a study of teacher and student perceptions. Stud. Educ. Eval. **83**, 101395 (2024)
40. Ayanwale, M.A., Adelana, O.P., Molefi, R.R., Adeeko, O., Ishola, A.M.: Examining artificial intelligence literacy among pre-service teachers for future classrooms. Comput. Educ. Open. **6**, 100179 (2024)
41. Dai, Y., Liu, A., Lim, C.P.: Reconceptualizing ChatGPT and generative AI as a student-driven innovation in higher education. Procedia CIRP. **119**, 84–90 (2023)
42. Darwin, D.R., Nur, M., Nunung, S., Ekaning, D.L.: Marzuki: critical thinking in the AI era: an exploration of EFL students' perceptions, benefits, and limitations. Cogent Educ. **11**(1), 2290342 (2024)
43. Gillings, M., Kohn, T., Mautner, G.: The rise of large language models: challenges for critical discourse studies. Crit. Discourse Stud. **22**(6), 625–641 (2024)
44. Mollick, E.R., Mollick, L.: Using AI to implement effective teaching strategies in classrooms: five strategies, including prompts. The Wharton School Research Paper, University of Pennsylvania. (2023).
45. Ivanov, S.: The dark side of artificial intelligence in higher education. Serv. Ind. J. **43**(15–16), 1055–1082 (2023)
46. Tzirides, A.O.O., et al.: Combining human and artificial intelligence for enhanced AI literacy in higher education. Comput. Educ. Open. **6**, 100184 (2024)
47. Moorhouse, B.L., et al.: Developing language teachers' professional generative AI competence. Syst. **125**, 103399 (2024)
48. Starkey, L., Yates, A.: Do digital competence frameworks align with preparing beginning teachers for digitally infused contexts? Eur. J. Teach. Educ. **45**(4), 476–492 (2022)
49. Gisbert Cervera, M., Caena, F.: Teachers' digital competence for global teacher education. Eur. J. Teach. Educ. **45**(4), 451–455 (2022)

50. Chiu, T.K.: Future research recommendations for transforming higher education with generative AI. Comput. Educ. Artif. Intell. **6**, 100197 (2024)
51. Xia, Q., Chiu, T.K., Lee, M., Sanusi, I.T., Dai, Y., Chai, C.S.: A self-determination theory (SDT) design approach for inclusive and diverse artificial intelligence (AI) education. Comput. Educ. **189**, 104582 (2022)
52. Khan, I., Ahmad, A.R., Jabeur, N., Mahdi, M.N.: An artificial intelligence approach to monitor student performance and devise preventive measures. Smart Learn. Environ. **8**, 1–18 (2021)
53. Porter, B., Grippa, F.: A platform for AI-enabled real-time feedback to promote digital collaboration. Sustainability. **12**(24), 10243 (2020)
54. Kim, H.S.: Is it beneficial to use AI chatbots to improve learners' speaking performance? J. Asia TEFL. **18**(1), 161–178 (2021)
55. Hashmi, N., Bal, A.S.: Generative AI in higher education and beyond. Bus. Horiz. **67**(5), 607–614 (2024)
56. Essien, A., Bukoye, O.T., O'Dea, X., Kremantzis, M.: The influence of AI text generators on critical thinking skills in UK business schools. Stud. High. Educ. **49**(5), 865–882 (2024)
57. Moorhouse, B.L., Yeo, M.A., Wan, Y.: Generative AI tools and assessment: guidelines of the world's top-ranking universities. Comput. Educ. Open. **5**, 100151 (2023)
58. Liu, Y., Pásztor, A.: Effects of problem-based learning instructional intervention on critical thinking in higher education: A meta-analysis. Think. Skills Creat. **45**, 101069 (2022)
59. Michel-Villarreal, R., Vilalta-Perdomo, E., Salinas-Navarro, D.E., Thierry-Aguilera, R., Gerardou, F.S.: Challenges and opportunities of generative AI for higher education as explained by ChatGPT. Educ. Sci. **13**(9), 856 (2023)
60. Sedlbauer, J., Cincera, J., Slavík, M., Hartlová, A.: Students' reflections on their experience with ChatGPT. J. Comput. Assist. Learn. **40**(4), 1526–1534 (2024)
61. Gammoh, L.A.: ChatGPT risks in academia: examining university educators' challenges in Jordan. Educ. Inf. Technol. **30**(3), 3645–3667 (2025)
62. Bond, M., Khosravi, H., De Laat, M., Bruijn, M.D., Kalz, M., Pardo, A.: A meta systematic review of artificial intelligence in higher education: a call for increased ethics, collaboration, and rigour. Int. J. Educ. Technol. High. Educ. **21**, 4 (2024)
63. Ruiz-Rojas, L.I., Salvador-Ullauri, L., Acosta-Vargas, P.: Collaborative working and critical thinking: adoption of generative artificial intelligence tools in higher education. Sustainability. **16**, 5367 (2024)
64. Thiga, M.M.: Generative AI and the development of critical thinking skills. In: 9th International Conference on AI in Education, pp. 1–12. Springer, Heidelberg (2024)
65. AlAfnan, M.A., Al-Mutairi, M.: Taxonomy of educational objectives: teaching, learning, and assessing in the information and artificial intelligence era. J. Curric. Teach. **13**(4), 173–191 (2024)
66. Peláez, C.A., et al.: Toolkit for inclusion of user experience design guidelines in the development of assistants based on generative artificial intelligence. Informatics. **12**(1), 10 (2025) MDPI
67. Holmes, W., Bialik, M., Fadel, C.: Artificial intelligence in education: promises and implications for teaching and learning. Center for Curriculum Redesign (2019)
68. Luckin, R.: Machine learning and human intelligence: the future of education for the 21st century. UCL IOE Press (2018)
69. Woolf, B.P.: Artificial intelligence and human learning: partners for the future. Int. J. Artif. Intell. Educ. **31**(1), 1–15 (2021)

Author Index

H. Luna-García et al. (Eds.): HCI-COLLAB 2025, CCIS 2850, pp. 353–354, 2027.
https://doi.org/10.1007/978-3-032-31223-5

The manufacturer's authorised representative in the EU is Springer Nature Customer Service Centre GmbH, Europaplatz 3, 69115 Heidelberg, Germany. If you have any concerns regarding our products, please contact ProductSafety@springernature.com

Printed and bound by CPI Group (UK) Ltd, Croydon, CR0 4YY
17/09/2026
02218434-0006